Microsoft Silverlight 4 and SharePoint 2010 Integration

Techniques, practical tips, hints, and tricks for Silverlight interactions with SharePoint

Gastón C. Hillar

[PACKT] enterprise

PUBLISHING

professional expertise distilled

BIRMINGHAM - MUMBAI

Microsoft Silverlight 4 and SharePoint 2010 Integration

First published: July 2010

Production Reference: 1160710

Published by Packt Publishing Ltd.
32 Lincoln Road
Olton
Birmingham, B27 6PA, UK.

ISBN 978-1-849680-06-6

www.packtpub.com

Cover Image by Sandeep Babu (sandyjb@gmail.com)

Credits

Author
Gastón C. Hillar

Reviewers
Marius Constantinescu
Laurent Duveau
Russell East
Vikram Pendse

Acquisition Editor
James Lumsden

Development Editor
Reshma Sundaresan

Technical Editors
Vinodhan Nair
Erika Fernandes

Indexer
Rekha Nair

Editorial Team Leader
Gagandeep Singh

Project Team Leader
Lata Basantani

Project Coordinator
Poorvi Nair

Proofreader
Chris Smith

Graphics
Nilesh Mohite

Production Coordinator
Adline Swetha Jesuthas

Cover Work
Adline Swetha Jesuthas

About the Author

Gastón C. Hillar has been working with computers since he was eight. He began programming with the legendary Texas TI-99/4A and Commodore 64 home computers in the early 80s.

He has a Bachelor's degree in Computer Science in which he graduated with honors and he also has an MBA (Master in Business Administration) in which he graduated with an outstanding thesis. He has worked as a developer, an architect, and project manager for many companies in Buenos Aires, Argentina. Now, he is an independent IT consultant and a freelance author looking for new adventures around the world. He also works with electronics (he is an electronics technician). He is always researching about new technologies and writing about them. He owns an IT and electronics laboratory with many servers, monitors, and measuring instruments.

He has written two additional books for Packt Publishing, *C# 2008 and 2005 Threaded Programming: Beginner's Guide* and *3D Game Development with Microsoft Silverlight 3: Beginner's Guide*.

He contributes to Dr. Dobb's Go Parallel programming portal `http://www.ddj.com/go-parallel/` and he is a guest blogger at Intel Software Network `http://software.intel.com/`.

In 2009, he was awarded an Intel® Black Belt Software Developer award.

He is the author of more than 40 books in Spanish about computer science, modern hardware, programming, systems development, software architecture, business applications, balanced scorecard applications, IT project management, the Internet, and electronics.

He lives with his wife, Vanesa and his son, Kevin. When not tinkering with computers, he enjoys developing and playing with wireless virtual reality devices and electronics toys with his father, his son, and his nephew Nico.

You can reach him at `gastonhillar@hotmail.com`.

You can follow him on Twitter at `http://twitter.com/gastonhillar`.

Gastón's blog is at `http://csharpmulticore.blogspot.com`.

Acknowledgement

While writing this book, I was fortunate to work with an excellent team at Packt Publishing, whose contributions vastly improved the presentation of this book. James Lumsden helped me to transform the idea in the final book and gave me first steps, while working with this book for Packt. Poorvi Nair made everything easier with both her incredible time management and patience. Reshma Sundaresan helped me realize my vision for this book and provided many sensible suggestions regarding the text, the format, and the flow. The reader will notice her great work. Vinodhan Nair and Erika Fernandes made the sentences, the paragraphs, the pictures and the code easier to read and to understand. They added great value to the final drafts.

I would like to thank my technical reviewers and proofreaders, for their thorough reviews and insightful comments. I was able to incorporate some of the knowledge and wisdom they have gained in their many years in the software development industry. The examples, the pictures, and the code include the great feedback provided by Marius Constantinescu, Laurent Duveau, Russell East, and Vikram Pendse. This book was possible, because they gave valuable feedback.

I must acknowledge David Barnes, Beginner's Guide Series Editor at Packt Publishing. His help in my first book published by Packt and his wisdom are also part of this new one.

I wish to acknowledge Hector A. Algarra, who always helped me to improve my writing.

Special thanks go to my wife, Vanesa S. Olsen, my son Kevin, my nephew Nicolas, my father Jose Carlos, who acted as a great sounding board and participated in many hours of technical discussions, my sister Silvina, and my mother Susana. They were always supporting me during the production of this book.

About the Reviewers

Marius Constantinescu is currently the Lead Architect on Microsoft Solutions for a professional IT services company based in Geneva, Switzerland and also has experience on commercial development dating back in the late nineties.

Having worked with .NET from its very early beta stages as well as with SharePoint platform ever since 2003, Marius C. has achieved number of prestigious roll-outs for large international organizations and private companies, providing consulting expertise on architectures based on .NET, SharePoint, and related software.

His passion for technology has made him a recipient of various prestigious awards, such as Technology Scout for 2005, while being Microsoft Solution architect for Siemens, as well as gaining the Siemens Certified Architect certification. Most recently, his focus has again shifted to the latest .NET technologies, such as Silverlight 4, SharePoint 2010, and Cloud Computing.

He has been performing technical reviewing for almost a decade with multiple publishing houses and prestigious authors around .NET technologies, including two best-sellers on ASP.NET 2.0 for the popular author Dino Esposito back in 2005. He also speaks at technology conferences and maintains a blog available at `http://nettitude.spaces.live.com`.

> I'd like to thank my fiancée, Réka K. for her immense patience and support through the long late nights I had to spend away and all the weekends traded in favor of my other passion—the .NET technology.

Laurent Duveau is an expert in Silverlight, a technology that fascinates him and the development of which he has followed since the very beginning in 2007. He has had the opportunity to give a multitude of Silverlight presentations at conferences such as TechDays, DevTeach, Code Camp, User Group, MSDN Tour, and W3C. Laurent has been a **Microsoft Certified Trainer (MCT)** since 2004 and is also a Silverlight MVP, Silverlight Partner, and Silverlight Insider. He is Vice-president of RunAtServer Consulting (`http://www.runatserver.com/`), a company based in Montreal, QC whose focus is Silverlight projects, coaching, and training.

Russell East's career spans over 15 long years in which he has led development teams and developed software for a number of companies in varying industries of various sizes. He has used various technologies and languages along the way. These days he has focused his skill set in application architecture, primarily, Windows development with a mix of web development using WPF, Silverlight, WCF, and ASP.NET MVC using C#. Currently, he is freelancing and building up an innovative software company called Razorbeam.

Vikram Pendse is a consistent Microsoft MVP and first Silverlight MVP in India. He is very passionate about Microsoft Technologies. He completed his Masters in Computer Management from IndSearch, Pune. He is also involved as a speaker in various Microsoft events like Tech Ed-India,Virtual TechDays, DevCon, and other community events like CSI Annual Meets, IT Expo, Architect Day, and so on. He actively works with Pune User Group (http://www.puneusergroup.org) as User Group Lead, which is supported by Microsoft and INETA. Silverlight and ASP.NET are his core areas of interest. In the past, he executed large-scale Web Applications for Healthcare and hospitals, which included Product Development and implementation of HL7 standards. He also created POCs for many banking projects and HealthCare applications using cutting-edge technologies such as Silverlight, WCF RIA, and LINQ. He blogs at http://pendsevikram.blogspot.com.

I am very thankful to my family and friends for supporting me all the time for my work and community activities. Also, I am very thankful to India MVP Program and Team Silverlight at Microsoft for their continuous support and encouragement.

I would like to dedicate this book to my son Kevin and my wife Vanesa

Table of Contents

Preface	**1**
Chapter 1: Integrating Silverlight 4 with SharePoint 2010	**7**
Understanding the benefits of integrating Silverlight with SharePoint	**8**
Creating a SharePoint solution	9
Preparing the development environment	**9**
Setting up the development environment	10
Discovering the rich controls offered by the Silverlight Toolkit	12
Browsing themes with sample controls	15
Preparing the server	**16**
Browsing SharePoint Site collections	18
Creating a Silverlight LOB (Line-of-Business) RIA	**20**
Creating rich User eXperiences (UX)	27
Building a Silverlight 4 RIA	29
Adding a Silverlight Web Part	**30**
Adding a Silverlight RIA as a shared document	30
Adding a Silverlight Web Part to display a Silverlight RIA	33
Working with many Silverlight Web Parts in a single page	39
Understanding client and server code	41
Summary	**42**
Chapter 2: Deploying and Debugging Techniques for Silverlight and SharePoint	**43**
Deploying a Silverlight RIA included in a SharePoint solution	**44**
Creating a list of tasks in SharePoint	44
Browsing SharePoint lists and fields with Visual Studio	47
Creating a Silverlight RIA to be linked with a SharePoint module	51
Working with the asynchronous methods and callbacks	58

Working with the ClientContext object 61
Linking a SharePoint module to a Silverlight RIA 65
Understanding the default deployment configuration 71
Debugging Silverlight and SharePoint **72**
Debugging Silverlight Web Parts 75
Taking advantage of Visual Studio 2010 multi-monitor support 80
Understanding 32-bit and 64-bit differences 81
Understanding scalability 82
Preparing applications for multiple-browser support 82
Summary **84**
Chapter 3: Interacting with Data on the SharePoint Server **85**
Managing data in a Silverlight RIA included in a SharePoint solution **86**
Working with the SharePoint 2010 Silverlight Client Object Model
to insert items 86
Inserting items in a SharePoint list with the Silverlight Web Part 94
Working with successful and failed asynchronous queries 98
Retrieving specific information about fields 102
Creating complex LOB applications composed of multiple Silverlight RIAs 112
Interacting with multiple Silverlight Web Parts in the same page 117
Understanding Line-Of-Business systems as independent Web Parts 119
Expanding LOB systems with delete operations 121
Understanding how to delete an item from a list 124
Expanding LOB systems with update operations 126
Updating an item in a list 129
Summary **131**
Chapter 4: Creating Dynamic Business Solutions **133**
Accessing an external database in a Silverlight RIA included in a SharePoint solution **134**
Creating a new database 134
Creating a new external content type to access data in a SQL Server
database 139
Browsing a SharePoint list with external content and its fields 149
Interacting with external data sources using the SharePoint
2010 Silverlight Client Object Model 150
Specifying the fields to include in a CAML query for an external list 158
Consuming Business Connectivity Services from a Silverlight Web Part 163
Understanding security issues related to Business Connectivity Services 166
Impersonating BCS calls 167
Applying dynamic filters in a CAML query 171
Running Silverlight RIAs as Out-of-Browser Applications 174

Interacting with workflows	**179**
Attaching a workflow to a list of tasks in SharePoint	180
Inserting and approving items in a list with an attached workflow	182
Using a Silverlight RIA to display a SharePoint workflow's status	185
Understanding workflows' status fields	189
Summary	**190**
Chapter 5: Working with WCF Data Services	**191**
Working with SharePoint 2010 WCF Data Services	**192**
Querying SharePoint 2010 lists in a web browser	193
Working with SharePoint 2010 WCF Data Services to display data from a list	203
Consuming SharePoint 2010 WCF Data Services from a Silverlight Web Part	**209**
Performing CRUD operations with SharePoint 2010 WCF Data Services	**213**
Deleting an item from a list with SharePoint 2010 WCF Data Services	223
Updating an item in a list with SharePoint 2010 WCF Data Services	225
Working with SharePoint 2010 WCF Data Services to insert items	227
Using LINQ to objects to perform joins	236
Debugging HTTP Requests with Fiddler	**240**
Analyzing Web Parts with SharePoint Developer Dashboard	**243**
Analyzing pages and Web Parts with SharePoint Developer Dashboard	**247**
Activating the Developer Dashboard On Demand display mode	247
Understanding the Developer Dashboard	249
Deactivating the Developer Dashboard	252
Summary	**253**
Chapter 6: Interacting with Rich Media and Animations	**255**
Bringing life to business applications and complex workflows	**256**
Creating asset libraries in SharePoint 2010	256
Adding content to an assets library	258
Browsing the structure for SharePoint Asset Libraries	262
Controlling the rich media library by using controls in a Visual Web Part	264
Creating a Silverlight RIA rendered in a SharePoint Visual Web Part	271
Linking a SharePoint Visual Web Part to a Silverlight RIA	285
Adding a SharePoint Visual Web Part in a Web Page	288
Organizing controls in a containing box	294
Reading files from an assets library	295
Working with interactive animations and effects	296
Adding and controlling videos	303
Video formats supported in Silverlight 4	307
Adding and controlling sounds and music	307
Audio formats supported in Silverlight 4	308

Changing themes in Silverlight and SharePoint   309
Summary   **312**
Index   **313**

Preface

Silverlight is a powerful development platform for creating engaging, interactive user experiences for web, desktop, and mobile applications. Integrating Silverlight RIAs in SharePoint 2010 offers amazing opportunities to combine the power and flexibility offered by SharePoint. It is easy to create great user experiences when you have a step-by-step guide to implement Silverlight 4 applications on SharePoint 2010 sites, isn't it?

This book begins with the fundamental concepts of integrating Silverlight 4 with SharePoint 2010, such as the preparation of the development environment to create applications using Silverlight 4 and the addition of one or more Silverlight RIAs to a SharePoint site.

Then, it moves into the SharePoint Silverlight Client Object Model world, using step-by-step examples to combine a Silverlight application and a SharePoint module. It explains to deploy and debug the Silverlight application while it runs as s Silverlight Web Part in a SharePoint page.

Then, it is time to interact with SharePoint lists to perform CRUD (Create, Read, Update, and Delete) operations and retrieve metadata information for the fields that compose lists. The book teaches to take advantage of the new features offered by Visual Studio 2010 to browse SharePoint lists.

Once you have control over the SharePoint Silverlight Client Object Model and its asynchronous operations in Silverlight applications, it is time to access external databases through the new Business Connectivity Services (BCS) and interact with workflows. Then, the book explains how to perform CRUD operations by consuming the new SharePoint 2010 WCF Data Services in Silverlight.

Then, consuming different kinds of multimedia files from the new SharePoint 2010 Digital Asset Libraries offers the final touches to the Silverlight 4 and SharePoint 2010 integration learning experience.

In each example, the book teaches to take advantage of unique features offered by Silverlight in order to create impressive User eXperiences that interact with SharePoint 2010. For example, themes, effects, animations, data-binding, and Silverlight 4 Out-of-Browser capabilities.

What this book covers

Chapter 1, Integrating Silverlight 4 with SharePoint 2010, briefs you about integration of Silverlight 4 applications with SharePoint 2010 sites and solutions. In this chapter, you will learn to prepare a development environment and look at the tools to work with Silverlight 4 RIAs. You will also configure the SharePoint 2010 server and add Silverlight Web Parts to a new page. Finally, you will create your first Silverlight RIA and then make it available in a SharePoint site.

Chapter 2, Deploying and Debugging Techniques for Silverlight and SharePoint, will help you create a new Silverlight 4 RIA that retrieves data from SharePoint through the SharePoint Silverlight Client Object Model. In this chapter, you will create your first Silverlight RIA that interacts with a list of tasks in SharePoint and learn a way to run and debug asynchronous queries to the SharePoint server run by using multiple threads.

Chapter 3, Interacting with Data on the SharePoint Server, covers advanced interaction with data on the SharePoint Server. In this chapter, you will create a new Silverlight 4 RIA that allows us to insert new items into a remote SharePoint list and later enhance this simple application to retrieve metadata information for the fields. You will also perform delete and update operations to the remote SharePoint list through the SharePoint Silverlight Client Object Model.

Chapter 4, Creating Dynamic Business Solutions, guides you to create dynamic business solutions by accessing external databases in a Silverlight RIA included in a SharePoint solution and interacting with workflows. You will also work with the new SharePoint 2010 approval workflows and enhance an existing Silverlight RIA to retrieve workflow status information and display it in a column of a grid.

Chapter 5, Working with WCF Data Services, helps you develop Silverlight 4 applications in SharePoint 2010 sites that interact with data in lists by performing insert, update, and delete operations with WCF Data Services. In this chapter, you will use Fiddler to inspect the communication between the Silverlight RIA and the SharePoint server. Finally, you will analyze the performance and resource usage information for pages and Web Parts with SharePoint Developer Dashboard.

Chapter 6, Interacting with Rich Media and Animations, will help you access asset libraries in a Silverlight RIA rendered in a SharePoint Visual Web Part. In this chapter, you will learn to take advantage of Silverlight 4 rich media features to add effects and interactive animations to images and videos.

What you need for this book

The following software products are used in this Microsoft Silverlight 4 and SharePoint 2010 Integration book:

- Visual Studio 2010 Professional, Premium, or Ultimate
- SharePoint 2010 Server or SharePoint 2010 Foundation, installed on the same computer that runs Visual Studio 2010
- SharePoint Designer 2010

Who this book is for

If you are an application developer who wants to implement Silverlight 4 applications within a SharePoint 2010 environment, this book is for you. We assume that the reader has prior knowledge of Silverlight and SharePoint 2010 and this book focuses on the integration of Silverlight with SharePoint 2010.

Conventions

In this book, you will find a number of styles of text that distinguish between different kinds of information. Here are some examples of these styles, and an explanation of their meaning.

Code words in text are shown as follows: "Add a new XML file to the project, `Projects.xml`."

A block of code is set as follows:

```
public class Project
{
    public int ProjectId { get; set; }
    public string Title { get; set; }
    public int EstimatedDaysLeft { get; set; }
    public string Status { get; set; }
    public string AssignedTo { get; set; }
    public int NumberOfTasks { get; set; }
}
```

When we wish to draw your attention to a particular part of a code block, the relevant lines or items are set in bold:

```
lblStatus.Content = "Started";
// Replace "http://gaston-pc" with
// your SharePoint Web site's URL
_context = new SP.ClientContext("http://gaston-pc");
_context.Load(_context.Web);
_context.ExecuteQueryAsync(OnConnectSucceeded, null);
```

New terms and **important words** are shown in bold. Words that you see on the screen, in menus or dialog boxes for example, appear in the text like this: "Click on **Create**; SharePoint will create the new list with no items".

[Warnings or important notes appear in a box like this.   ]

[Tips and tricks appear like this.   ]

Reader feedback

Feedback from our readers is always welcome. Let us know what you think about this book—what you liked or may have disliked. Reader feedback is important for us to develop titles that you really get the most out of.

To send us general feedback, simply send an e-mail to feedback@packtpub.com, and mention the book title via the subject of your message.

If there is a book that you need and would like to see us publish, please send us a note in the **SUGGEST A TITLE** form on www.packtpub.com or e-mail suggest@packtpub.com.

If there is a topic that you have expertise in and you are interested in either writing or contributing to a book, see our author guide on www.packtpub.com/authors.

Customer support

Now that you are the proud owner of a Packt book, we have a number of things to help you to get the most from your purchase.

> **Downloading the example code for the book**
>
> You can download the example code files for all Packt books you have purchased from your account at http://www.PacktPub.com. If you purchased this book elsewhere, you can visit http://www.PacktPub.com/support and register to have the files e-mailed directly to you.

Errata

Although we have taken every care to ensure the accuracy of our content, mistakes do happen. If you find a mistake in one of our books — maybe a mistake in the text or the code — we would be grateful if you would report this to us. By doing so, you can save other readers from frustration and help us improve subsequent versions of this book. If you find any errata, please report them by visiting http://www.packtpub.com/support, selecting your book, clicking on the **let us know** link, and entering the details of your errata. Once your errata are verified, your submission will be accepted and the errata will be uploaded on our website, or added to any list of existing errata, under the Errata section of that title. Any existing errata can be viewed by selecting your title from http://www.packtpub.com/support.

Piracy

Piracy of copyright material on the Internet is an ongoing problem across all media. At Packt, we take the protection of our copyright and licenses very seriously. If you come across any illegal copies of our works, in any form, on the Internet, please provide us with the location address or website name immediately so that we can pursue a remedy.

Please contact us at copyright@packtpub.com with a link to the suspected pirated material.

We appreciate your help in protecting our authors, and our ability to bring you valuable content.

Questions

You can contact us at questions@packtpub.com if you are having a problem with any aspect of the book, and we will do our best to address it.

1
Integrating Silverlight 4 with SharePoint 2010

We want to include Silverlight 4 **RIAs (Rich Internet Applications)** in SharePoint 2010. RIAs provide rich experience for users, both through their browsers and outside them. Integrating Silverlight RIAs in SharePoint 2010 offers amazing opportunities to combine the power and flexibility offered by SharePoint with great user experiences. In fact, many interfaces shown in SharePoint 2010 are developed in Silverlight. We want to integrate Silverlight RIAs into SharePoint 2010. First, we must understand some of the fundamentals that are related to various tools and their configurations. In this chapter, we will cover many topics to help us understand the new tools and techniques involved in creating Silverlight RIAs for SharePoint 2010 sites. We will:

- Understand the benefits of integrating Silverlight with SharePoint
- Prepare the development environment to develop applications for SharePoint 2010 using Silverlight 4
- Prepare the SharePoint 2010 server to host Silverlight applications
- Create a Silverlight Line of Business RIA
- Learn to add a Silverlight RIA to a SharePoint site
- Understand the advantage of creating rich user experiences for SharePoint solutions
- Work with shared documents to store a Silverlight application in SharePoint sites
- Work with many Silverlight applications in a single page
- Learn the differences between client and server code

Understanding the benefits of integrating Silverlight with SharePoint

The following list shows many benefits of integrating Silverlight with SharePoint 2010:

- **Rich UX**: Silverlight RIAs can offer a rich user experience. You can take full advantage of the rich visual capabilities offered by Silverlight and include them in a SharePoint site. The rich and interactive content offers an incredible new world of possibilities in SharePoint. For example, you can offer an interactive balanced scorecard with animated graphs, rich navigation capabilities, and context menus.

- **Code runs on the client**: You can take advantage of the power of the client computers accessing the SharePoint server. You can use threading and asynchronous calls to offer responsive user interfaces and to take advantage of modern multi-core microprocessors found in client computers. You can offer great response times without the need to wait for the server to load another page. You can take advantage of rich controls, animations, and exciting multimedia effects. The processing removes load from the server and enables you to use both the server and the client in your solutions. Additionally, Silverlight 4 is cross-browser capable and we can take advantage of the improved Out of Browser features to create applications that interact with the SharePoint 2010 server but run in the Windows desktop, out of the web browser.

- **Efficient applications**: As you can work with the power offered by the client, you can process data without the need to make requests to the server all the time. This way, you can create load-balanced solutions.

- **Access to the Client OM (Client Object Model)**: When you have to access data and services offered by the SharePoint 2010 server, you don't need to create your own complex infrastructure. There is no need to add additional layers. You can take advantage of the new Client Object Model, also known as Client OM. As you can work with asynchronous calls to the Client OM, you can still offer great responsive applications when consuming services from the server. Users can interact with SharePoint data without requiring server calls as they would from traditional pages. Lots of the processing can be pushed down to the client. This way, as previously explained, you can remove load from the SharePoint server and create load-balanced solutions.

- **Leverage your existing Silverlight knowledge, components, and applications**: You can build new capabilities quickly from existing Silverlight components and applications, integrating them with SharePoint 2010.

Considering the aforementioned benefits, we will work hard to learn all the possibilities offered by the integration of Silverlight and SharePoint 2010 in later parts of the book.

Creating a SharePoint solution

Now, when we design a new SharePoint 2010 solution, we will be able to consider Silverlight RIAs as new components for the global solution. We have to consider the aforementioned benefits of integrating Silverlight with SharePoint and decide which parts would be convenient to create as Silverlight RIAs.

This way, we can focus on preparing the SharePoint 2010 infrastructure and then we can access data and services offered by the server through Silverlight RIAs. For example, you can view the images found in an assets library defined in SharePoint through a Silverlight application.

> Once you start integrating Silverlight with SharePoint, you will find a new exciting way of enhancing SharePoint solutions.

Preparing the development environment

We want to take full advantage of modern technologies. First of all, we must install the latest tools and begin working on configurations. Later, we will be able to use our existing knowledge to create different kinds of RIAs for SharePoint 2010, using Silverlight 4 — the newest kid-on-the-block from Microsoft.

> Silverlight 4 is backward-compatible with its previous version, Silverlight 3. Therefore, when an example uses a feature found only in Silverlight 4, you will find a note explaining this situation. Most of the examples work for both Silverlight versions. However, we will also take advantage of some of the new features found in Silverlight 4.

The only requirements underpinning the development and integration of RIAs into SharePoint 2010 sites are understanding the basics of the C# programming language, ASP.NET, XAML code, and the Visual Studio IDE. We will cover any other requirements in our journey through the creation of many different kinds of RIAs to run in a SharePoint 2010 site. First, we must download and install various Silverlight development tools. We need Visual C# 2010 Professional, Premium, or Ultimate installed, in order to successfully complete the installations explained in the following section. Visual C# 2010 allows us to choose the desired Silverlight version (for example, version 3 or version 4). The following sections and chapters will show Visual Studio 2010 Ultimate screenshots. If you use other versions, some elements that appear in the screenshots could be different but the steps are all valid for the aforementioned versions.

Setting up the development environment

Follow these steps to prepare the development environment:

1. Download the following files:

Application's name	Download link	File name	Description
Silverlight 4 Tools for Visual Studio 2010	http://www. microsoft.com/ downloads/details. aspx?FamilyID= eff8a0da-0a4d-48e8- 8366-6ddf2ecad801& displaylang=en	Silverlight4_ Tools.exe	We must install Silverlight 4 Tools in order to create Silverlight 4 applications in the Visual Studio 2010 IDE, using XAML and C#. It will co-exist with previous Silverlight SDKs (Software Development Kits). This new version of Silverlight Tools also includes the WCF RIA Services package.

Application's name	Download link	File name	Description
Silverlight 4 Offline Documentation (in CHM format)	`http://www. microsoft.com/ downloads/details. aspx?familyid= B6127B9B-968C-46C2- 8CB6-D228E017AD74& displaylang=en`	`Silverlight_ Documentation. EXE`	We must download and run this file to decompress its content, because we will need access to Silverlight 4 official documentation in due course.
Expression Blend for .NET 4	`http://www.microsoft. com/downloads/ details. aspx?FamilyID= 88484825-1b3c-4e8c- 8b14-b05d025e1541& displaylang=en`	`Blend_Trial_ en.exe`	This tool will enable us to create content that targets Silverlight 4 and to create rapid prototypes with the SketchFlow tool.
Silverlight Toolkit (Updated for Silverlight 4 compatibility)	`http://codeplex.com/ Silverlight`	`Silverlight_4_ Toolkit_ April_2010.msi`	It is convenient to download the latest stable release. This toolkit provides a nice collection of Silverlight controls, components, and utilities made available outside the normal Silverlight release cycle. It will be really helpful to use these controls to provide even more attractive user interfaces. Besides, it includes more Silverlight themes.

2. Run the installers in the same order in which they appear in the above table and follow the steps to complete the installation wizards.

3. Once the installations have successfully finished, run Visual Studio 2010 or Visual Web Developer 2010 (or later).

4. Select **File | New | Project...** or press *Ctrl+Shift+N*. Select **Visual C# | Silverlight** under **Installed Templates** in the **New Project** dialog box. You will see many Silverlight templates, including **Silverlight Business Application** and **WCF RIA Services Class Library**, as shown in the following screenshot:

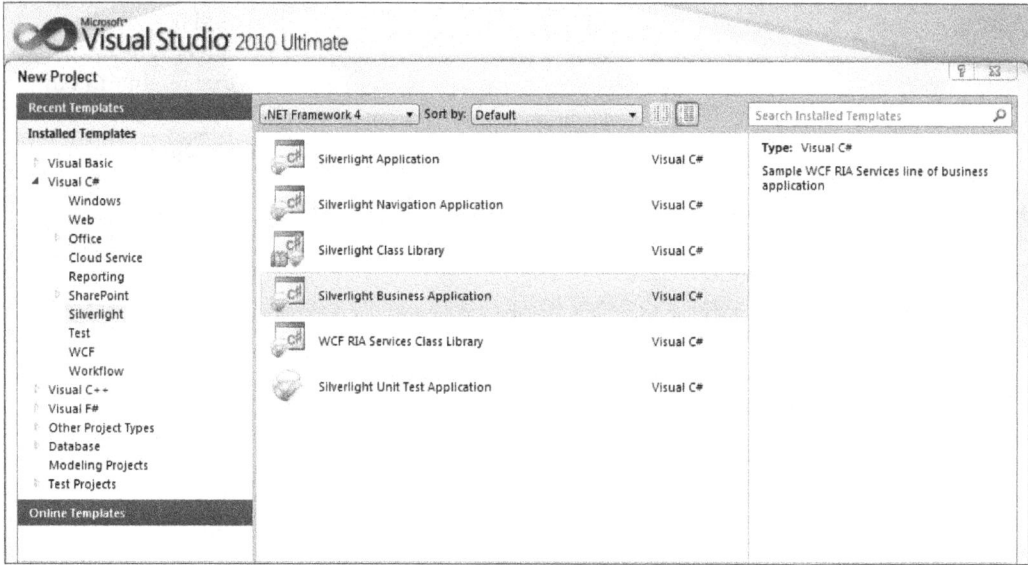

Discovering the rich controls offered by the Silverlight Toolkit

Silverlight Toolkit is a Microsoft project offering many rich controls, components, and utilities that can help us to enhance our Silverlight UI (User Interface). As we want to create a very attractive UI for SharePoint, it is convenient to get familiar with its features. Follows these steps to see the controls in action and to change the values for many of their properties.

1. Select **Start | All Programs | Microsoft Silverlight 4 Toolkit April 2010 | Toolkit Samples** and your default web browser will display a web page with a Silverlight application displaying a list of the controls organized in ten categories as follows:
   - Controls
   - Data
   - DataForm
   - Data Input

- ° DataVisualization
- ° Input
- ° Layout
- ° Navigation
- ° Theming
- ° Toolkit

> By default, the `default.htm` web page is located at `C:\Program Files (x86)\Microsoft SDKs\Silverlight\v4.0\Toolkit\Apr10\Samples` in 64-bit Windows versions.

2. Click on a control name under the desired category and the right panel will display the control with different values assigned for its properties, creating diverse instances of the control. For example, the following screenshot shows many instances of the `Rating` control under the **Input** category.

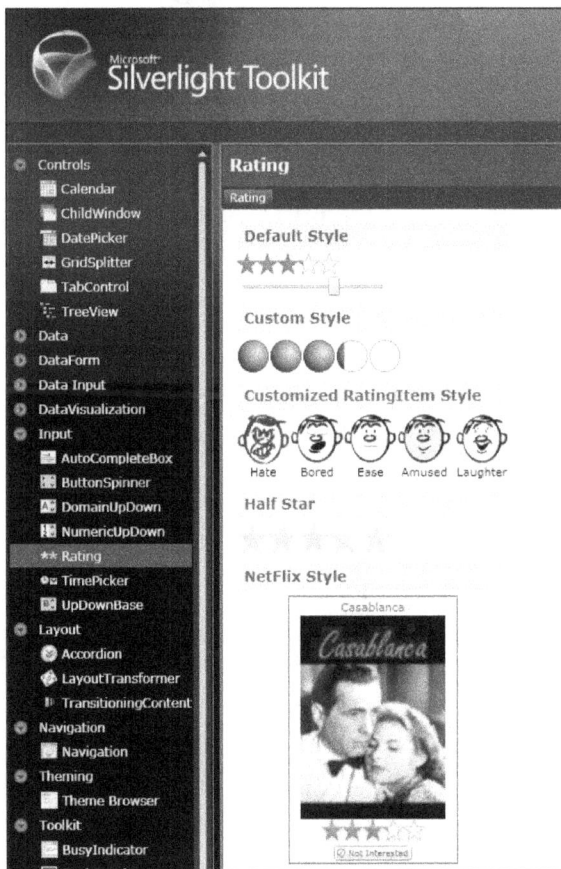

3. Click on the buttons shown at the bottom of the web page and you will be able to see both the XAML and the C# code used to create the sample for the control. For example, the following screenshot shows the XAML code for the DataGrid control example, DataGridSample.xaml. You can also click on DataGridSample.xaml.cs and check the C# part. This control appears under the **Data** category.

Browsing themes with sample controls

Silverlight Toolkit also includes 11 themes that allow us to change and improve the overall look-and-feel for our Silverlight UI. They are:

- Bubble Creme
- Bureau Black
- Bureau Blue
- Expression Dark
- Expression Light
- Rainier Purple
- Rainier Orange
- Shiny Blue
- Shiny Red
- Twilight Blue
- Whistler Blue

Click on **Theme Browser** under the **Theming** category and you will be able to select one of the themes shown in the previous list to preview the look-and-feel of many controls. The following screenshot shows the preview for the **Whistler Blue** theme:

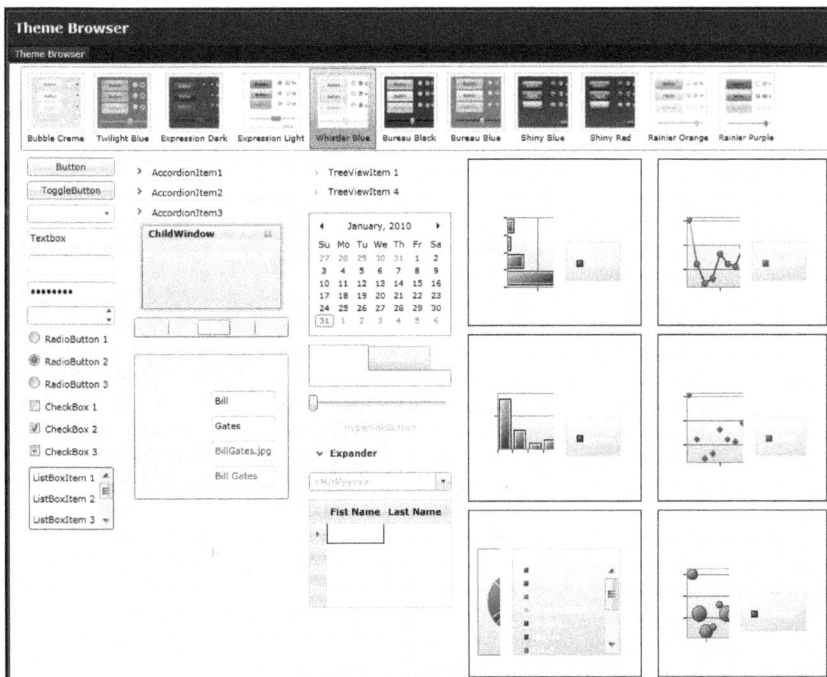

Preparing the server

So far, we have prepared the development environment. Now, it is time to make sure that we have the necessary configuration for the SharePoint 2010 server in which we are going to integrate Silverlight applications.

In order to complete all the examples that we will develop throughout this book, you must be an administrator of a SharePoint site collection. SharePoint Server 2010 or SharePoint Foundation 2010 must be installed in the same computer that runs Visual Studio 2010. You can check the necessary steps to perform a SharePoint Server 2010 or SharePoint Foundation 2010 installation for your development computer at `http://msdn.microsoft.com/en-us/library/ee554869.aspx`. Follow these steps to ensure that you are a site collection administrator:

1. Open your default web browser, view the SharePoint site, and log in with your username and password. You have to enter the SharePoint server URL. In our examples, we will use `http://xpsgaston` as our default SharePoint 2010 site. However, you have to replace it with your SharePoint 2010 site URL. Your default site will appear, in this case, `http://xpsgaston/SitePages/Home.aspx`, as shown in the following screenshot:

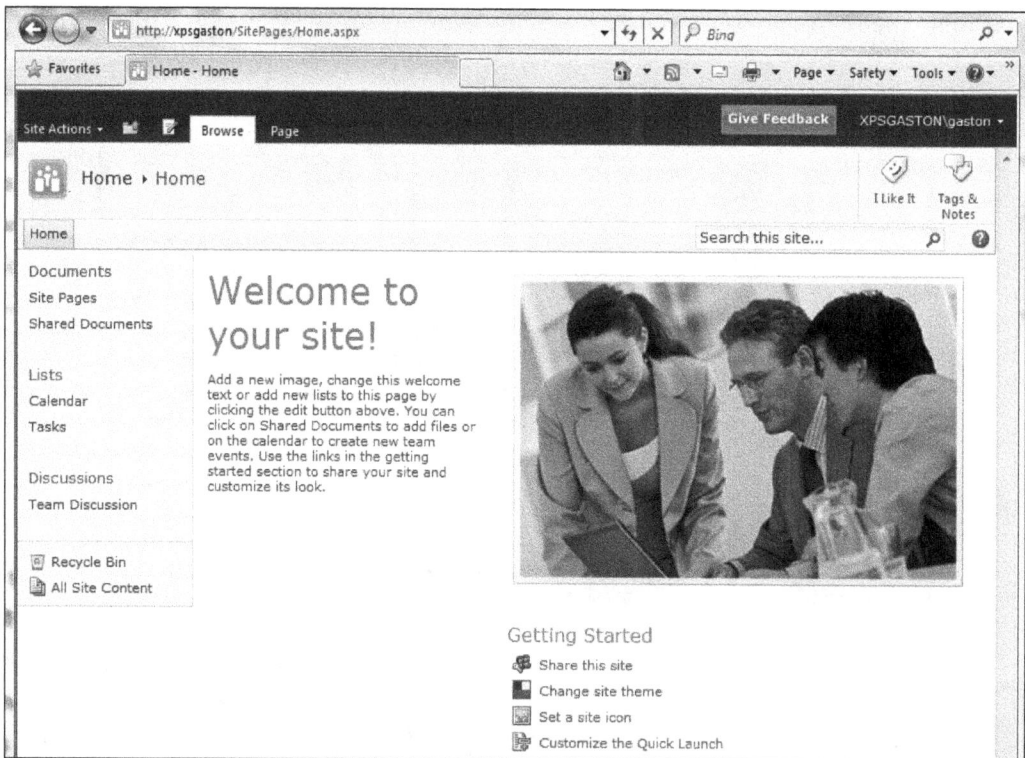

2. Click **Site Actions | Site Permissions** and a list of users with their permission levels will appear.

3. Now, click on **Site Collection Administrators** in the ribbon. A new dialog box with the names of the users with administrator rights on this site collection will appear.

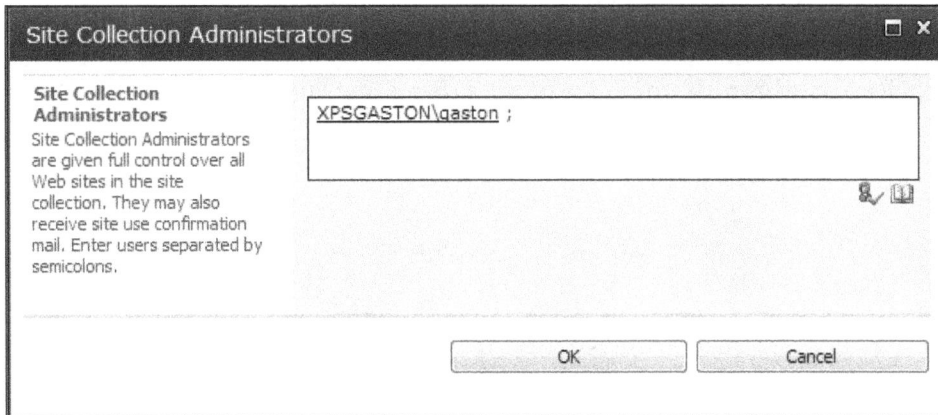

4. If your user name appears in the text box, you are a Site Collection Administrator.

> If you cannot see the **Site Collection Administrators** button in the ribbon, it means that you don't have site collection administrator privileges on the site. In this case, you have to request this permission from the SharePoint site administrator.

Browsing SharePoint Site collections

Once we have ensured that our username is a Site Collection Administrator, we can use **Server Explorer** in Visual Studio to browse a SharePoint site.

1. Start Visual Studio as a system administrator user. In Windows Server 2008 R2, 2008, and 2003, if you are already logged as Administrator on the machine you can simply run the application. However, in Windows 7 or Windows Vista, you can do it by right-clicking on its shortcut and selecting **Run as administrator** in the context menu that appears, as shown:

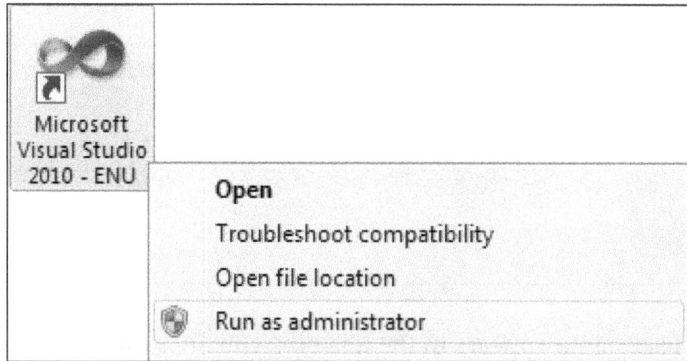

2. Activate the **Server Explorer** palette. If it isn't visible, you have to select **View | Server Explorer** in the main menu.

3. Click on the expand button for **SharePoint Connections**. If the name of your desired SharePoint 2010 server doesn't appear in the list, you can manually connect to the server. You can do it by right-clicking on **SharePoint Connections** and selecting **Add Connection...** in the context menu that appears. Then, you have to enter the URL for the server, for example, http://xpsgaston and click **OK** in the dialog box that appears. If your user has the previously explained privileges, the server will appear in the list.

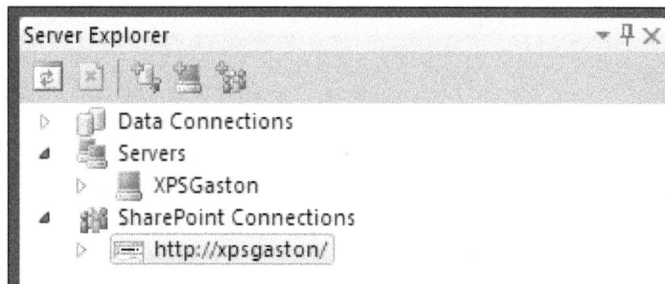

4. Now, click on the expand button for the SharePoint server and you will be able to browse its different nodes. Every component of a SharePoint site is represented by a node in the **Server Explorer** tree view. You can inspect the properties for each node, as shown in the following screenshot:

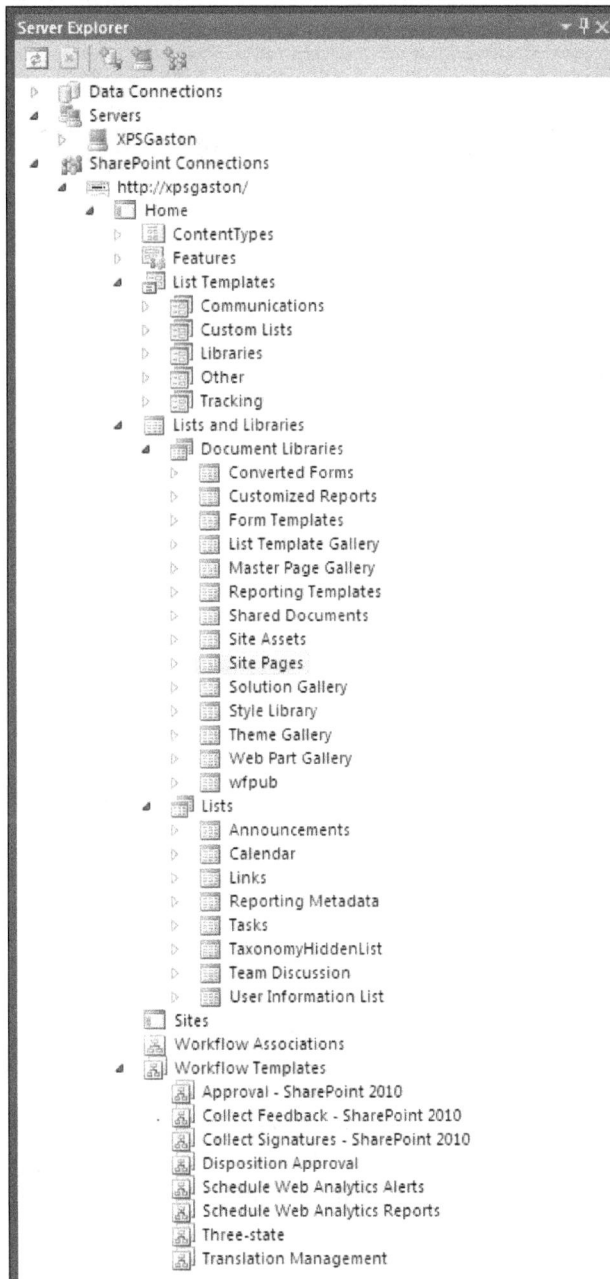

5. You can view some lists in your default web browser by right-clicking on a node and then selecting **View in Browser** in the context menu that appears. For example, you can do it for the node **Home | Lists and Libraries | Site Pages** and your default web browser will display all the pages. In this case, the URL shown is `http://xpsgaston/SitePages/Forms/AllPages.aspx`.

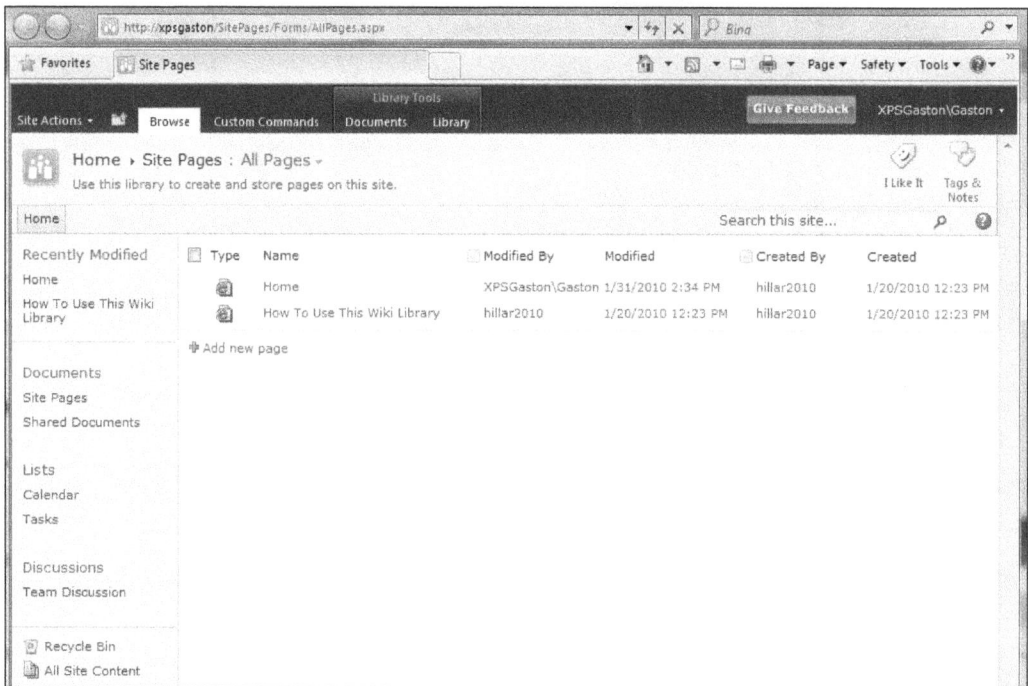

[💡 Remember to run Visual Studio as a system administrator user in order to interact with SharePoint for all the examples covered in this book.]

Creating a Silverlight LOB (Line-of-Business) RIA

Now, we are going to create a very simple Silverlight **LOB (Line-Of-Business)** RIA that retrieves data, displays a grid with a list of projects, and allows the users to navigate through the data. Then, we are going to integrate this Silverlight UI in SharePoint.

1. Create a new Visual C# project using the **Silverlight | Silverlight Application** template. Use `SilverlightProjects` as the project's name.

2. Deactivate the **Host the Silverlight application in a new Web site** checkbox in the **New Silverlight Application** dialog box. We want the Silverlight application to run in a simple HTML web page. As you have installed Silverlight 4 Tools, the dialog box will offer you a combo box with the possibility to choose the desired Silverlight version. Select **Silverlight 4** as we want to take advantage of the new features offered by this version.

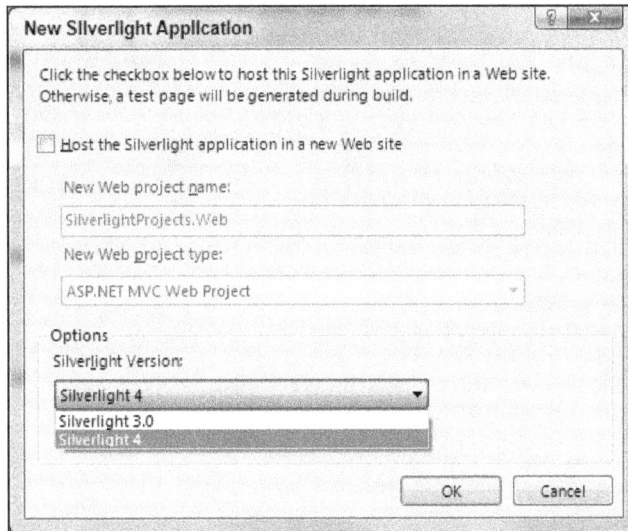

3. Add a new XML file to the project, `Projects.xml`. The following lines define properties and values for five `project` instances. This way, we have some data in XML format for our simple LOB application.

```xml
<?xml version="1.0" encoding="utf-8" ?>
<projects>
  <project projectId="0">
    <title>Creating a Silverlight 4 UI</title>
    <estimatedDaysLeft>4</estimatedDaysLeft>
    <status>Delayed</status>
    <assignedTo>Jon Share</assignedTo>
    <numberOfTasks>5</numberOfTasks>
  </project>
  <project projectId="1">
    <title>Creating a Complex Silverlight LOB RIA</title>
    <estimatedDaysLeft>5</estimatedDaysLeft>
    <status>Delayed</status>
```

```
      <assignedTo>James Point</assignedTo>
      <numberOfTasks>35</numberOfTasks>
    </project>
    <project projectId="2">
      <title>Creating a New SharePoint Site</title>
      <estimatedDaysLeft>3</estimatedDaysLeft>
      <status>Delayed</status>
      <assignedTo>Vanessa Dotcom</assignedTo>
      <numberOfTasks>8</numberOfTasks>
    </project>
    <project projectId="3">
      <title>Installing a New SharePoint 2010 Server</title>
      <estimatedDaysLeft>3</estimatedDaysLeft>
      <status>Delayed</status>
      <assignedTo>Michael Desktop</assignedTo>
      <numberOfTasks>25</numberOfTasks>
    </project>
    <project projectId="4">
      <title>Testing the New Silverlight LOB RIA</title>
      <estimatedDaysLeft>4</estimatedDaysLeft>
      <status>Delayed</status>
      <assignedTo>Jon Share</assignedTo>
      <numberOfTasks>35</numberOfTasks>
    </project>
  </projects>
```

4. Add a new class to the project called `Project` in a new class file, `Project.cs`. The following lines define the new class, with six properties. This way, you will be able to create instances of this class to hold the values defined in the previously created XML file.

```
public class Project
{
    public int ProjectId { get; set; }
    public string Title { get; set; }
    public int EstimatedDaysLeft { get; set; }
    public string Status { get; set; }
    public string AssignedTo { get; set; }
    public int NumberOfTasks { get; set; }
}
```

5. Open `MainPage.xaml`, define a new width and height for the `Grid` as `800` and `600`, add the following controls located in the **Toolbox** under **All Silverlight Controls**, and align them as shown in the screenshot. Remember that Visual Studio 2010 allows us to drag-and-drop controls from the toolbox to the Silverlight `UserControl` in the design view and it will automatically generate the XAML code.

   ◦ Two `Label` controls.

   ◦ One `DataGrid` control and set its name to `dataGridProjects`. Set its `AutoGenerateColumns` property to `true`.

   ◦ One `Slider` control, `sliGridFontSize`. Set its `Minimum` property to `8`, `Maximum` to `72`, and `Value` to `11`.

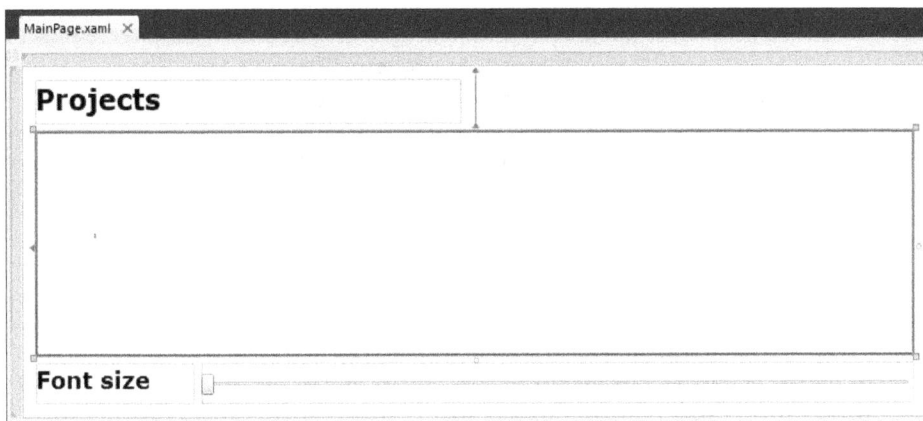

6. Apply data binding to the font size for the `DataGrid` control, `dataGridProjects`. In order to do so, select `dataGridProjects`, activate the **Properties** panel, display them in alphabetical order, right-click on the **FontSize** property, and select **Apply Data Binding** in the context menu that appears. Then, select `ElementName` in **Source**, `sliGridFontSize`, and then `Value` in **Path**. This way, when the user moves the slider, the font size for the data grid will change. The code that defines the data binding is as follows:

```
FontSize="{Binding ElementName=sliGridFontSize, Path=Value}"
```

7. The complete XAML markup code for `MainPage.xaml` will be similar to the following lines:

```xml
<UserControl x:Class="SilverlightProjects.MainPage"
    xmlns="http://schemas.microsoft.com/winfx/2006/xaml/
      presentation"
    xmlns:x="http://schemas.microsoft.com/winfx/2006/xaml"
    xmlns:d="http://schemas.microsoft.com/expression/blend/2008"
    xmlns:mc="http://schemas.openxmlformats.org/markup-
      compatibility/2006"
    mc:Ignorable="d"
    d:DesignWidth="800" d:DesignHeight="600" xmlns:data=
      "clr-namespace:System.Windows.Controls;
      assembly=System.Windows.Controls.Data" xmlns:dataInput=
      "clr-namespace:System.Windows.Controls;
      assembly=System.Windows.Controls.Data.Input">

    <Grid x:Name="LayoutRoot" Background="White">
        <data:DataGrid AutoGenerateColumns="True" Height="491"
            HorizontalAlignment="Left" Margin="12,56,0,0"
            Name="dataGridProjects" VerticalAlignment="Top"
            Width="776" FontSize="{
            Binding ElementName=sliGridFontSize, Path=Value}" />

        <dataInput:Label Height="38" HorizontalAlignment="Left"
            Margin="12,12,0,0" Name="label1"
            VerticalAlignment="Top" Width="376"
            FontWeight="Bold" FontSize="24"
            Content="Projects" />

        <Slider Height="35" HorizontalAlignment="Left"
            Margin="158,553,0,0" Name="sliGridFontSize"
            VerticalAlignment="Top" Width="630" Value="11"
            Maximum="72" Minimum="11" />

        <dataInput:Label Content="Font size" FontSize="20"
            FontWeight="Bold" Height="35" HorizontalAlignment="Left"
            Margin="12,553,0,0" Name="label2"
            VerticalAlignment="Top" Width="140" />
    </Grid>
</UserControl>
```

8. Now, it is necessary to add code to retrieve data from the XML file and assign a value to the `ItemsSource` property of the `DataGrid` control. First, you have to add a reference to `System.Xml.Linq.dll`. Then, you can add the new `InitializeGrid` method and call it from the class constructor as shown in the following lines for `MainPage.xaml.cs`.

```
using System;
using System.Collections.Generic;
using System.Linq;
using System.Net;
using System.Windows;
using System.Windows.Controls;
using System.Windows.Documents;
using System.Windows.Input;
using System.Windows.Media;
using System.Windows.Media.Animation;
using System.Windows.Shapes;
// Added
using System.Xml.Linq;

namespace SilverlightProjects
{
    public partial class MainPage : UserControl
    {
        private void InitializeGrid()
        {
            XDocument docProjects =
                    XDocument.Load("Projects.xml");
            var projectsData = from el in
                    docProjects.Descendants("project")
                                select new Project
                                {
                                    ProjectId = Convert.
ToInt32(el.Attribute("projectId").Value),
                                    Title = Convert.ToString(el.
Element("title").Value),
                                    EstimatedDaysLeft = Convert.
ToInt32(el.Element("estimatedDaysLeft").Value),
                                    Status = Convert.ToString(el.
Element("status").Value),
                                    AssignedTo = Convert.
ToString(el.Element("assignedTo").Value),
                                    NumberOfTasks = Convert.
ToInt32(el.Element("numberOfTasks").Value)
                                };
            dataGridProjects.ItemsSource = projectsData;
        }

        public MainPage()
```

```
        {
            InitializeComponent();
            InitializeGrid();
        }
    }
}
```

9. Build and run the solution. The default web browser will appear showing a grid with headers and the five rows defined in the previously added XML file, as shown in the following screenshot:

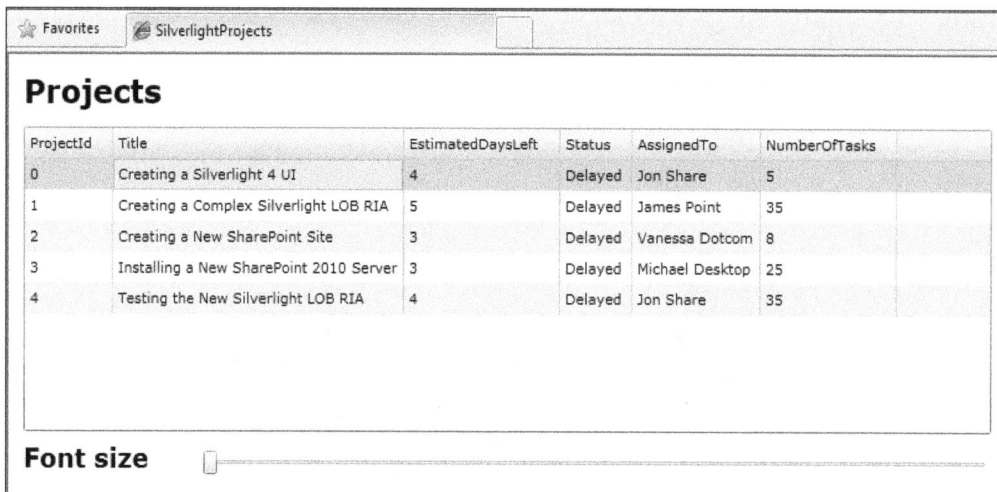

ProjectId	Title	EstimatedDaysLeft	Status	AssignedTo	NumberOfTasks
0	Creating a Silverlight 4 UI	4	Delayed	Jon Share	5
1	Creating a Complex Silverlight LOB RIA	5	Delayed	James Point	35
2	Creating a New SharePoint Site	3	Delayed	Vanessa Dotcom	8
3	Installing a New SharePoint 2010 Server	3	Delayed	Michael Desktop	25
4	Testing the New Silverlight LOB RIA	4	Delayed	Jon Share	35

Favorites | SilverlightProjects

Projects

Font size

It is a very simple Silverlight LOB RIA displaying a data grid with rows that are read from the XML file included in the project, `Projects.xml`.

First, we added the XML file with the definitions for the five projects. Then, we added a class with the necessary properties to hold the values defined in this XML file.

The `InitializeGrid` method loads the projects from the `Projects.xml` XML file (embedded and compressed in the `.xap` file).

```
XDocument docProjects = XDocument.Load("Projects.xml");
```

Then, it uses a LINQ to XML query to create instances of the `Project` class and assign values to their properties. Finally, it assigns this query to the `ItemsSource` property of the `DataGrid`:

```
dataGridProjects.ItemsSource = projectsData;
```

> C# 3.0 (Visual C# 2008) introduced LINQ and it is very useful for processing queries for many different data sources. The features of LINQ and its usage in real-life scenarios are described in depth in *LINQ Quickly (A Practical Guide to Programming Language Integrated Query with C#)* by N. Satheesh Kumar from Packt Publishing.

Creating rich User eXperiences (UX)

We can click on one of the headers and the grid will sort the data in ascending order. Then, we can click again to sort the data into descending order.

When we drag the slider located at the bottom, the font size for the grid will change, as shown in the following screenshot:

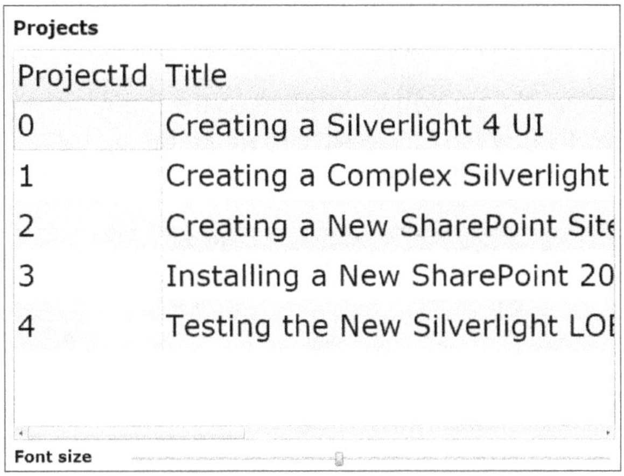

Projects

ProjectId	Title
0	Creating a Silverlight 4 UI
1	Creating a Complex Silverlight
2	Creating a New SharePoint Site
3	Installing a New SharePoint 20
4	Testing the New Silverlight LOI

Font size

As previously explained, we can also take advantage of the themes included in Silverlight's Toolkit to offer the user a more exciting UI. Follow these steps to apply a theme to the main `UserControl` for the Silverlight UI:

1. Select **Start | All Programs | Microsoft Silverlight 4 Toolkit | Binaries** and Windows will open the folder that contains the Silverlight Toolkit binaries. By default, they are located at `C:\Program Files (x86)\Microsoft SDKs\Silverlight\v4.0\Toolkit\Apr10\Bin` in 64-bit Windows versions. Its parent folder contains the Themes sub-folder, `C:\Program Files (x86)\Microsoft SDKs\Silverlight\v4.0\Toolkit\Apr10\Themes`. In 32-bit Windows versions, the default folders are `C:\Program Files\Microsoft SDKs\Silverlight\v4.0\Toolkit\Apr10\Bin` and `C:\Program Files\Microsoft SDKs\Silverlight\v4.0\Toolkit\Apr10\Themes`.

2. Add a reference to `System.Windows.Controls.Theming.Toolkit.dll`. Remember that it is located in the aforementioned `Bin` sub-folder.

3. Add a reference to the DLL for the desired theme in the `Themes` sub-folder. For example, if you want to apply the `ShinyBlue` theme, add `System.Windows.Controls.Theming.ShinyBlue`, located in the aforementioned `Themes` sub-folder.

4. Add the following line to include the namespace that defines the theme in the `UserControl` defined in `MainPage.xaml`:

```
xmlns:shinyBlue=
    "clr-namespace:System.Windows.Controls.Theming;
    assembly=System.Windows.Controls.Theming.ShinyBlue"
```

5. Add the following line before the definition of the main `Grid`, `LayoutRoot`:

```
<shinyBlue:ShinyBlueTheme>
```

6. Add the following line after the definition of the main `Grid`, `LayoutRoot`:

```
</shinyBlue:ShinyBlueTheme>
```

This way, the `ShinyBlue` theme will be applied to the main `Grid`, `LayoutRoot` and all its child controls. It wasn't necessary to make great changes to offer a more attractive rich user experience. Let's see the revised look in the following screenshot:

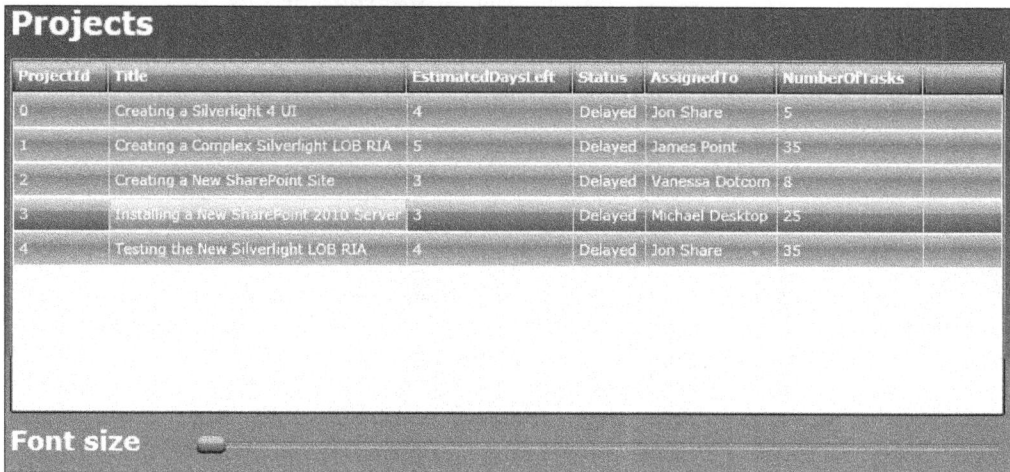

ProjectId	Title	EstimatedDaysLeft	Status	AssignedTo	NumberOfTasks
0	Creating a Silverlight 4 UI	4	Delayed	Jon Share	5
1	Creating a Complex Silverlight LOB RIA	5	Delayed	James Point	35
2	Creating a New SharePoint Site	3	Delayed	Vanessa Dotcom	8
3	Installing a New SharePoint 2010 Server	3	Delayed	Michael Desktop	25
4	Testing the New Silverlight LOB RIA	4	Delayed	Jon Share	35

Font size

Building a Silverlight 4 RIA

When we build a Silverlight project, Visual Studio or Expression Blend creates many folders with a lot of sub-folders and files.

In this case, we want to add the simple Silverlight RIA to a page in SharePoint 2010. Thus, we are interested in the `SilverlightProjects.xap` file. This is a compressed file, that is, a ZIP file with a `.xap` extension, and it contains all the necessary files for the Silverlight application.

You can find this file in the `Debug` or the `Release` sub-folder, according to your active solution configuration. For example, if the project is located in a `SilverlightProjects` folder, the relative path for the release `SilverlightProjects.xap` file would usually be `...\SilverlightProjects\Bin\Release`. If you want to be sure about the location of the generated `.xap` file, you can follow these steps after building the project:

1. Activate the **Solution Explorer**.

2. Click on the **Show All Files** button, the second button located at the top of the **Solution Explorer** palette. Now, expand the `Bin` folder and then the `Debug` or `Release` sub-folder, according to your active solution configuration, as shown in the following screenshot:

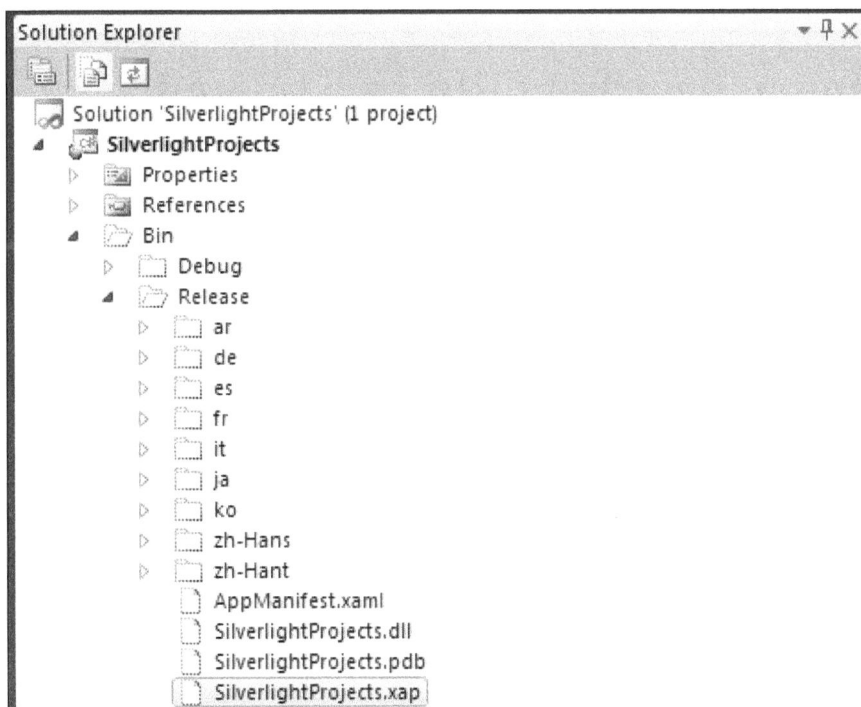

3. Right-click on the `SilverlightProjects.xap` file and, and select **Properties** in the context menu that appears or press *F4*. The **Properties** palette will appear and you will be able to see the value for its **Full Path** property. This way, you can get the exact path for this file, as shown in the next screenshot. You will need it later to integrate it with SharePoint.

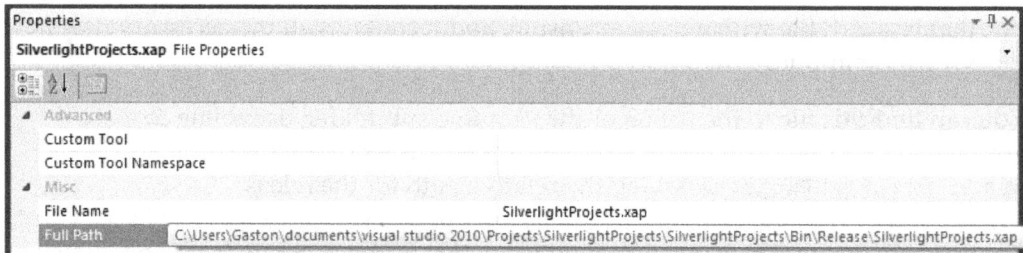

Adding a Silverlight Web Part

We now want to add the Silverlight RIA to a SharePoint site. This Silverlight application doesn't interact with the SharePoint services. It displays information about projects saved in the same `.xap` file.

In this case, we can add a **Silverlight Web Part** to a SharePoint site.

Adding a Silverlight RIA as a shared document

First, follow these steps to add the Silverlight RIA as a shared document in a SharePoint site:

1. Open your default web browser, view the SharePoint site, and log in with your username and password.

2. Click **Site Actions | View All Site Content** and SharePoint will display all sites, lists, and libraries in the active site.

3. Click on **Shared Documents** under **Documents** on the panel located at the left of the web page. SharePoint will display the shared documents library. These are the documents shared with the team.

4. Click on **Add new document**. The **Upload Document** dialog box will appear. Click on the **Browse...** button and enter the full path for the `SilverlightProjects.xap` file. Then, click **Open** and the document's name will be the `.xap` file and its path, as shown in the next screenshot:

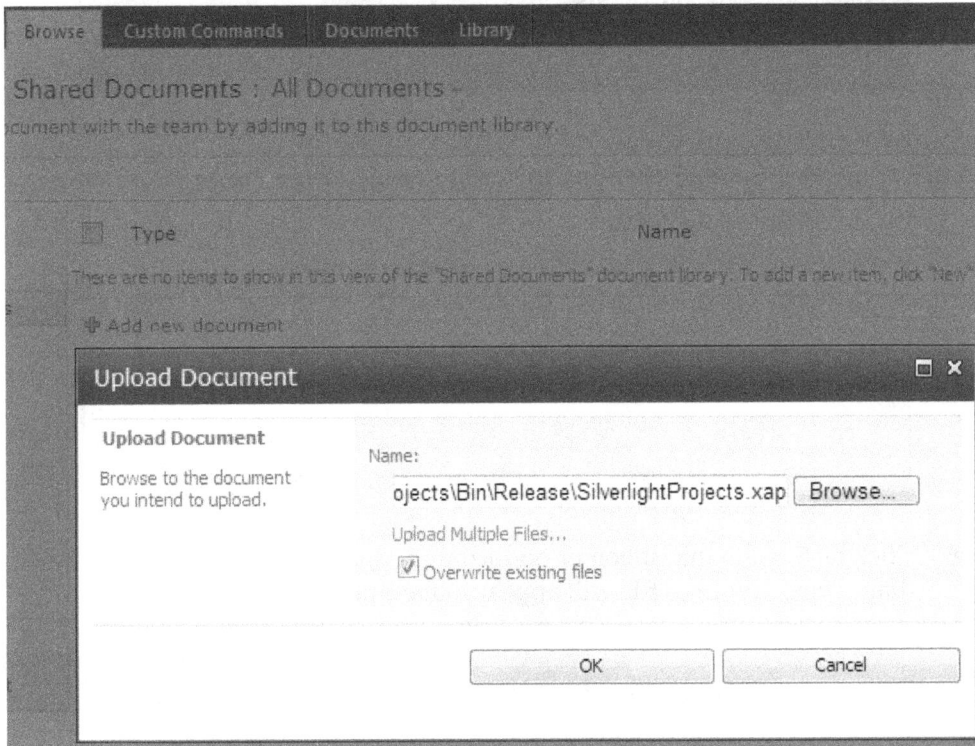

Browse	Custom Commands	Documents	Library

Shared Documents : All Documents ~

document with the team by adding it to this document library.

	Type		Name

There are no items to show in this view of the "Shared Documents" document library. To add a new item, click "New"

✦ Add new document

Upload Document   ☐ ✕

Upload Document

Browse to the document   Name:
you intend to upload.
                               ojects\Bin\Release\SilverlightProjects.xap [Browse...]

                               Upload Multiple Files...

                               ☑ Overwrite existing files

                               [OK   ]   [Cancel   ]

5. Click **OK**. Once the file finishes the upload process, the dialog box to define its properties as a shared document will appear. Enter `Silverlight projects` in **Title** and `Silverlight` in **Managed Keywords**.

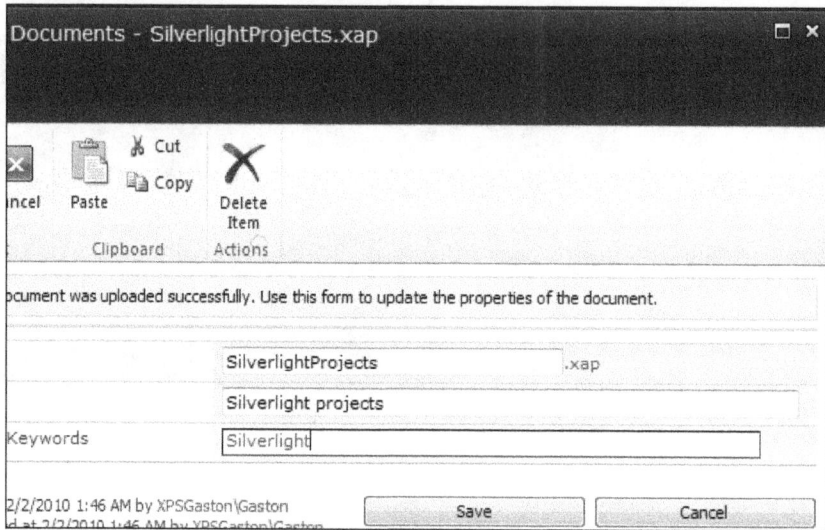

6. Click on **Save** in the ribbon or on the button located at the bottom of the dialog box. The `.xap` file will appear in the **Shared Documents** list.

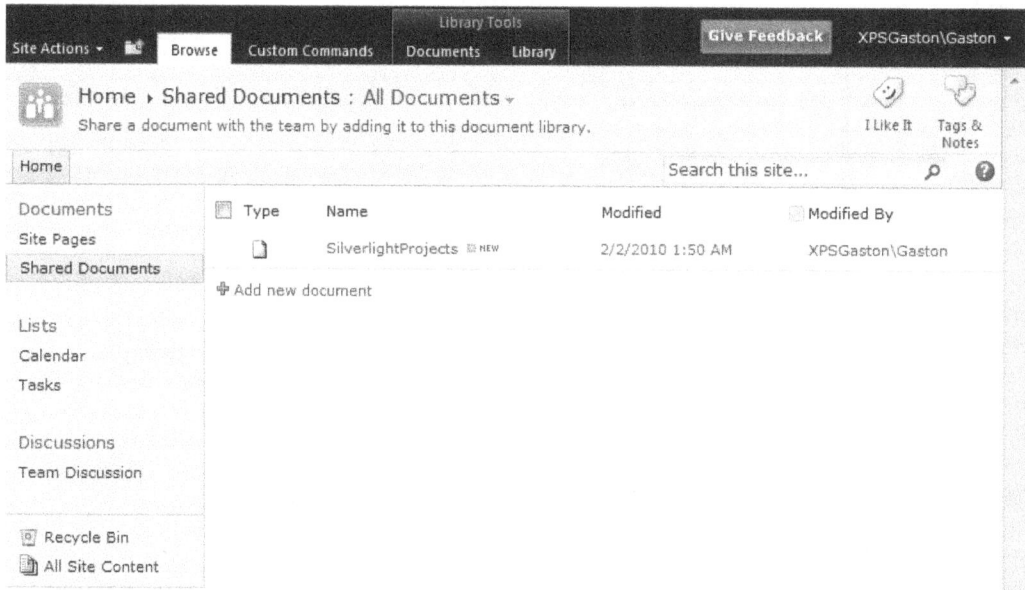

7. Right-click on the new document name, `SilverlightProjects`, and select **Copy Shortcut** from the context menu that appears. This way, you will copy the URL for this shared document in the clipboard and you will be able to paste it when SharePoint asks you for its URL. In this case, the copied URL is `http://xpsgaston/Shared%20Documents/SilverlightProjects.xap`.

Adding a Silverlight Web Part to display a Silverlight RIA

The `.xap` file is available as a shared document. Now, follow these steps to add a Silverlight Web Part to display the Silverlight RIA in a SharePoint site:

1. Click **Site Actions | New Page** and SharePoint will display a new dialog box requesting a name for the new page. Enter `Projects Grid` and click on **Create**. SharePoint will display the **Editing Tools** for the new page.

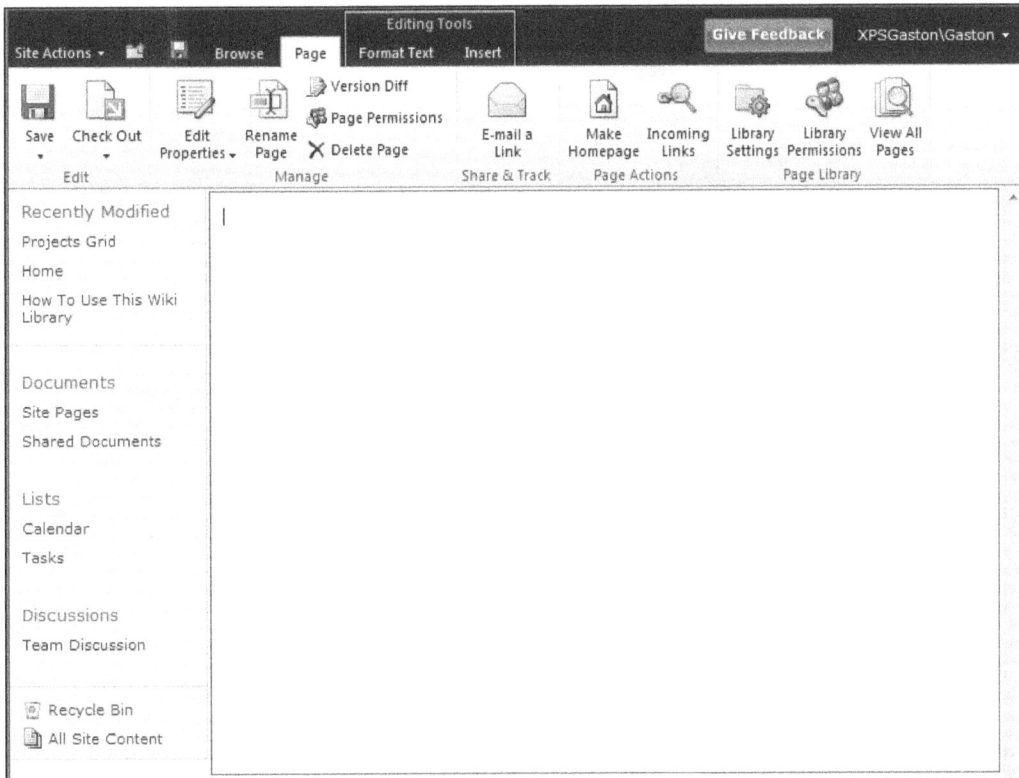

2. Click **Insert | Web Part** in the ribbon and a new panel will appear. Select **Media and Content** in **Categories** and then **Silverlight Web Part** in **Web Parts**, as shown in the following screenshot:

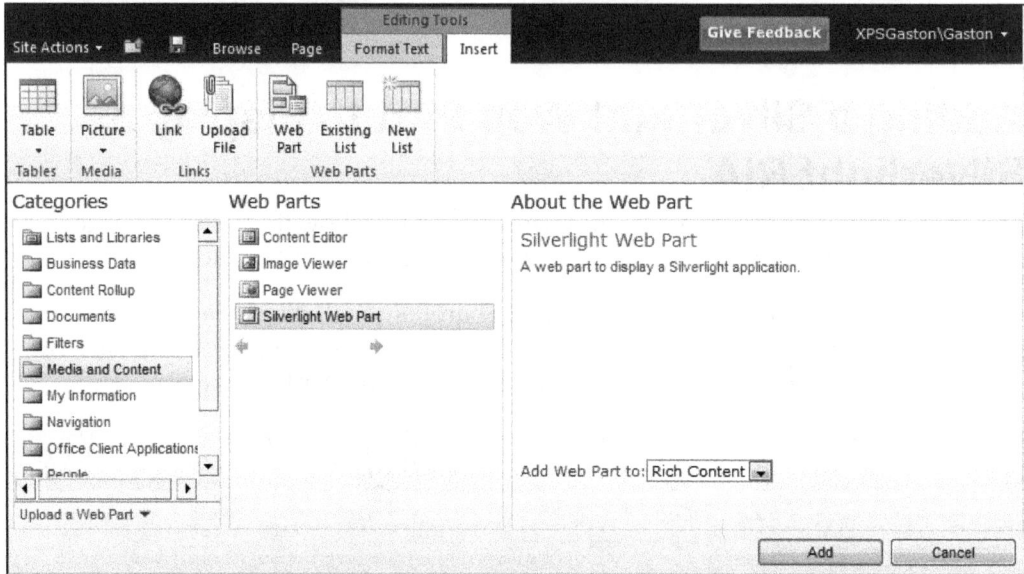

3. Click **Add**. The **Silverlight Web Part** dialog box will appear. Paste the previously copied URL for the shared document, the `.xap` file. In this case, it is `http://xpsgaston/Shared%20Documents/SilverlightProjects.xap`, as shown in the next screenshot:

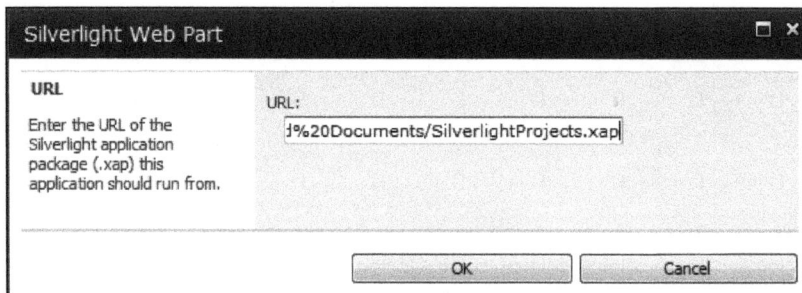

> If you don't have the URL for the the `.xap` file copied to the clipboard, you can open a new tab or a new browser window and access the shared documents as previously explained. Then, you can right-click on the desired document name and select **Copy Shortcut** from the context menu that appears. This way, you will be able to paste the URL in the **Silverlight Web Part** dialog box.

4. Click **OK**.

> In certain SharePoint 2010 pre-release versions, the following error message could appear, **Could not download the Silverlight application or the Silverlight Plugin did not load. To re-configure the Web Part or to provide a different Silverlight application (.xap), open the tool pane and then click Configure.**

5. If the error appears, click on **open the tool pane** or click on the down arrow, located at the top and then select **Edit Web Part**.

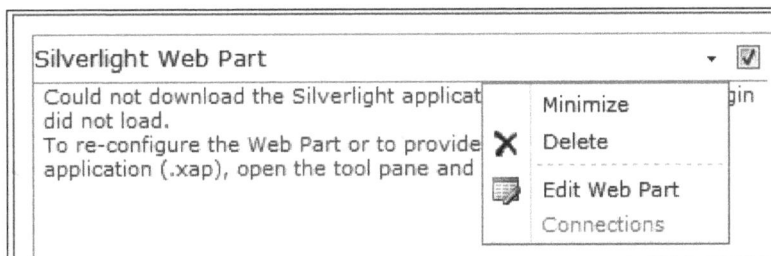

Silverlight Web Part	▾ ☑
Could not download the Silverlight applicat did not load. To re-configure the Web Part or to provide application (.xap), open the tool pane and	Minimize gin ✖ Delete ▨ Edit Web Part Connections

6. The **Silverlight Web Part** pane will appear on the right. It will enable us to define many properties that affect the appearance and behavior for the Silverlight UI.

7. Enter `Projects List Viewer` in **Title**.

8. Click on **Yes** in **Should the Web Part have a fixed height?** and enter `600` in **Pixels**.

9. Click on **Yes** in **Should the Web Part have a fixed width?** and enter `800` in **Pixels**.

```
◄ Silverlight Web Part                    ✕
Application                                ☆

To provide a Silverlight application (.xap)
to use, click Configure.

              [ Configure... ]

⊟  Appearance

Title
[ Projects List Viewer              ]

Height
Should the Web Part have a fixed height?
◉ Yes      [ 600 ] [ Pixels    ▼ ]
◯ No. Adjust height to fit zone.

Width
Should the Web Part have a fixed width?
◉ Yes      [ 800 ] [ Pixels    ▼ ]
◯ No. Adjust width to fit zone.

Chrome State
◯ Minimized
◉ Normal

Chrome Type
[ Default         ▼ ]

⊞  Layout
⊞  Advanced
⊟  Other Settings

Custom Initialization Parameters
[                                   ]

       [ OK ]  [ Cancel ]  [ Apply ]
```

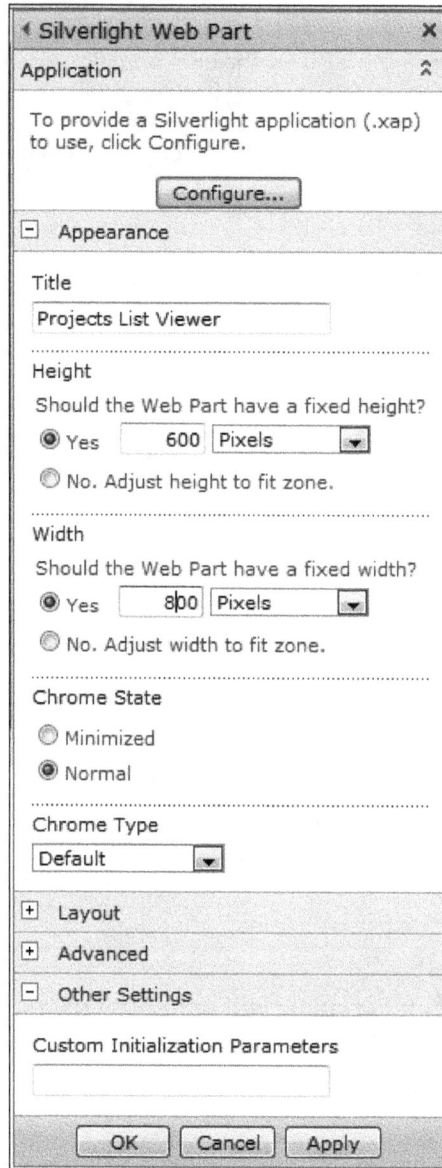

10. Click **OK**. The title for the Web Part will change but the same error message will appear. Don't worry about that.

11. Click on the **Save** button in the ribbon. Now, the new page will appear displaying the previously created Silverlight RIA. However, the title won't appear as expected, as shown in the next screenshot:

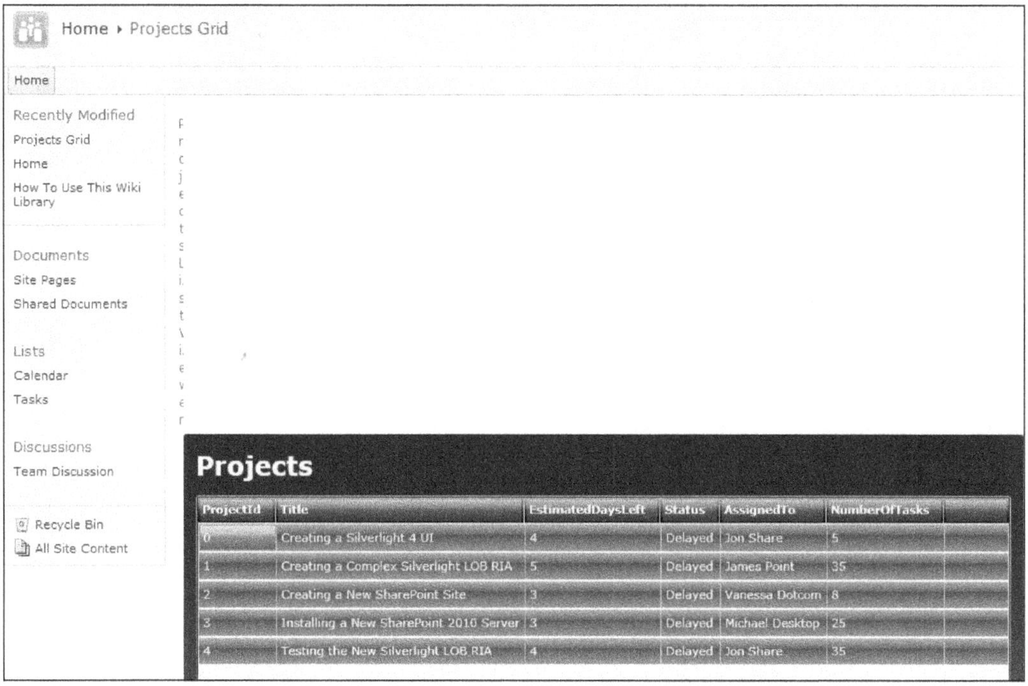

12. Click **Site Actions | Edit Page**. This time, SharePoint will display the Silverlight RIA alive in the editing mode instead of the previously shown error message.

13. Click on the down arrow, located at the top, and then select **Edit Web Part**. The **Silverlight Web Part** pane will appear on the right.

14. Click on **No. Adjust width to fit zone.** in **Should the Web Part have a fixed width?**

15. Click **OK** and then on the **Save** button in the ribbon. Now, the new page will appear displaying the previously created Silverlight RIA with the title appearing as expected.

16. The Silverlight Web Part added to the page holds a running and active Silverlight application. Click on one of the grid rows and you will see the gradient animations for the selected theme. Click on a column header and the rows will be sorted according to it.

Working with many Silverlight Web Parts in a single page

Following the previously explained steps, we can upload many Silverlight RIAs as shared documents and then add various Silverlight Web Parts to a single page. For example, we can rename the `.xap` file for the previous version of the `SilverlightProjects` application, without the application of the theme, to `SilverlightProjectsNoTheme.xap`. Then, we can follow the necessary steps to edit the page and add it as a new Silverlight Web Part to allow the users to choose between the different looks-and-feels to display the list of active projects.

Projects List Viewer (No Theme)

Projects

ProjectId	Title ▲	EstimatedDaysLeft	Status	AssignedTo	Num
1	Creating a Complex Silverlight LOB RIA	5	Delayed	James Point	35
2	Creating a New SharePoint Site	3	Delayed	Vanessa Dotcom	8
0	Creating a Silverlight 4 UI	4	Delayed	Jon Share	5
3	Installing a New SharePoint 2010 Server	3	Delayed	Michael Desktop	25
4	Testing the New Silverlight LOB RIA	4	Delayed	Jon Share	35

Font size

Projects List Viewer

Projects

ProjectId	Title ▲	EstimatedDaysLeft ▲	Status	AssignedTo	NumberOfTasks	
2	Creating a New SharePoint Site	3	Delayed	Vanessa Dotcom	8	
3	Installing a New SharePoint 2010 Server	3	Delayed	Michael Desktop	25	
0	Creating a Silverlight 4 UI	4	Delayed	Jon Share	5	
4	Testing the New Silverlight LOB RIA	4	Delayed	Jon Share	35	
1	Creating a Complex Silverlight LOB RIA	5	Delayed	James Point	35	

This way, you can make many Silverlight applications available to SharePoint users by following very simple steps. SharePoint 2010 added the new Silverlight Web Part to simplify adding Silverlight applications as part of SharePoint pages.

When the user moves the slider, the font size for the data grid will change, as previously experienced with the Silverlight RIA running in a simple web page. However, this time, the application is running as a Silverlight Web Part in a SharePoint site, as shown. Each Silverlight Web Part offers a very responsive application to the user because they don't have to wait for server responses to refresh the Web Part.

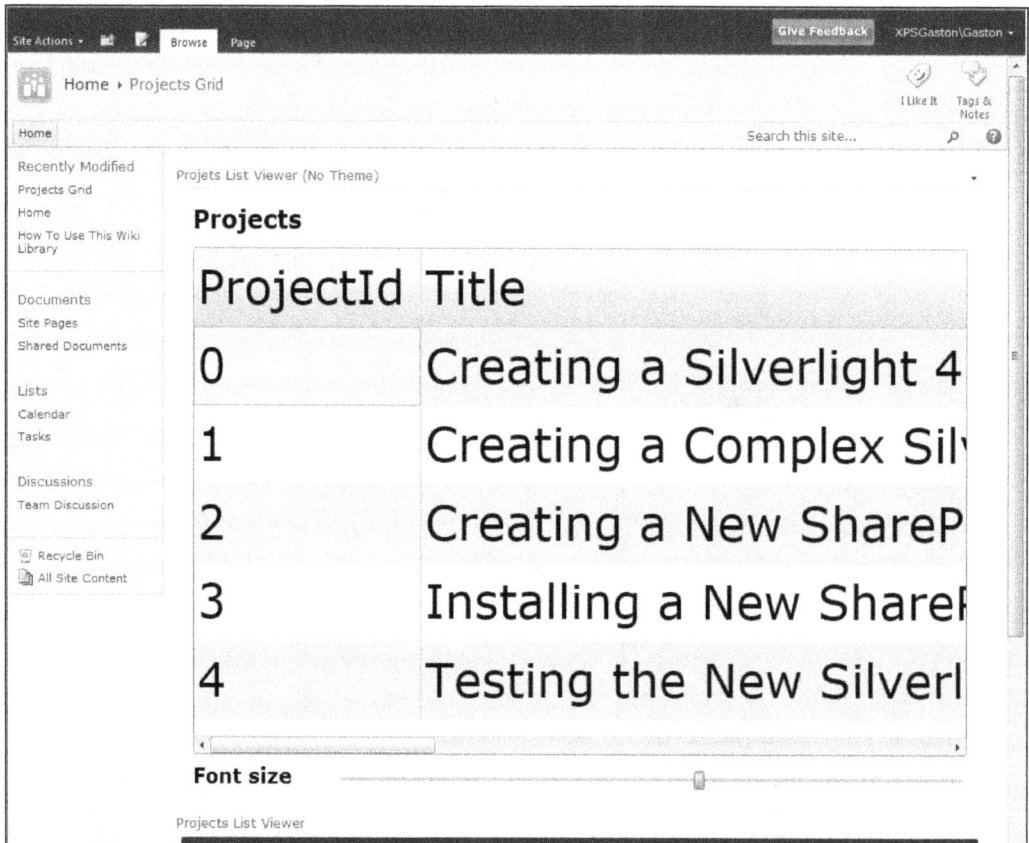

It is easy for a SharePoint user to consume a Silverlight Application. Now, all the users that have access to the new page will be able to interact with the Silverlight UIs added to this page.

It is possible to add Silverlight applications to SharePoint through many different alternatives:

- **As a Silverlight Web Part**
- **Included in a SharePoint Module**
- **Included in a SharePoint Visual Web Part**

The previous steps explained how to work with the first alternative. In the next chapters we will analyze the other two alternatives.

Understanding client and server code

As previously explained, when we integrate Silverlight with SharePoint, there is going to be code running on both the client and the server. The Silverlight applications appear on the SharePoint pages. However, once the .xap files are downloaded, their code runs on the client. Each client will require the Silverlight 4 client runtime installed in order to be able to run the application. If it isn't installed, a message will appear indicating that it requires Silverlight.

When you see an animation in a Silverlight RIA, it is consuming processing power found in the client and it is not adding load to the SharePoint server. When you add code to interact with the SharePoint server, the requests consume processing power from the server. However, when the Silverlight application processes the results from a request this code is running on the client.

All the code that presents graphics on the screen runs on the client. When you move the mouse cursor over an element, the animations and the events run on the client. Therefore, you don't add huge processing power from the server when adding Silverlight applications to a SharePoint solution.

Summary

We learned a lot in this chapter about the integration of Silverlight 4 applications with SharePoint 2010 sites and solutions. Specifically, we prepared a development environment and the tools to work with Silverlight 4 RIAs. We configured the SharePoint 2010 server and added Silverlight Web Parts to a new page. We understood the differences between client and server code and the benefits of integrating Silverlight with SharePoint.

We created our first Silverlight RIA and then, we made it available in a SharePoint site. Now, we are ready to begin adding simple Silverlight RIAs as part of SharePoint solutions.

Now that we have learned about the principles of the integration of Silverlight with SharePoint, we are ready to learn the techniques to work with deploying and debugging for this integration process, which is the topic of the next chapter.

2
Deploying and Debugging Techniques for Silverlight and SharePoint

We already know how to consume a Silverlight RIA in a SharePoint page. Now, we want to create Silverlight RIAs that interact with SharePoint data and services. However, as it requires learning many new classes, it is very important to simplify the deployment process and learn techniques to debug the code that runs in the Silverlight RIA when it is executed in a SharePoint page. In this chapter, we will cover many topics that help us understand the new deployment and debugging techniques involved in integrating Silverlight RIAs with SharePoint 2010 sites.

We will:

- Deploy a Silverlight RIA included in a SharePoint solution by using the new SharePoint deployment features offered by Visual Studio 2010
- Link a Silverlight RIA to a SharePoint module
- Use the SharePoint Silverlight Client Object Model to retrieve data from a SharePoint list in a Silverlight RIA
- Work with asynchronous SharePoint requests and queries, along with the debugging of their execution
- Work with a central object to access SharePoint data and services
- Debug a Silverlight RIA running in a Silverlight Web Part
- Learn to take advantage of Visual Studio 2010 multi-monitor support
- Test applications for multiple-browser support

Deploying a Silverlight RIA included in a SharePoint solution

So far, we have been able to consume a Silverlight RIA in SharePoint 2010. However, the Silverlight RIA did not interact with the SharePoint server. SharePoint offers the possibility to create lists and to edit their data. The predefined list of tasks is appropriate for managing projects and their related tasks. Therefore, we can create a new list of tasks, add the projects to this list, and then create a Silverlight RIA to retrieve and display data from this list in a grid.

There are many different ways to deploy a Silverlight RIA included in a SharePoint solution with Visual Studio 2010. We will analyze diverse alternatives to simplify the deployment process and show how to debug a Silverlight RIA that queries data from a SharePoint server.

Creating a list of tasks in SharePoint

First, follow these steps to add a list of tasks in a SharePoint site and fill it with some items:

1. Open your default web browser, view the SharePoint site, and log in with your username and password.

2. Click **Site Actions | More Options...** in the ribbon and the **Create** dialog box will appear.

3. Select **List** and **Tracking** under **Filter By:** and then **Tasks** in **Installed Items**, as shown in the following screenshot:

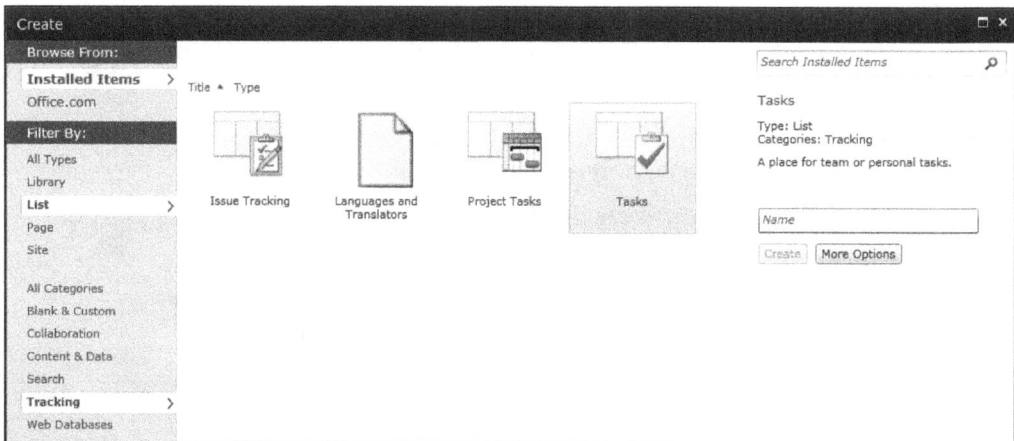

4. Enter ProjectsList2010 in the **Name** textbox.

5. Click on **More Options**. SharePoint will display a new panel with additional options for the new list.

6. Enter `Projects and tasks for year 2010` in the **Description** field and select **Yes** in **Display this list on the Quick Launch?**

Click on **Create**. SharePoint will create the new list with no items. It will show the following fields (columns) for the new list of tasks in the **Standard View**:

Field	Description
Type	The type of project
Title	Describes the task or project.
Assigned To	Refers to the person to whom the task or project is assigned. They can be any existing user in the SharePoint server.
Status	The possible values for the status are: `Not Started, In Progress, Completed, Deferred` or `Waiting on Someone Else`.
Priority	The possible values for the priority are: `(1) High, (2) Normal, (3) Low`.
Due Date	The due date for the project or task.
% Complete	The percentage completed of the total work for the project or task.
Predecessors	The list of predecessor tasks. It is possible to select one or many existing tasks as predecessors.

The shortcut for **ProjectsList2010**, appears under **Lists**, in the panel located on the left:

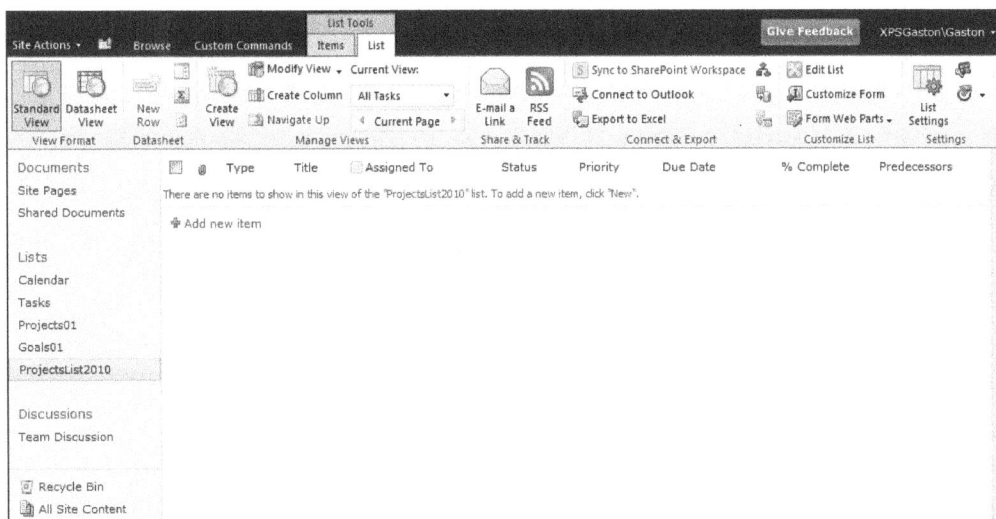

7. Click on **Add new item**. The **ProjectsList2010 - New Item** dialog box will appear. Enter the data for each field that appears in this dialog box to define a new project as a task. You can add some of the projects defined in the `Projects.xml` file used in the project, explained in the previous chapter. The following screenshot shows the dialog box with all the fields and some values to add the new item to the list of tasks:

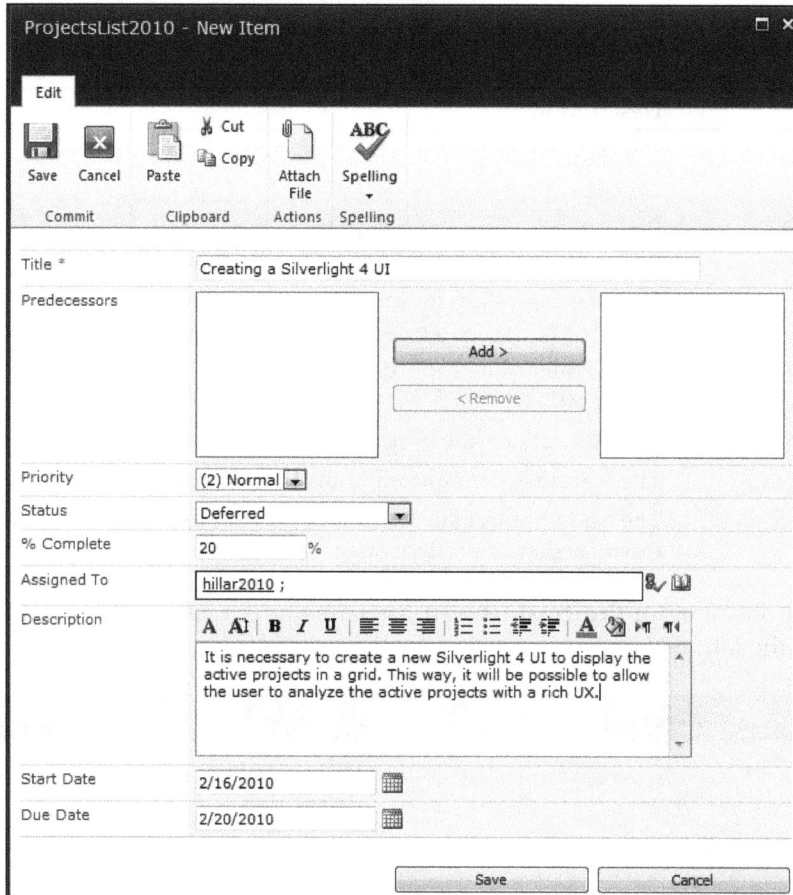

8. Click on **Save** and the new item will appear in the list:

9. Repeat the aforementioned steps (7 and 8) to add items to the list of tasks. This way, you will have a list of tasks, **ProjectsList2010**, with many items:

		Type	Title	Assigned To	Status	Priority	Due Date	% Complete	Predecessors
			Creating a Silverlight 4 UI ⬚ NEW	hillar2010	Deferred	(2) Normal	2/20/2010	20 %	
			Creating a Complex Silverlight LOB RIA ⬚ NEW	XPSGaston\Gaston	Deferred	(1) High	3/2/2010	30 %	
			Creating a New SharePoint Site ⬚ NEW	hillar2010	In Progress	(1) High	2/25/2010	35 %	

➕ Add new item

The SharePoint Site has a new list of tasks, ProjectsList2010, with many fields of different types. This new list has many items and we are going to be able to read them from a Silverlight application.

> Visual Studio 2010 allows us to browse a local SharePoint server. This means that SharePoint Server or SharePoint Foundation must be running on the same computer where we are executing Visual Studio 2010.

Browsing SharePoint lists and fields with Visual Studio

Once we have created the list of tasks in SharePoint, we can use **Server Explorer** in Visual Studio to analyze the new list's structure. Follow these steps to check the properties for each of the fields that compose the SharePoint list.

1. Start Visual Studio as a system administrator user.

2. Activate the Server Explorer by clicking **View | Server Explorer**.

3. Click on the expand button for **SharePoint Connections** and then on the expand button for your SharePoint server URL.

4. Expand **Home | Lists and Libraries | Lists** and you will be able to browse all the lists, including the previously created one, **ProjectsList2010**:

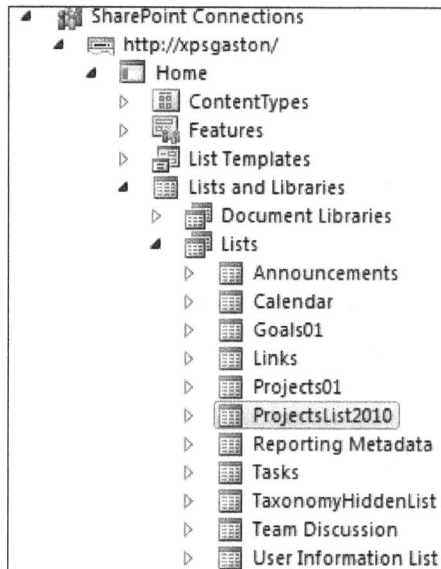

```
◢ 🏭 SharePoint Connections
   ◢ 🖳 http://xpsgaston/
      ◢ 🔲 Home
         ▷ 🔢 ContentTypes
         ▷ 📑 Features
         ▷ 📑 List Templates
         ◢ 🔢 Lists and Libraries
            ▷ 📑 Document Libraries
            ◢ 📑 Lists
               ▷ 🔢 Announcements
               ▷ 🔢 Calendar
               ▷ 🔢 Goals01
               ▷ 🔢 Links
               ▷ 🔢 Projects01
               ▷ 🔢 ProjectsList2010
               ▷ 🔢 Reporting Metadata
               ▷ 🔢 Tasks
               ▷ 🔢 TaxonomyHiddenList
               ▷ 🔢 Team Discussion
               ▷ 🔢 User Information List
```

5. Now, expand **ProjectsList2010** and then its **Fields** node. This way, you will see all the fields for this list:

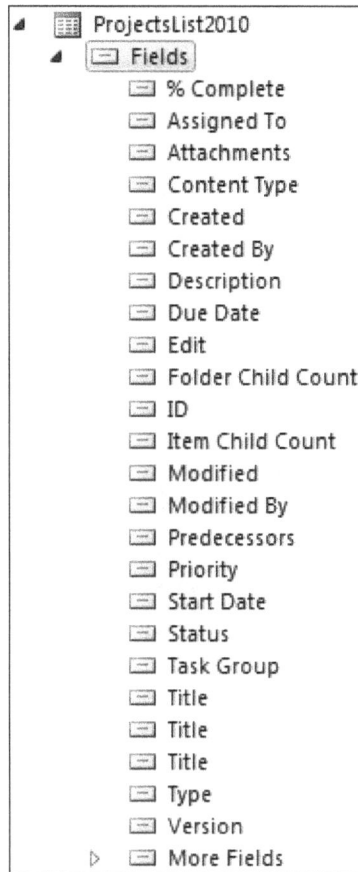

6. Now, click on each field name in the **Fields** list that you want to retrieve for this list in a Silverlight application. Display its properties in the **Properties** palette and check the value for its `InternalName` and `FieldValueType` properties.

The **Title** field is the value shown in the expanded list and it is the value for its `Title` property:

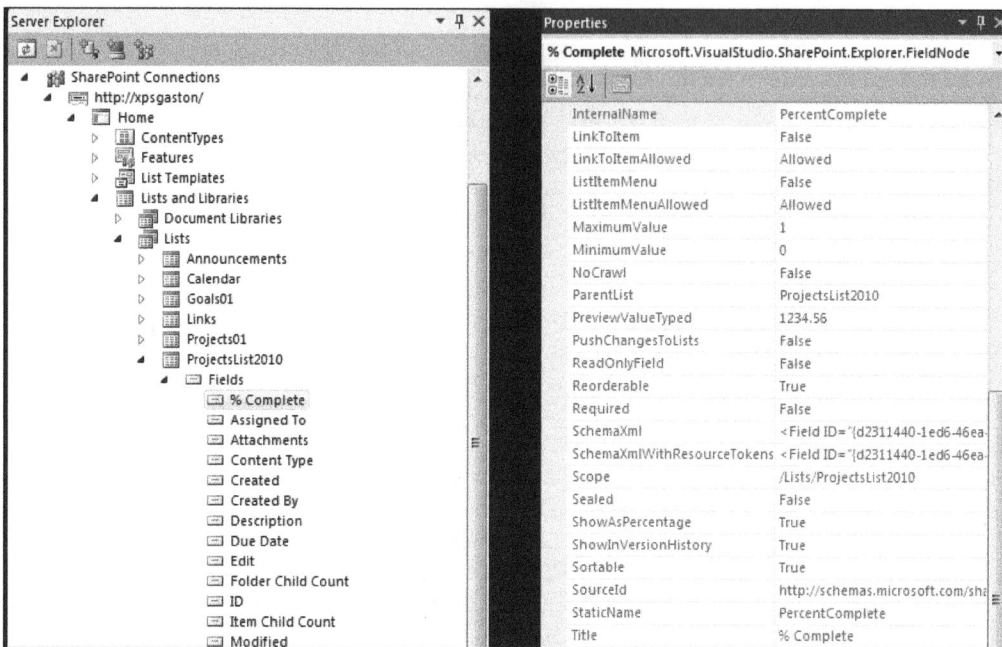

> Many fields in the same list can have the same value for the
> Title property, and therefore it is important to use its unique
> InternalName to access each field.

The Title field that appears in the table is the second **Title** value that
appears in the expanded list in the screenshot in step no. 5. The following
table shows the InternalName and FieldValueType values for each field
that we want to retrieve in our next Silverlight application:

Field title (Title property value)	InternalName property value	FieldValueType property value
ID	ID	Counter (doesn't have a FieldValueType property)
Title	Title	System.String
Start Date	StartDate	System.DateTime
Due Date	DueDate	System.DateTime
Status	Status	System.String
Assigned To	AssignedTo	Microsoft.SharePoint. SPFieldUserValue

We now have the information needed to create a new solution for deploying a Silverlight application that retrieves information from the new list.

Creating a Silverlight RIA to be linked with a SharePoint module

We are now going to create a new solution in Visual Studio that will include the following two new projects:

- A Silverlight application project, `SLTasksViewer`
- An empty SharePoint 2010 project with a module, `SPTasksViewer`

Follow these steps to create the new Silverlight RIA that accesses the list from the SharePoint server:

1. Start Visual Studio as a system administrator user.

2. Select **File | New | Project...** or press *Ctrl+Shift+N*. Expand **Other Project Types** and then select **Visual Studio Solutions** under **Installed Templates** in the **New Project** dialog box. Then, select **Blank Solution**, make sure that **.NET Framework 4** version is selected and enter `TasksViewer` as the project's name and click **OK**. Visual Studio will create a blank solution with no projects, as shown in the following **Solution Explorer** snapshot:

3. Right-click on the solution's name in **Solution Explorer** and select **Add | New Project...** from the context menu that appears.

4. Expand **Visual C#** and then select **Silverlight** under **Installed Templates** in the **Add New Project** dialog box. Then, select **Silverlight Application**, enter `SLTasksViewer` as the project's name, and click **OK**.

5. Deactivate the **Host the Silverlight application in a new Web site** checkbox in the **New Silverlight Application** dialog box and select **Silverlight 4** in **Silverlight Version**. Then, click **OK**. Visual Studio will add the new Silverlight application project to the existing solution.

6. We have to access data and services offered by the SharePoint 2010 server and therefore, we will use the new SharePoint 2010 Silverlight Client OM (Client Object Model) and add these references:

    ○   `Microsoft.SharePoint.Client.Silverlight.dll`

    ○   `Microsoft.SharePoint.Client.Silverlight.Runtime.dll`

7. You will need to browse to the `ClientBin` subfolder where the reference assemblies to the SharePoint Silverlight Client OM are located. By default, the location for the assemblies is `C:\Program Files\Common Files\microsoft shared\Web Server Extensions\14\TEMPLATE\LAYOUTS\ClientBin`. The following screenshot shows the **SLTasksViewer** project in the **Solution TasksViewer** with the two references added:

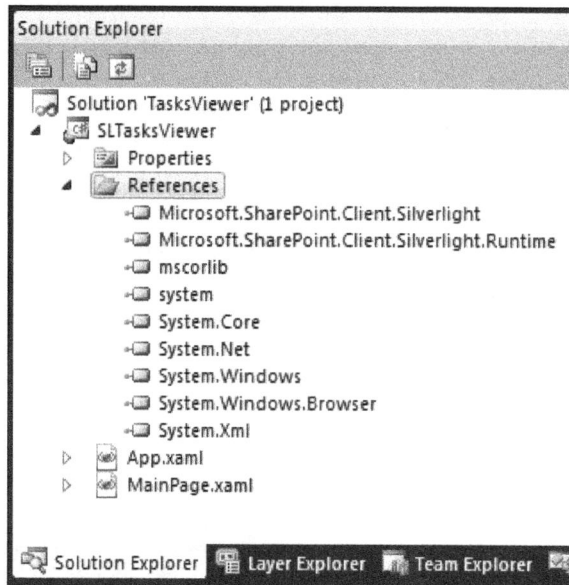

8. Open `App.xaml.cs` and add the following statement:

    ```
    using Microsoft.SharePoint.Client;
    ```

9. It is necessary to add some code in the `StartUp` event handler to initialize the `Microsoft.SharePoint.Client.ApplicationContext` with the same initialization parameters and the synchronization context for the current thread (the UI thread). This way, it is also possible to pass initialization parameters from the page to the Silverlight application.

```
private void Application_Startup(object sender, StartupEventArgs e)
{
    this.RootVisual = new MainPage();
    // Initialize the ApplicationContext
    ApplicationContext.Init(e.InitParams, System.Threading.
                    SynchronizationContext.Current);
}
```

10. Add a new class to the project, **Project**, in a new class file, `Project.cs`. The following lines define the new class, with nine properties. This time, we will fill its properties with the values of the fields retrieved from the list of tasks in SharePoint.

```
public class Project
{
    public int ProjectId { get; set; }
    public string Title { get; set; }
    public DateTime StartDate { get; set; }
    public DateTime DueDate { get; set; }
    public int EstimatedDaysLeft { get; set; }
    public string Priority { get; set; }
    public string Status { get; set; }
    public string AssignedTo { get; set; }
    public int NumberOfTasks { get; set; }
}
```

11. Open `MainPage.xaml`, define a new `width` and `height` for the `Grid`, `800` and `600`, and add the following controls:

    ○ One `Label` control, `lblStatus`.

    ○ One `DataGrid` control, `dataGridProjects`. Set its `AutoGenerateColumns` property to `true`.

12. Open `MainPage.xaml.cs`. Now, it is necessary to add a `using` statement to include the `Microsoft.SharePoint.Client` namespace, as we want to work with the SharePoint Silverlight Client OM. As this namespace includes some duplicate items that exist in other namespaces, we use a reference to it with an `SP.` prefix to make it easier to reference an item for this namespace. For example, `List` is included in `System.Generic.Collections` and also in `Microsoft.SharePoint.Client`, but they are completely different classes. Thus, `SP.List` is going to be `Microsoft.SharePoint.Client.List`. Add the following lines of code:

```
using Microsoft.SharePoint.Client;
using SP = Microsoft.SharePoint.Client;
```

Add the following four private variables:

```
private SP.ClientContext _context;
private SP.ListItemCollection _projectsItemCol;
private SP.List _projects;
private List<Project> _projectsList;
```

13. Now, it is necessary to add code to execute the following tasks:

1. Connect to the SharePoint server using the `Connect` method.

2. Connect to the lists available in the SharePoint server using the `ConnectLists` method.

3. Retrieve data from the `ProjectsList2010` list, `GetListData` method.

4. Load all the available items for the `ProjectsList2010` list, `LoadItems` method.

5. Store a local variable in a list of project instances, one for each item in the `ProjectsList2010` list, fill its properties, and then bind the results list to the `dataGridProjects` DataGrid to display the retrieved data, using the `ShowItems` method.

```
private void Connect()
{
  // Runs in the UI Thread
  lblStatus.Content = "Started";
  _context = new SP.ClientContext
    (SP.ApplicationContext.Current.Url);
  //_context = new SP.ClientContext("http://xpsgaston");
  _context.Load(_context.Web);
  //_context.Load(_context.Web, website => website.Title);
  _context.ExecuteQueryAsync(OnConnectSucceeded, null);
}
private void ConnectLists()
{
```

```
    // Runs in the UI Thread
    lblStatus.Content = "Web Connected. Connecting to Lists...";
    _context.Load(_context.Web.Lists);
    _context.ExecuteQueryAsync(OnConnectListsSucceeded, null);
}

private void GetListData()
{
    // Runs in the UI Thread
    lblStatus.Content = "Lists Connected. Getting List data...";
    // ProjectsList2010 is the list of tasks
    _projects = _context.Web.Lists.GetByTitle("ProjectsList2010");
    _context.Load(_projects);
    _context.Load(_projects.RootFolder);
    _context.ExecuteQueryAsync(OnGetListDataSucceeded, null);
}

private void LoadItems()
{
    // Runs in the UI Thread
    lblStatus.Content = String.Format("Loading {0} items...",
                         _projects.RootFolder.ItemCount);
    var camlQuery = new SP.CamlQuery();
    camlQuery.ViewXml = "<View/>";
    _projectsItemCol = _projects.GetItems(camlQuery);
    _context.Load(_projectsItemCol);
    _context.ExecuteQueryAsync(OnLoadItemsSucceeded, null);
}

private void ShowItems()
{
    // Runs in the UI Thread
    lblStatus.Content = "Showing items...";
    _projectsList = new List<Project>();
    foreach (SP.ListItem listItem in _projectsItemCol)
    {
        _projectsList.Add(
        new Project()
        {
            ProjectId = Convert.ToInt32(listItem["ID"]),
            Title = listItem["Title"].ToString(),
            StartDate = Convert.ToDateTime(listItem["StartDate"]),
            DueDate = Convert.ToDateTime(listItem["DueDate"]),
            EstimatedDaysLeft =
            (Convert.ToDateTime(listItem["DueDate"])
            .Subtract(Convert.ToDateTime(listItem["StartDate"]))).Days),
            Status = listItem["Status"].ToString(),
```

```
        AssignedTo = (listItem["AssignedTo"] as FieldUserValue).
            LookupValue,
        NumberOfTasks = Convert.ToInt32(listItem["ItemChildCount"]),
        Priority = listItem["Priority"].ToString()
      });
  }
  dataGridProjects.ItemsSource = _projectsList;
}
```

14. All the previously added methods are going to run in the UI thread. However, when they execute asynchronous queries to the SharePoint server, both the successful and failed requests fire asynchronous callbacks that are going to run in another thread, different from the UI thread. Thus, if you have to update the UI, it is necessary to invoke the code to run in the UI thread. The following methods, which are going to be fired as asynchronous callbacks, schedule the execution of other methods to continue with the necessary program flow in the UI thread:

    ° When the connection to the SharePoint server, requested by the Connect method, is successful, the OnConnectSucceeded method schedules the execution of the ConnectLists method in the UI thread.

    ° When the connection to the lists available in the SharePoint server, requested by the ConnectLists method, is successful, the OnConnectListsSucceeded method schedules the execution of the GetListData method in the UI thread.

    ° When the retrieval of data from the ProjectsList2010 list, requested by the GetListData method, is successful, the OnGetListDataSucceeded method schedules the execution of the LoadItems method in the UI thread.

    ° Finally, when the loading of all the available items for the ProjectsList2010 list, requested by the LoadItems method, is successful, the OnLoadItemsSucceeded method schedules the execution of the ShowItems method in the UI thread.

```
private void OnConnectSucceeded(Object sender, SP.ClientRequestSuc
ceededEventArgs args)
{
  // This callback isn't called on the UI thread
  Dispatcher.BeginInvoke(ConnectLists);
}

private void OnConnectListsSucceeded(Object sender, SP.ClientReque
stSucceededEventArgs args)
{
  // This callback isn't called on the UI thread
  Dispatcher.BeginInvoke(GetListData);
}

private void OnGetListDataSucceeded(Object sender, SP.ClientReques
tSucceededEventArgs args)
{
  // This callback isn't called on the UI thread
  Dispatcher.BeginInvoke(LoadItems);
}

private void OnLoadItemsSucceeded(Object sender, SP.ClientRequestS
ucceededEventArgs args)
{
  // This callback isn't called on the UI thread
  Dispatcher.BeginInvoke(ShowItems);
}
```

15. Add the following line to the LayoutRoot_Loaded event:

```
Connect();
```

Working with the asynchronous methods and callbacks

The following sequence diagram shows the interaction between the methods defined in `MainPage` that are going to run in the UI thread, the `Microsoft.SharePoint.Client.ClientContext` instance, `_context`, and the methods defined in `MainPage` that are going to run in another thread, that is , a worker thread. This sequence represents the situation in which all the asynchronous operations against the SharePoint server have a successful completion:

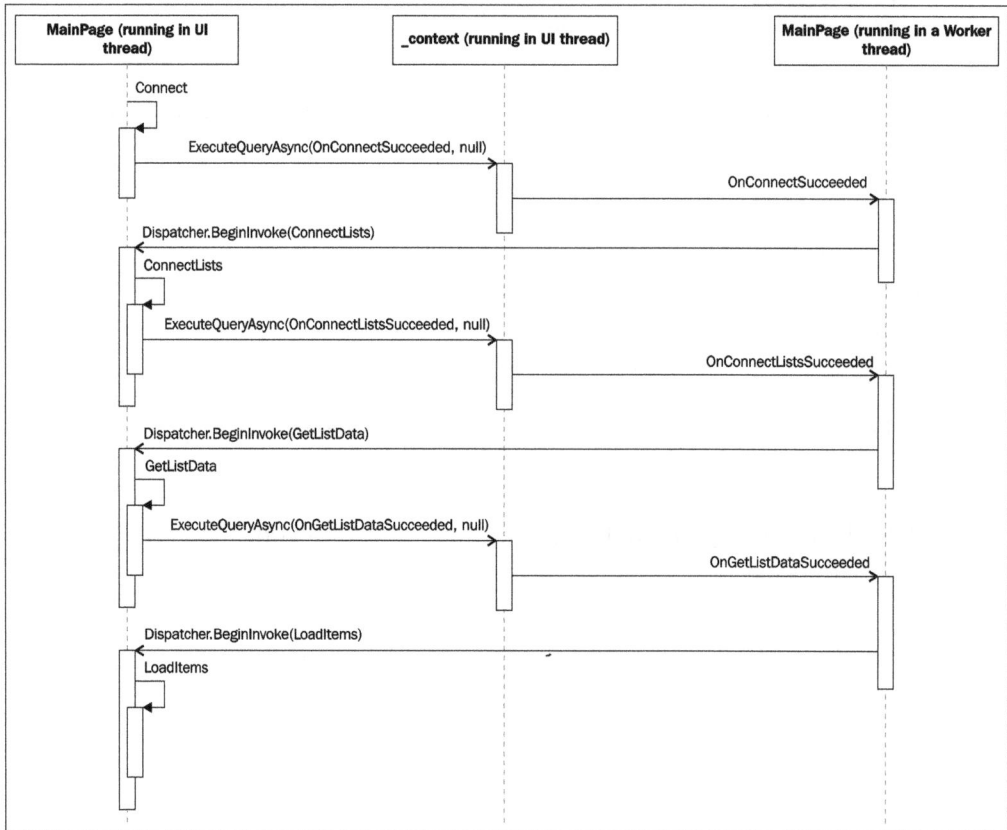

```
MainPage (running in UI          _context (running in UI thread)          MainPage (running in a Worker
       thread)                                                                      thread)

    Connect

            ExecuteQueryAsync(OnConnectSucceeded, null)
                                                                        OnConnectSucceeded

    Dispatcher.BeginInvoke(ConnectLists)

    ConnectLists

            ExecuteQueryAsync(OnConnectListsSucceeded, null)
                                                                        OnConnectListsSucceeded

    Dispatcher.BeginInvoke(GetListData)

    GetListData

            ExecuteQueryAsync(OnGetListDataSucceeded, null)
                                                                        OnGetListDataSucceeded

    Dispatcher.BeginInvoke(LoadItems)

    LoadItems
```

Each call to the `_context.ExecuteQueryAsync` method runs a query to the SharePoint server in another worker thread, different from the UI thread, with an asynchronous execution. When an asynchronous method is called, it runs in an independent way and the program flow in the caller thread (in this case the UI thread) goes on with the execution of the next instruction located after the asynchronous method called before. The execution of the next instruction doesn't mean that the query has finished its execution, because the code in the `ExecuteQueryAsync` method runs concurrently and potentially in parallel with the main program flow in the UI thread. Therefore, this method receives delegates for two callback methods with different parameters, defined in `Microsoft.SharePoint.Client`:

- `ClientRequestSucceededEventHandler` (`succeededCallback`): If the request succeeded, the delegate method receives `Object sender` and `ClientRequestSucceededEventArgs args` as parameters.
- `ClientRequestFailedEventHandler` (`failedCallback`): If the request failed, the delegate method receives `Object sender` and `ClientRequestFailedEventArgs args` as parameters.

The last line of the `Connect` method calls the `_context.ExecuteQueryAsync` with the `OnConnnectSucceeded` delegate method as the first parameter. The second parameter is `null` and therefore, if something goes wrong, the asynchronous query won't fire a callback.

```
_context.ExecuteQueryAsync(OnConnectSucceeded, null);
```

> In this case, the multiple calls to the `_context.ExecuteQueryAsync` method do not specify a delegate method with the `ClientRequestFailedEventHandler` definition. It is not a good practice, because the asynchronous query execution could fail and it is a good idea to do something when it fails. As we are working with many complex asynchronous executions, we have specified a `null` in the second parameter to simplify the explanation. In the next examples, we will include delegate methods with the `ClientRequestFailedEventHandler` definition.

The `OnConnectSucceeded` method uses the definition provided by the `ClientRequestSucceededEventHandler` delegate method:

```
private void OnConnectSucceeded(Object sender, SP.ClientRequestSucceed
edEventArgs args)
```

The code is a bit complicated, because some parts run in the UI thread and others in another thread or threads. A Silverlight application contains one or more threads. The execution of a Silverlight application implies the generation of a main thread and other worker threads. Additional threads can be created, according to needs. Each thread represents the basic unit to which the operating system assigns a processing time. A thread belongs to the Silverlight application process and therefore, shares its context and is able to access the entire private process' memory space.

A thread generated in the Silverlight application can execute any part of its code, including parts being executed by other threads. Each thread can be assigned to a different logical core or logical processor. This task is performed by the **CLR** (**Common Language Runtime**) and the operating system scheduler.

It is not possible to update the UI controls in a worker thread. Therefore, in order to update the UI controls, it is necessary to execute an asynchronous delegate on the UI thread. It is possible to do it with a single line by using the `System.Windows.Threading.Dispatcher`, created for managing the queue of work items, for the UI thread. When we call the `BeginInvoke` method for the `Dispatcher`, created in the `MainPage UserControl`, accessible through `this.Dispatcher` or simply `Dispatcher`, we can queue a delegate to be executed asynchronously in the UI thread from any other worker thread.

For example, the following line schedules the asynchronous execution of the `ConnectLists` method in the UI thread from a worker thread that runs the code after the connection succeeded.

```
private void OnConnectSucceeded(Object sender, SP.ClientRequestSucceed
edEventArgs args)
{
    Dispatcher.BeginInvoke(ConnectLists);
}
```

> As the `Dispatcher` accessed by the previous method is created for the `MainPage UserControl`, it is associated with the UI thread.

Working with the ClientContext object

The `ClientContext` object is the main entry point for accessing the new SharePoint 2010 Silverlight Client OM. It manages the requests and actions within a SharePoint Site Collection. Therefore, in order to obtain and work with sites and their data, it begins by retrieving a context object. The application defines a private variable to hold the instance of `ClientContext`, `_context`. This way, it is possible to access it in the methods defined in the `MainPage UserControl`.

The `Connect` method creates a new `ClientContext` instance, considering the `Current.Url` property of the `ApplicationContext`.

```
_context = new SP.ClientContext(SP.ApplicationContext.Current.Url);
```

It is also possible to initiate a new `ClientContext` object for a specific site collection, which creates it for the `ProjectsWeb` site collection in the `xpsgaston` SharePoint server, as shown in the following line:

```
_context = new SP.ClientContext("http://xpsgaston/ProjectsWeb");
```

The SharePoint 2010 Silverlight Client OM uses a programming pattern similar to the SQL requests. Once you have created the `ClientContext` object, you must follow the following pattern to interact with SharePoint:

1. Build one or more SharePoint queries or method invocations with the client library. This way, you can define the actions to be performed by using the objects that are returned through the `ClientContext` object. It is possible to accumulate many queries before executing them.

2. Execute the SharePoint queries or method invocations. In this way, it is possible to run them with a synchronous execution by using the `ClientContext` object's `ExecuteQuery` method. However, the synchronous execution cannot work in the UI thread. Therefore, if we want to start it in the UI thread, it is necessary to run it with an asynchronous execution by calling the `ClientContext` object's `ExecuteQueryAsync` method and using the previously explained callbacks.

3. Read the results from SharePoint.

After creating the `ClientContext` object, `_context`, the `Connect` method calls the `Load` method to build a query and then the `ExecuteQueryAsync` to run it with an asynchronous execution.

```
_context.Load(_context.Web);
_context.ExecuteQueryAsync(OnConnectSucceeded, null);
```

The `Load` method is very powerful because we can include LINQ expressions as a second parameter. Here is its definition:

```
public void Load<T>(
  T clientObject,
  params Expression<Func<T, Object>>[] retrievals
)
where T : ClientObject
```

The function `T` has to be a `ClientObject`. In the previous lines, the `Load` method receives `_context.Web` as the `ClientObject` to a query. In this example, there are no LINQ expressions as the second parameter when we call the `Load` method.

The result of calling the `Load` method and then executing this query, is the possibility to access the `_context.Web ClientObject`, which means that after the successful execution of the query, we can access `_context.Web` in Silverlight. For example, we could access `_context.Web.Title` to get the title for the website. However, the previous query requested *Load all the properties* for the `_context.Web ClientObject`. If we retrieved all the properties to read just a single one, the code would be really inefficient. The following line shows an example of using a LINQ expression to limit the information that has to be retrieved, because we just want the value for the `Title` property:

```
_context.Load(_context.Web, website => website.Title);
```

Now, let's go back to our example. If everything worked as expected, the `OnConnectSucceeded` method is going to schedule the execution of the `ConnectLists` method in the UI thread. This method follows the aforementioned pattern to query for the SharePoint lists collection:

```
_context.Load(_context.Web.Lists);
_context.ExecuteQueryAsync(OnConnectListsSucceeded, null);
```

It was necessary to call the `Load` method for `_context.Web` before calling the `Load` method for `_context.Web.Lists`. In this case, we want to update the `lblStatus Label` with each operation that is being performed. However, as previously explained it could be possible to call two `Load` methods and then run the `ExecuteQueryAsync` method. The following lines would query the lists in the website:

```
// First, Web
_context.Load(_context.Web);
// Then, Web.Lists
_context.Load(_context.Web.Lists);
_context.ExecuteQueryAsync(OnConnectListsSucceeded, null);
```

The `_context.Web.Lists` is a `Microsoft.SharePoint.Client.ListCollection` and it allows access to many `Microsoft.SharePoint.Client.List` instances, identified as `SP.List` in the code. However, it is necessary to query the list and its `RootFolder` property to access its `ItemCount` property and then another query can retrieve the desired items.

The `GetListData` method calls the `GetByTitle` method to save a reference to the `ProjectsList2010` list, previously created in the SharePoint server in the `_projects` private variable. However, it is necessary to query it, before accessing its properties:

```
_projects = _context.Web.Lists.GetByTitle("ProjectsList2010");
_context.Load(_projects);
_context.Load(_projects.RootFolder);
_context.ExecuteQueryAsync(OnGetListDataSucceeded, null);
```

Then, the `LoadItems` method updates the `lblStatus` Label with the number of items that it is going to load, because, at this point, it can access the `_projects.RootFolder.ItemCount` property. It can do it, because the `_project.RootFolder` was included in the previous query. After that, it is necessary to define a query against the list data. In this case, we want to return all the data for the `_projects` `SP.List` and therefore, we define a very simple **Collaborative Application Markup Language (CAML)** query. This query isn't going to filter data from the list, it will simply return all the values. The `camlQuery` local variable holds a new `SP.CamlQuery` instance with its `ViewXml` property set to `<View/>`. We will work with more complex queries later.

```
var camlQuery = new SP.CamlQuery();
camlQuery.ViewXml = "<View/>";
```

> CAML is a complex and powerful XML-based language. You can check the definitions for all the query schema elements for CAML that you can use to query SharePoint 2010 at `http://msdn.microsoft.com/en-us/library/ms467521(v=office.14).aspx`.

Then, the method calls the `GetItems` method with the previously defined `camlQuery` as a parameter to save a reference to the list item collection for the `_projects` list in the `_projectsItemCol` private variable. However, as expected, it is necessary to query it before accessing its individual items:

```
_context.Load(_projectsItemCol);
_context.ExecuteQueryAsync(OnLoadItemsSucceeded, null);
```

_projectsItemCol is a Microsoft.SharePoint.Client.ListItemCollection and it allows access to many Microsoft.SharePoint.Client.ListItem instances, identified as SP.ListItem in the code. Each of these items contain the value for the fields in one row in the SharePoint list.

Finally, it is time to run the ShowItems method that iterates through each SP.ListItem instance in _projectsItemCol and this creates a new instance of the Project class with the necessary values to show in the dataGridProjects DataGrid. As we already checked the value of both the InternalName and FieldValueType properties for each field that we wanted to access, we use the InternalName as the string to access a desired field and we consider its FieldValueType property to perform the necessary type conversions. The _projectsList private variable is a new List<Project>, with the SharePoint field values loaded to the properties of each Project instance. This way, it is possible to bind this List to the dataGridProjects DataGrid. The value for EstimatedDaysLeft calculates the difference between the DueDate and the StartDate. In this case, it is not considering the % Complete field value, to keep things simple.

```
_projectsList = new List<Project>();
foreach (SP.ListItem listItem in _projectsItemCol)
{
  _projectsList.Add(
  new Project()
  {
    ProjectId = Convert.ToInt32(listItem["ID"]),
    Title = listItem["Title"].ToString(),
    StartDate = Convert.ToDateTime(listItem["StartDate"]),
    DueDate = Convert.ToDateTime(listItem["DueDate"]),
    EstimatedDaysLeft =
    (Convert.ToDateTime(listItem["DueDate"])
    .Subtract(Convert.ToDateTime(listItem["StartDate"])).Days),
    Status = listItem["Status"].ToString(),
    AssignedTo = (listItem["AssignedTo"] as FieldUserValue).
              LookupValue,
    NumberOfTasks = Convert.ToInt32(listItem["ItemChildCount"]),
    Priority = listItem["Priority"].ToString()
  });
}
dataGridProjects.ItemsSource = _projectsList;
```

The `AssignedTo` field has a `Microsoft.SharePoint.SPFieldUserValue` value in its `FieldValueType` property. Therefore, it is necessary to cast it to a `FieldUserValue` and access its `LookupValue` property to show the username to which the task is assigned:

```
AssignedTo = (listItem["AssignedTo"] as FieldUserValue).LookupValue
```

> We have worked with many new classes to make it possible to display data from a SharePoint list in a `DataGrid`. Some of these classes are really complex and we will cover more details about their advanced usage in the next examples in this chapter itself and in the next chapters.

Linking a SharePoint module to a Silverlight RIA

Follow these steps to create a new SharePoint module and link it to the Silverlight RIA, `SLTasksViewer`:

1. Stay in Visual Studio as a system administrator user.

2. Right-click on the solution's name in **Solution Explorer** and select **Add | New Project...** from the context menu that appears.

3. Expand **Visual C#** and then expand **SharePoint** and then select **2010** under **Installed Templates** in the **New Project** dialog box. Then, select **Empty SharePoint Project** and then enter `SPTasksViewer` as the project's name and click **OK**. The **SharePoint Customization Wizard** dialog box will appear.

4. Enter the URL for the SharePoint server and site in **What local site do you want to use for debugging?**

5. Click on **Deploy as a sandboxed solution**. Then, click on **Finish** and the new **SPTasksViewer** empty SharePoint 2010 project will be added to the solution. The next screenshot shows the components for this new project in the **Solution Explorer**:

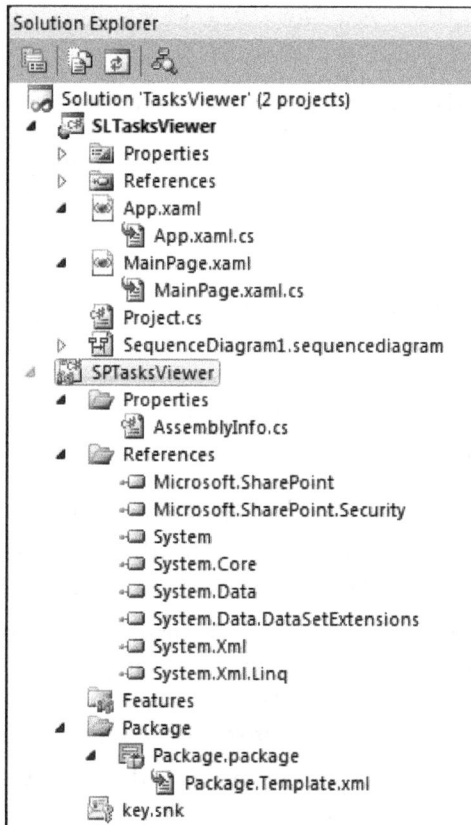

6. Add a new item to the project, that is, a SharePoint 2010 module, `Module1`.

7. Expand the new SharePoint 2010 module, `Module1`, in the **Solution Explorer** and delete the `Sample.txt` file.

8. Open the `Elements.xml` file. The following lines are the initial contents of this XML file. They describe the elements that compose this SharePoint 2010 module.

```xml
<?xml version="1.0" encoding="utf-8"?>
  <Elements xmlns="http://schemas.microsoft.com/sharepoint/">
    <Module Name="Module1">
    </Module>
  </Elements>
```

9. Now, right-click on **Module1** and select **Properties** in the context menu that appears. You will see the values for its properties in the **Properties** panel:

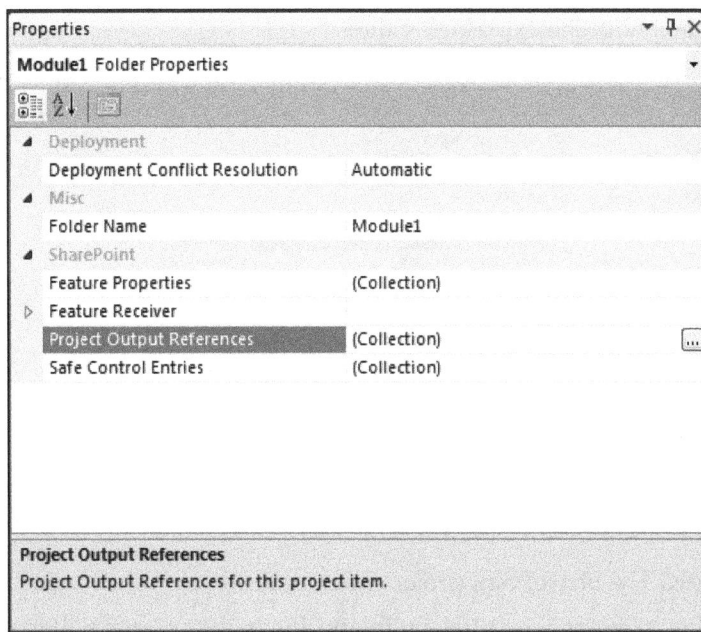

Properties	▾ ⇤ ×
Module1 Folder Properties	▾

⊿ Deployment	
Deployment Conflict Resolution	Automatic
⊿ Misc	
Folder Name	Module1
⊿ SharePoint	
Feature Properties	(Collection)
▷ Feature Receiver	
Project Output References	(Collection) ...
Safe Control Entries	(Collection)

Project Output References
Project Output References for this project item.

10. In the **Properties** palette, click the ellipsis (**...**) button for the **Project Output References** property. The **Project Output References** dialog box will appear.

11. Click on **Add** below the **Members** list. The empty SharePoint 2010 project's name, **SPTasksViewer**, will appear as a new member.

12. Go to its properties, shown on the list located at the right. Select the Silverlight application project's name, **SLTasksViewer**, in the **Project Name** drop-down list.

13. Select **Element File** in the **Deployment Type** drop-down list. The following value will appear in **Deployment Location**, `{SharePointRoot}\Template\ Features\{FeatureName}\Module1\`. The following screenshot shows the dialog box with the explained values:

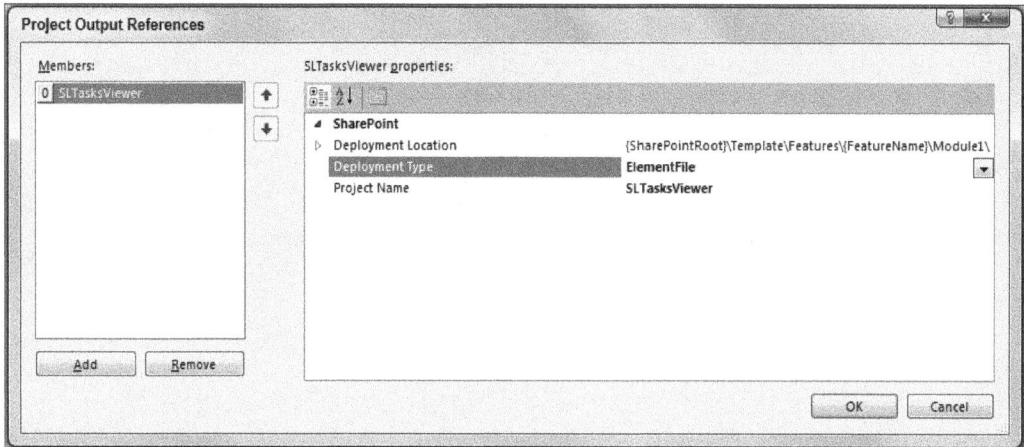

14. Click **OK**. The SharePoint project now includes `SLTasksViewer`.

15. Open the `Elements.xml` file again and the new contents will include a new line with a reference to the linked Silverlight project `.xap` file, `SLTasksViewer.xap`, which is a new element for this SharePoint 2010 module. During the deployment process, the `SLTasksViewer.xap` file will be located in the `Module1` folder in the **SharePoint package file**, also known as the **WSP package**, because it has a `.wsp` extension. Thus, the WSP package will also deploy the Silverlight application to the SharePoint server. The value for `Url` is the location in the website where it will be placed when this feature is activated.

```xml
<?xml version="1.0" encoding="utf-8"?>
<Elements xmlns="http://schemas.microsoft.com/sharepoint/">
  <Module Name="Module1">
    <File Path="Module1\SLTasksViewer.xap" Url="Module1/
        SLTasksViewer.xap" />
  </Module>
</Elements>
```

16. Now, right-click on `SPTasksViewer` and select **Properties** in the context menu. Click on the **SharePoint** tab in the properties panel and different options for the SharePoint deployment configuration will be shown. Activate the **Enable Silverlight debugging (instead of Script debugging)** checkbox. We want to debug the code in the Silverlight application that accesses the data in SharePoint server.

17. Right-click on the solution's name in **Solution Explorer** and select **Properties** from the context menu that appears. Select **Startup Project** in the list on the left, activate **Single startup project**, and choose **SPTasksViewer**. This way, the solution is going to start with the SharePoint project and not with the Silverlight application. This is very important, because it will allow us to debug the Silverlight application when it runs in a SharePoint site. Then, click **OK**.

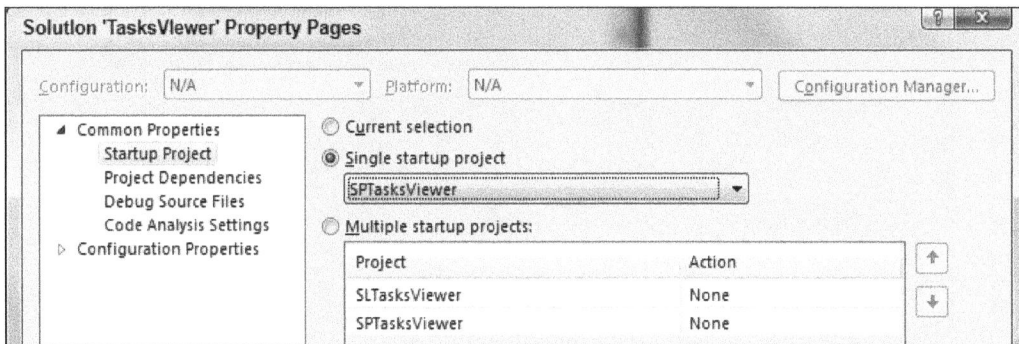

18. Expand **Features | Feature1** in Solution Explorer and double-click on **Feature1.feature**. Visual Studio will display a new panel with the feature title, description, scope, and its items. Make sure that **Module1** is included in the **Items in the feature** list:

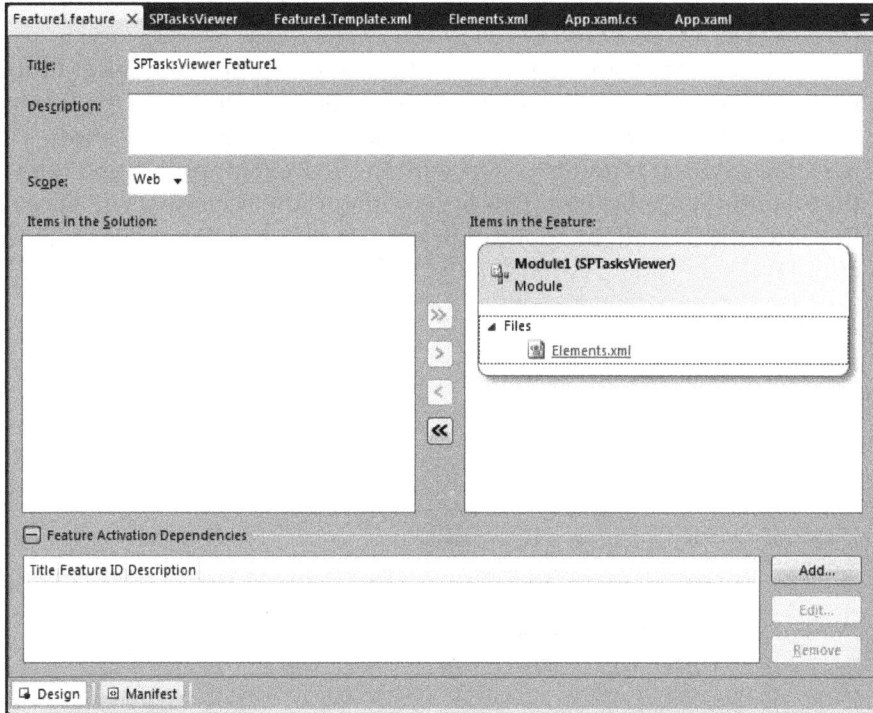

19. Select **Build | Build Solution**, to build the complete solution.

20. Select **Build | Deploy Solution** from Visual Studio's main menu, to deploy the solution to the previously chosen SharePoint server and site. Visual Studio will run the active deployment configuration. It will deploy the WSP package, SPTasksViewer.wsp and will activate Feature1 (SPTasksViewer_ Feature1). This way, the Silverlight RIA will be available in the SharePoint site and we will be able to debug our application.

If you deploy the solution many times, the default deployment configuration will retract a solution with the same name and then it will deploy the new version. Thus, it is easy to update an existing Silverlight RIA for SharePoint by deploying its link to a SharePoint module and a feature. Each Web Part that has references to the Silverlight RIA will be automatically updated when the new version is deployed.

Understanding the default deployment configuration

The default deployment configuration for SharePoint performs the following steps:

1. Run a pre-deployment command. By default, there is no command defined.

2. Create the WSP package file.

3. Recycle the IIS Application Pool.

4. Retract any existing solution with the same name. When it is necessary to uninstall an existing package, the IIS Application Pool will be recycled and the solution retracted.

5. Add the solution.

6. Activate its features.

7. Run a post-deployment command. By default, there is no command defined.

It is possible to check the detailed status of the deployment process by reading the information written in the output window. The following lines show the output text for the solution when it is deployed for the second time. The output headers group the actions performed for each of the aforementioned steps and appear as highlighted lines in the next text:

```
Output
Show output from: Build
------ Deploy started: Project: SPTasksViewer, Configuration: Debug Any CPU ------
Active Deployment Configuration: Default
Run Pre-Deployment Command:
  Skipping deployment step because a pre-deployment command is not specified.
Recycle IIS Application Pool:
  Skipping application pool recycle because a sandboxed solution is being deployed.
Retract Solution:
  Retracting solution 'SPTasksViewer.wsp'...
  Deleting solution 'SPTasksViewer.wsp'...
Add Solution:
  Adding solution 'SPTasksViewer.wsp'...
  Deploying solution 'SPTasksViewer.wsp'...
Activate Features:
  Activating feature 'Feature1' ...
Run Post-Deployment Command:
  Skipping deployment step because a post-deployment command is not specified.
========== Build: 2 succeeded or up-to-date, 0 failed, 0 skipped ==========
========== Deploy: 1 succeeded, 0 failed, 0 skipped ==========

  Output   Error List
```

The results show that two builds and one deployment succeeded. The two builds correspond to the two projects that compose the solution and the generated WSP package, which is deployed as a single unit.

> Visual Studio 2010 allows you to perform automated deployments only to a local SharePoint server. This means that SharePoint Server or SharePoint Foundation must be running on the same computer where we are executing Visual Studio 2010. Then, the SharePoint administrator must deploy the WSP packages to the production SharePoint server and activate the features included in the WSP packages by following the necessary steps. The SharePoint administrator can automate the necessary tasks but you cannot use Visual Studio 2010 for remote deployment.

Debugging Silverlight and SharePoint

Now that the WSP package has been deployed to the SharePoint site, follow these steps to create a new web page, add a Silverlight Web Part, and include the Silverlight RIA in it. In this case, it is not necessary to upload the .xap file because it was already deployed with the WSP package.

1. Click **Site Actions | New Page** and SharePoint will display a new dialog box requesting a name for the new page. Enter `SilverlightProjectsList2010` and click on **Create**. SharePoint will display the editing tools for the new page.

2. Click **Insert | Web Part** in the ribbon and a new panel will appear. Select **Media and Content** in **Categories** and then **Silverlight Web Part** in **Web Parts**.

3. Click **Add** and the **Silverlight Web Part** dialog box will appear. Enter the URL and the name for the .xap file. In this case, it was deployed in the Url value, added in the Elements.xml file, inside the site collection entered when we specified the SharePoint server and site when creating the solution. The Url value was `Module1/SLTasksViewer.xap` and therefore, if you specified the server name without a site, the value for Url should be `/Module1/SLTasksViewer.xap`. If you specified a site collection, you will have to include it in the Url. For example, if you deployed the solution to the `ProjectsWeb` site collection, the value for the Url should be `/ProjectsWeb/Module1/SLTasksViewer.xap`. If you have doubts about the Url value to enter, you can deploy the solution many times and the output window will display the complete Url for the deleted .xap file, as shown in the following lines. You just have to remove the server name.

```
Add Solution:
  Found 1 deployment conflict(s).  Resolving conflicts ...
  Deleted file 'http://xpsgaston/Module1/SLTasksViewer.xap'
    from server.
  Adding solution 'SPTasksViewer.wsp'...
  Deploying solution 'SPTasksViewer.wsp'...
```

4. Click **OK**.

> In pre-release SharePoint 2010 versions, the following error message could appear:
>
> **Could not download the Silverlight application or the Silverlight Plugin did not load. To reconfigure the Web Part or to provide a different Silverlight application (.xap), open the tool pane and then click Configure.**

5. Click on **open the tool pane** or click on the down arrow, located at the top, and then select **Edit Web Part**.

6. The **Silverlight Web Part** pane will appear at the right. It will enable us to define many properties that affect the appearance and behavior of Silverlight UI.

7. Enter Silverlight SharePoint Tasks Viewer in **Title**.

8. Click on **Yes** in **Should the Web Part have a fixed height?** and enter 600 in **Pixels**.

9. Click on **No. Adjust width to fit zone.** in **Should the Web Part have a fixed width?**

10. Click the **Save** button in the ribbon. Now, the new page will appear, displaying the previously created Silverlight RIA. This application is going to load and display its different status values in the label located at the bottom:

    ° **Started**

    ° **Web Connected. Connecting to Lists...**

    ° **Lists Connected. Getting List data...**

    ° **Loading n items...**

    ° **Showing items...**

11. Finally, the grid in the Silverlight RIA will display the data retrieved from the list of tasks previously created in SharePoint, **ProjectsList2010**.

Silverlight SharePoint Tasks Viewer

ProjectId	Title	StartDate	DueDate	EstimatedDaysLeft	Priority	Stat
2	Creating a Silverlight 4 UI	2/16/2010 3:00:00 AM	2/20/2010 3:00:00 AM	4	(2) Normal	Defe
3	Creating a Complex Silverlight LOB RIA	2/17/2010 3:00:00 AM	3/2/2010 3:00:00 AM	13	(1) High	Defe
4	Creating a New SharePoint Site	2/18/2010 3:00:00 AM	2/25/2010 3:00:00 AM	7	(1) High	In P

Showing items...

12. Now, open a new tab in your web browser and add a new item to the list of tasks in SharePoint by using the list editor. Then, go back to the tab that is displaying the page with the Silverlight Web Part and refresh it. The new item will appear in the grid:

Silverlight SharePoint Tasks Viewer

ProjectId	Title	StartDate	DueDate	EstimatedDaysLeft	Priority	Stat
2	Creating a Silverlight 4 UI	2/16/2010 3:00:00 AM	2/20/2010 3:00:00 AM	4	(2) Normal	Defe
3	Creating a Complex Silverlight LOB RIA	2/17/2010 3:00:00 AM	3/2/2010 3:00:00 AM	13	(1) High	Defe
4	Creating a New SharePoint Site	2/18/2010 3:00:00 AM	2/25/2010 3:00:00 AM	7	(1) High	In P
5	New Project	3/1/2010 3:00:00 AM	3/20/2010 3:00:00 AM	19	(3) Low	Not

In this case, it was necessary to refresh the page and reload the application. However, if we added a refresh button to the Silverlight RIA, it wouldn't be necessary to reload the Silverlight Web Part to refresh the grid.

Debugging Silverlight Web Parts

We added some status information in the label located at the bottom of the grid. However, we want to debug a Silverlight RIA running in a Silverlight Web Part. We already activated the options to allow Silverlight code debugging before deploying the solution. Follow these steps to debug the Silverlight RIA while it runs in the page:

1. Stay in Visual Studio as a system administrator user.

2. Open `MainPage.xaml.cs` in the `SLTasksViewer` project.

3. Insert a breakpoint at the first line of the `Connect` method:

   ```
   lblStatus.Content = "Started";
   ```

4. Insert a breakpoint at each line that calls the `Dispatcher.BeginInvoke` method, in the following methods:

   ° `OnConnectSucceeded`
   ° `OnConnectListsSucceeded`
   ° `OnGetListDataSucceeded`
   ° `OnLoadItemsSucceeded`

5. Select **Debug | Start Debugging** from Visual Studio's main menu or press *F5* to start debugging the solution.

6. Visual Studio will display a new window for your default web browser with the server and site collection in which you deployed the WSP package.

7. Enter the URL for the previously added page that contains the Silverlight Web Part in the web browser. This way, Silverlight RIA will start and Visual Studio will stop in the breakpoint established in the `Connect` method and the web browser will show **Not Responding** as part of its title:

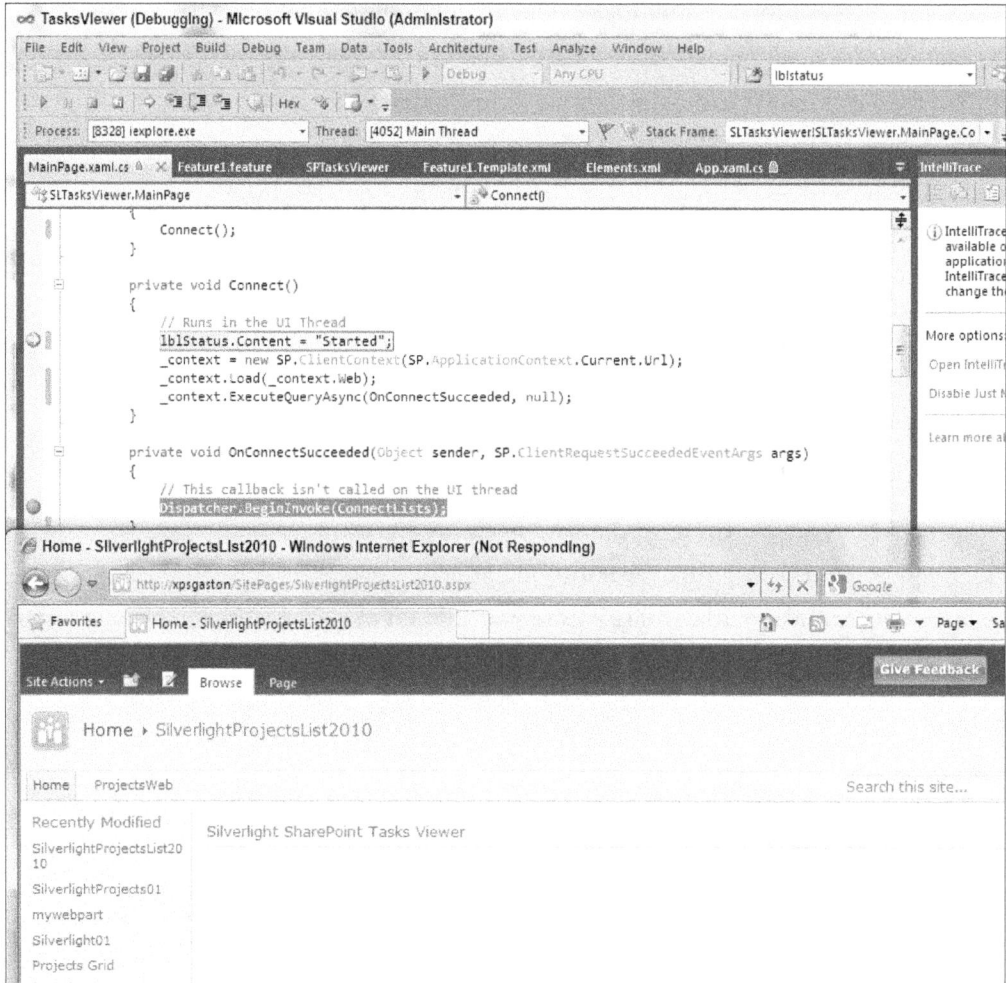

8. Select **Debug | Windows | Thread** or press *Ctrl+Alt+H*. Visual Studio will display the **Threads** window and you will be able to see the thread in which the current code is running. A yellow arrow located at the left of the current thread indicates that it is the active thread for the current statement. The following screenshot shows the code for the `Connect` method running in the UI thread.

```
MainPage.xaml.cs    ×   Feature1.feature    SPTasksViewer    Feature1.Template.xml    Elements.xml    App.xaml.cs
SLTasksViewer.MainPage                                    Connect()
            {
                Connect();
            }

            private void Connect()
            {
                // Runs in the UI Thread
                lblStatus.Content = "Started";
                _context = new SP.ClientContext(SP.ApplicationContext.Current.Url);
                _context.Load(_context.Web);
                _context.ExecuteQueryAsync(OnConnectSucceeded, null);
            }

            private void OnConnectSucceeded(Object sender, SP.ClientRequestSucceededEventArgs args)
            {
                // This callback isn't called on the UI thread
                Dispatcher.BeginInvoke(ConnectLists);
            }
100 %
```

Threads

Search: X Search Call Stack   Group by: Process Name   Columns

	ID	Managed ID	Category	Name	Location	Priority
▲ iexplore.exe (id = 8328) : C:\PROGRA~2\INTERN~1\iexplore.exe						
→	4052	1	Main Thread	Main Thread	SLTasksViewer.MainPage.Connect	Normal
▲ SPUCWorkerProcess.exe (id = 1492) : C:\Program Files\Common Files\Microsoft Shared\Web Server Extensions\14\UserCode\SPUCWorkerProces						
	7768	1	Main Thread	Main Thread	[In a sleep, wait, or join]	Normal
	7644	2	Worker Thread	<No Name>	<not available>	Highest
	7224	0	Worker Thread	<No Name>	<not available>	Normal
	3208	4	Worker Thread	<No Name>	[Managed to Native Transition]	Normal
	4244	5	Worker Thread	<No Name>	<not available>	Normal
	8440	0	Worker Thread	<No Name>	<not available>	Normal
	8480	0	Worker Thread	<No Name>	<not available>	Normal
	2120	8	Worker Thread	<No Name>	<not available>	Normal

Autos   Locals   Watch 1   Threads   Call Stack   Breakpoints   Command Window   Immediate Window   Output

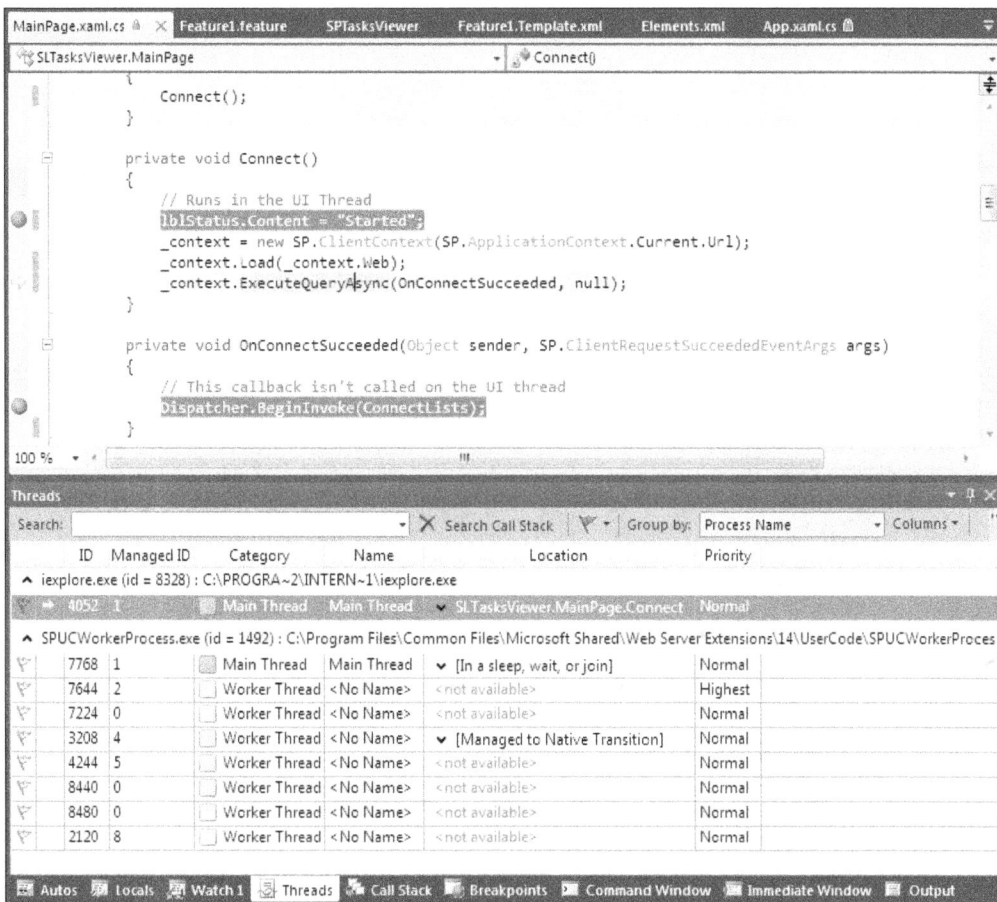

9. Press *F5* and the execution will stop in the breakpoint set in the
    OnConnectSucceeded method. In this case, as previously explained,
    the code for the method is running in a different thread, that is, in one
    of the worker threads:

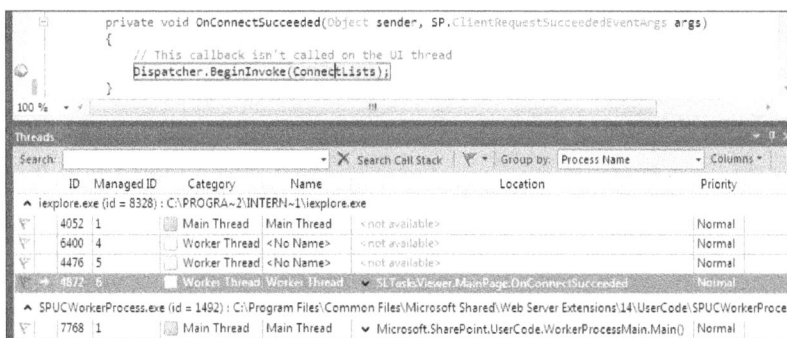

```
            private void OnConnectSucceeded(Object sender, SP.ClientRequestSucceededEventArgs args)
            {
                // This callback isn't called on the UI thread
                Dispatcher.BeginInvoke(ConnectLists);
            }
100 %
```

Threads

Search: X Search Call Stack   Group by: Process Name   Columns

	ID	Managed ID	Category	Name	Location	Priority
▲ iexplore.exe (id = 8328) : C:\PROGRA~2\INTERN~1\iexplore.exe						
	4052	1	Main Thread	Main Thread	<not available>	Normal
	6400	4	Worker Thread	<No Name>	<not available>	Normal
	4476	5	Worker Thread	<No Name>	<not available>	Normal
→	4872	6	Worker Thread	Worker Thread	SLTasksViewer.MainPage.OnConnectSucceeded	Normal
▲ SPUCWorkerProcess.exe (id = 1492) : C:\Program Files\Common Files\Microsoft Shared\Web Server Extensions\14\UserCode\SPUCWorkerProces						
	7768	1	Main Thread	Main Thread	Microsoft.SharePoint.UserCode.WorkerProcessMain.Main()	Normal

10. Insert a breakpoint at the first line of the `ConnectLists` method. Press *F5* and the execution will stop in this new breakpoint. In this case, as previously explained, the code for the method is running in the UI thread again because it was called by the `Dispatcher.BeginInvoke`:

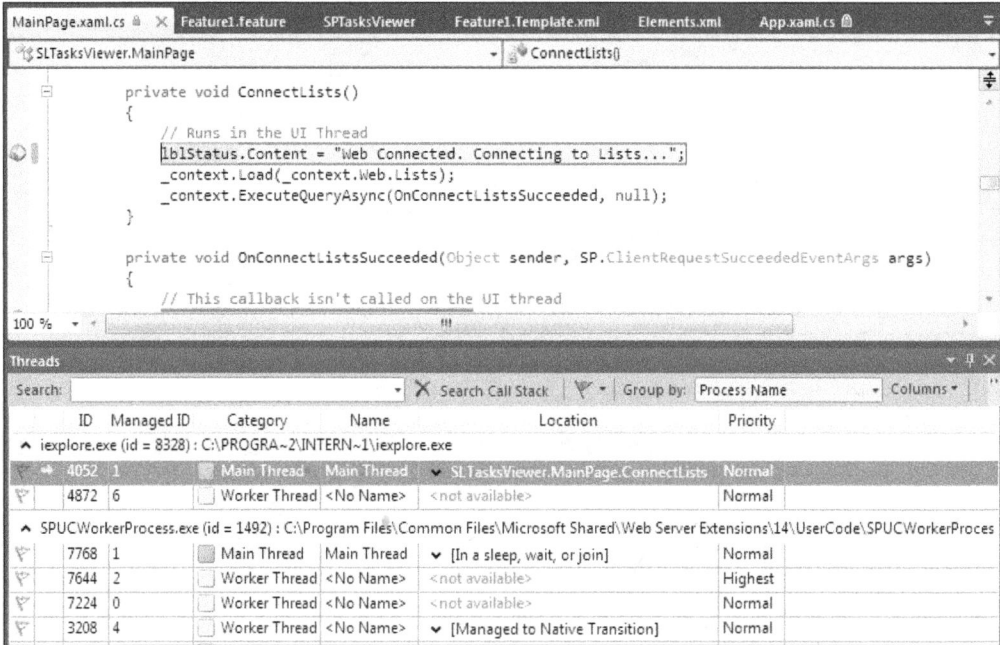

11. At this point, the code in the `ConnectLists` method is preparing to query the SharePoint server to load the `SP.ListCollection _context.Web.List`. The `_context.Web` is already loaded but `_context.Web.List` is not loaded yet.

12. Select **Debug | Windows | Immediate Window** or press *Ctrl+Atl+I*. Enter the following line and press *Enter*:

    `_context.Web.Title`

13. The title for the Web will appear, because `_context.Web` is already loaded and therefore, it is possible to access its `Title` property.

14. Now, enter the following line and press *Enter*:

    `_context.Web.RootFolder.ItemCount`

15. A `PropertyOrFieldNotInitializedException` will be raised, because `_context.Web.RootFolder` was not loaded:

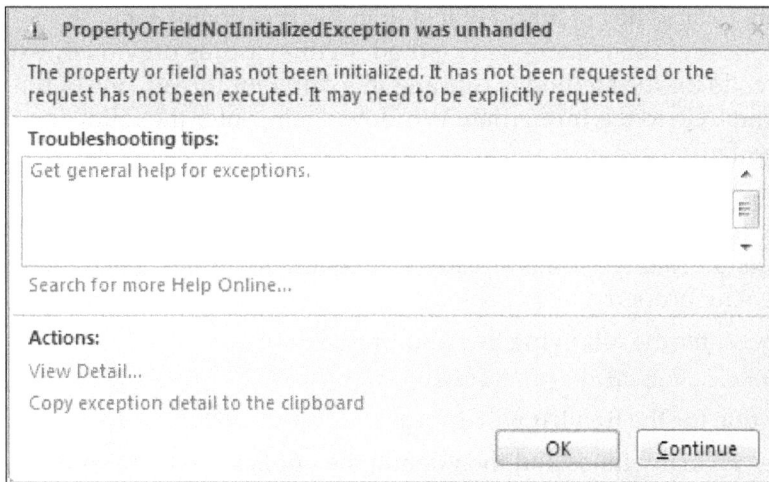

16. The `PropertyOrFieldNotInitializedException` is raised when you want to access a property or field that has not been initialized in a SharePoint Silverlight Client OM object. When this exception appears, it means that you have to query for this specific property or field before accessing it. This means that you have to load `_context.Web` and then `_context.Web. RootFolder`.

17. Now, enter the following line and press *Enter*:

    `_context.Web.Lists.Count`

18. A `CollectionNotInitializedException` will be raised, because the `ListCollection _context.Web.Lists` was not loaded:

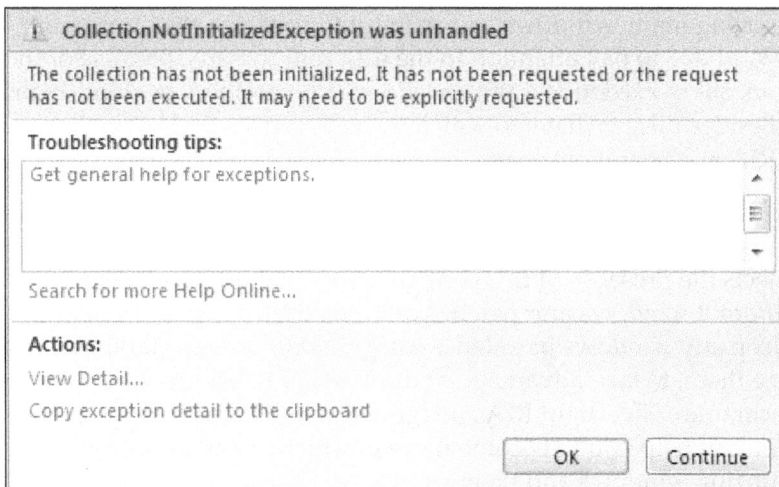

19. Press *F5* and the execution will stop in the breakpoint set in the `OnConnectListsSucceeded` method. In this case, as previously explained, the code for the method is running in a different thread, one of the worker threads. Go to the **Immediate Window** again, enter the following line and press *Enter*:

```
_context.Web.Lists.Count
```

20. The number of lists defined in SharePoint will appear, because at this point `_context.Web.Lists` is already loaded and therefore, it is possible to access its `Count` property.

21. Now, enter the following line and press *Enter*:

```
_context.Web.Lists[0].Title
```

   The title for the first list will appear.

22. Press *F5* many times and then debug the application by running it step-by-step. This way, you will be able to understand the way the SharePoint Silverlight Client OM works.

> It is easy to debug a Silverlight RIA with the new SharePoint deployment features found in Visual Studio 2010. As the code runs many different threads, it is very important to use breakpoints to make sure that the execution is going to stop in a certain statement.

Taking advantage of Visual Studio 2010 multi-monitor support

When we deploy and debug Silverlight RIAs integrated to SharePoint, we find ourselves moving many windows and palettes to organize the information on our screen. We have to pay attention to the different threads, because of the asynchronous query executions. We have to watch variables, evaluate expressions, and so on. Besides this, we have to watch the web browser window that shows the Silverlight RIA in a SharePoint page.

If you have the opportunity to work with two monitors connected to the same computer, Visual Studio 2010 has added support for dual-monitor configurations. When it detects the presence of this configuration, it allows you to simply drag-and-drop the different windows and palettes onto the desired screen. This way, you can drag-and-drop any windows or palettes integrated in the development environment and organize them, to take advantage of the extended desktop size. If you work with many complex Silverlight RIAs integrated with SharePoint, a dual-monitor configuration can help you to become more productive and avoid spending a lot of time reorganizing windows and palettes.

> If you disconnect the second monitor, all the windows and palettes that were displayed on that monitor will automatically move to the single visible screen area.

Understanding 32-bit and 64-bit differences

We already know that SharePoint Server 2010 is a 64-bit application that only runs on specific 64-bit Windows versions. However, if you try to access the page that contains the Silverlight RIA in a 64-bit browser, you will see the **Install Microsoft Silverlight** button, as shown in the following screenshot:

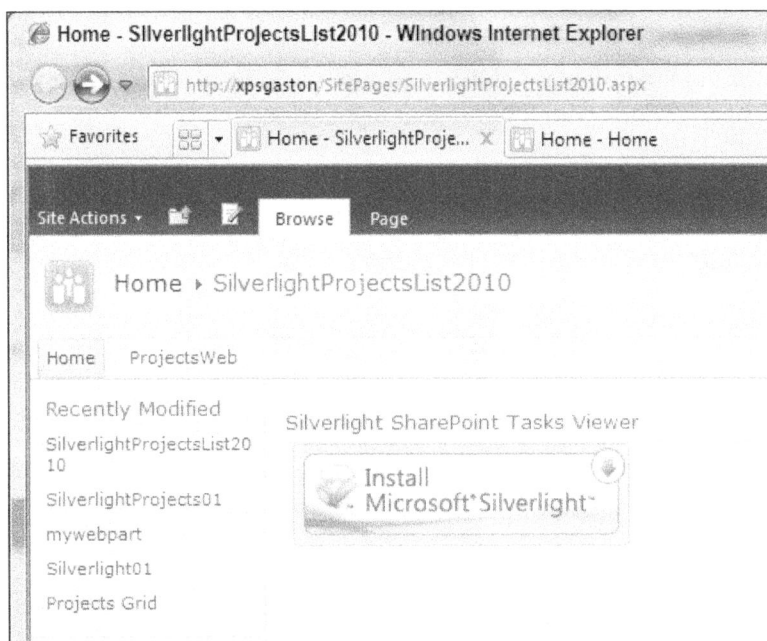

So far, Silverlight 4 doesn't offer a plugin for 64-bit web browsers and therefore, you have to use a 32-bit web browser to access the pages that contain Silverlight Web Parts.

The Silverlight RIA is going to run as a 32-bit application. However, it will be able to access the services provided by the SharePoint server, which is running as a collection of many 64-bit applications and services.

Understanding scalability

In this case, we worked with a simple example and executed many queries to the SharePoint server through the SharePoint Silverlight Client OM. Each asynchronous query will use the network connection and will require the server to send a response with the requested data. Once you start integrating Silverlight RIAs with SharePoint, you will find new opportunities for many new exciting applications. Therefore, it is very important to apply the same principle used when working with database servers—only request necessary data from the server.

> Avoid unnecessary requests for data, because it could reduce the scalability of serving more users running Silverlight RIAs that consume SharePoint data and services.

Silverlight developers must take into account the *number of users* that are going to consume RIAs in order to avoid performance problems with their final deployment.

Preparing applications for multiple-browser support

SharePoint 2010 improved multiple web browser support. Thus, if our Silverlight Web Parts had to be compatible with different web browsers, it is clearly necessary to test them in multiple browsers before any final deployment.

If a web browser supports Silverlight and is included in the list of SharePoint 2010 compatible browsers, you shouldn't face any unexpected results. Silverlight 4 supports the following web browsers:

- Internet Explorer
- Mozilla Firefox
- Google Chrome
- Apple Safari

Mozilla Firefox and Google Chrome are compatible with both SharePoint 2010 and Silverlight RIAs. The following screenshots show the pages that contain the Silverlight Web Part running in Mozilla Firefox and Google Chrome:

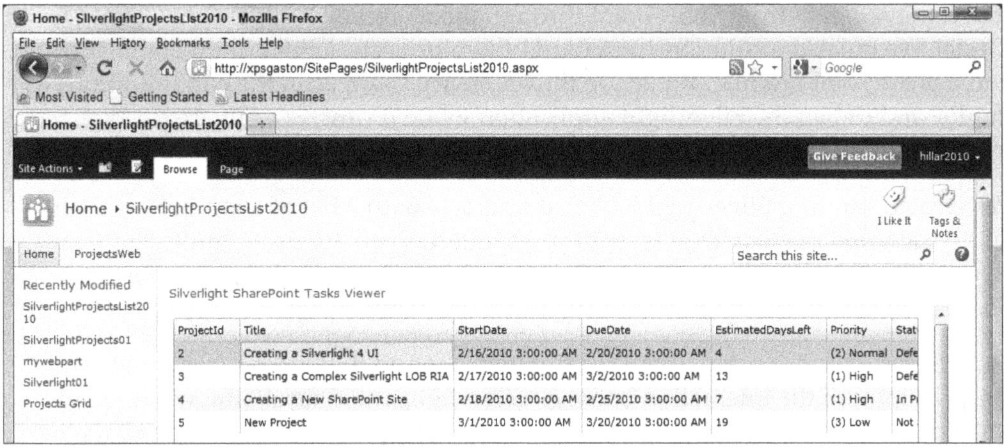

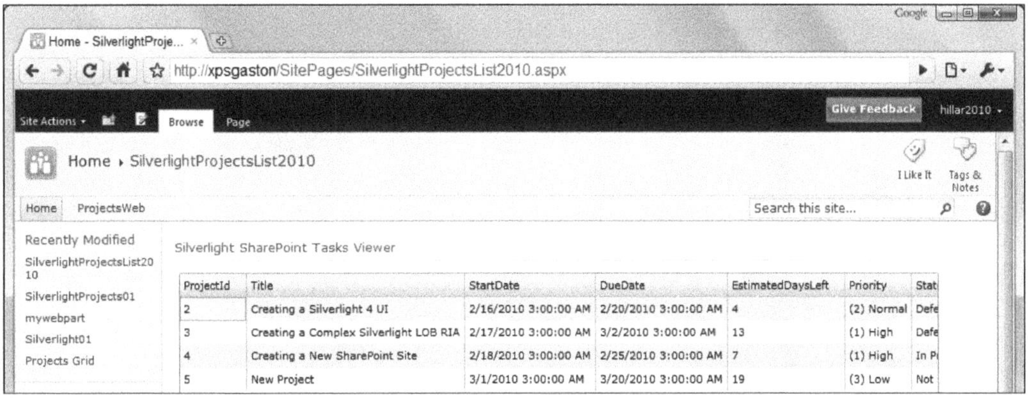

Summary

We learned a lot in this chapter about deploying and debugging Silverlight 4 applications in SharePoint 2010 sites. Specifically, we created a new Silverlight 4 RIA that retrieved data from SharePoint through the SharePoint Silverlight Client Object Model. We created a solution composed of two projects, a Silverlight application and a SharePoint module. We made the necessary changes in the configurations to deploy and debug the Silverlight application while it runs as a Silverlight Web Part in a SharePoint page.

We created our first Silverlight RIA that interacts with a list of tasks in SharePoint and we learned the way that asynchronous queries run, by using multiple threads. Now, we are able to begin adding Silverlight RIAs that read data from the SharePoint server and deploy them by following simple steps.

Now that we have learned about the deployment and debugging techniques and the principles of the interaction between Silverlight and SharePoint, we are ready to learn to interact with data on the SharePoint server, which is the topic of the next chapter.

3
Interacting with Data on the SharePoint Server

We already know how to develop, deploy, and debug Silverlight RIAs that read data, request services, and access remote objects from the SharePoint server. Now, we want to interact with this data by performing insert, update, and delete operations. In this chapter, we will cover many topics that help us create simple and complex Line-Of-Business Silverlight RIAs that run as Silverlight Web Parts to interact with data in the SharePoint Server.

In this chapter, we will:

- Use a Silverlight RIA to insert items into a SharePoint list
- Retrieve and process metadata information about a SharePoint list
- Prepare code to handle errors when remote operations fail
- Work with messages to allow multiple Silverlight RIAs to communicate with each other
- Work with Visual Studio 2010 code editor features to track the execution flow
- Enhance a Silverlight RIA to delete specific items from a SharePoint list
- Enhance a Silverlight RIA to update specific fields for an item in a SharePoint list

Managing data in a Silverlight RIA included in a SharePoint solution

So far, we have been able to create, deploy, and debug a Silverlight RIA that read data from a list in the SharePoint server. It is also possible to insert, update, and remove items from these lists. In fact, the typical **LOB (Line-Of-Business)** RIA performs **CRUD (Create, Read, Update, and Delete)** operations. Therefore, we can create a Silverlight RIA to perform some of the CRUD operations with the existing list of tasks, by using more features provided by the SharePoint 2010 Silverlight Client OM.

We could improve our existing Silverlight RIA that displays data from the existing list in a grid. However, we are going to create a new Silverlight RIA and then, we will improve both applications to work together to offer a complex LOB solution.

We will analyze diverse alternatives to simplify the deployment process and show how to debug a Silverlight RIA that queries data from a SharePoint server.

Working with the SharePoint 2010 Silverlight Client Object Model to insert items

Now, we are going to create a new solution in Visual Studio as we learned in the previous chapter. It will include two new projects:

- A Silverlight application project, SLTasksCRUD
- An empty SharePoint 2010 project with a module, SPTasksCRUD

Follow these steps to create the new Silverlight RIA that allows a user to insert a new item into the list in the SharePoint server:

> This example requires the ProjectsList2010 list created in SharePoint. We created this list in *Chapter 2, Deploying and Debugging Techniques for Silverlight and SharePoint*.

1. Start Visual Studio as a system administrator user.

2. Select **File | New | Project...** or press *Ctrl+Shift+N*. Select **Other Project Types | Visual Studio Solutions** under **Installed Templates** in the **New Project** dialog box. Then, select **Blank Solution** and enter TasksCRUD as the project's name and click **OK**. Visual Studio will create a blank solution with no projects.

3. Right-click on the solution's name in **Solution Explorer** and select **Add |
New Project...** from the context menu that appears.

4. Select **Visual C# | Silverlight** under **Installed Templates** in the **New Project**
dialog box. Then, select **Silverlight Application**, enter SLTasksCRUD as the
project's name and click **OK**.

5. Deactivate the **Host the Silverlight application in a new Web site** checkbox
in the **New Silverlight Application** dialog box and select **Silverlight 4**
in **Silverlight Version**. Then, click **OK**. Visual Studio will add the new
Silverlight application project to the existing solution.

6. Follow the necessary steps to add the following two references to access the
new SharePoint 2010 Silverlight Client OM:

    ° Microsoft.SharePoint.Client.Silverlight.dll

    ° Microsoft.SharePoint.Client.Silverlight.Runtime.
      dll

7. Open App.xaml.cs and add the following using statement:

```
using Microsoft.SharePoint.Client;
```

8. Add the following code in the StartUp event handler to initialize the
Microsoft.SharePoint.Client.ApplicationContext with the same
initialization parameters and the synchronization context for the current
thread (the UI thread).

```
private void Application_Startup(object sender, StartupEventArgs
e)
{
    this.RootVisual = new MainPage();
    // Initialize the ApplicationContext
    ApplicationContext.Init(e.InitParams,
      System.Threading.SynchronizationContext.Current);
}
```

9. Open MainPage.xaml, define a new width and height for the Grid, 800 and
600, add the following controls, and align them as shown in the following
screenshot:

    ° Six Label controls aligned at the left with the following
      values for their Content properties. They are Title,
      Priority, Status, % Complete, Start Date and Due Date.

    ° One Label control, located at the bottom, lblStatus.

    ° One TextBox control, txtTitle.

- ° One ComboBox control, cboPriority.

- ° One ComboBox control, cboStatus.

- ° One Slider control, sldPercentComplete. Set LargeChange to 10, Maximum to 100, and Minimum to 0. This slider will allow the user to set the percentage of the total work that has been completed.

- ° One DatePicker control, dtStartDate.

- ° One DatePicker control, dtDueDate.

- ° One Button control, butInsert. Set its Title property to Insert.

10. Select the Grid, LayoutRoot. Click on the **Categorized** button to arrange the properties by category. Then, click on **Brushes | Background** and a color palette with many buttons located at the top and the bottom will appear. Click on the **Gradient Brush** button, located at the top and then on the **Vertical Gradient** one, located at the bottom. Define both the start and the stop colors. The rectangle that defines the background Grid will display a nice linear gradient, as shown in the previous screenshot.

11. Open `MainPage.xaml.cs` and add the following `using` statements to include the `Microsoft.SharePoint.Client` namespace:

```
using Microsoft.SharePoint.Client;
using SP = Microsoft.SharePoint.Client;
Add the following two private variables
private SP.ClientContext _context;
private SP.List _projects;
```

Add the following method to fill the drop-down lists that will display the different options for the priority and the status:

```
private void FillComboBoxes()
{
    cboPriority.Items.Add("(1) High");
    cboPriority.Items.Add("(2) Normal");
    cboPriority.Items.Add("(3) Low");
    cboStatus.Items.Add("Not Started");
    cboStatus.Items.Add("In Progress");
    cboStatus.Items.Add("Completed");
    cboStatus.Items.Add("Deferred");
    cboStatus.Items.Add("Waiting on someone else");
}
```

> It is possible to retrieve the possible choices for both the **Priority** and **Status** fields. However, we will improve this application later. In this case, we add the possible values in this method and then we will learn how to retrieve the choices through queries to the SharePoint server.

12. Add the following line to the page `MainPage` constructor:

```
public MainPage()
{
    InitializeComponent();
    FillComboBoxes();
}
```

13. Now, it is necessary to add code to execute the following tasks:

   i. Connect to the SharePoint server and load the current user that logged on the server, `ConnectAndAddItemToList` method.

ii. Add a new item to the `ProjectsList2010` list, considering the values entered by the user in the controls, `AddItemToList` method.

```
private void ConnectAndAddItemToList()
{
  // Runs in the UI Thread
  lblStatus.Content = "Started";
  _context = new
      SP.ClientContext(SP.ApplicationContext.Current.Url);
  _context.Load(_context.Web);
  // Load the current user
  _context.Load(_context.Web.CurrentUser);
  _context.ExecuteQueryAsync(OnConnectSucceeded, null);
}

private void AddItemToList()
{
  // Runs in the UI Thread
  lblStatus.Content = "Web Connected. Adding new item to List...";
  _projects = _context.Web.Lists.GetByTitle("ProjectsList2010");
  ListItem listItem = _projects.AddItem(new
    ListItemCreationInformation());
  listItem["Title"] = txtTitle.Text;
  listItem["StartDate"] =
      Convert.ToString(dtStartDate.SelectedDate);
  listItem["DueDate"] = Convert.ToString(dtDueDate.SelectedDate);
  listItem["Status"] = "Not Started";
  var fieldUserValue = new FieldUserValue();
  // Assign the current user to the Id
  fieldUserValue.LookupId = _context.Web.CurrentUser.Id;
  listItem["AssignedTo"] = fieldUserValue;
  listItem["Priority"] = "(2) Normal";
  listItem["PercentComplete"] =
      Convert.ToString(Math.Round(sldPercentComplete.Value, 0)/100);
  listItem.Update();
  // Just load the list Title proprty
  _context.Load(_projects, list => list.Title);
  _context.ExecuteQueryAsync(OnAddItemToListSucceeded,
      OnAddItemToListFailed);
}
```

14. All the previously added methods are going to run in the UI thread, as we learned in *Chapter 2*. The following methods, which are going to be fired as asynchronous callbacks, schedule the execution of other methods to continue with the necessary program flow in the UI thread:

    ° When the connection to the SharePoint server, requested by the `ConnectAndAddItemToList` method, is successful, the `OnConnectSucceeded` method schedules the execution of the `AddItemToList` method in the UI thread. If the `ConnectAndAddItemToList` method fails, the `OnConnectFailed` method schedules the execution of the `ShowErrorInformation` method in the UI thread, sending the `ClientRequestFailedEventArgs args` instance as a parameter to the delegate.

    ° When the insert operation performed on the list available in the SharePoint server, requested by the `AddItemToList` method, is successful, the `OnAddItemToListSucceeded` method schedules the execution of the `ShowInsertResult` method in the UI thread. If the `AddItemToList` method fails, the `OnAddItemToList` method schedules the execution of the `ShowErrorInformation` method in the UI thread, sending the `ClientRequestFailedEventArgs args` instance as a parameter to the delegate.

```
private void ShowErrorInformation(ClientRequestFailedEventArgs
args)
{
  System.Windows.Browser.HtmlPage.Window.Alert(
      "Request failed. " + args.Message + "\n" +
    args.StackTrace + "\n" +
 args.ErrorDetails + "\n" + args.ErrorValue);
}

private void ShowInsertResult()
{
  lblStatus.Content = "New item added to " + _projects.Title;
}

private void OnConnectSucceeded(Object sender, SP.ClientRequestSuc
ceededEventArgs args)
{
  // This callback isn't called on the UI thread
```

```
    Dispatcher.BeginInvoke(AddItemToList);
}

private void OnConnectFailed(object sender,
ClientRequestFailedEventArgs args)
{
  // This callback isn't called on the UI thread
  // Invoke a delegate and send the args instance as a parameter
  Dispatcher.BeginInvoke(() => ShowErrorInformation(args));
}

private void OnAddItemToListSucceeded(Object sender, SP.ClientRequ
estSucceededEventArgs args)
{
  // This callback isn't called on the UI thread
  //Dispatcher.BeginInvoke(GetListData);
  Dispatcher.BeginInvoke(ShowInsertResult);
}

private void OnAddItemToListFailed(object sender,
ClientRequestFailedEventArgs args)
{
  // This callback isn't called on the UI thread
  // Invoke a delegate and send the args instance as a parameter
  Dispatcher.BeginInvoke(() => ShowErrorInformation(args));
}
```

Add the following line to the `Click` event for the `butInsert Button`. This way, when the user clicks on this button, the application will connect to the SharePoint server and will insert the new item.

```
private void butInsert_Click(object sender, RoutedEventArgs e)
{
  ConnectAndAddItemToList();
}
```

Now, follow these steps to create a new SharePoint module and link it to the previously created Silverlight RIA, SLTasksCRUD.

1. Stay in Visual Studio as a system administrator user.

2. Right-click on the solution's name in **Solution Explorer** and select **Add | New Project...** from the context menu that appears.

3. Select **Visual C# | SharePoint | 2010** under **Installed Templates** in the **New Project** dialog box. Then, select **Empty SharePoint Project**, enter SPTasksCRUD as the project's name, and click **OK**. The **SharePoint Customization Wizard** dialog box will appear.

4. Enter the URL for the SharePoint server and site in **What local site do you want to use for debugging?**

5. Click on **Deploy as a sandboxed solution**. Then, click on **Finish** and the new SPTasksCRUD empty SharePoint 2010 project will be added to the solution.

6. Add a new item to the project, that is a SharePoint 2010 module, Module1.

7. Expand the new SharePoint 2010 module, Module1, in the **Solution Explorer** and delete the Sample.txt file.

8. Now, right-click on Module1 and select **Properties** in the context menu that appears. In the **Properties** palette, click the ellipsis (...) button for the **Project Output References** property. The **Project Output References** dialog box will appear.

9. Click on **Add**, below the **Members** list. The empty SharePoint 2010 project's name, SPTasksCRUD, will appear as a new member.

10. Go to its properties, shown in the list, located at the right. Select the Silverlight application project's name, SLTasksCRUD, in the **Project Name** drop-down list.

11. Select ElementFile in the **Deployment Type** drop-down list. The following value will appear in Deployment Location: {SharePointRoot}\Template\ Features\{FeatureName}\Module1\, as shown in the next screenshot:

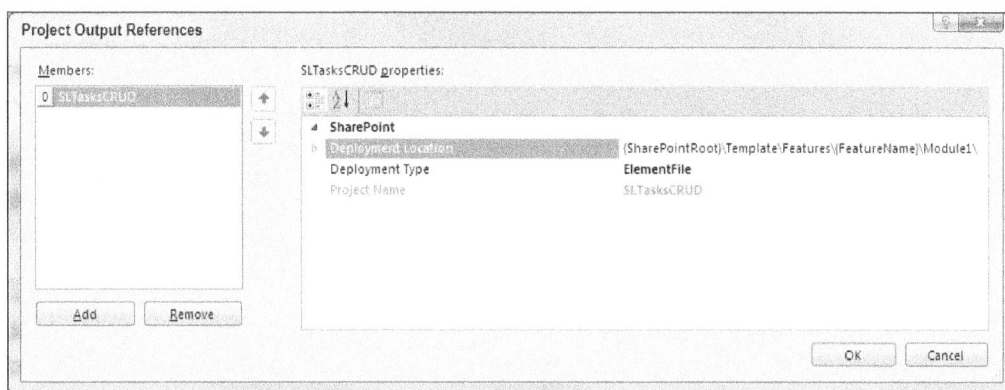

Click **OK** and the SharePoint project now includes the Silverlight application project, SLTasksCRUD.

12. Now, right-click on the SharePoint 2010 project, SPTasksCRUD, and select **Properties** in the context menu that appears. Click on the **SharePoint** tab in the properties panel and different options for the SharePoint deployment configuration will be shown.

13. Activate the **Enable Silverlight debugging (instead of Script debugging)** checkbox. Remember that this option will allow us to debug code in the Silverlight application that adds items to the list in the SharePoint server.

14. Right-click on the solution's name in **Solution Explorer** and select **Properties** from the context menu that appears. Select **Startup Project** in the list on the left, activate **Single startup project**, and choose the SharePoint project's name in the drop-down list below it, SPTasksCRUD. Then, click **OK**.

15. Build and deploy the solution.

16. Now that the WSP package has been deployed to the SharePoint site, follow the necessary steps to create a new web page, add the Silverlight Web Part, and include the Silverlight RIA in it. Remember that in this case, it is not necessary to upload the .xap file because it was already deployed with the WSP package.

Inserting items in a SharePoint list with the Silverlight Web Part

Now, follow these steps to insert an item with the recently deployed Silverlight RIA running in a Silverlight Web Part.

1. Enter the URL for the previously added page that contains the Silverlight Web Part in the web browser. This way, the Silverlight RIA will appear.

2. Enter a value for the **Title**. Select a value for both the **Priority** and the **Status** drop-down lists and use the slider to specify the percentage of the work completed so far and select both the **Start Date** and the **Due Date** by clicking on the datetime pickers. The following screenshot shows some values and the elegant drop-down list that offers the five alternatives for **Status**:

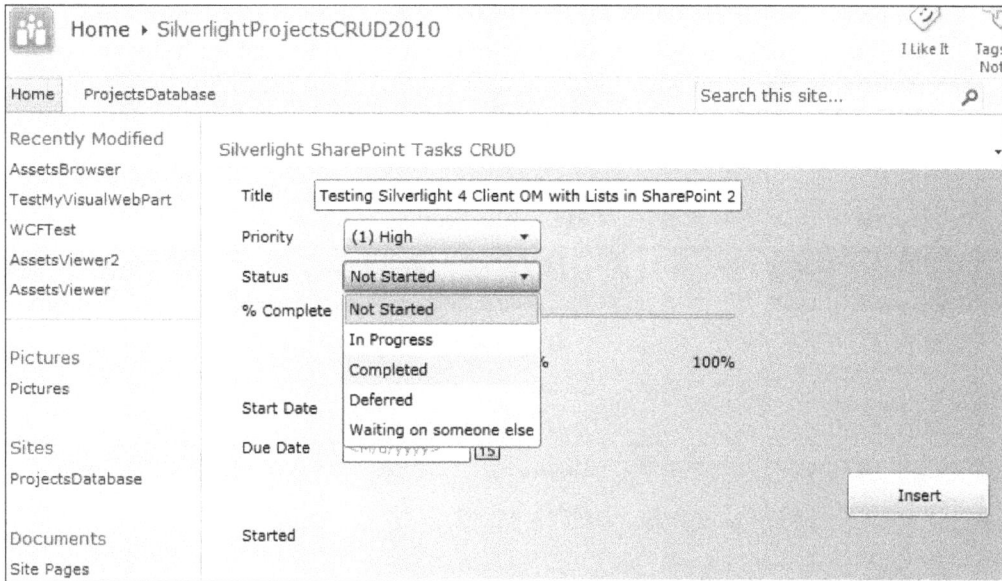

3. Click on the **Insert** button. The application is going to display its different status values in the label located at the bottom:

   ° **Ready**

   ° **Started**

   ° **Web Connected. Adding new item to List...**

   ° **New item added to ProjectsList2010**

4. Open or refresh the items for the list in the corresponding SharePoint 2010 page and you will see the new item added to the list with the values entered in the application and the user logged on to the SharePoint server in the **Assigned To** column. The following screenshot shows the new item in the list:

5. The Silverlight RIA doesn't include code to validate the data that is going to be added to the list in the SharePoint server. Thus, the user can enter inappropriate values for the fields. Enter a new title and delete the value for **Start Date**. Then, click on the **Insert** button and a new dialog box will appear, indicating that the request failed, because the String was not recognized as a valid DateTime. The problem is that the StartDate field has the invalid value 0. The following screenshot shows the dialog box with the error message:

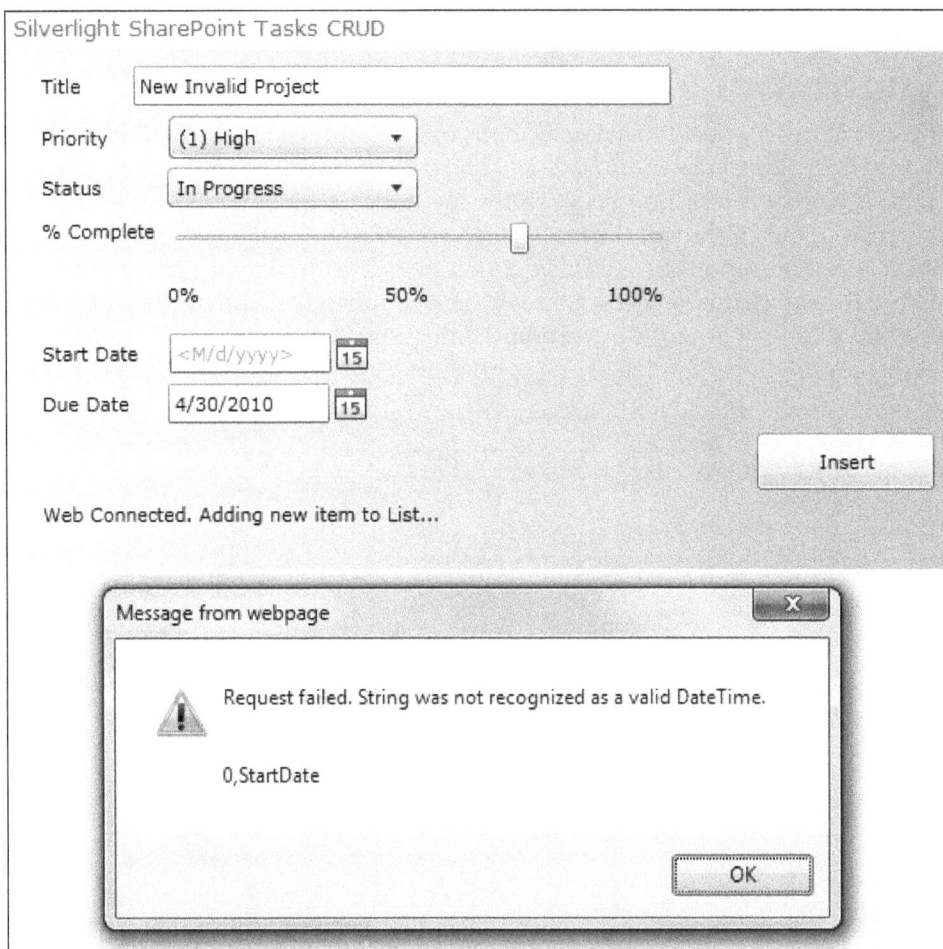

This dialog box is the result of the execution of the `OnAddItemToListFailed` callback, the second parameter of the `_context.ExecuteQueryAsync` method in `AddItemToList`. As something went wrong, this callback invokes a delegate that send the `args` instance as a parameter to the `ShowErrorInformation` method.

```
Dispatcher.BeginInvoke(() => ShowErrorInformation(args));
```

6. Debug the Silverlight RIA, following the steps explained in *Chapter 2*, in the *Debugging Silverlight Web Parts* section.

    This way, you will be able to understand the different steps that we are going to analyze in the following section.

Working with successful and failed asynchronous queries

We already learned about the asynchronous queries and callbacks in *Chapter 2*, in the *Working with the asynchronous methods and callbacks* section. The following sequence diagram shows the interaction between the methods defined in `MainPage` that are going to run in the UI thread, the `Microsoft.SharePoint.Client.ClientContext` instance, `_context`, and the methods defined in `MainPage` that are going to run in another thread, that is, a worker thread. This sequence represents the situation in which all the asynchronous operations against the SharePoint server have a successful completion:

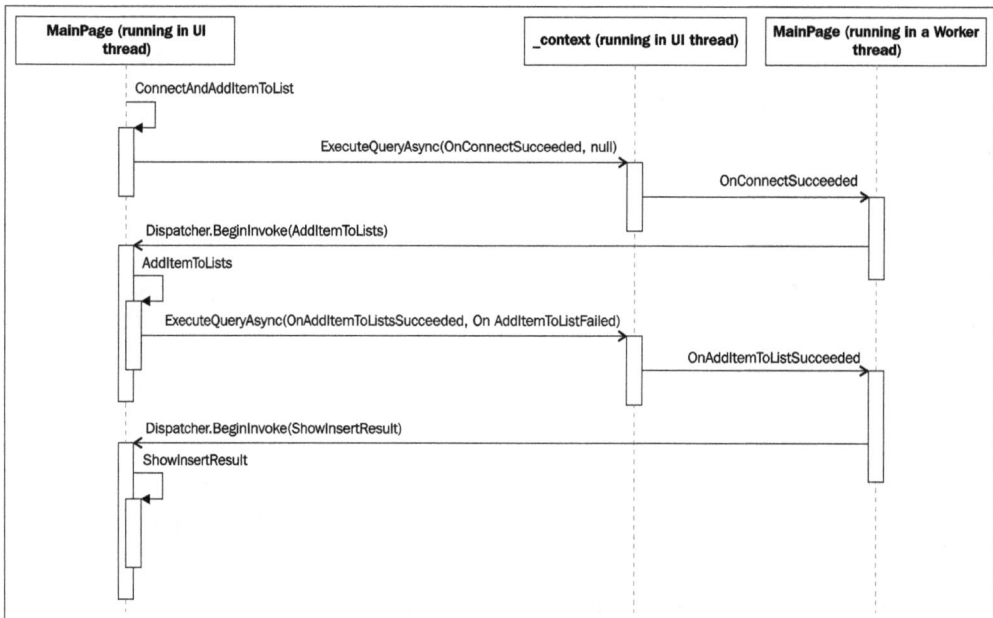

When the user clicks the **Insert** button, the `Click` event handler calls the `ConnectAndAddItemToList` method, in the UI thread. This method uses the current URL to generate a `ClientContext` instance, saved in the `private_context` variable. Then, it calls the `Load` method to build a query to load the `Web` and its current user, the user that logged on to the SharePoint site. Then, it calls the `ExecuteQueryAsync` to run it with an asynchronous execution.

```
_context.Load(_context.Web);
_context.Load(_context.Web.CurrentUser);
```

If the query has a successful execution, the `OnConnectSucceeded` callback schedules the asynchronous execution of the `AddItemToList` method in the UI thread from a worker thread that runs this code after the query has succeeded.

```
private void OnConnectSucceeded(Object sender, SP.ClientRequestSucceed
edEventArgs args)
{
    Dispatcher.BeginInvoke(AddItemToList);
}
```

In this example, we also specified the `OnConnectFailed` callback and used it as the second parameter for the `ExecuteQueryAsync` method. If something goes wrong, it invokes a delegate that calls the `ShowErrorInformation` method and sends the `ClientRequestFailedEventArgs args` instance as a parameter to it. The code uses a **lambda expression** to define the delegate:

```
private void OnConnectFailed(object sender,
ClientRequestFailedEventArgs args)
{
    Dispatcher.BeginInvoke(() => ShowErrorInformation(args));
}
```

> Remember that a lambda expression, introduced in C# 3.0, is an anonymous function that can contains expressions and statements and can be used to create delegates or expression tree types. They are useful to simplify the code when we use delegates. All lambda expressions use the lambda operator => (read as **goes to**). Lambda expressions are described in depth in *WCF Multi-tier Services Development with LINQ* by Mike Liu, Packt Publishing.

The following lines show equivalent code to define a delegate and invoke it to run asynchronously in the UI thread without using a lambda expression. It requires more lines of code, because it is necessary to declare a `delegate` type, create a new instance with the method to run, use the `Dispatcher.BeginInvoke` method to call the delegate instance, and send the `args` instance as a parameter encapsulated in an array of `object`.

```
private delegate void ShowErrorInformationCaller
(ClientRequestFailedEventArgs args);

private void OnConnectFailed(object sender,
ClientRequestFailedEventArgs args)
{
    // This callback isn't called on the UI thread
    // Create the delegate instance
    ShowErrorInformationCaller ShowErrorInformationD =
    new ShowErrorInformationCaller(ShowErrorInformation);
    // Invoke the delegate
    Dispatcher.BeginInvoke(
    ShowErrorInformationD, new object[] { args });
}
```

It is convenient to use lambda expressions, because they require less code to achieve the same goal. However the previously shown lines make it easier to understand the way the method is called in the delegate.

If everything works as expected, then the `AddItemToList` method is going to run in the UI thread. This method calls the `GetByTitle` method to save a reference to the `ProjectsList2010` list that was previously created in the SharePoint server in the preceding chapter, in the `_projects` private variable. Then, it calls its `AddItem` method to add a new `ListItemCreationInformation` empty instance. This method returns a new `ListItem` instance that allows us to access the fields for the new item in the list and fill their values.

```
_projects = _context.Web.Lists.GetByTitle("ProjectsList2010");
ListItem listItem = _projects.AddItem(new
ListItemCreationInformation());
```

Then, the code completes the value for each field by using its `InternalName` and assigning a string value, as shown in the next line.

```
listItem["Title"] = txtTitle.Text;
```

The `AssignedTo` field is a special case, because it is a `FieldUserValue` that references a SharePoint server user through a lookup ID. Remember that this field had a `Microsoft.SharePoint.SPFieldUserValue` value in its `FieldValueType` property. Thus, it is necessary to use the `Id` for the user currently logged on the SharePoint server to assign it to the `LookupId` property of a new `FieldUserValue` instance, `fieldUserValue`. Then, it is possible to assign `fieldUserValue` to `listItem["AssignedTo"]` to store the current user as the value for this field.

```
var fieldUserValue = new FieldUserValue();
fieldUserValue.LookupId = _context.Web.CurrentUser.Id;
listItem["AssignedTo"] = fieldUserValue;
```

> Remember, it is possible to access the `_context.Web.CurrentUser.Id` property because we queried `_context.Web.CurrentUser` in the `ConnectAndAddItemToList` method.

Once all the fields are filled with the corresponding values, the code calls the `Update` method for the new `ListItem` instance that holds the new row, `listItem`. At this point, the new item isn't still inserted in the list, because it is necessary to execute the query. The code requests the `Title` for the list as a response and then calls the `ExecuteQueryAsync` method:

```
listItem.Update();
_context.Load(_projects, list => list.Title);
_context.ExecuteQueryAsync(OnAddItemToListSucceeded,
OnAddItemToListFailed);
```

The following diagram shows the detailed execution flowchart for the asynchronous query that adds the item to the list. Besides, it indicates the code that runs in the UI thread. If the query execution isn't successful, the application will run the `OnAddItemToListFailed` callback and it will display information about the error that made the query fail in a dialog box. If the query execution succeeds, the application will run the `OnAddItemToListSucceeded` callback and it will display status information to let the user know that the item was inserted in the list.

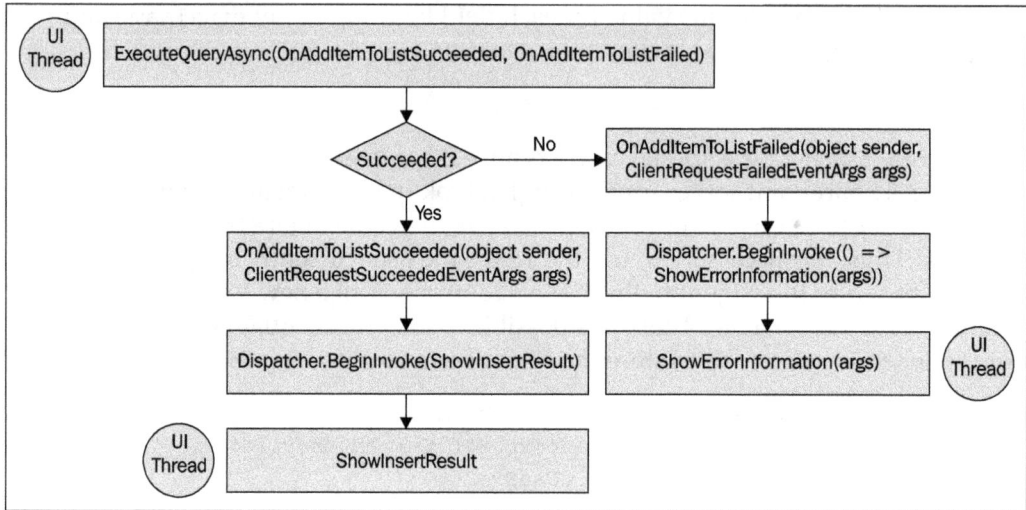

Retrieving specific information about fields

If we examine the default dialog box that allows a user to insert items into the list in the SharePoint server, we will notice that there is a default value for both the **Priority** and **Status** fields, as shown in the following screenshot:

- **(2) Normal** for **Priority**
- **Not Started** for **Status**

Besides, when we use this dialog box to insert a new item or edit an existing one, the two drop-down lists offer many choices as their possible values.

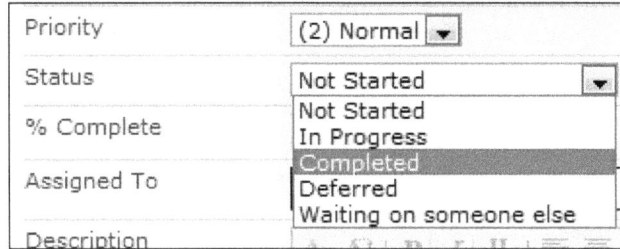

Follow these steps to access the value for the SchemaXml property in the **Priority** and **Status** fields by using Server Explorer.

1. Stay in Visual Studio as a system administrator user.

2. Activate the **Server Explorer** palette and navigate to the previously created list, **ProjectsList2010**.

3. Now, expand the list of tasks, **ProjectsList2010**, and then expand its **Fields** node. This way, you will see all the fields for this list.

4. Now, click on the **Priority** field, display its properties, and check the value for its SchemaXml property. As the content for this property is XML markup, you won't be able to analyze all the information in the **Properties** palette, because you will see only the first characters

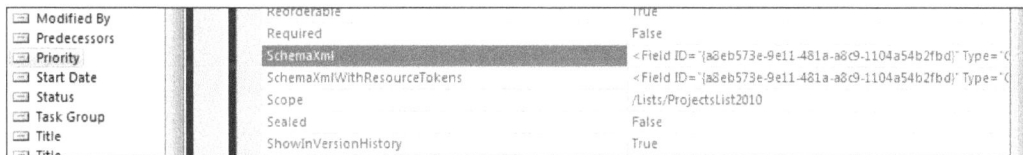

5. You can copy the value for the SchemaXml property and paste it in a new **XML File** in Visual Studio. This way, you will be able to see the three choices and their mappings, and a default value, as shown in the following lines and in the next screenshot with the contents pasted in a Visual Studio XML File that organizes the markup code.

```
XMLFile2.xml*  ✕   MainPage.xaml.cs*      SequenceDiagram1.sequencediagram      N
    ⊟<Field ID="{a8eb573e-9e11-481a-a8c9-1104a54b2fbd}"
            Type="Choice" Name="Priority" DisplayName="Priority"
            SourceID="http://schemas.microsoft.com/sharepoint/v3"
            StaticName="Priority" ColName="nvarchar3">
    ⊟  <CHOICES>
         <CHOICE>(1) High</CHOICE>
         <CHOICE>(2) Normal</CHOICE>
         <CHOICE>(3) Low</CHOICE>
       </CHOICES>
    ⊟  <MAPPINGS>
         <MAPPING Value="1">(1) High</MAPPING>
         <MAPPING Value="2">(2) Normal</MAPPING>
         <MAPPING Value="3">(3) Low</MAPPING>
       </MAPPINGS>
       <Default>(2) Normal</Default>
     </Field>|
```

```
<Field ID="{a8eb573e-9e11-481a-a8c9-1104a54b2fbd}"
        Type="Choice" Name="Priority" DisplayName="Priority"
        SourceID="http://schemas.microsoft.com/sharepoint/v3"
        StaticName="Priority" ColName="nvarchar3">
  <CHOICES>
    <CHOICE>(1) High</CHOICE>
    <CHOICE>(2) Normal</CHOICE>
    <CHOICE>(3) Low</CHOICE>
  </CHOICES>
  <MAPPINGS>
    <MAPPING Value="1">(1) High</MAPPING>
    <MAPPING Value="2">(2) Normal</MAPPING>
    <MAPPING Value="3">(3) Low</MAPPING>
  </MAPPINGS>
  <Default>(2) Normal</Default>
</Field>
```

6. Now, repeat the aforementioned steps (4 and 5) with the **Status** field. You will be able to see the five choices and their mappings, as shown in the following lines:

```
<Field Type="Choice"
        ID="{c15b34c3-ce7d-490a-b133-3f4de8801b76}"
        Name="Status" DisplayName="Status"
        SourceID="http://schemas.microsoft.com/sharepoint/v3"
        StaticName="Status" ColName="nvarchar4">
```

```
<CHOICES>
  <CHOICE>Not Started</CHOICE>
  <CHOICE>In Progress</CHOICE>
  <CHOICE>Completed</CHOICE>
  <CHOICE>Deferred</CHOICE>
  <CHOICE>Waiting on someone else</CHOICE>
</CHOICES>
<MAPPINGS>
  <MAPPING Value="1">Not Started</MAPPING>
  <MAPPING Value="2">In Progress</MAPPING>
  <MAPPING Value="3">Completed</MAPPING>
  <MAPPING Value="4">Deferred</MAPPING>
  <MAPPING Value="5">Waiting on someone else</MAPPING>
</MAPPINGS>
<Default>Not Started</Default>
</Field>
```

We now have the information that we need to enhance the Silverlight LOB RIA.
Follow these steps to add new code that retrieves the choices defined in the
SharePoint list for both the **Priority** and **Status** fields and uses their default values.

1. Stay in Visual Studio as a system administrator user, in the
   `TasksCRUD` solution.

2. Open `MainPage.xaml.cs` and add the following private variable:
   ```
   private SP.FieldCollection _collField;
   ```

3. Now, it is necessary to add code to execute the following tasks:

   1. Connect to the SharePoint server and load information about
      the **Priority** and **Status** fields from the `ProjectsList2010`,
      `ConnectAndFillComboBoxes` method.

   2. Iterate through a collection of fields, find and return a `FieldChoice`
      instance, according to an `InternalName` value, received as a
      parameter, `ReturnFieldByInternalName` method.

   3. Add each choice defined for the retrieved **Priority** and **Status**
      `FieldChoice` fields as a new item in the corresponding combo
      boxes and set their default value, `AddFieldChoicesToComboBoxes`
      method.

   ```
   private void ConnectAndFillComboBoxes()
   {
     // Runs in the UI Thread
   ```

```
        lblStatus.Content = "Started";
        _context = new SP.ClientContext(
           SP.ApplicationContext.Current.Url);
        // Load the Web
        _context.Load(_context.Web);
        // Get the ProjectsList2010 list
        _projects = _context.Web.Lists.
          GetByTitle("ProjectsList2010");
        _context.Load(_projects);
        // Just load the two necessary fields for the List:
        // Status and Priority
        _collField = _projects.Fields;
        _context.Load(_collField,
        fields => fields.Where(
        field => field.InternalName == "Status"
        || field.InternalName == "Priority")
        .IncludeWithDefaultProperties());
        _context.ExecuteQueryAsync(
        OnConnectAndFillComboBoxesSucceeded,
        OnConnectAndFillComboBoxesFailed);
    }

    private SP.FieldChoice ReturnFieldByInternalName(string
    internalName)
    {
      for (int i = 0; i < _collField.Count; i++)
      {
        if (_collField[i].InternalName == internalName)
        {
          return (_collField[i] as FieldChoice);
        }
      }
      return null;
    }

    private void AddFieldChoicesToComboBoxes()
    {
      // Runs in the UI Thread
      SP.FieldChoice statusField =
      ReturnFieldByInternalName("Status");
      SP.FieldChoice priorityField =
```

```
ReturnFieldByInternalName("Priority");
// Add each choice to the corresponding ComboBox control
foreach (string item in statusField.Choices)
{
  cboStatus.Items.Add(item);
}
foreach (string item in priorityField.Choices)
{
  cboPriority.Items.Add(item);
}
// Set default values
cboStatus.SelectedValue = statusField.DefaultValue;
cboPriority.SelectedValue = priorityField.DefaultValue;
}
```

4. All the previously added methods are going to run in the UI thread, as explained in *Chapter 2*, in *Working with the asynchronous methods and callbacks*. The following methods, which are going to be fired as asynchronous callbacks, schedule the execution of other methods to continue with the necessary program flow in the UI thread:

   ° When the connection to the SharePoint server and the query execution, requested by the ConnectAndFillComboBoxes method, is successful, the OnConnectAndFillComboBoxesSucceeded method schedules the execution of the AddFieldChoicesToComboBox method in the UI thread.

   ° If the ConnectAndFillComboBoxes method fails, the OnConnectAndFillComboBoxesFailed method schedules the execution of the ShowErrorInformation method in the UI thread, sending the ClientRequestFailedEventArgs args instance as a parameter to the delegate.

```
private void OnConnectAndFillComboBoxesSucceeded(Object sender,
  SP.ClientRequestSucceededEventArgs args)
{
    // This callback isn't called on the UI thread
    Dispatcher.BeginInvoke(AddFieldChoicesToComboBoxes);
}

private void OnConnectAndFillComboBoxesFailed(object sender,
  ClientRequestFailedEventArgs args)
{
```

```
        // This callback isn't called on the UI thread
        // Invoke a delegate and send the args instance as a parameter
        Dispatcher.BeginInvoke(() => ShowErrorInformation(args));
}
```

Replace the code in the `MainPage` constructor with the following lines to fill the combo boxes by calling the new `ConnectAndFillComboBoxes` method instead of the previously defined `FillComboBoxes`:

```
public MainPage()
{
        InitializeComponent();

        ConnectAndFillComboBoxes();
}
```

5. Build and deploy the solution.

6. Enter the URL for the previously added page that contains the Silverlight Web Part in the Web browser. This way, the updated Silverlight RIA will appear and it will load the choices and default values for the `Priority` and `Status` fields from the information retrieved from the list in the SharePoint server:

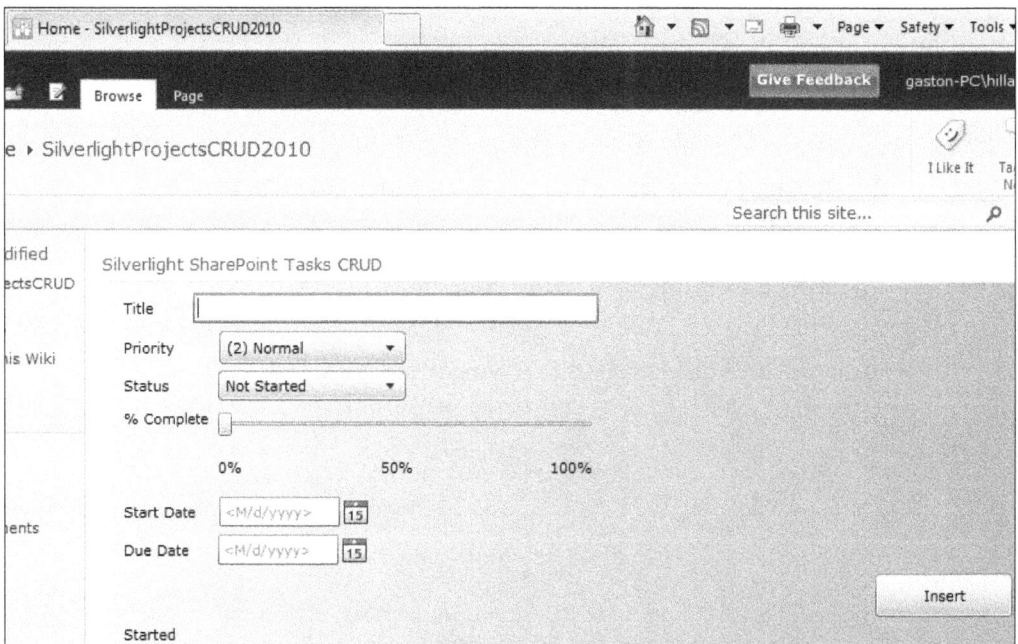

The following diagram shows the detailed execution flowchart for the asynchronous query that retrieves information for both the `Priority` and `Status` fields. The diagram indicates the code that runs in the UI thread. If the query execution isn't successful, the application will run the `OnConnectAndFillComboBoxesFailed` callback and it will display information about the error that made the query fail in a dialog box. If the query execution succeeds, the application will run the `OnConnectAndFillComboBoxesSucceeded` callback and it will fill the two combo boxes with the retrieved choices and will set their default values.

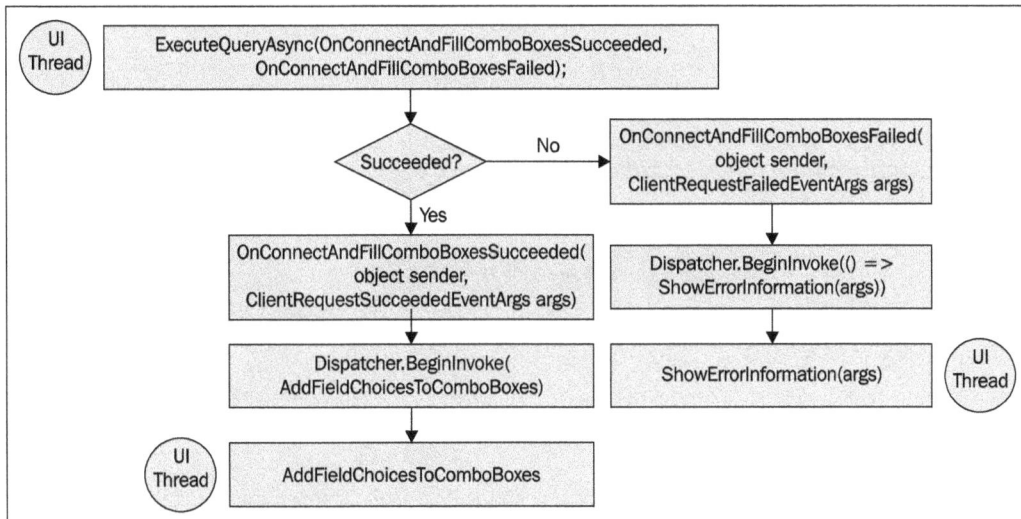

As the asynchronous executions make it a bit difficult to track the execution flow, we can use one of the features offered by the Visual Studio code editor to help us. Locate the cursor over a method's name and press *F12* or right-click on it and select **Go To Definition** in the context menu that appears. For example, you can do it for `OnConnectAndFillComboBoxesSucceeded` in the line that sends this callback as a parameter to the `_context.ExecuteQueryAsync` method.

```
SLTasksCRUD.MainPage

        private void ConnectAndFillComboBoxes()
        {
            // Runs in the UI Thread
            lblStatus.Content = "Started";
            _context = new SP.ClientContext(SP.ApplicationContext.Current.Url);
            // Load the Web
            _context.Load(_context.Web);
            // Get the ProjectsList2010 list
            _projects = _context.Web.Lists.GetByTitle("ProjectsList2010");

            _context.Load(_projects);

            // Just load the two necessary fields for the List:
            // Status and Priority
            _collField = _projects.Fields;

            _context.Load(_collField,
                fields => fields.Where(
                    field => field.InternalName == "Status"
                        || field.InternalName == "Priority")
                        .IncludeWithDefaultProperties());
            _context.ExecuteQueryAsync(
                OnConnectAndFillComboBoxesSucceede
                OnConnectAndFillComboBoxesFailed).
        }
```

View Designer	
Refactor	▶
Organize Usings	▶
Create Unit Tests...	
Generate Sequence Diagram...	
Insert Snippet...	Ctrl+K, Ctrl+X
Surround With...	Ctrl+K, Ctrl+S
Go To Definition	F12

This way, the code editor will locate the cursor at the line that defines the selected method's name, `OnConnectAndFillComboBoxesSucceeded`. You can take advantage of this feature to track the execution flow by accessing the code for the different methods involved in the sequence.

```
MainPage.xaml.cs* ✕  SequenceDiagram1.sequencediagram    MainPage.xaml

SLTasksCRUD.MainPage

        private void OnConnectAndFillComboBoxesSucceeded(Object sender,
            SP.ClientRequestSucceededEventArgs args)
        {

            // This callback isn't called on the UI thread
            Dispatcher.BeginInvoke(AddFieldChoicesToComboBoxes);
        }
```

Now, the `MainPage` constructor calls the new `ConnectAndFillComboBoxes` method that creates a new `ClientContext` instance, requests it to load the `Web` and the list, `ProjectsList2010`. Then, it is necessary to load just two fields, `Priority` and `Status`, and therefore, we specified a LINQ expression as the second parameter for the `Load` method to limit the information that has to be retrieved. We used a lambda expression as a parameter of the `Where` method to filter the sequence of values based on a predicate. We just wanted to retrieve the fields whose `InternalName` property value was `Status` or `Priority`. We added the call to the `IncludeWithDefaultProperties` extension method without parameters, because we just want to retrieve the default properties for the two `Field` instances in the `_collField FieldCollection`.

```
_context.Load(_collField,
    fields => fields.Where(
        field => field.InternalName == "Status"
            || field.InternalName == "Priority")
                .IncludeWithDefaultProperties());
```

This way, we query for two fields and we request their default properties. Once this query is successful, the `AddFieldChoicesToComboBoxes` method retrieves the two fields from the `_collField FieldCollection` as `FieldChoice` instances, `statusField` and `prioriryField`. The `ReturnFieldByInternalName` method receives a string with the required value for the `InternalName` property and returns the field from the `_collField FieldCollection` that satisfies this simple condition as a `FieldChoice` instance. The `FieldChoice` class, `Microsoft.SharePoint.Client.FieldChoice`, represents a choice field control. As this is the real class for the two field instances, it is necessary to cast them to `FieldChoice` to access the specific field and properties that allow us to retrieve the choices.

```
SP.FieldChoice statusField =
                        ReturnFieldByInternalName("Status");
SP.FieldChoice priorityField =
                        ReturnFieldByInternalName("Priority");
```

Then, the code adds a new item to each combo box, `cboStatus` and `cboPriority`, for each string in the `FieldChoice` instance `Choices` string array. The following lines show the `foreach` loop that adds items to the `cboStatus ComboBox`:

```
foreach (string item in statusField.Choices)
{
    cboStatus.Items.Add(item);
}
```

Once the code has filled the two combo boxes with the possible choices, it assigns the value for each field `DefaultValue` property to the `ComboBox SelectedValue` property. This way, the drop-down list displayed by these controls will show the same default value as the dialog box that allows inserting items in the SharePoint list.

```
cboStatus.SelectedValue = statusField.DefaultValue;
```

Creating complex LOB applications composed of multiple Silverlight RIAs

One of the interesting features provided by Silverlight applications is the possibility to establish a simple communication channel between them and use it to send messages between many applications. This feature is very useful when we have many Silverlight applications included in Web Parts. Silverlight applications running on the same computer can communicate over the boundaries of tabs inside a web browser and even over the limits of web browser instances.

Follow these steps to add new code that sends a message to a listener application when the application inserts a new item in the list:

1. Stay in Visual Studio as a system administrator user, in the `TasksCRUD` solution.

2. Open `MainPage.xaml.cs` and add the following `using` statements to include the `System.Windows.Messaging` namespace:

   ```
   using System.Windows.Messaging;
   ```

3. Add the following two private constants:

   ```
   private const string MSG_RECEIVER_NAME = "MessageReceiver";
   private const string MSG_TASKSCRUD_NEWITEM = "TASKSCRUD_NEWITEM";
   ```

4. Add the following method that sends the message received as a parameter to the receiver:

   ```
   private void SendMessage(string message)
   {
       // Create a new LocalMessageSender instance
       // with the receiver name as a parameter
       LocalMessageSender messageSender =
                       new LocalMessageSender(MSG_RECEIVER_NAME);

       // Attach a SendCompletedEventArgs handler
       messageSender.SendCompleted +=
                       (object s, SendCompletedEventArgs args) =>
   ```

```
    {
        // Update the status label
        lblStatus.Content = "Message sent successfully. " +
                        "Response: " + args.Response;
    };
    // Send the asynchronous message to the receiver
    messageSender.SendAsync(message);
}
```

5. Add the following line in the `ShowInsertResult` method to send a message to another Silverlight application when the item was successfully added to the list:

```
private void ShowInsertResult()
{
    lblStatus.Content =
                    "New item added to " + _projects.Title;
    // Send a message to another Silverlight RIA
    // in order to force a refresh
    SendMessage(MSG_TASKSCRUD_NEWITEM);
}
```

6. Build and deploy the solution.

Now, follow these steps to add new code that listens to the messages sent by the previously modified Silverlight application and runs code as a response to them:

1. Stay in Visual Studio as a system administrator user or run a new instance.

2. Open the `TasksViewer` solution, created in *Chapter 2*, in the *Creating a Silverlight RIA to be linked with a SharePoint module* section.

3. Open `MainPage.xaml.cs` and add the following `using` statements to include the `System.Windows.Messaging` namespace:

```
using System.Windows.Messaging;
```

4. Add the following two private constants:

```
private const string MSG_RECEIVER_NAME = "MessageReceiver";
private const string MSG_TASKSCRUD_NEWITEM = "TASKSCRUD_NEWITEM";
```

5. Add the following code to the `MainPage` constructor that starts receiving messages and refreshes the items from the list shown in the `DataGrid`, `dataGridProjects`, each time it receives the `MSG_TASKSCRUD_NEWITEM` message:

```
public MainPage()
{
  InitializeComponent();
  LocalMessageReceiver messageReceiver =
        new LocalMessageReceiver(MSG_RECEIVER_NAME);
    messageReceiver.MessageReceived +=
        ( object sender, MessageReceivedEventArgs e ) =>
        {
            if (e.Message == MSG_TASKSCRUD_NEWITEM)
            {
                Connect();
            }
            e.Response = "OK";
        };
    try
    {
        messageReceiver.Listen();
    }
    catch (ListenFailedException)
    {
        // There is another receiver with the same name
        // and the application cannot receive messages
        lblStatus.Content = "Cannot receive messages.";
    }
}
```

6. Build and deploy the solution.

Follow these steps to test the two Silverlight Web Parts in different web browser instances:

1. Start two web browser instances.

2. Load the SharePoint page that shows `SLTasksViewer.xap` as a Silverlight Web Part in one web browser's window, `SilverlightProjectsList2010.aspx`.

3. Load the SharePoint page that shows `SLTasksCRUD.xap` as a Silverlight Web Part in the other web browser's window, `SilverlightProjectsCRUD2010.aspx`. Make both Web Parts visible at the same time.

4. Complete the data to insert a new item in the list and click on the **Insert** button. The new item will be added to the list and the Silverlight Web Part that displays the grid will refresh its contents to show the new item, because it receives the message from the other Silverlight Web Part. The status label at the bottom of SLTasksCRUD.xap will display **Message sent successfully. Response: OK.**, because it receives OK as a response from SLTasksViewer. xap, the listener application:

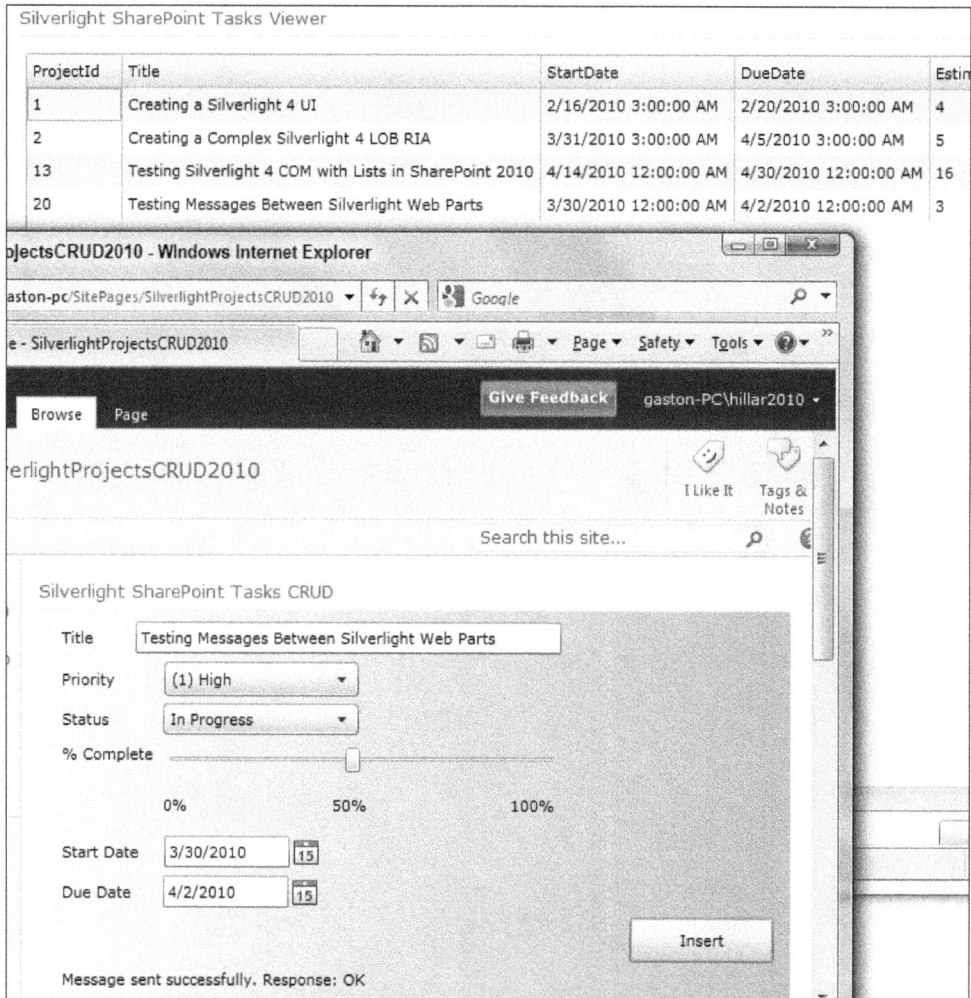

5. Test the behavior by showing each Web Part in a different browser tab and you will achieve the same results.

Interacting with multiple Silverlight Web Parts in the same page

We took advantage of Silverlight's messaging capabilities to establish a communication channel between multiple Silverlight Web Parts in SharePoint. This way, it is possible to create complex solutions composed of multiple Silverlight Web Parts that interact with each other. Then, we can decide the best layout for these Silverlight Web Parts in one or many SharePoint pages.

Follow these steps to test the two Silverlight Web Parts in the same SharePoint page:

1. Open the web page that shows `SLTasksCRUD.xap` as a Silverlight Web Part in the other web browser's window, `SilverlightProjectsCRUD2010.aspx`.

2. Click **Site Actions** | **Edit Page** and SharePoint will display the editing tools for this page.

3. Follow the necessary steps to insert a second Silverlight Web Part to this page, `SLTasksViewer.xap`. This way, the page will show `SLTasksCRUD.xap` at the top and `SLTasksViewer.xap` at the bottom.

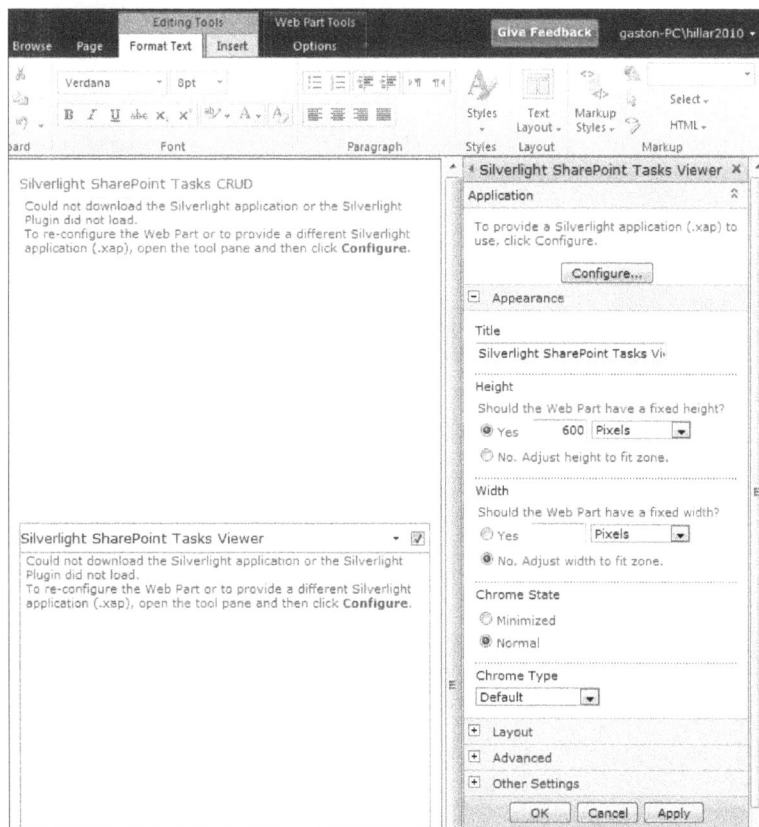

4. Remember to apply the settings learned in the previous examples to the new Silverlight Web Part and click on the **Save** button in the ribbon. Now, the new page will appear, displaying the two previously created Silverlight RIAs running as two Silverlight Web Parts in the same page.

5. Complete the data to insert a new item in the list and click on the **Insert** button. The new item will be added to the list and the Silverlight Web Part that displays the grid at the bottom of the page will refresh its contents to show the new item, because it receives the message from the other Silverlight Web Part.

Silverlight SharePoint Tasks CRUD

Title	Testing Two Silverlight Web Parts Interacting in the Sam
Priority	(2) Normal ▾
Status	In Progress ▾
% Complete	

0%   50%   100%

Start Date	3/29/2010 [15]
Due Date	4/21/2010 [15]

Insert

Message sent successfully. Response: OK

Silverlight SharePoint Tasks Viewer

ProjectId	Title	StartDate	DueDate	EstimatedDa
1	Creating a Silverlight 4 UI	2/16/2010 3:00:00 AM	2/20/2010 3:00:00 AM	4
2	Creating a Complex Silverlight 4 LOB RIA	3/31/2010 3:00:00 AM	4/5/2010 3:00:00 AM	5
13	Testing Silverlight 4 COM with Lists in SharePoint 2010	4/14/2010 12:00:00 AM	4/30/2010 12:00:00 AM	16
20	Testing Messages Between Silverlight Web Parts	3/30/2010 12:00:00 AM	4/2/2010 12:00:00 AM	3
26	Testing Two Silverlight Web Parts Interacting in the Same Page	3/29/2010 12:00:00 AM	4/21/2010 12:00:00 AM	23

The user inserts a new item into the list and doesn't need to refresh the Silverlight Web Part that displays the data for the list, because the application receives the message and updates its content.

This simple example demonstrates one of the most interesting possibilities offered by Silverlight RIAs included as Silverlight Web Parts: they make it simpler to refresh content without having to reload a page in the Web browser.

Understanding Line-Of-Business systems as independent Web Parts

The `System.Windows.Messaging` namespace offers the necessary classes and event types that allowed us to send messages between two Silverlight Web Parts running on the same computer.

The `SendMessage` method in the `SLTasksCRUD` Silverlight application receives the message to be sent as a `string` parameter. It creates a new `LocalMessageSender` instance (`System.Windows.Messaging.LocalMessageSender`) with the receiver name, defined in the `MSG_RECEIVER_NAME` constant, as a parameter for the constructor.

```
LocalMessageSender messageSender =
                        new LocalMessageSender(MSG_RECEIVER_NAME);
```

Then, it attaches a `SendCompleted` event handler to the `SendCompleted` event for the `LocalMessageSender` instance, `messageSender`. In this case, a lambda expression defines the code to run in the event handler that receives the `SendCompletedEventArgs args` as the second parameter. This event will fire when the message has been sent. If everything worked as expected, `args.Response` will contain the response added by the receiver to acknowledge the message's reception. The code just updates the text shown in the `lblStatus` Label and adds the value for `args.Response` to this text. This value should be `OK` if the `SLTasksViewer` Silverlight application received the message.

```
messageSender.SendCompleted +=
                        (object s, SendCompletedEventArgs args) =>
{
    // Update the status label
    lblStatus.Content = "Message sent successfully. " +
                        "Response: " + args.Response;
};
```

If the message wasn't received, the `args.Error` property would be set to a `SendFailedException` instance. In this case, in order to keep the example simple, the code doesn't consider this situation. However, when you work with more complex Silverlight Web Parts, it is convenient to add more code to handle the potential exceptions that could be thrown.

Then, the code sends the `string` received as a parameter, `message`, as an asynchronous message to the previously specified receiver. Remember that the code defined in the previously explained event handler will run after the receiver receives the asynchronous message.

```
messageSender.SendAsync(message);
```

Each time a user adds a new item to a list, the `SLTasksCRUD` Silverlight application calls the `SendMessage` method to send the `MSG_TASKSCRUD_NEWITEM` string to the registered listener.

```
SendMessage(MSG_TASKSCRUD_NEWITEM);
```

The `MainPage` constructor in the `SLTasksViewer` Silverlight application creates a new `LocalMessageReceiver` instance (`System.Windows.Messaging.LocalMessageReceiver`) with the receiver name, defined in the `MSG_RECEIVER_NAME` constant, and with the same value as the one defined in `SLTasksCRUD`, as a parameter for the constructor.

```
LocalMessageReceiver messageReceiver =
new LocalMessageReceiver(MSG_RECEIVER_NAME);
```

Then, the code performs the following sequence:

It attaches a `MessageReceived` event handler to the `MessageReceived` event for the `LocalMessageReceiver` instance, `messageReceiver`.

A lambda expression defines the code to run in the event handler that receives the `MessageReceivedEventArgs e` as the second parameter.

The event will fire if the `Listen` method was called and a message was received for the registered receiver. `e.Message` contains a string with the received message and it is possible to send a response to the sender by assigning a string to `e.Response`.

If the message received is `MSG_TASKSCRUD_NEWITEM`, it means that the `SLTasksCRUD` Silverlight application added a new item to the list that this application is showing in a `DataGrid`. Thus, it is necessary to refresh the data shown in the grid and the code calls the `Connect` method to query the data from the SharePoint server and assigns `OK` as a response to the sender to acknowledge the message's reception.

```
messageReceiver.MessageReceived += ( object sender,
MessageReceivedEventArgs e ) =>
{
  if (e.Message == MSG_TASKSCRUD_NEWITEM)
  {
    Connect();
  }
```

```
      e.Response = "OK";
   };
```

In order to be able to receive messages, it is necessary to call the `Listen` method for the `LocalMessageReceiver` instance, `messageReceiver`. This method will throw a `ListenFailedException`, if something goes wrong. For example, if there is another receiver registered with the same name, this application is not going to be able to receive messages targeting the indicated receiver. Thus, the code encloses the call to the `Listen` method in a `try-catch` block.

If the call to the `Listen` method is successful, each time a message is sent to the registered receiver, this application will run the code in the previously explained `MessageReceived` attached event handler. In this case, in order to keep things simple, the application doesn't use flags to determine whether a received message that suggests a data refresh is being processed or not. However, as the refresh process can take some time, because it requests data from the SharePoint server and at the same time, other messages can arrive, it is convenient to add some kind of mechanism to run only one refresh process at a time.

Expanding LOB systems with delete operations

So far, we have created Silverlight Web Parts that can retrieve the items from a list in the SharePoint server, add new items to this list, and communicate between themselves to refresh the data shown to the user when necessary.

Now, follow these steps to add a new button in the `SLTasksViewer` Silverlight application to allow the user to delete the item selected in the DataGrid from the list in the SharePoint server, `ProjectsList2010`.

1. Stay in Visual Studio as a system administrator user, in the `TasksViewer` solution.

2. Open `MainPage.xaml`, add a new `Button` control, `butDelete`, and set its `Content` property to `Delete`.

3. Add a new `DataPager` control, `dataPager` and locate it at the bottom of the `dataGridProjects` DataGrid. Set its `DisplayMode` property to `Numeric` and `PageSize` to 5. This control will simplify the navigation and will display 5 items per page.

4. Apply data binding to the `Source` property for the `DataPager` control, `dataPager`. Click **Apply Data Binding...**, select `ElementName` in `Source`, `dataGridProjects` and then `ItemsSource` in `Path`. This way, the `Source` property will be set to `dataGridProjects.ItemsSource`. The XAML markup that defines the data binding will be the following:

    ```
    Source="{Binding ElementName=dataGridProjects, Path=ItemsSource}"
    ```

5. Open `MainPage.xaml.cs` and add the following private variable:

    ```
    private System.Windows.Data.PagedCollectionView
    _projectsPagedView;
    ```

6. Replace the line that assigns the value for `ItemSource` in the `ShowItems` method, `dataGridProjects.ItemsSource = _projectsList;`, with the following lines. Now, the `ItemsSource` property will have a representation of a view of `_projectsList` for navigating a paged data collection.

    ```
    _projectsPagedView = new System.Windows.Data.PagedCollectionView(
    _projectsList);
    dataGridProjects.ItemsSource = _projectsPagedView;
    ```

7. Now, add the following code to the `Click` event for the `butDelete Button`. This way, when the user clicks on this button, the application will retrieve the `Project` instance selected in the `dataGridProjects DataGrid`, and use its ID to retrieve and delete the item form the list in the SharePoint server.

    ```csharp
    private void butDelete_Click(object sender, RoutedEventArgs e)
    {
        _context = new
            SP.ClientContext(SP.ApplicationContext.Current.Url);
        _projects =
            _context.Web.Lists.GetByTitle("ProjectsList2010");
        var selectedProject =
            (dataGridProjects.SelectedItem as Project);

        SP.ListItem listItem =
            _projects.GetItemById(selectedProject.ProjectId);

        // Remove the item from the list
        listItem.DeleteObject();

        _context.ExecuteQueryAsync(
            OnDeleteSucceeded, OnDeleteFailed);
    }
    ```

8. The code in the `Click` event for the `butDelete Button` is going to run in the UI thread. The following methods, which are going to be fired as asynchronous callbacks, schedule the execution of other methods to continue with the necessary program flow in the UI thread:

    ○   When the connection to the SharePoint server and the query execution that deletes an item from the list, requested by the `butDelete_Click` method, is successful, the `OnDeleteSucceeded` method schedules the execution of the `Connect` method in the UI thread, to refresh the data shown in the `dataGridProjects DataGrid`.

    ○   If the `butDelete_Click` method fails, the `OnDeleteFailed` method schedules the execution of the `ShowErrorInformation` method in the UI thread, sending the `ClientRequestFailedEventArgs args` instance as a parameter to the delegate.

```
private void ShowErrorInformation(ClientRequestFailedEventArgs
args)
{
    MessageBox.Show("Request failed. " + args.Message + "\n"
+ args.StackTrace + "\n" + args.ErrorDetails + "\n" + args.
ErrorValue);
}


private void OnDeleteSucceeded(Object sender, SP.ClientRequestSucc
eededEventArgs args)
{
    // This callback isn't called on the UI thread
    Dispatcher.BeginInvoke(Connect);
}


private void OnDeleteFailed(Object sender,
SP.ClientRequestFailedEventArgs args)
{
    // This callback isn't called on the UI thread
    // Invoke a delegate and send the args instance as a parameter
    Dispatcher.BeginInvoke(() => ShowErrorInformation(args));
}
```

9. Build and deploy the solution.

10. Load the SharePoint page that shows `SLTasksViewer.xap` as a Silverlight Web Part, `SilverlightProjectsList2010.aspx`.

11. Click on the row that you want to delete in the grid and then click on the **Delete** button.

Silverlight SharePoint Tasks Viewer

ProjectId	Title	StartDate	DueDate	EstimatedDaysL
1	Creating a Silverlight 4 UI	2/16/2010 3:00:00 AM	2/20/2010 3:00:00 AM	4
2	Creating a Complex Silverlight 4 LOB RIA	3/31/2010 3:00:00 AM	4/5/2010 3:00:00 AM	5
13	Testing Silverlight 4 Client OM with Lists in SharePoint 2010	4/14/2010 12:00:00 AM	4/30/2010 12:00:00 AM	16
20	Testing Messages Between Silverlight Web Parts	3/30/2010 12:00:00 AM	4/2/2010 12:00:00 AM	3
26	Testing the Delete Operation in a SharePoint List	3/28/2010 3:00:00 AM	4/20/2010 3:00:00 AM	23

Showing items...   1 2 3   Delete

12. The application will request the SharePoint server to delete the selected item from the list and then it will refresh the data shown in the grid. If the operation was successful, the row will not appear in the grid.

Silverlight SharePoint Tasks Viewer

ProjectId	Title	StartDate	DueDate	EstimatedDa
1	Creating a Silverlight 4 UI	2/16/2010 3:00:00 AM	2/20/2010 3:00:00 AM	4
2	Creating a Complex Silverlight 4 LOB RIA	3/31/2010 3:00:00 AM	4/5/2010 3:00:00 AM	5
13	Testing Silverlight 4 COM with Lists in SharePoint 2010	4/14/2010 12:00:00 AM	4/30/2010 12:00:00 AM	16
20	Testing Messages Between Silverlight Web Parts	3/30/2010 12:00:00 AM	4/2/2010 12:00:00 AM	3
26	Testing Two Silverlight Web Parts Interacting in the Same Page	3/29/2010 12:00:00 AM	4/21/2010 12:00:00 AM	23

Understanding how to delete an item from a list

When the user clicks the **Delete** button, the `Click` event handler, `butDelete_Click`, runs in the UI thread. It uses the current URL to generate a `ClientContext` instance, saved in the private `_context` variable. Then, it calls the `GetByTitle` method to save a reference to the `ProjectsList2010` list that was previously created in the SharePoint server in the preceding chapter, in the private `_projects` variable.

```
_context = new SP.ClientContext(SP.ApplicationContext.Current.Url);
_projects = _context.Web.Lists.GetByTitle("ProjectsList2010");
```

Then, it assigns the value for the data item corresponding to the selected row in the dataGridProjects DataGrid to the selectedProject local variable. It does so by accessing the dataGridProjects.SelectedItem property and casting it to Project, because it represents a Project instance.

```
var selectedProject = (dataGridProjects.SelectedItem as Project);
```

The next line calls the GetItemById method for the reference to the ProjectsList2010 list, _projects. This method receives the value for the unique ID field, an int or string, and returns a reference to the ListItem instance that is going to be retrieved when the query is executed. In this case, the value for ID was set in selectedProject.ProjectID and it is an int.

```
SP.ListItem listItem =
    _projects.GetItemById(selectedProject.ProjectId);
```

Once the code has a reference to the desired item in the list, it calls the DeleteObject method to remove it. Remember that at this point, we don't have access to the ListItem instance properties, because the query hasn't yet been executed. However, we can schedule many queries in a single call to ExecuteQueryAsync.

```
listItem.DeleteObject();
```

The call to the ExecuteQueryAsync will perform the following actions in the SharePoint server:

Retrieve the element with the specified ID value from the ProjectsList2010 list. If found, delete it.

If the query has a successful execution, the OnDeleteSucceeded callback schedules the asynchronous execution of the Connect method in the UI thread from a worker thread that runs this code after the query succeeds. It will refresh the data shown in the dataGridProjects DataGrid to reflect the new contents of the ProjectsList2010 list.

```
private void OnDeleteSucceeded(Object sender, SP.ClientRequestSucceede
dEventArgs args)
{
    Dispatcher.BeginInvoke(Connect);
}
```

In this example, we also specified the OnDeleteFailed callback and used it as the second parameter for the ExecuteQueryAsync method. If something goes wrong, it invokes a delegate that calls the ShowErrorInformation method and sends the ClientRequestFailedEventArgs args instance as a parameter to it.

Expanding LOB systems with update operations

Now, follow these steps to add a new feature in the SLTasksViewer Silverlight application to allow the user to edit and update the value for the Title row in the item selected in the DataGrid from the list in the SharePoint server, ProjectsList2010.

1. Stay in Visual Studio as a system administrator user, in the TasksViewer solution.

2. Open MainPage.xaml.cs and add the following code to the CellEditEnded event for the dataGridProjects DataGrid. This way, when the user finishes editing the cell corresponding to the Title row, the application will retrieve the Project instance selected in the dataGridProjects DataGrid and use its ID to update the value for the Title field in the corresponding item in the list in the SharePoint server.

```
private void dataGridProjects_CellEditEnded(object sender,
DataGridCellEditEndedEventArgs e)
{
  if ((e.EditAction == DataGridEditAction.Commit) &&
      (e.Column.Header.Equals("Title")))
  {
    _context = new SP.ClientContext(
      SP.ApplicationContext.Current.Url);
    _projects = _context.Web.Lists.GetByTitle("ProjectsList2010");
    var selectedProject = (dataGridProjects.SelectedItem as
      Project);
    SP.ListItem listItem = _projects.GetItemById(selectedProject.
      ProjectId);
    // Assign the new value for the Title field
    listItem["Title"] = selectedProject.Title;
    // Update the item in the list
    listItem.Update();
    _context.ExecuteQueryAsync(
    OnUpdateSucceeded,
    OnUpdateFailed);
  }
}
```

3. The code in the `CellEditEnded` event for the `dataGridProjects DataGrid` is going to run in the UI thread, as described in *Chapter 2*, in the *Working with the asynchronous methods and callbacks* section. The following methods, which are going to be fired as asynchronous callbacks, schedule the execution of other methods to continue with the necessary program flow in the UI thread:

   ○ When the connection to the SharePoint server and the query execution that updates an item in the list, requested by the `dataGridProjects_CellEditEnded` method, is successful, the `OnUpdateSucceeded` method schedules the execution of a delegate defined in the UI thread with a lambda expression that updates the text shown in the `lblStatus Label`. The lambda expression appears highlighted in the next code snippet.

   ○ If the `dataGridProjects_CellEditEnded` method fails, the `OnUpdateFailed` method schedules the execution of the `ShowErrorInformation` method in the UI thread, sending the `ClientRequestFailedEventArgs args` instance as a parameter to the delegate.

```
private void OnUpdateSucceeded(Object sender, SP.ClientRequestSucc
eededEventArgs args)
{
    // This callback isn't called on the UI thread
    Dispatcher.BeginInvoke(
        () =>
        {
            // This code will run on the UI thread
            lblStatus.Content =
            "The title field was updated successfully.";
        }
    );
}


private void OnUpdateFailed(Object sender,
SP.ClientRequestFailedEventArgs args)
{
    // This callback isn't called on the UI thread
    // Invoke a delegate and send the args instance as a parameter
    Dispatcher.BeginInvoke(
        () => ShowErrorInformation(args)
    );
}
```

4. Build and deploy the solution.

5. Load the SharePoint page that shows `SLTasksViewer.xap` as a Silverlight Web Part, `SilverlightProjectsList2010.aspx`.

6. Double-click on the cell that contains the title that you want to update and you will enter in the edit mode:

Silverlight SharePoint Tasks Viewer

ProjectId	Title	StartDate
1	Creating a Silverlight 4 UI	2/16/2010
2	Creating a Complex Silverlight 4 LOB RIA	3/31/2010
13	Testing Silverlight 4 COM with Lists in SharePoint 2010	4/14/2010
20	Testing Messages Between Silverlight Web Parts	3/30/2010
26	Testing the New Feature that Allows a User to Update|	3/29/2010

7. Press *Tab* and the application will request the SharePoint server to update the value for the `Title` field of the selected item from the list. If the operation was successful, the status label will display the following message, **The title field was updated successfully**.

Silverlight SharePoint Tasks Viewer

ProjectId	Title	StartDate
1	Creating a Silverlight 4 UI	2/16/2010 3:00:00 AM
2	Creating a Complex Silverlight 4 LOB RIA	3/31/2010 3:00:00 AM
13	Testing Silverlight 4 COM with Lists in SharePoint 2010	4/14/2010 12:00:00 AM
20	Testing Messages Between Silverlight Web Parts	3/30/2010 12:00:00 AM
26	Testing the New Feature that Allows a User to Update a Title	3/29/2010 12:00:00 AM

The title field was updated successfully.

8. You can access the page for the list to check that the value for the `Title` field also appears updated in this view:

	📎	Type	Title		Assigned To	Status	Priority
☐							
		🗋	Creating a Silverlight 4 UI		gaston-PC\hillar2010	Not Started	(2) Normal
		🗋	Creating a Complex Silverlight 4 LOB RIA		gaston-PC\hillar2010	Not Started	(2) Normal
		🗋	Testing Silverlight 4 COM with Lists in SharePoint 2010 ❄ NEW		gaston-PC\hillar2010	Not Started	(2) Normal
		🗋	Testing Messages Between Silverlight Web Parts ❄ NEW		gaston-PC\hillar2010	Not Started	(2) Normal
☐		🗋	Testing the New Feature that Allows a User to Update a Title ❄ NEW	▼	gaston-PC\hillar2010	Not Started	(2) Normal
✚ Add new item							

Updating an item in a list

When the user finishes editing a cell in the `dataGridProjects DataGrid`, the `CellEditEnded` event handler, `dataGridProjects_CellEditEnded`, runs in the UI thread. If the edited column was the one corresponding to the `Title` field and the user committed the edit action, it runs the necessary code to update the corresponding item in the list with the new value for the `Title` field. It uses the values provided in the `EditAction` and `Column.Header` properties from the `DataGridCellEditEndedEventArgs e` parameter to determine that the conditions are satisfied.

```
if ((e.EditAction == DataGridEditAction.Commit) &&
    (e.Column.Header.Equals("Title")))
```

It uses the current URL to generate a `ClientContext` instance, saved in the private `_context` variable. Then, it calls the `GetByTitle` method to save a reference to the `ProjectsList2010` list, in the private `_projects` variable.

```
_context = new SP.ClientContext(SP.ApplicationContext.Current.Url);
_projects = _context.Web.Lists.GetByTitle("ProjectsList2010");
```

As it needs to access the new value for the `Title` field, it assigns the value for the data item corresponding to the selected row in the `dataGridProjects` DataGrid to the `selectedProject` local variable. It does so by accessing the `dataGridProjects.SelectedItem` property and casting it to `Project`, because it represents a `Project` instance. At this point, the new value is available in the `selectedProject.Title` property.

```
var selectedProject = (dataGridProjects.SelectedItem as Project);
```

The next line calls the `GetItemById` method for the reference to the `ProjectsList2010` list, `_projects`, with `selectedProject.ProjectID` as the ID for `ListItem` instance to retrieve from the list.

```
SP.ListItem listItem =
  _projects.GetItemById(selectedProject.ProjectId);
```

Once the code has a reference to the desired item in the list, it assigns the new value for the `Title` field to the `ListItem` instance:

```
listItem["Title"] = selectedProject.Title;
```

The next step is to call the `Update` method for the `ListItem` instance to update this row with the new value for the `Title` field. Remember that at this point, we don't have access to the `ListItem` instance properties because the query hasn't yet been executed. However, we can assign new values to its contents and then perform all the operations that require many queries in a single call to `ExecuteQueryAsync`.

```
listItem.Update();
```

The call to `ExecuteQueryAsync` will perform the following actions in the SharePoint server:

- Retrieve the element with the specified ID value from the `ProjectsList2010` list.
- If found, assign the new value to the `Title` field for the row and update it.

If the query has a successful execution, the `OnUpdateSucceeded` callback schedules the asynchronous execution of the delegate defined through a lambda expression in the UI thread from a worker thread that runs this code after the query has succeeded. In this case, the code is written inside the lambda expression that defines the delegate and displays a message in the `lblStatus` Label, indicating that the update operation was successful.

```
private void OnUpdateSucceeded(Object sender, SP.ClientRequestSucceede
dEventArgs args)
{
    // Code that runs in a worker thread
```

```
Dispatcher.BeginInvoke((() =>
{
  // The code inside this delegate
  // runs in the UI thread
  lblStatus.Content =
                "The title field was updated successfully.";
});
// Back in the worker thread
}
```

We also specified the OnUpdateFailed callback and used it as the second parameter for the ExecuteQueryAsync method. If something goes wrong, it invokes a delegate that calls the ShowErrorInformation method and sends the ClientRequestFailedEventArgs args instance as a parameter to it.

Summary

In this chapter, we learned about developing and deploying Silverlight 4 applications in SharePoint 2010 sites that interact with data in lists by performing insert, update, and delete operations. Specifically, we created a new Silverlight 4 RIA that allowed us to insert new items into a remote SharePoint list. Then, we enhanced this simple application to retrieve metadata information for the fields that compose the list to offer the possible choices and default values for some of the fields.

We worked with messages to allow multiple Silverlight Web Parts to communicate when some events occur. Besides, we performed delete and update operations on the remote SharePoint list through the SharePoint Silverlight Client Object Model. Now, we are able to begin adding Silverlight RIAs that interact with data from the SharePoint server and deploy them by enhancing the examples learned in this chapter.

Now that we have learned about advanced interaction with data on the SharePoint server, we are ready to learn to create dynamic business solutions by working with workflows, which is the topic of the next chapter.

4
Creating Dynamic Business Solutions

We want to create dynamic business solutions by interacting with external data and working with workflows. In this chapter, we will cover many topics that help us create complex solutions that can interact with the powerful SharePoint workflows and access data in databases that aren't included in the SharePoint data model. We will:

- Create a new external content type to access data in external databases
- Access an external database in a Silverlight RIA included in a SharePoint solution
- Interact with external data sources linked to lists
- Create queries to filter fields and specify conditions
- Configure security issues related to external data sources
- Run Silverlight RIAs that interact with SharePoint 2010 outside the web browser
- Create and interact with workflows and their status
- Retrieve information about workflows in Silverlight RIAs

Accessing an external database in a Silverlight RIA included in a SharePoint solution

So far, we have been able to add many Silverlight RIAs that interact with data from the SharePoint Server and use their messaging capabilities to make them work together to offer a complex LOB solution. Sometimes, we need to access data residing in external databases that are closely related to data in the SharePoint Server.

SharePoint 2007 introduced the **Business Data Catalog (BDC)** to enable connectivity between SharePoint and an external data store so that it could be mapped and rendered in a Web Part. It made it easy to surface external data inside a SharePoint portal experience. It was easy to read external data but it was not so simple to enable users to make changes to the data and write them back to the external data store.

SharePoint 2010 improves the BDC introduced in the previous SharePoint version and offers the new **Business Connectivity Services (BCS)**. BCS streamlines the process of connecting to external data and interacting with it from SharePoint. It includes out of box features, services, and tools that simplify the development of solutions with deep integration of external data and services. This way, it is easier to create rich and interactive solutions that integrate with existing systems.

We will take advantage of BCS and its related tools to develop a Silverlight RIA that connects to an external database and performs operations on one of its tables. BCS make it easy to interact with external data as you are used to working with SharePoint lists. However, when you access these new lists that represent external data, it is necessary to make some changes to the way you work with them through the SharePoint Silverlight Client Object Model.

Creating a new database

Firstly, we are going to create a new SQL Server database and a new table that will hold the information for events. This table won't be part of the SQL Server instance and the database that supports the SharePoint Server data model.

You require a SQL Server installation to run this example. By default, Visual Studio 2010 installs SQL Server 2008 Express Edition. However, you can also use other versions. Besides, it is very important that you consider the necessary security measures to avoid unexpected problems when you create a new database. The following example is going to cover the necessary steps to create a new database and a new table to work in a developer workstation. You can also create the new database using SQL Server Management Studio or the command-line tools.

Follow these steps to create a new SQL Server database and a simple table to use as an external data source.

1. Make sure that the required SQL Server service is running. You can check this by running **Sql Server Configuration Manager** and clicking on **SQL Server Services**. By default, the SQL Server 2008 Express Edition instance is SQLEXPRESS. You can start the **SQL Server (SQLEXPRESS)** service in this application. You have to make sure that the value shown in the **State** column for the corresponding service is **Running**, as shown in the following screenshot:

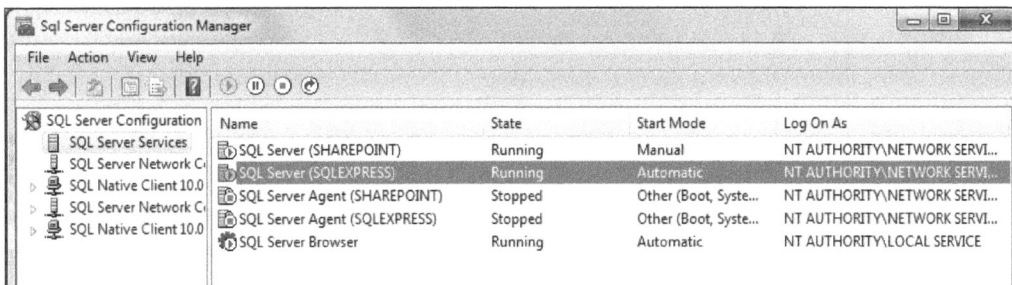

2. Start Visual Studio as a system administrator user.

3. Activate the **Server Explorer** palette and right-click on **Data Connections**. Select **Create New SQL Server Database...** in the context menu that appears and Visual Studio will show a new dialog box.

4. Select the server name and the SQL Server instance from the **Server name** drop-down list or enter the information. For example, the SQLEXPRESS instance running in GASTON-PC will be GASTON-PC\SQLEXPRESS. Make sure that you don't select the instance that is storing the SharePoint Server data model. By default, a SharePoint 2010 installation creates its own instance named SHAREPOINT.

5. Select the most convenient authentication option to log on to the SQL server instance. You have to make sure that your user has the required rights in the SQL Server instance. In a developer workstation, it is convenient to select **Use Windows Authentication** whenever possible. However, the most convenient option will depend on the security measures in the environment in which you are working. You can also use **SQL Server Authentication** and specify the **User name** and **Password**. However, it is very important that you understand the security requirements when you work with a specific authentication mechanism.

6. Enter the desired name for the new database in **New database name**, events2, as shown in the following screenshot, and click **OK**.

7. Expand the new connection that appears within the **Data Connections** root node and right-click on **Tables**. Select **Add New Table** in the context menu that appears and Visual Studio will display a new grid. Fill this grid with the values shown in the following table to create the new events table. The next screenshot shows the diagram for this table.

Column Name	Data Type	Allows Null
ID	int	False
Title	nvarchar(50)	False
DateTime	datetime	True
Description	text	False

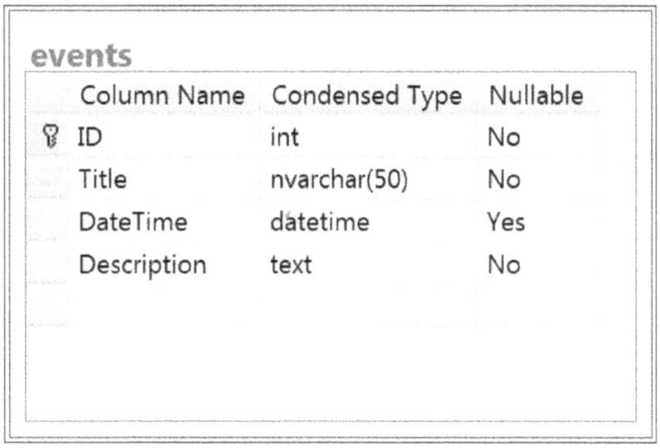

events

Column Name	Condensed Type	Nullable
ID	int	No
Title	nvarchar(50)	No
DateTime	datetime	Yes
Description	text	No

8. Right-click on the row for the `ID` column and select **Set Primary Key** in the context menu that appears. Then, go to the **Column Properties** panel, expand **Identity Specification**, and set `Yes` to **(Is Identity)**, `1` to **Identity Increment**, and `1` to **Identity Seed**, as shown in the following picture. This way, the `ID` column will be an auto-increment primary key, starting with `1` and incrementing its value in steps of `1`.

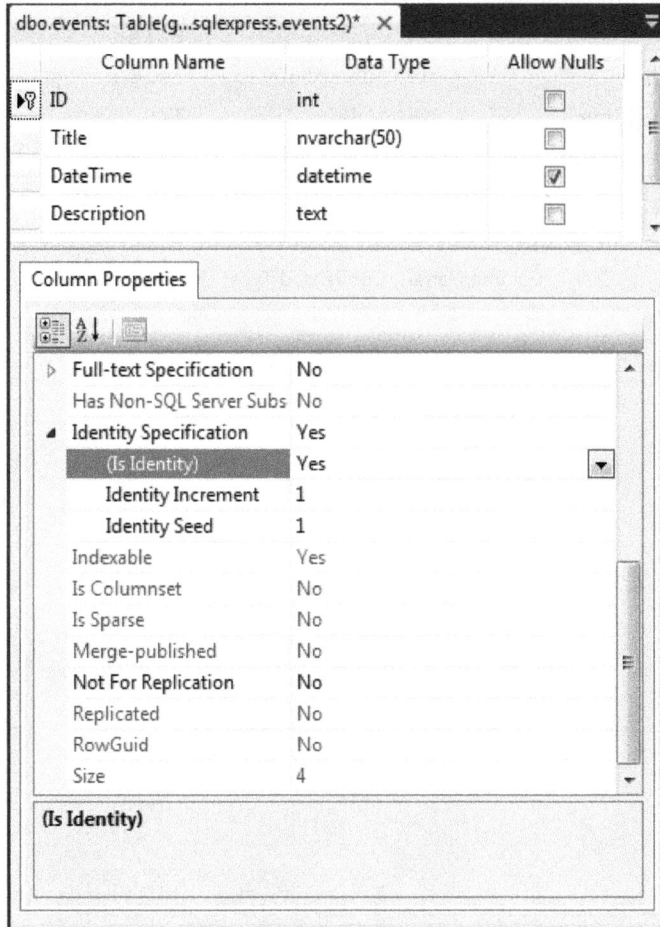

9. Right-click on the table columns and select **Indexes/Keys...** in the context menu that appears. Visual Studio will display a new dialog box to define additional indexes. The index for the primary key is already added. You can add a unique index for the `Title` column and a non-unique index for `DateTime`.

10. Save the new table as `events`.

11. Now, right-click on the recently added table in **Server Explorer** and select **Show Table Data**.

12. Use the grid shown in Visual Studio to add three records to the new table to represent events, as shown in the following screenshot:

ID	Title	DateTime	Description
5	Silverlight 4 Ever	5/4/2010 5:00:00 PM	New challenges for developer to create exciting User eXperiences
6	SharePoint 2010 External Data	4/20/2010 3:30:00 PM	Case Study: The new Business Connectivity Services (BCS) in Silverlight RIAs
7	Out-of-Browser Silverlight 4 RIAs	4/21/2010 4:15:00 PM	Case Study: Out-of-Browser Silverlight 4 RIAs that interact with SharePoint 2010
NULL	NULL	NULL	NULL

We have created a new SQL Server database, `events2`, with one table, `events`. Then, we populated this table with a few records that represent events. This table is going to be our external data source and we will access it from a Silverlight RIA running in SharePoint.

Creating a new external content type to access data in a SQL Server database

Now, we are going to use SharePoint Designer 2010 to create a new **external content type**, capable of consuming data from and writing data to the recently created SQL Server table.

> It is also possible to create a Business Data Connectivity Model project for SharePoint 2010 with Visual Studio 2010. However, in this case, we will use SharePoint Designer because we have a simple table and we don't need the flexibility offered by the BDC Model project.

1. Open your default Web browser, view the SharePoint site, and log in with your username and password.

2. Click **Site Actions | Edit Site in SharePoint Designer** in the ribbon. If you don't have SharePoint Designer 2010, a dialog box will offer you the possibility to download and install it. SharePoint Designer 2010 will display its main window showing information about the site and the list of the **Site Objects** in the **Navigation** panel located on the left, as shown in the following screenshot:

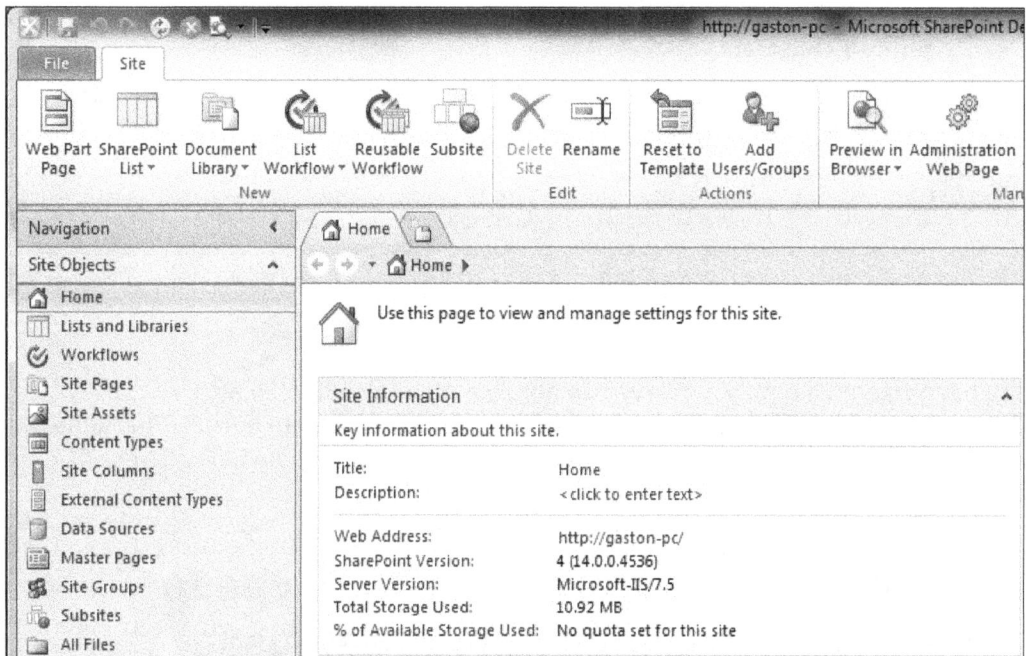

3. Click **External Content Types** under **Site Objects**. A new tab will display the external content types registered in the BDC.

4. Click **External Content Types | External Content Type** in the ribbon, located over the **New** label. A new page with all the settings for the new external content type will appear.

5. Click **New External Content Type** at the left of **Name**, under **External Content Type Information**. A textbox will appear and you will be able to enter a **Name**; enter ExternalEvents. Do the same for **Display Name**.

6. Select Generic List in the **Office Item Type** drop-down list.

7. Select `Enabled` in the **Offline Sync for External List** drop-down list, as shown in the following screenshot:

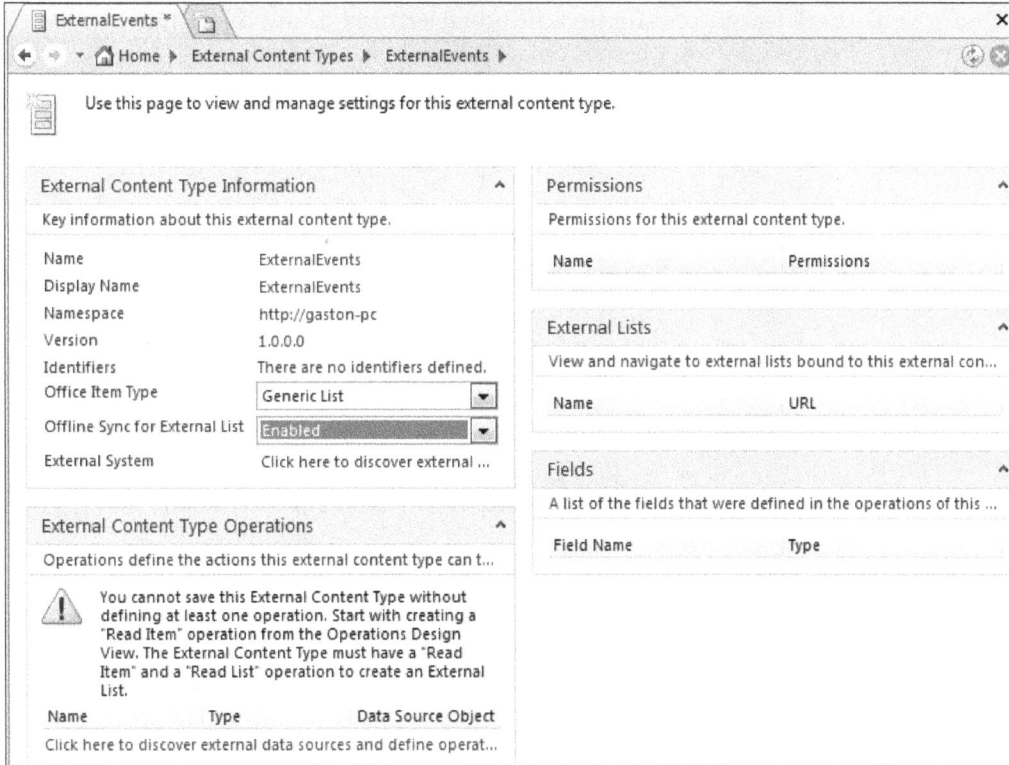

8. Now, click on **Click here to discover external data sources and define operations** on the right of **External System**. A new page will appear displaying the available connections to external data sources.

9. Click **Add Connection**. A new dialog box will appear with a **Data Source Type** drop-down list.

10. Select **SQL Server** and click **OK**. A new dialog box will appear asking for the parameters to establish a SQL Server connection to an existing database in a server.

11. Enter the following information in this dialog box, as shown in the next screenshot and then click **OK**.

    ° The server name and the SQL Server instance in **Database Server**.

    ° The database name, `events2`, in **Database Name**.

° Select the **Connect with User's Identity** radio button. This isn't the best choice but we're going to use it to run the solution in a developer's workstation. In the next sections, we will learn to configure additional security issues related to connections with external data sources.

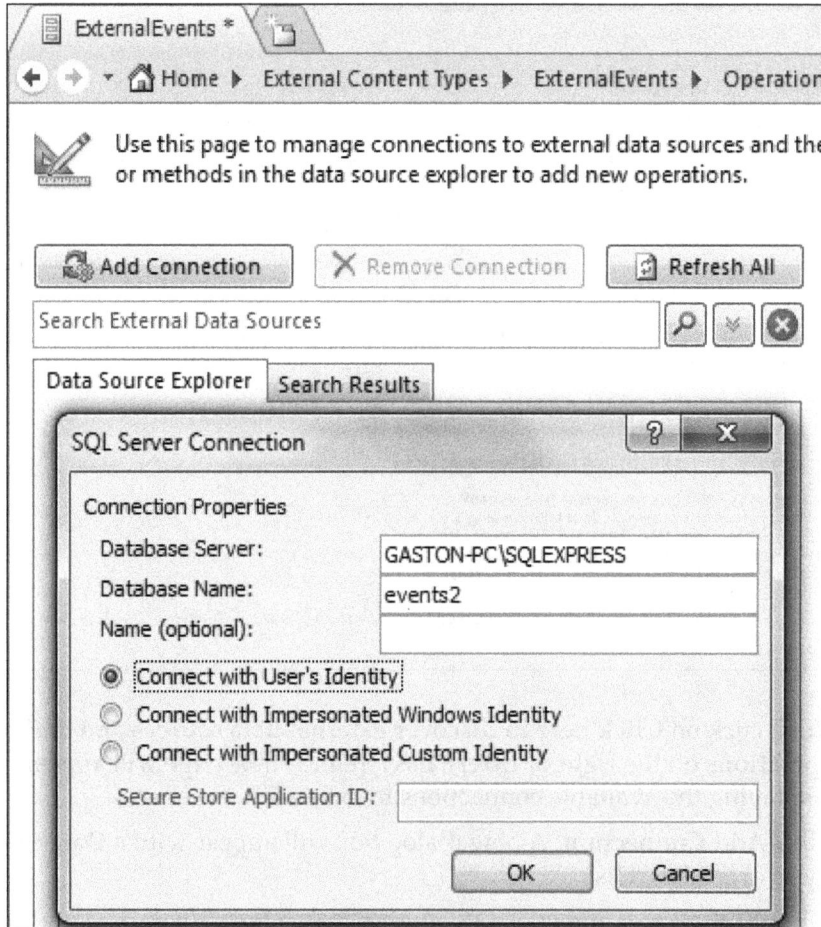

12. The database specified in the previous step will appear in the **Data Source Explorer** tab. Expand **events2 | Tables** and select **events**. Right-click on **events** and select **Create All Operations** in the context menu that appears, as shown in the following screenshot:

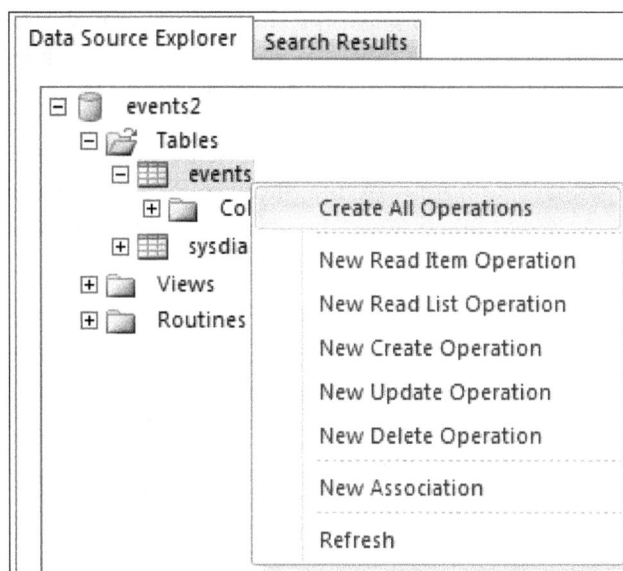

13. A new wizard that will create all operations required to create, read, update, delete, and query data for the external content type will appear. It is going to define five operations with the following names:

   ° Create

   ° Read Item

   ° Update

   ° Delete

   ° Read List

14. The wizard will allow us to select the columns that we want to expose from the external content type. In this case, we want to expose all the fields. Click **Next**; the wizard will display the field names in the **Data Source Elements** list and the **Properties** for the selected element on the right. For example, the **Map to Identifier** checkbox will appear activated for the ID field because it is the table's primary key. Activate the **Show in Picker** checkbox for this field and the warning displayed under **Errors and Warnings** will disappear, as shown in the next screenshot:

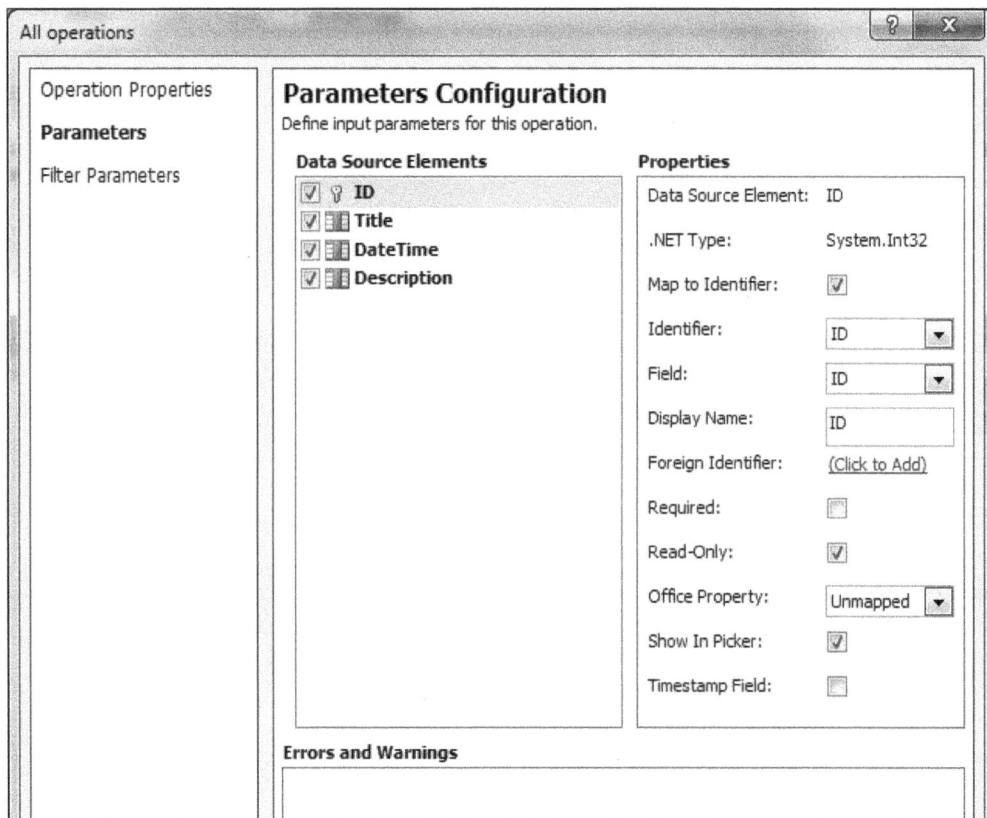

15. Click **Next** and the wizard will offer the possibility to define the configuration for filter parameters. In this case, we are going to define a limit filter to restrict the number of rows returned to 100.

> When you work with tables that can have more than 100 records, it is convenient to consider applying a limit filter or including conditions in the code that interacts with this external data source when the Silverlight application reads its contents.

16. Click on the **Add Filter Parameter** button and a new row will appear under **Filter Parameters**. Click on the **(Click to Add)** link under **Properties** and the **Filter Configuration** dialog box will appear.

17. Select `Limit` in **Filter Type** and `ID` in **Filter Field**. Then click on **OK**.

18. Enter `100` in **Default Value** under **Properties**. This way, the filter will limit the result sets to 100 records for the `Read List` operation.

19. Click **Finish** and SharePoint Designer will create the aforementioned five operations and will display their relationship with the data source object, the `events` table, in the **External Content Type Operations** panel. The next screenshot shows the five operations with their **Name**, **Type**, and **Data Source Object**. You can change parameters, properties, and filters for each individual operation by double-clicking on it in this list.

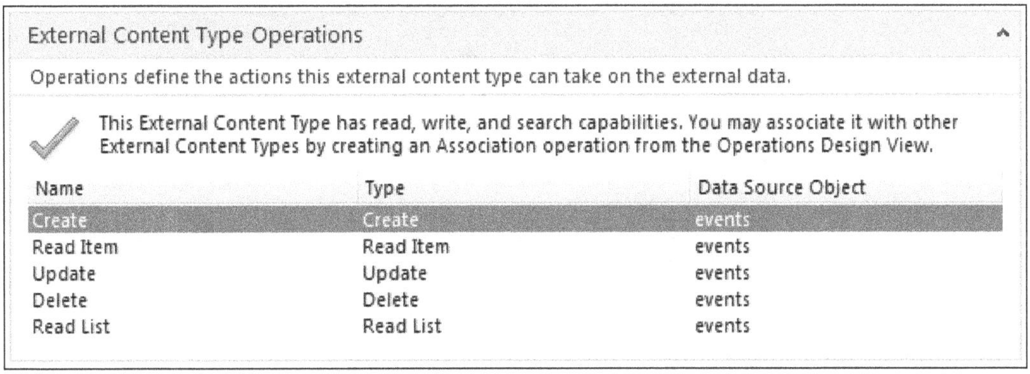

External Content Type Operations

Operations define the actions this external content type can take on the external data.

This External Content Type has read, write, and search capabilities. You may associate it with other External Content Types by creating an Association operation from the Operations Design View.

Name	Type	Data Source Object
Create	Create	events
Read Item	Read Item	events
Update	Update	events
Delete	Delete	events
Read List	Read List	events

---

20. Now, click **Create Lists and Form** in the ribbon, located over the **Lists & Form** label. SharePoint Designer will display a dialog box asking you to save the previously created new external content type. Click **Yes** and it will save it in the BDC metadata store for the SharePoint server. Then, the **Create List and Form** for the `ExternalEvents` external content type, representing a table in an external database, will appear.

21. Select the **Create New External List** radio button. Enter SharedEvents in **List Name**. This will be the list name in the SharePoint server that will access the data in the events table. Read Item will appear in the **Read Item Operation** drop-down list and events2, the database name, in **System Instance**, as shown in the following screenshot:

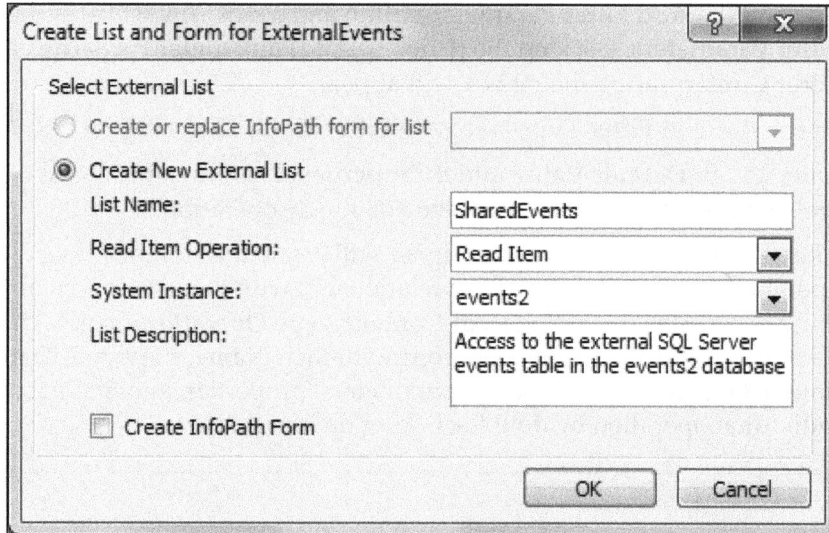

22. Click on **OK**. SharePoint designer will create the new SharedEvents list, linked to the previously defined external content and the new forms to access the different operations.

23. Click **Lists and Libraries** under **Site Objects**. A new tab will display the lists and libraries defined in the SharePoint site. A link for the recently added list, SharedEvents, will appear under **External Lists**. Click on this link and a new tab will display its properties, views, and forms.

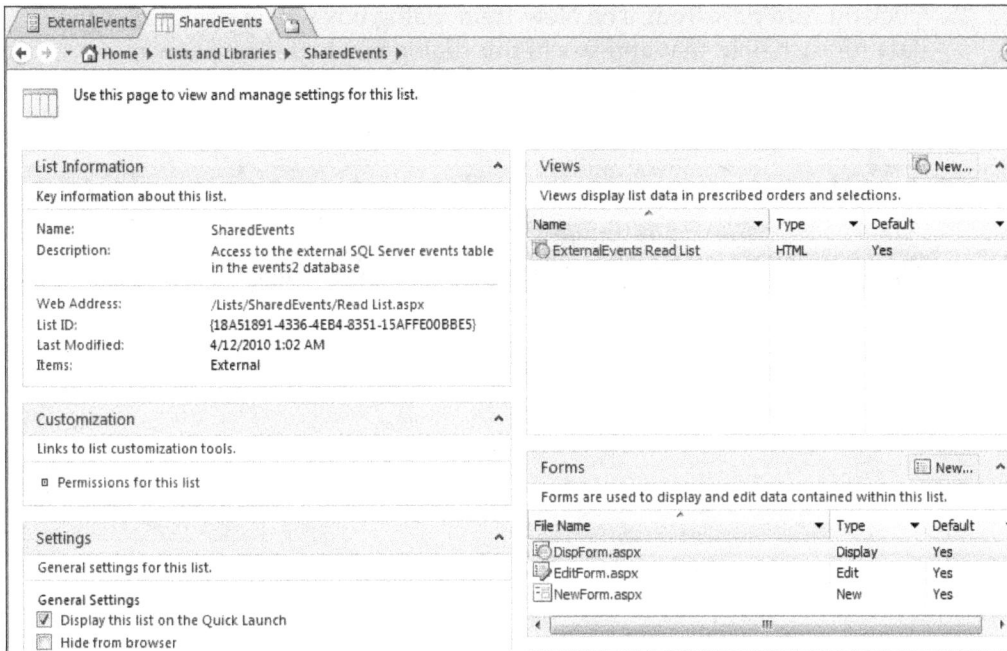

24. Click **Preview in Browser** in the ribbon, located over the **Manage** label. Your default web browser will display the page that reads the `SharedEvents` list and it will show the three items that were previously added to the underlying database table. The next screenshot shows the page that displays the items for the list.

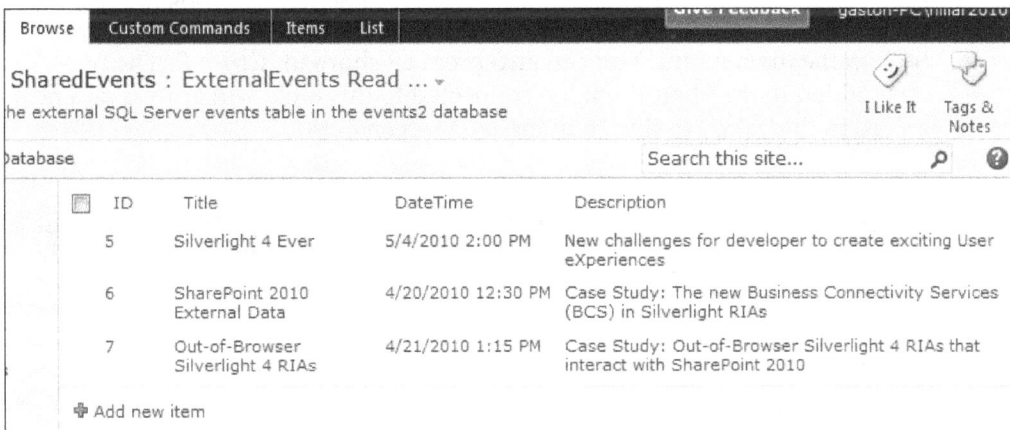

25. Click on **Add new item**. The **New Item** dialog box will appear. Enter the data for each field that appears in this dialog box to define a new event. The following screenshot shows the dialog box with all the fields and some values to add the new item to the list of events.

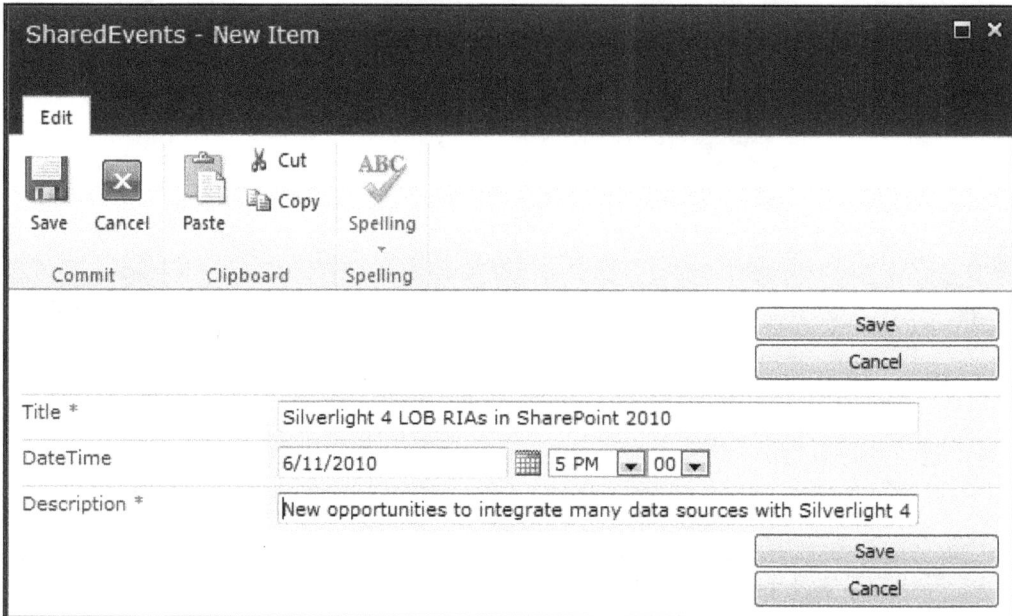

26. Click on **Save** and the new item will appear in the list.

27. Now, go back to Visual Studio 2010 and display the data for the events table or refresh the contents of the grid by selecting **Query Designer | Execute SQL** in the main menu. You can also press its shortcut, *Ctrl + R*. The new item added in the SharePoint list connected to this table will appear as a new record in this table, as shown in the next screenshot:

Browsing a SharePoint list with external content and its fields

Once we have created the data source, the external content type, and the list of events associated to the external content in SharePoint, we can use **Server Explorer** in Visual Studio to analyze the new list's structure. It is a SharePoint list but it has many differences with our previously studied lists that didn't access external data sources. Thus, it is a good idea to use **Server Explorer** to learn about these differences before working in a new Silverlight application. Follow these steps to use Visual Studio to browse a SharePoint list with external content and its fields.

1. Stay in Visual Studio as a system administrator user.

2. Activate the **Server Explorer** palette.

3. Click on the expand button for **SharePoint Connections** and then on the expand button for the SharePoint server.

4. Expand **Home | Lists and Libraries | Lists** and you will be able to browse all the lists, including the previously created one, **SharedEvents**.

5. Select the **SharedEvents** list and activate the **Properties** panel. The value for the HasExternalDataSource property is going to be True and this means that it is an external list, linked to an external data source.

6. Now, expand **SharedEvents** and then expand its **Fields** node. This way, you will see all the fields for this list.

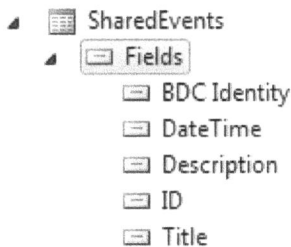

7. You will notice that there is an additional field that isn't part of the database table, BDC Identity. If you select any of the fields that are part of the database table, you will notice that the **Properties** palette displays neither properties nor values for these fields, as shown in the following screenshot. Thus, we will use the field name that appears under Fields in **Server Explorer** to access each field in this external list.

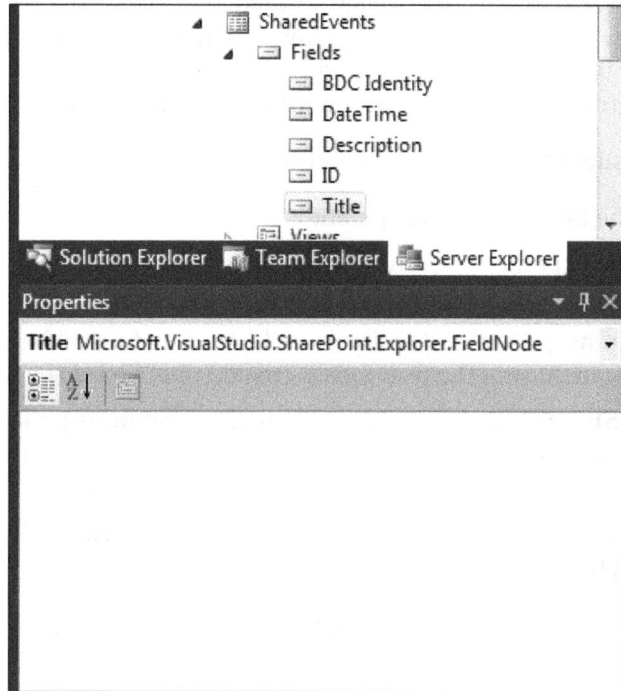

Interacting with external data sources using the SharePoint 2010 Silverlight Client Object Model

We are now going to create a new solution in Visual Studio as we learned in the previous chapters. It will include two new projects:

- A Silverlight application project, SLEventsViewer

- An empty SharePoint 2010 project with a module, SPEventsViewer

Follow these steps to create the new Silverlight RIA that allows a user to retrieve and delete rows from an external list in the SharePoint server, connected to an external data source:

1. Stay in Visual Studio as a system administrator user.

2. Follow the previously learned steps to create a new **Blank Solution**, EventsViewer.

3. Add a new Silverlight Application project to the solution. Use SLEventsViewer as the new project's name. Remember to select the options used in the previous examples.

4. Follow the necessary steps to add the two references to access the new SharePoint 2010 Silverlight COM.

5. Open App.xaml.cs and add the following using statement:

```
using Microsoft.SharePoint.Client;
```

6. Add the following code in the StartUp event handler to initialize Microsoft.SharePoint.Client.ApplicationContext with the same initialization parameters and the synchronization context for the current thread (the UI thread):

```
private void Application_Startup(object sender, StartupEventArgs e)
{
    this.RootVisual = new MainPage();
    // Initialize the ApplicationContext
    ApplicationContext.Init(e.InitParams,
      System.Threading.SynchronizationContext.Current);
}
```

7. Add a new class to the project, Event, in a new class file, Event.cs. The following lines define the new class, with four properties. This way, you will be able to create instances of this class to hold the values retrieved from the external list.

```
public class Event
{
    public int EventId { get; set; }
    public string Title { get; set; }
    public DateTime EventDateTime { get; set; }
    public string Description { get; set; }
}
```

8. Open `MainPage.xaml`, define a new `width` and `height` for the Grid as `800` and `600`, and add the following controls:
   - One `Label` control, `lblStatus`.
   - One `DataGrid` control, `dataGridEvents`. Set its `AutoGenerateColumns` property to `true`.
   - One Button control, `butDelete`. Set its `Content` property to `Delete`.
   - One Button control, `butRefresh`. Set its `Content` property to `Refresh`.

9. Open `MainPage.xaml.cs` and add the following lines of code to include our well-known SharePoint Silverlight COM necessary namespaces:

   ```
   using Microsoft.SharePoint.Client;
   using SP = Microsoft.SharePoint.Client;
   ```

10. Add the following `private` constant that defines the name of the external list, `SharedEvents`:

    ```
    private const string EXTERNAL_LIST_NAME = "SharedEvents";
    ```

11. Add the following four `private` variables:

    ```
    private SP.ListItemCollection _eventsItemCol;
    private ClientContext _context;
    private SP.List _events;
    private List<Event> _eventsList;
    ```

12. Now, it is necessary to add code to execute the following tasks:
    - Connect to the SharePoint server, `Connect` method.
    - Connect to the lists available in the SharePoint server, `ConnectLists` method.
    - Retrieve data from the `SharedEvents` external list (`EXTERNAL_LIST_NAME`), `GetListData` method.
    - Load all the available items for the `SharedEvents` list, `LoadItems` method.
    - Create a local list of `Event` instances, one for each item in the `SharedEvents` list, fill its properties and then bind the results list to the `dataGridEvents` DataGrid to display the retrieved data, `ShowItems` method.
    - Display information about any errors that occur in the asynchronous callbacks, `ShowErrorInformation`.

The code for this is as follows:

```
private void Connect()
{
    // Runs in the UI Thread
    lblStatus.Content = "Started";
    _context = new SP.ClientContext(
        SP.ApplicationContext.Current.Url);
    _context.Load(_context.Web);
    _context.ExecuteQueryAsync(OnConnectSucceeded, null);
}

private void ConnectLists()
{
    // Runs in the UI Thread
    lblStatus.Content =
        "Web Connected. Connecting to Lists...";
    _context.Load(_context.Web.Lists);
    _context.ExecuteQueryAsync(OnConnectListsSucceeded, null);
}

private void GetListData()
{
    // Runs in the UI Thread
    lblStatus.Content =
        "Lists Connected. Getting List data...";
    _events =
        _context.Web.Lists.GetByTitle(EXTERNAL_LIST_NAME);
    _context.Load(_events);
    _context.Load(_events.RootFolder);

    _context.Load(_events.Fields);

    _context.ExecuteQueryAsync(OnGetListDataSucceeded, null);
}

private void LoadItems()
{
    // Runs in the UI Thread
    lblStatus.Content =
        String.Format("Loading {0} items...",
        _events.RootFolder.ItemCount);
    var camlQuery = new SP.CamlQuery();
    camlQuery.ViewXml = @"<View >
```

```
                              <Method Name='Read List'/>
                              <Query/>
                              <ViewFields>
                                 <FieldRef Name='ID' />
                                 <FieldRef Name='Title'/>
                                 <FieldRef Name='DateTime'/>
                                 <FieldRef Name='Description'/>
                              </ViewFields>
                           </View>";
     _eventsItemCol = _events.GetItems(camlQuery);
     _context.Load(_eventsItemCol);
     _context.ExecuteQueryAsync(
         OnLoadItemsSucceeded,
         OnLoadItemsFailed);
}

private void ShowItems()
{
    // Runs in the UI Thread
    lblStatus.Content = "Showing items...";

    _eventsList = new List<Event>();
    foreach (SP.ListItem listItem in _eventsItemCol)
    {
        _eventsList.Add(
            new Event()
            {
                EventId = Convert.ToInt32(listItem["ID"]),
                Title = listItem["Title"].ToString(),
                EventDateTime =
                    Convert.ToDateTime(listItem["DateTime"]),
                Description =
                    listItem["Description"].ToString(),
            });
    }
    dataGridEvents.ItemsSource = _eventsList;
}

private void ShowErrorInformation(
    ClientRequestFailedEventArgs args)
{
    MessageBox.Show("Request failed. " +
        args.Message + "\n" + args.StackTrace + "\n" +
```

```
        args.ErrorDetails + "\n" + args.ErrorValue);
}
```

13. All the previously added methods are going to run in the UI thread. The following methods, which are going to be fired as asynchronous callbacks, schedule the execution of other methods to continue with the necessary program flow in the UI thread:

   i.   When the connection to the SharePoint server, requested by the `Connect` method, is successful, the `OnConnectSucceeded` method schedules the execution of the `ConnectLists` method in the UI thread.

   ii. When the connection to the lists available in the SharePoint server, requested by the `ConnectLists` method, is successful, the `OnConnectListsSucceeded` method schedules the execution of the `GetListData` method in the UI thread.

   iii. When the retrieval of data from the `SharedEvents` external list, requested by the `GetListData` method, is successful, the `OnGetListDataSucceeded` method schedules the execution of the `LoadItems` method in the UI thread.

   iv. Finally, when the loading of all the available items for the `SharedEvents` external list, requested by the `LoadItems` method, is successful, the `OnLoadItemsSucceeded` method schedules the execution of the `ShowItems` method in the UI thread.

Add the following methods to support the aforementioned program flow:

```csharp
private void OnConnectSucceeded(Object sender,
  SP.ClientRequestSucceededEventArgs args)
{
    // This callback isn't called on the UI thread
    Dispatcher.BeginInvoke(ConnectLists);
}

private void OnConnectListsSucceeded(Object sender,
  SP.ClientRequestSucceededEventArgs args)
{
    // This callback isn't called on the UI thread
    Dispatcher.BeginInvoke(GetListData);
}

private void OnGetListDataSucceeded(Object sender,
  SP.ClientRequestSucceededEventArgs args)
{
    // This callback isn't called on the UI thread
    Dispatcher.BeginInvoke(LoadItems);
}
```

```
private void OnLoadItemsFailed(Object sender,
  SP.ClientRequestFailedEventArgs args)
{
    // This callback isn't called on the UI thread
    // Invoke a delegate and send the args instance as a parameter
    Dispatcher.BeginInvoke(() => ShowErrorInformation(args));
}
private void OnLoadItemsSucceeded(Object sender,
  SP.ClientRequestSucceededEventArgs args)
{
    // This callback isn't called on the UI thread
    Dispatcher.BeginInvoke(ShowItems);
}
```

14. Add the following line to the `LayoutRoot_Loaded` event:

```
Connect();
```

15. Define a `Click` event handler for the `butRefresh Button` and add the following code in it. This way, when the user clicks on this button, the application will query the external list and will refresh the contents of the data shown in the grid.

```
private void butRefresh_Click(object sender, RoutedEventArgs e)
{
    Connect();
}
```

16. Now define a `Click` event handler for the `butDelete Button` and add the following code in it. This way, when the user clicks on this button, the application will retrieve the `Event` instance selected in the `dataGridEvents DataGrid`, and use its `ID` to retrieve and delete the item from the external list in the SharePoint server.

```
private void butDelete_Click(object sender, RoutedEventArgs e)
{
    _context = new
        SP.ClientContext(SP.ApplicationContext.Current.Url);
    _events =
        _context.Web.Lists.GetByTitle(EXTERNAL_LIST_NAME);
    var selectedEvent =
        (dataGridEvents.SelectedItem as Event);

    // It is possible to call the GetItemsById method
    // because the underlying table has an ID field
    SP.ListItem listItem =
        _events.GetItemById(selectedEvent.EventId);

    // Remove the item from the list
    listItem.DeleteObject();
```

```
_context.ExecuteQueryAsync(
    OnDeleteSucceeded, OnDeleteFailed);
}
```

17. The code in the `Click` event for the `butDelete Button` is going to run in the UI thread. The following methods, which are going to be fired as asynchronous callbacks, schedule the execution of other methods to continue with the necessary program flow in the UI thread:

   ° When the connection to the SharePoint server and the query execution that deletes an item from the external list, requested by the `butDelete_Click` method, is successful, the `OnDeleteSucceeded` method schedules the execution of the `Connect` method in the UI thread, to refresh the data shown in the `dataGridEvents DataGrid`.

   ° If the `butDelete_Click` method fails, the `OnDeleteFailed` method schedules the execution of the `ShowErrorInformation` method in the UI thread, sending the `ClientRequestFailedEventArgs args` instance as a parameter to the delegate.

Add the following methods to support the aforementioned program flow:

```
private void OnDeleteSucceeded(Object sender,
   SP.ClientRequestSucceededEventArgs args)
{
    // This callback isn't called on the UI thread
    Dispatcher.BeginInvoke(Connect);
}

private void OnDeleteFailed(Object sender,
   SP.ClientRequestFailedEventArgs args)
{
    // This callback isn't called on the UI thread
    // Invoke a delegate and send the args instance as a parameter
    Dispatcher.BeginInvoke(() => ShowErrorInformation(args));
}
```

18. Now, follow the steps learned in *Chapter 2*, in the section *Creating a Silverlight RIA to be linked with a SharePoint module,* to create a new SharePoint module and link it to the previously created Silverlight RIA, SLEventsViewer. Use SPEventsViewer as the new **Empty SharePoint Project**.

[✎ Remember to enable Silverlight debugging instead of the default script debugging capabilities.]

19. Right-click on the solution's name in **Solution Explorer** and select **Properties** from the context menu that appears. Select **Startup Project** in the list on the left, activate **Single startup project**, and choose the SharePoint SPEventsViewer in the drop-down list below it. Then, click **OK**.

20. Build and deploy the solution.

21. Now that the WSP package has been deployed to the SharePoint site, follow the necessary steps to create a new web page, add the Silverlight Web Part, and include the Silverlight RIA in it.

[✎ Remember that in this case, it isn't necessary to upload the .xap file because it was already deployed with the WSP package.]

We created, built, and deployed a Silverlight RIA that uses the SharePoint Silverlight Client OM to retrieve and delete rows from an external list in the SharePoint server. The external list is connnected to an external data source, the previously created events table in the events2 SQL Server database.

Specifying the fields to include in a CAML query for an external list

Most of the code is very similar to the code written in previous examples. The Silverlight application works with the SharePoint list as a Microsoft.SharePoint. Client.List instance, _events, defined with SP.List in the code. However, when the code queries the list and its RootFolder property to access its ItemCount property, it will always return 0 elements. The ItemCount property doesn't offer valid information with an external list. Thus, the value shown in the lblStatus Label with the number of items that it is going to load is always going to be 0.

In this case, we want to return all the data for the _events SP.List, but we cannot use the simple <View/> CAML query used in the previous examples. In order to retrieve data from an external list, we must specify the Method Name to read the list, Read List, and the name of the fields that we want to retrieve within ViewFields in the CAML query.

This query isn't going to filter data from the list. It will simply return all the values for four fields (ID, Title, DateTime, and Description), by using the Read List method. The camlQuery local variable holds a new SP.CamlQuery instance with its ViewXml property set to the following XML markup:

```
"<View>
    <Method Name='Read List'/>
    <Query/>
    <ViewFields>
        <FieldRef Name='ID' />
        <FieldRef Name='Title'/>
        <FieldRef Name='DateTime'/>
        <FieldRef Name='Description'/>
    </ViewFields>
</View>";
```

In this case, the external list has four fields. However, in other cases, it could have dozens of fields and it could require more work to write the CAML query. It is possible to use SharePoint Designer to help us in the creation of the CAML query. Follow the next steps to obtain the XML for ViewFields for an external list already defined in SharePoint:

1. Open your default web browser, view the SharePoint site, and log in with your username and password.

2. Click **Site Actions | Edit Site in SharePoint Designer** in the ribbon. SharePoint Designer 2010 will display its main window showing information about the site and the list of the **Site Objects** in the **Navigation** panel located on the left.

3. Click **Home** under **Site Objects**. A new tab will display the settings for the SharePoint site.

4. Click **Web Part Page** in the ribbon located over the **New** label and a new dialog box will appear. Enter `SharedEventsCAMLHelper` as the name for the new Web Part page and click **OK**. SharePoint designer will display the markup for the new `SharedEventsCAMLHelper.aspx` Web Part page, as shown in the following screenshot:

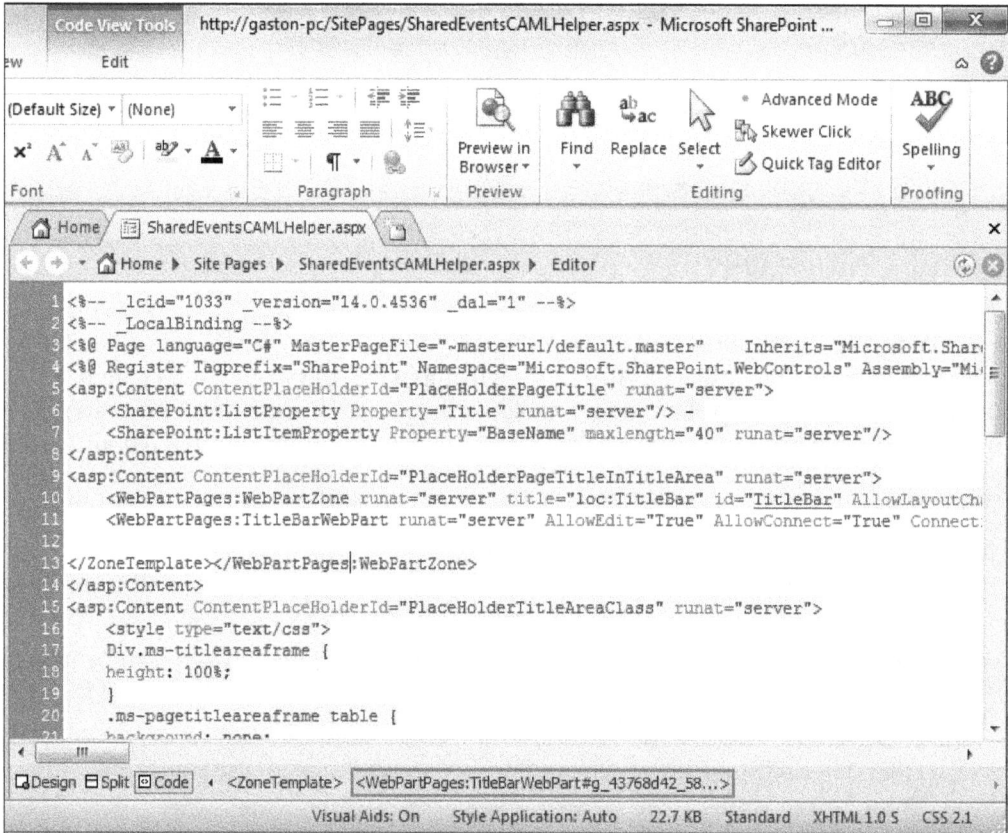

5. Switch to the Design view by clicking on the **Design** button located on the lower-left corner of the `SharedEventsCAMLHelper.aspx` editor, as shown in the next screenshot:

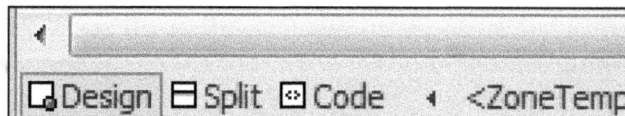

6. Click on the second rectangle inside **PlaceHolderMain (Custom)**.

7. Click **Insert | Data View** in the ribbon and a drop-down list with all the available data sources will appear. The recently added `SharedEvents` external list will appear under **External Lists**.

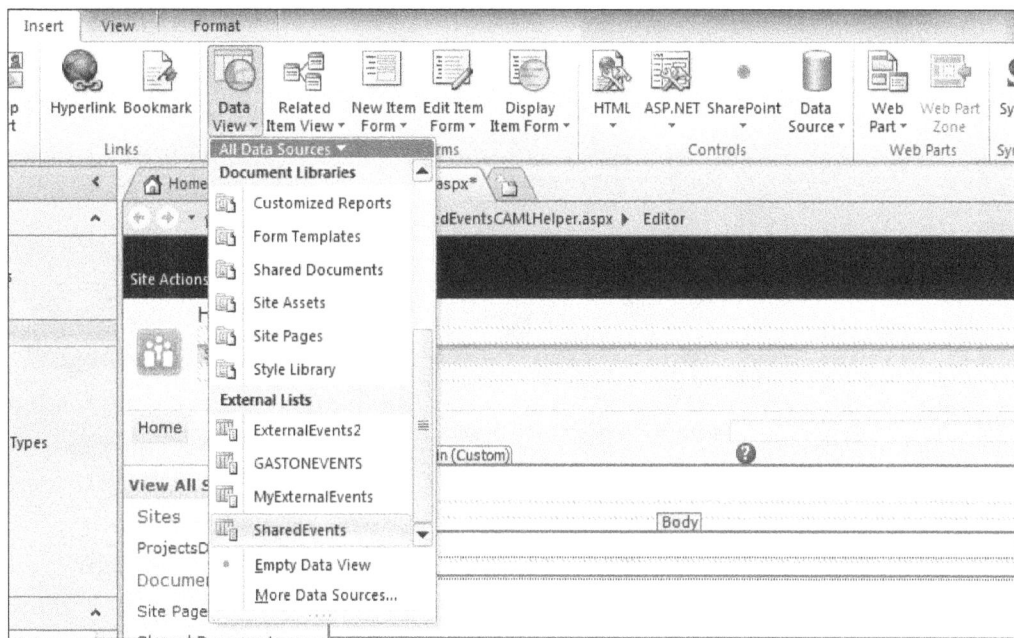

8. Select `SharedEvents` from the drop-down list and a new `WebPartPages:XsltListViewWebPart` element will be added. The Design view will display the items for the external list in the page, organized in a table.

9. Switch to the Code view by clicking on the **Code** button located on the lower-left corner of the `SharedEventsCAMLHelper.aspx` editor and the lines that define the new `WebPartPages:XsltListViewWebPart` element will appear selected, as shown in the next screenshot:

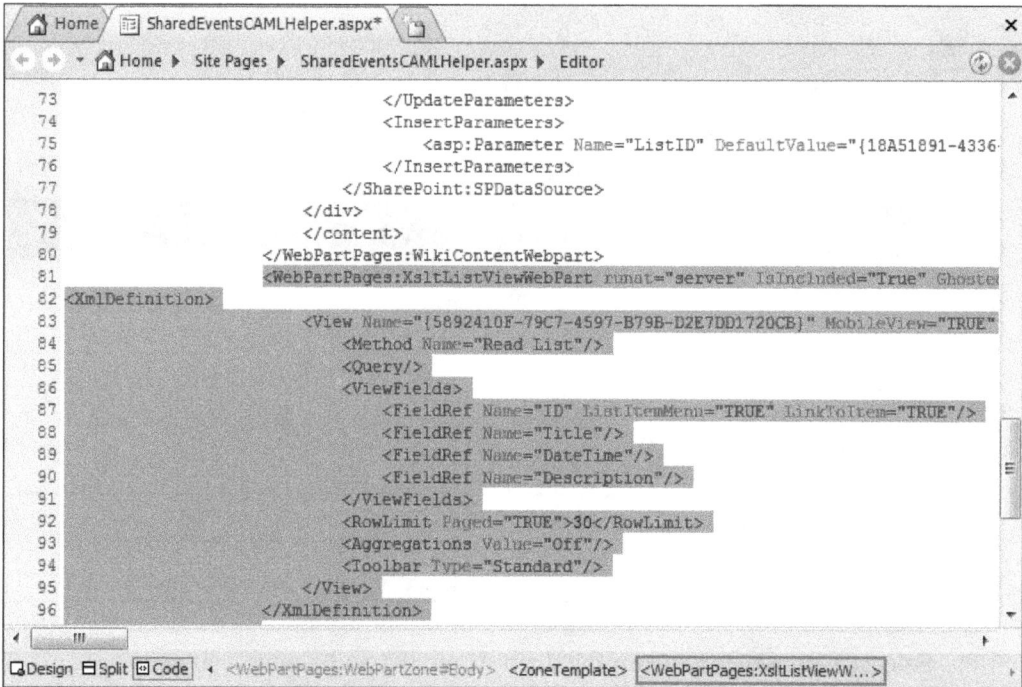

10. Copy the code from `<View Name>` to `</View>`. The following lines show the code that defines `View`:

```
<View Name="{5892410F-79C7-4597-B79B-D2E7DD1720CB}"
  MobileView="TRUE" Type="HTML" DisplayName="ExternalEvents Read
  List" Url="/Lists/SharedEvents/Read List.aspx" Level="1"
  BaseViewID="1" ContentTypeID="0x"
  ImageUrl="/_layouts/images/generic.png">
    <Method Name="Read List"/>
    <Query/>
    <ViewFields>
        <FieldRef Name="ID" ListItemMenu="TRUE"
            LinkToItem="TRUE"/>
        <FieldRef Name="Title"/>
        <FieldRef Name="DateTime"/>
        <FieldRef Name="Description"/>
    </ViewFields>
```

```
    <RowLimit Paged="TRUE">30</RowLimit>
    <Aggregations Value="Off"/>
    <Toolbar Type="Standard"/>
</View>
```

11. Some code defines values for attributes that we don't need in the CAML query. Thus, we can remove them and we will have our CAML query with the necessary `ViewFields` definition. We can replace the first line with `<View>`, remove the content after `</ViewFields>` and before `</View>` and delete the values defined for the `ListItemMenu` and `LinkToItem` attributes in the `FieldRef` elements. This way, you can use SharePoint Designer to help you to create the final CAML query for your Silverlight application that consumes the external list. The following lines show the final CAML query:

```
<View>
    <Method Name="Read List"/>
    <Query/>
    <ViewFields>
        <FieldRef Name="ID"/>
        <FieldRef Name="Title"/>
        <FieldRef Name="DateTime"/>
        <FieldRef Name="Description"/>
    </ViewFields>
</View>
```

12. You can delete the `SharedEventsCAMLHelper` Web Part page after preparing the XML code for the CAML query.

Consuming Business Connectivity Services from a Silverlight Web Part

Follow these steps to test the Silverlight Web Part that allows a user to read data and delete items from the `events` table in the `events2` database by using SharePoint BCS.

1. Start your default web browser and load `SilverlightEventsList.aspx`, which shows `SLEventsViewer.xap` as a Silverlight Web Part.

2. The Web Part will display the four items in the grid, as shown in the following screenshot:

External Events

EventId	Title	EventDateTime	Description
5	Silverlight 4 Ever	5/4/2010 2:00:00 PM	New challenges for developer to create exciting User eXperien
6	SharePoint 2010 External Data	4/20/2010 12:30:00 PM	Case Study: The new Business Connectivity Services (BCS) in
7	Out-of-Browser Silverlight 4 RIAs	4/21/2010 1:15:00 PM	Case Study: Out-of-Browser Silverlight 4 RIAs that interact wi
8	Silverlight 4 LOB RIAs in SharePoint 2010	6/11/2010 2:00:00 PM	New opportunities to integrate many data sources with Silverl

Showing items...   [Refresh]   [Delete]

3. Insert a new item in the `events` database table using Visual Studio 2010. Then, go back to the Web Part and click **Refresh**. The Web Part will display the five items in the grid, as shown in the next screenshot:

External Events

EventId	Title	EventDateTime	Description
5	Silverlight 4 Ever	5/4/2010 2:00:00 PM	New challenges for developer to create exciting User eXperien
6	SharePoint 2010 External Data	4/20/2010 12:30:00 PM	Case Study: The new Business Connectivity Services (BCS) in
7	Out-of-Browser Silverlight 4 RIAs	4/21/2010 1:15:00 PM	Case Study: Out-of-Browser Silverlight 4 RIAs that interact wi
8	Silverlight 4 LOB RIAs in SharePoint 2010	6/11/2010 2:00:00 PM	New opportunities to integrate many data sources with Silverl
13	Visual Studio 2010 with Silverlight 4	7/11/2010 1:15:00 PM	New Visual Studio 2010 features that allow developers to debu

4. Click on the cell of one of the rows in the grid and then click **Delete**. The Web Part will remove the selected row. The related record in the `events` table will also be deleted.

EventId	Title	EventDateTime	Description
6	SharePoint 2010 External Data	4/20/2010 12:30:00 PM	Case Study: The new Business Connectivity Services (BCS) in
7	Out-of-Browser Silverlight 4 RIAs	4/21/2010 1:15:00 PM	Case Study: Out-of-Browser Silverlight 4 RIAs that interact w
8	Silverlight 4 LOB RIAs in SharePoint 2010	6/11/2010 2:00:00 PM	New opportunities to integrate many data sources with Silverli
13	Visual Studio 2010 with Silverlight 4	7/11/2010 1:15:00 PM	New Visual Studio 2010 features that allow developers to deb

The code that deletes the selected item, written in the `butDelete_Click` event handler, calls the `GetItemById` method to retrieve the corresponding element from the external list, `_events`, and then delete it.

```
SP.ListItem listItem =
    _events.GetItemById(selectedEvent.EventId);
```

In this case, it was possible to use this method because the related table has an `ID` field as the primary key. This method works with the `ID` field and it cannot work against an external list with a different name as the primary key field. For example, if the field's name was `EventsId`, the call to this method would fail.

> When we need more customization, we can create a new SharePoint 2010 Business Data Connectivity Model project in Visual Studio 2010. This kind of project will allow us to link an external list in SharePoint 2010 to any external data source and enable create, read, update, and delete functions on it. Besides, it allows us to provide operations that process data for multiple data sources. The possibility to add code makes it more complex to create the operations but it offers more customization possibilities.

BCS allows the definition of three external data source types:

- .NET type
- SQL Server
- WCF Service

In our example, we worked against a SQL Server database. However, we can use the same techniques learned in the example to work with external lists linked to the other two external data source types.

Understanding security issues related to Business Connectivity Services

As previously explained, it is very important to take into account the different applications that work together to provide services when we work with SharePoint 2010 BCS. The situation in a developer workstation is different than the real-life scenarios with users consuming a Silverlight Web Part that accesses an external list. It is very important to restrict the access to each BCS data source to the appropriate users.

When you have to deploy a Silverlight Web Part that will consume a SharePoint 2010 BCS, the SharePoint Server administrator has to set the necessary permissions for the corresponding objects in the BDC metadata store. The administrator can do it by following these steps:

1. Start the SharePoint 2010 Central Administration Web Application.

2. Click **Application Management** on the panel located on the left, and then click **Manage Service Application** under **Service Application** on the panel located on the right. A list with all the service applications, their type, and status will appear, as shown in the next screenshot:

Operations	Sharing	
Name	Type	Status
Access Services	Access Services Web Service Application	Started
Access Services	Access Services Web Service Application Proxy	Started
Application Discovery and Load Balancer Service Application	Application Discovery and Load Balancer Service Application	Started
Application Discovery and Load Balancer Service Application Proxy_c2820c6e-b2b9-4518-8d85-47ac8a27d9ff	Application Discovery and Load Balancer Service Application Proxy	Started
Application Registry Service	Application Registry Service	Started
Application Registry Service	Application Registry Proxy	Started
Business Data Connectivity	Business Data Connectivity Service Application	Started
Business Data Connectivity	Business Data Connectivity Proxy	Started

3. Click **Business Data Connectivity** and a new page will display the list of objects defined in the BDC metadata store, including the previously added `ExternalEvents` external content type.

4. Move the mouse pointer over the desired element, `ExternalEvents` and a down arrow will appear on the right. Click on it and a drop-down menu will appear displaying many options, as shown in the following screenshot.

5. Select **Set Permissions** and define the desired permissions for each user that has to use this object.

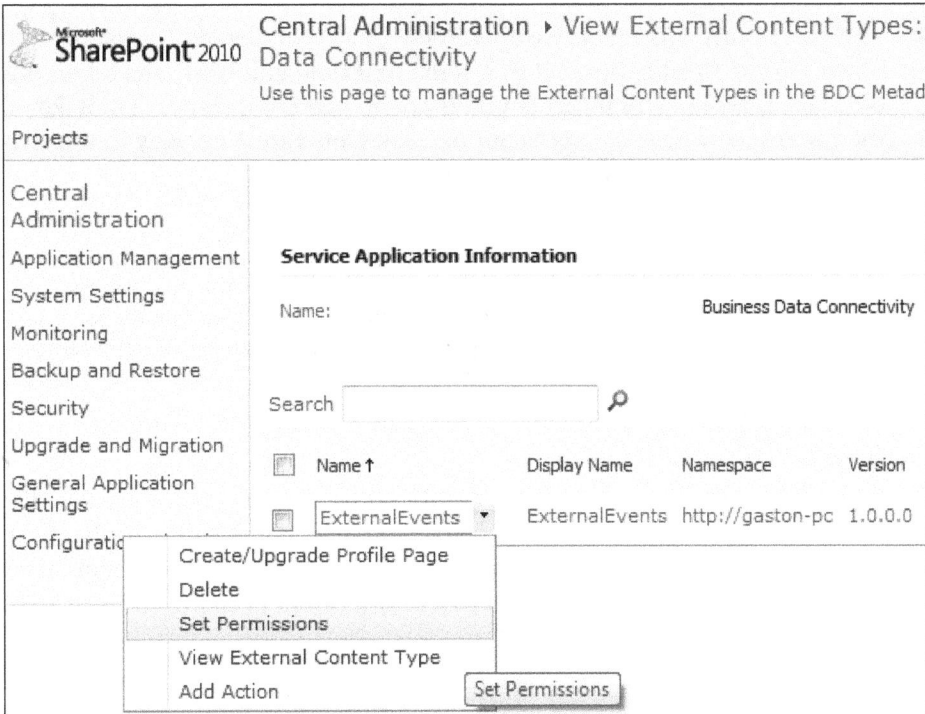

Impersonating BCS calls

SharePoint makes Windows security integration possible by using .NET impersonation. When using impersonation, an application can optionally execute with the identity of the client on whose behalf it is operating.

The SharePoint Server administrator can also activate a secure store service application that allows us to **impersonate** specific services, including BCS. If you want to impersonate BCS calls, the administrator can configure it by following these steps:

1. Start the SharePoint 2010 Central Administration Web Application.

2. Click **Application Management** on the panel located on the left, and then click **Manage Service Application** under **Service Application** on the panel located on the right. A list with all the service applications, their type, and status will appear.

3. Make sure that **Secure Store Service** appears as **Started**. If it shows the **Stopped** status, click on **Start** on the right.

4. Click on **Secure Store Service** and a new page will display the list of Secure Store Target Applications. If this is the first time you have clicked on this option, a message will indicate you that you need to generate a new key for the Secure Store Service Application. Click **Generate New Key** in the ribbon, enter and confirm a pass phrase, and click **OK**.

> This pass phrase is case-sensitive and it won't be stored. Thus, the administrator has to make sure that he or she records the pass phrase and stores it safely because it will be required to add new Secure Store Service Servers and for restoring to a backed-up Secure Store database.

5. Now, click **New** in the ribbon to create a new Secure Store Target Application.

6. Enter ExternalSQL as the **Target Application ID**, ExternalSQL as its display name, and the contact e-mail address. Select Group in **Target Application Type**, as shown in the next screenshot, to enable you to assign members the accounts of which will be impersonated by another account that you are going to specify. Then, click **Next**.

Central Administration ▸ Create New Secure Store Target Application

Specify the settings for the new Secure Store Target Application. The settings that you specify here can be changed later at Secure Store Target Application page.

I Like It   Tags & Notes

Target Application Settings

The Secure Store Target Application ID is a unique identifier. You cannot change this property after you create the Target Application.

The display name is used for display purposes only.

The contact e-mail should be a valid e-mail address of the primary contact for this Target Application.

The Target Application page URL can be used to set the values for the credential fields for the Target Application by individual users.

The Target Application type determines whether this application uses a group mapping or individual mapping. Ticketing indicates whether tickets are used for this Target Application. You cannot change this property after you create the Target Application.

Target Application ID

> ExternalSQL

Display Name

> ExternalSQL

Contact E-mail

> gastonhillar@hotmail.com

Target Application Type

> Group ▾

Target Application Page URL

○ Use default page

○ Use custom page

> [   ]

◉ None

Next   Cancel

7. By default, the next page will offer the **Windows User Name** and the **Windows Password** as the credential fields. You can select the fields you want to mask and add additional fields you could require. Make sure that you activate the **Masked** checkbox for the **Windows Password** credential field and click **Next**.

8. Enter the administrator users for this Target Application and the users and groups that are mapped to the credentials defined for it. The former should be added to **Target Application Administrators** and the latter to **Members**. The **Members** should include all the users that are going to use impersonation for BCS services. Then, click **OK** and the new Target Application will appear in the list.

9. Move the mouse pointer over the desired element, `ExternalSQL` and a down arrow will appear on the right. Click on it and a drop-down menu will appear displaying many options, as shown in the following screenshot:

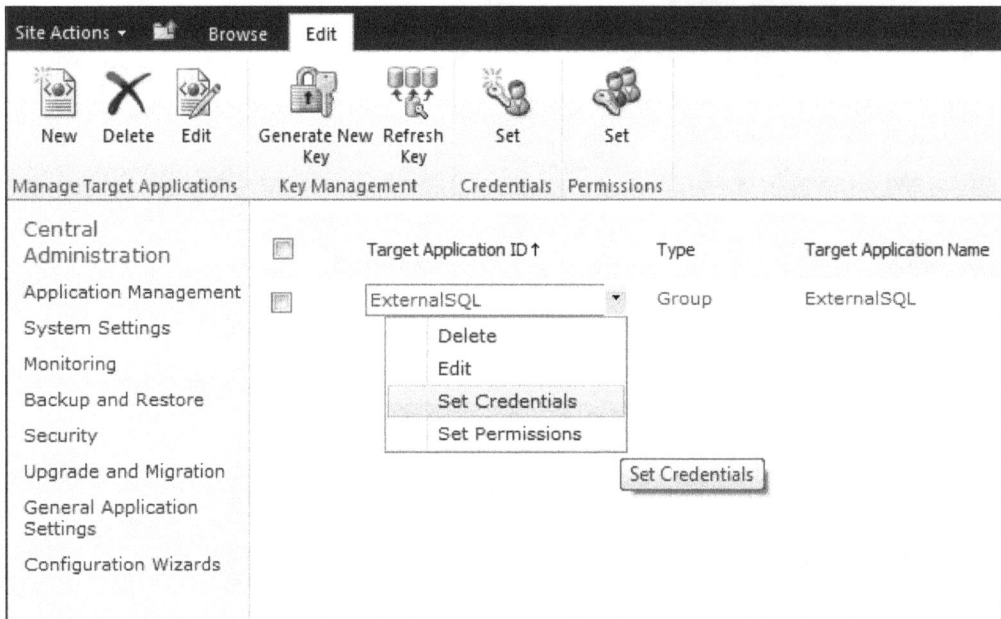

10. Add the users that will be the Credential Owners and then specify the **Windows User Name** and **Windows Password** that should be used for impersonation by the Secure Store Target Application. Then, click **OK** and the credentials will be set.

11. This way, when you define the connection properties in SharePoint Designer for the external content type, you can select **Connect with Impersonated Windows Identity** and enter the Secure Store Target Application, `ExternalSQL`, in **Secure Store Application ID**, as shown in the next screenshot:

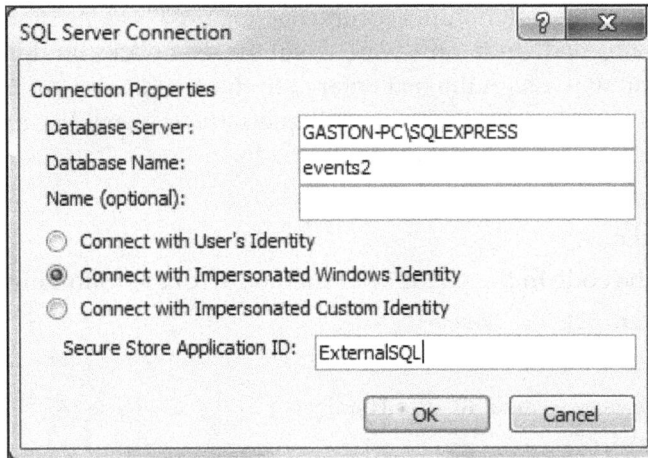

If your SharePoint administrator configures the previously explained security issues, you can use Impersonated Windows Identity to allow multiple SharePoint users to use a Silverlight Web Part that consumes BCS and connects to a SQL Server database. If you don't have the right security configuration, you can get unexpected errors when the Silverlight Web Part tries to consume BCS.

Applying dynamic filters in a CAML query

We are now going to add a few controls and the necessary code to our previous Silverlight RIA to allow the user to filter the data retrieved from the external grid and shown in the grid.

1. Stay in the `EventsViewer` project in Visual Studio as a system administrator user.

2. Open `MainPage.xaml` and add the following control at the top of the list:
   - One `Label` control, `lblFilterLabel`. Set its `Content` property to `Title`.
   - One `TextBox` control, `txtTitleFilter`.
   - One `Button` control, `butApplyFilter`. Set its `Content` property to `Apply Filter`.

3. Open `MainPage.xaml.cs` and add the following private variable:
   ```
   private string _titleFilter = "";
   ```

4. Define a `Click` event handler for the `butApplyFilter Button` and add the following code in it. This way, when the user clicks on this button, the application will assign the text entered in the `txtFilter TextBox` in the `_titleFilter` private string, will query the external list, and will refresh the contents of the data shown in the grid.

```
_titleFilter = txtTitleFilter.Text.Trim();
Connect();
```

5. Replace the code in the `LoadItems` method with the following lines:

```
// Runs in the UI Thread
lblStatus.Content = String.Format("Loading {0} items...");

var camlQuery = new SP.CamlQuery();

camlQuery.ViewXml = @"<View >
                        <Method Name='Read List'/>
                        <Query>" +
                      ((_titleFilter != "") ?
                          @"<Where>
                              <Contains>
                                  <FieldRef Name='Title'/>
                                  <Value Type='Text'>" +
                                  _titleFilter +  @"</Value>
                              </Contains>
                          </Where>"
                          : "") +
                      @"<OrderBy>
                              <FieldRef Name='DateTime'/>
                          </OrderBy>
                        </Query>
                        <ViewFields>
                            <FieldRef Name='ID' />
                            <FieldRef Name='Title'/>
                            <FieldRef Name='DateTime'/>
                            <FieldRef Name='Description'/>
                        </ViewFields>
                      </View>";

_eventsItemCol = _events.GetItems(camlQuery);
_context.Load(_eventsItemCol);
_context.ExecuteQueryAsync(
    OnLoadItemsSucceeded, OnLoadItemsFailed);
```

6. Build and deploy the solution.

7. Start your default web browser and load the `SilverlightEventsList.aspx` page that shows `SLEventsViewer.xap` as a Silverlight Web Part.

8. The Silverlight RIA running in the Web Part will display the four items in the grid ordered by the `DateTime` field. Enter some text that appears in one or more rows in the `Title` field, in the **Title** textbox. Then, click **Apply Filter** and the application is going to display only the rows that contain the entered text in the `Title` field, ordered by `DateTime`, as shown in the following screenshot:

External Events

Title	SharePoint 2010		Apply Filter	
EventId	Title		EventDateTime	Description
6	SharePoint 2010 External Data		4/20/2010 12:30:00 PM	Case Study: The new
8	Silverlight 4 LOB RIAs in SharePoint 2010		6/11/2010 2:00:00 PM	New opportunities to

When the user doesn't enter text in the `txtTitleFilter` TextBox, `_titleFilter` will hold an empty string. Thus, the CAML query won't include a `Where` condition, and the value for `camlQuery.ViewXml` will be the following:

```
<View >
    <Method Name='Read List'/>
    <Query>
        <OrderBy>
            <FieldRef Name='DateTime'/>
        </OrderBy>
    </Query>
    <ViewFields>
        <FieldRef Name='ID' />
        <FieldRef Name='Title'/>
        <FieldRef Name='DateTime'/>
        <FieldRef Name='Description'/>
    </ViewFields>
</View>
```

There is an `OrderBy` tag with a `FieldRef Name` set to `DateTime`, defined within the `Query` tag. Therefore, the query will order the results by `DateTime`.

When the user enters text in the `txtTitleFilter` TextBox, `_titleFilter` will hold the trimmed string. Thus, the CAML query will include a `Where` condition to filter the rows that have this text value in the `Title` field. If `_titleFilter` is equal to `"SharePoint 2010"`, the value for `camlQuery.ViewXml` will be the following:

```
<View >
    <Method Name='Read List'/>
    <Query>
        <Where>
            <Contains>
                <FieldRef Name='Title'/>
                <Value Type='Text'>SharePoint 2010</Value>
            </Contains>
        </Where>
        <OrderBy>
            <FieldRef Name='DateTime'/>
        </OrderBy>
    </Query>
    <ViewFields>
        <FieldRef Name='ID' />
        <FieldRef Name='Title'/>
        <FieldRef Name='DateTime'/>
        <FieldRef Name='Description'/>
    </ViewFields>
</View>
```

The `Query` defines a `Where` and the previously explained `OrderBy`. The `Where` defines a `Contains`, the `FieldRef Name` set to `Title`, the `Value Type` set to `Text`, and the text value that the field has to contain to be part of the result set.

> Remember that as we are working with an external list, it is always necessary to include the required fields in `ViewFields`.

Running Silverlight RIAs as Out-of-Browser Applications

We are going to make a few changes to our previous Silverlight RIA to allow the user to install the Silverlight RIA that appears in the Silverlight Web Part in his or her computer to run it outside the Web browser, as a desktop application. Follow these steps to configure the Out-of-Browser features for the previously created Silverlight RIA:

1. Stay in the `EventsViewer` project in Visual Studio as a system administrator user.

2. Replace the code in the `Connect` method with the following lines. Replace `"http://gaston-pc"` with the SharePoint website's URL.

```
// Runs in the UI Thread
lblStatus.Content = "Started";
// Replace "http://gaston-pc" with
// your SharePoint Web site's URL
_context = new SP.ClientContext("http://gaston-pc");
_context.Load(_context.Web);
_context.ExecuteQueryAsync(OnConnectSucceeded, null);
```

3. Now, right-click on the SLEventsViewer project, and select **Properties** in the context menu that appears. Click on the **Silverlight** tab in the properties panel and different options for the Silverlight application configuration will be shown. Activate the **Enable running application out of the browser** checkbox, as shown in the following screenshot:

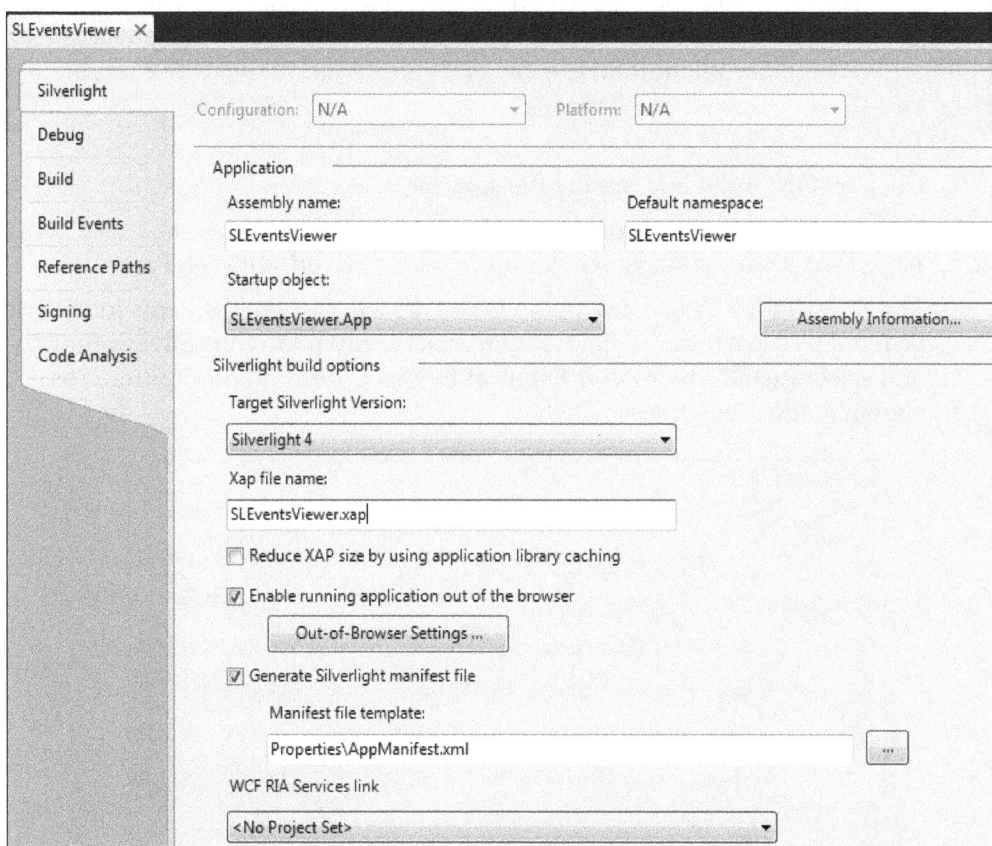

4. Click **Out-of-Browser Settings…** and a new dialog box will appear. This dialog box enables us to define specific properties for the Silverlight application when it runs out of the web browser.

5. Enter `SharePoint External Events Viewer` in **Window Title**, **Shortcut name**, and **Application Description**.

6. In this case, we are going to use the default icon. However, you can define `16 x 16`, `32 x 32`, `48 x 48`, and `128 x 128` icons for the application to use it in the different menus and shortcuts to which it is added.

7. Activate the **Use GPU Acceleration** checkbox. In this application, it won't make a difference but in the applications that we are going to create in the next chapter, this option will improve performance when the RIA runs out of the web browser. Therefore, it is a good idea to activate this checkbox.

> Silverlight 4 improved the **Out-of-Browser Settings**. You can also activate the **Require elevated trust when running outside the browser** checkbox if the application needs to interact with client devices or system resources. In addition, when you activate this option, you can select an appropriate **Window Style** — `Default`, `No Border`, `Single Border`, or `Borderless Round Corners`.

8. Click on **OK**. Build and deploy the solution.

9. Start your default web browser and load the `SilverlightEventsList.aspx` page, which shows `SLEventsViewer.xap` as a Silverlight Web Part.

10. The Silverlight RIA running in the Web Part will display the items in the grid ordered by the `DateTime` field. Right-click on any part of the Silverlight RIA and select **Install SharePoint External Events ... onto this computer...**, as shown in the following screenshot:

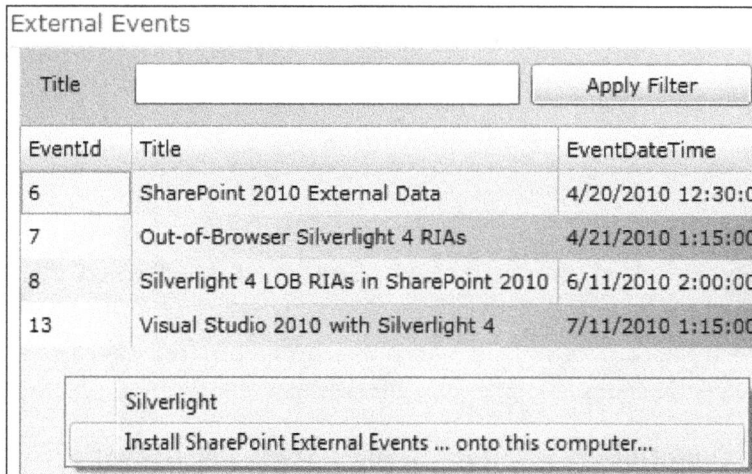

External Events

Title		Apply Filter

EventId	Title	EventDateTime
6	SharePoint 2010 External Data	4/20/2010 12:30:0(
7	Out-of-Browser Silverlight 4 RIAs	4/21/2010 1:15:00
8	Silverlight 4 LOB RIAs in SharePoint 2010	6/11/2010 2:00:00
13	Visual Studio 2010 with Silverlight 4	7/11/2010 1:15:00

Silverlight

Install SharePoint External Events ... onto this computer...

11. An **Install application** dialog box will appear, displaying information about the application you are about to install. You can activate the necessary checkboxes to add shortcuts to the **Start menu** and/or the **Desktop**, as shown in the next screenshot. In this case, the default icon appears on the left. However, remember that you can customize the icon.

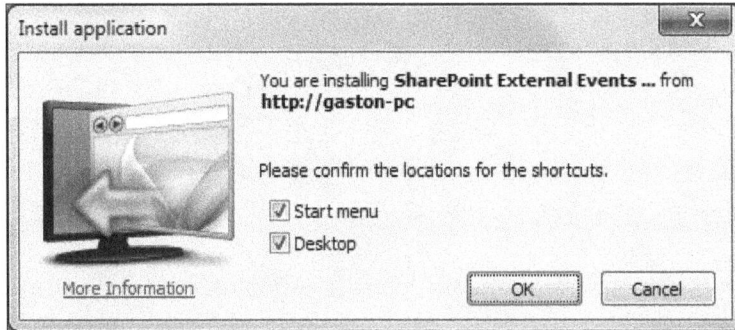

12. Click **OK**. The application will be installed to run without a web browser and a new window with the Silverlight RIA will appear on your desktop. The following screenshot shows the desktop shortcut icon that enables us to launch this application and the window that runs the Silverlight RIA out of the web browser.

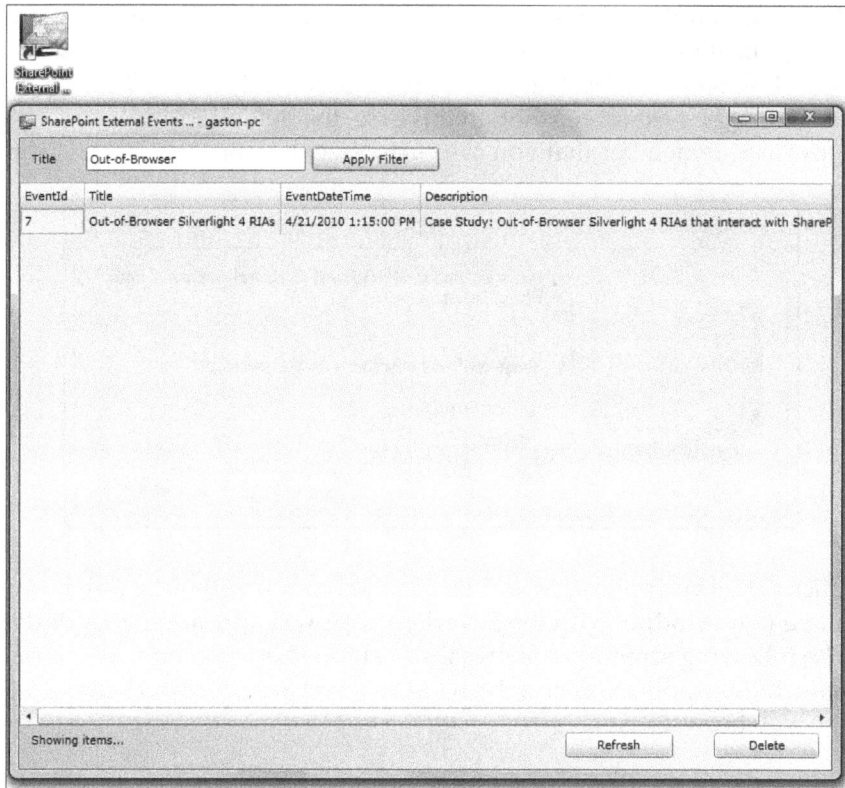

13. Now, close this window and the web browser, and use the new shortcut to launch the application. The Silverlight RIA's window will appear and you'll be able to filter data from the SharedEvents external list. As you can see, we don't need the Silverlight Web Part to run the application out of the web browser. We can launch this application whenever we want to.

14. If you right-click on any part of the Silverlight RIA, the context menu will display a **Remove this application...** option. If you select this option, the next time you show the Silverlight Web Part in the SharePoint web page and you right-click on the Silverlight RIA, the **Install SharePoint External Events ... onto this computer...** option will appear again because the application was uninstalled from your computer.

We made some changes and activated a few options to make it possible to run our Silverlight RIA as an **Out-of-Browser** application (also known as **OOB** application). As the application doesn't run within a web browser, there isn't a current URL. Thus, it cannot access ApplicationContext.Current.Url to send it as a parameter to the ClientContext constructor:

```
_context =
    new SP.ClientContext(SP.ApplicationContext.Current.Url);
```

It was necessary to replace the code in the `Connect` method to send the URL for the SharePoint server to the `ClientContext` constructor. You have to replace `http://gaston-pc` by your SharePoint server's URL.

```
_context = new SP.ClientContext("http://gaston-pc");
```

This way, when the Silverlight RIA runs as an OOB application, it knows the URL for the SharePoint server in order to create the `ClientContext` instance.

The OOB settings will generate a new file, `OutOfBrowserSettings.xml`, within the `Properties` folder in the Silverlight project. This XML file defines the values for the properties that appear in the **Out-of-Browser Settings** dialog box. The following lines show the contents for this file in the previously explained example:

```
<OutOfBrowserSettings ShortName="SharePoint External Events Viewer"
    EnableGPUAcceleration="True" ShowInstallMenuItem="True">
    <OutOfBrowserSettings.Blurb>SharePoint External Events
      Viewer</OutOfBrowserSettings.Blurb>
    <OutOfBrowserSettings.WindowSettings>
      <WindowSettings Title="SharePoint External Events Viewer" />
    </OutOfBrowserSettings.WindowSettings>
    <OutOfBrowserSettings.Icons />
</OutOfBrowserSettings>
```

Interacting with workflows

A **workflow** is a system that helps drive processes that require a chain of steps, along with tracking the status of these processes and their related events. A workflow provides visibility into what is happening with a process. SharePoint includes predefined workflows that help users get started with common processes. For example, an approval workflow routes a document for its approval. Approvers can approve or reject the document, reassign the approval task, or request changes to the document. When a document has an associated approval workflow, this workflow starts under certain conditions, or when a user creates or uploads a document.

SharePoint 2010 introduced many new features for workflows. Now, a workflow can run without a SharePoint list, and it is possible to define reusable workflows. You can create a workflow and then attach it to different lists. Besides, SharePoint Designer 2010 offers an improved workflow designer.

The SharePoint Silverlight Client Object Model allows us to read information from the fields and the lists associated to a workflow and their instances. Thus, it is possible to create a Silverlight Web Part that displays a workflow status for each item in a list.

Attaching a workflow to a list of tasks in SharePoint

First, follow these steps to add a new list of tasks in a SharePoint site and add a workflow to it that routes documents for their approval:

1. Open your default web browser, view the SharePoint site, and log in with your username and password.

2. Click **Site Actions | More Options...** in the ribbon and the **Create** dialog box will appear.

3. Select **List** and then **Tracking** under **Filter By**, and then **Tasks** in **Installed Items**.

4. Enter `ProjectsListWW` in the **Name** textbox.

5. Click on **More Options**. SharePoint will display a new panel with additional options for the new list.

6. Enter `Projects and tasks for year 2010 With Workflow` in **Description** and select **Yes** in **Display this list on the Quick Launch?**

7. Click on **Create**; SharePoint will create the new list with no items. It will show the same files as the previously created `ProjectsList2010` for the new list of tasks in the **Standard View**. Besides, the shortcut for the new list, `ProjectsListWW`, appears under **Lists** in the panel located at the left.

8. Click on **List Tools | List | Workflow Settings** in the ribbon and a drop-down menu will appear. Select **Add a Workflow**, as shown in the next screenshot:

9. Select `Approval - SharePoint 2010` in the **Select a workflow template** list. This way, an instance of this workflow template, which routes a document for approval, will be attached to the `ProjectsListWW` list. Approvers can approve or reject each new item in the list, reassign the approval task, or request changes to the item.

10. Enter `ProjectApproval` in **Type a unique name for this workflow**.

11. Select `New task list` in **Select a task list**. This way, the tasks related to this new workflow will be stored in a new task list for you or your team.

12. Select `Workflow History` in **Select a history list**. This way, the `Workflow History` list will store a log related with this new workflow, with the actions performed by the different users.

13. Activate **Start this workflow when a new item is created**, as shown in the next screenshot. This way, each time a new item is added to the `ProjectsListWW`, this workflow will start for this item to request its approval. Then, click **Next** and a new page with additional options for this workflow will appear.

Content Type		
Select the type of items that you want this workflow to run on. Content type workflows can only be associated to a list content type, not directly to the list.	Run on items of this type: All (Selecting a different type will navigate you to the Add a Workflow page for that content type.)	
Workflow		Description:
Select a workflow to add to this list. If the workflow template you want does not appear, contact your administrator to get it added to your site collection or workspace.	Select a workflow template: Disposition Approval Three-state Collect Signatures - SharePoint 2 Approval - SharePoint 2010	Routes a document for approval. Approvers can approve or reject the document, reassign the approval task, or request changes to the document.
Name		
Type a name for this workflow. The name will be used to identify this workflow to users of this list.	Type a unique name for this workflow: ProjectApproval	
Task List		Description:
Select a task list to use with this workflow. You can select an existing task list or request that a new task list be created.	Select a task list: Tasks	Use the Tasks list to keep track of work that you or your team needs to complete.
History List		Description:
Select a history list to use with this workflow. You can select an existing history list or request that a new history list be created.	Select a history list: Workflow History	History list for workflow.
Start Options		
Specify how this workflow can be started.	☑ Allow this workflow to be manually started by an authenticated user with Participate permissions. ☐ Require Manage Lists Permissions to start the workflow. ☐ Start this workflow to approve publishing a major version of an item. ☑ Start this workflow when a new item is created. ☐ Start this workflow when an item is changed.	

Next	Cancel

14. Select the users that will act as approvers for each item added to the list. Enter one or more users in the **Assign To** textbox. Select One at a time (serial) in **Order**.

15. Enter Do you approve this new project? in **Notification Message**. There are many additional options that allow you to define parameters that determine this workflow's behavior.

16. Click **Save** and the new workflow will be attached to the previously created list, ProjectsListWW.

We added a new list of tasks in a SharePoint site, ProjectsListWW, and we then attached it to a workflow that routes documents for their approval. SharePoint will create a new list, ProjectApproval Tasks, and store all the tasks related to the new approval workflow.

Inserting and approving items in a list with an attached workflow

Follow these steps to add a few items to the list of tasks with an attached approval workflow:

1. Display the previously created list, ProjectsListWW, in your web browser.

2. Click on **Add new item**. The **New Item** dialog box will appear. Enter the data for each field that appears in this dialog box to define a new project as a task. You can add some of the projects added in our previous examples.

3. Click on **Save** and the new item will appear in the list. A new column, ProjectApproval, will display the **In Progress** value, as shown in the following screenshot. This means that the ProjectApproval workflow created a new instance of the workflow associated to this new element to request its approval.

		Type	Title		Assigned To	Status	Priority	Due Date	% Complete	Predecessors	ProjectApproval
			Creating a Silverlight 4 UI ☑ NEW		gaston-PC\hillar2010	Deferred	(2) Normal	6/11/2010			In Progress

✦ Add new item

4. Click on **In Progress** and SharePoint will display a new page with the workflow status and the item assigned for approval to the approver user.

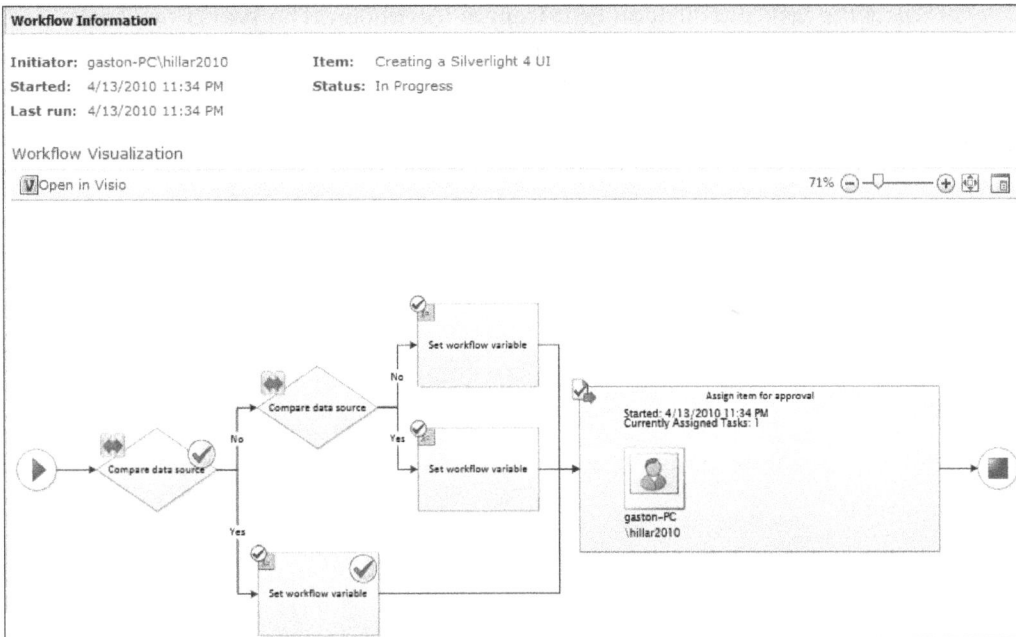

5. Scroll down and you will see the new task assigned to the participants of this workflow under **Tasks**. This new task will also appear in the `ProjectApproval Tasks` list.

6. Display the aforementioned list, `ProjectApproval Tasks`, in a new tab or a new window. An item requesting the approval of the related content, the new item added to the `ProjectsListWW` list, will appear, as shown in the next screenshot. Notice that the task's **Status** is **Not Started** and its **Outcome** is empty.

7. Select the task and click on **Edit Item** in the ribbon. The **Workflow Task** dialog box will appear and it will display the information about the task, the item that it applies to, and many buttons located at the bottom.

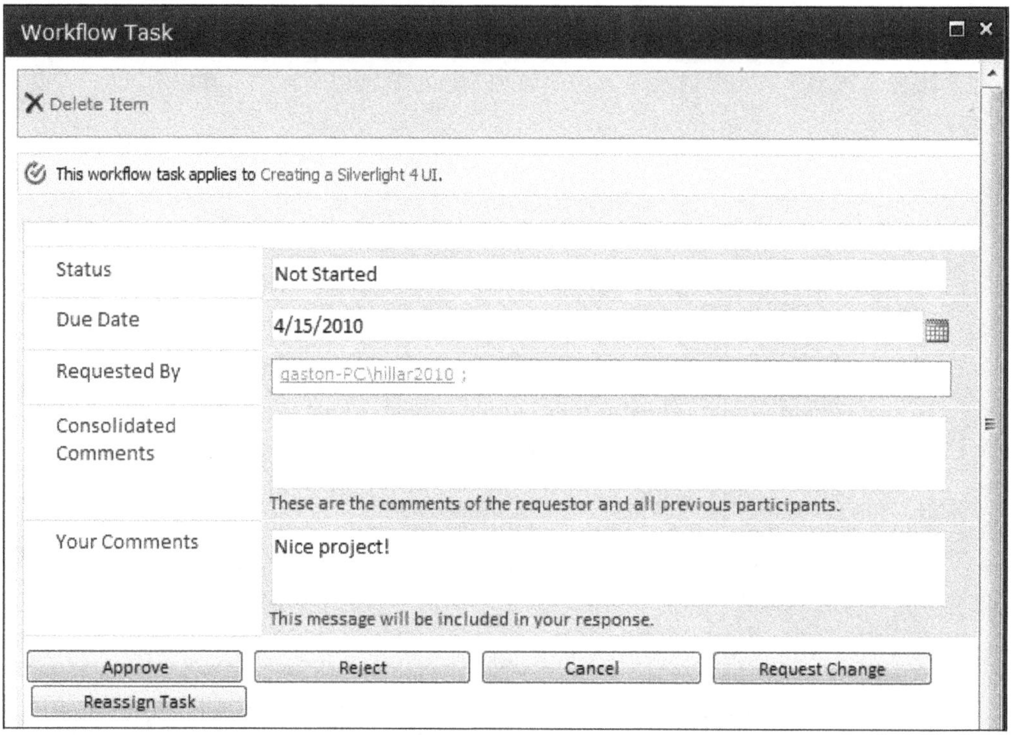

8. Enter the desired comments and click on **Approve** or **Reject**. Now, the task list will show a value for **Outcome** and will appear as completed.

9. Now, refresh the tab or window that was displaying all the items for the `ProjectsListWW` list. The `ProjectApproval` column will display a value according to the button clicked in the previous dialog box. The following screenshot shows an approved item. If you click on the value shown in this column, SharePoint will display a new page with the workflow status.

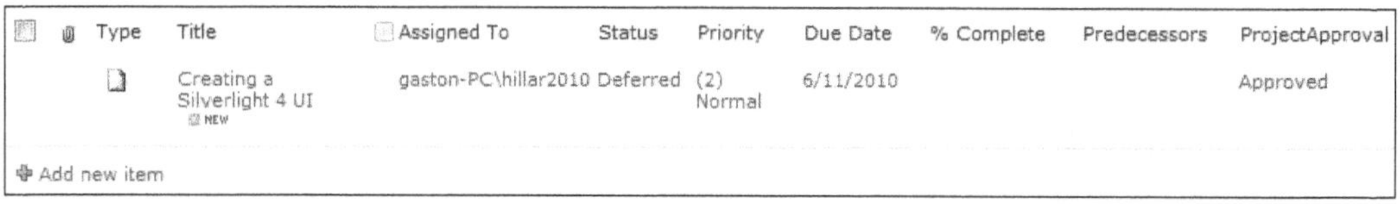

	Type	Title	Assigned To	Status	Priority	Due Date	% Complete	Predecessors	ProjectApproval
		Creating a Silverlight 4 UI [NEW]	gaston-PC\hillar2010	Deferred	(2) Normal	6/11/2010			Approved

Add new item

10. Repeat the aforementioned steps to insert many items and approve or reject many of them.

We inserted many items into the `ProjectsListWW` list. We approved and rejected many of these items because the list has an attached approval workflow. Now, we have a list with approved and rejected items and we can use a Silverlight RIA to read the workflow's status for this list.

Using a Silverlight RIA to display a SharePoint workflow's status

We are now going to improve one of our previously created Silverlight RIAs to interact with the `ProjectsListWW` list, retrieve, and display information about the status of each item in the workflow.

1. Stay in Visual Studio as a system administrator user.

2. Activate the **Server Explorer** palette and navigate to `ProjectsListWW`.

3. Now, expand the list of tasks for `ProjectsListWW`, and then expand its **Fields** node. This way, you will see all the fields for this list.

4. Now, click on the `ProjectApproval` field, display its properties, and check the value for its `SchemaXml` property. As previously explained, the content for this property is XML markup, and therefore, you won't be able to analyze all the information in the **Properties** palette because you will only see the first characters. When you attached the approval workflow, it added this field to the list.

5. You can copy the value for the `SchemaXml` property and paste it in a new **XML File** in Visual Studio. This way, you will be able to see all the choices, as shown in the following lines:

```
<Field DisplayName="ProjectApproval" Type="WorkflowStatus"
  Required="FALSE" ID="{821d8a8b-3139-4ef4-9a71-24da49b93849}"
  SourceID="{5284e895-fd48-4627-a229-46c875296566}"
  StaticName="ProjectA" Name="ProjectA" ColName="nvarchar5"
  RowOrdinal="0" Version="2"
  WorkflowStatusURL="_layouts/WrkStat.aspx" ReadOnly="TRUE">
<CHOICES>
  <CHOICE>Starting</CHOICE>
  <CHOICE>Failed on Start</CHOICE>
  <CHOICE>In Progress</CHOICE>
  <CHOICE>Error Occurred</CHOICE>
  <CHOICE>Canceled</CHOICE>
  <CHOICE>Completed</CHOICE>
  <CHOICE>Failed on Start (retrying)</CHOICE>
  <CHOICE>Error Occurred (retrying)</CHOICE>
  <CHOICE />
  <CHOICE />
  <CHOICE />
  <CHOICE />
```

```
        <CHOICE />
        <CHOICE />
        <CHOICE />
        <CHOICE>Canceled</CHOICE>
        <CHOICE>Approved</CHOICE>
        <CHOICE>Rejected</CHOICE>
      </CHOICES>
    </Field>
```

6. Now, expand the **Workflow Associations** node for the list. The `ProjectApproval` workflow association node will appear. Click on it and you will be able to see the values for its properties. The properties that hold the title for the related history and tasks lists are important. The following list shows the property names and their values for this `ProjectApproval` workflow association:

    ° `HistoryListTitle`: Has a value `Workflow History`.

    ° `TaskListTitle`: Has a value `ProjectApproval Tasks`.

7. Open `SLTasksViewer` project in the `TasksViewer` solution, created and enhanced in the previous chapters.

8. Open `Project.cs` and add the following property to the `Project` class:

    `public string ApprovalStatus { get; set; }`

9. Open `MainPage.xaml.cs` and replace `ProjectsList2010` with `ProjectsListWW` because we want the application to work against the new list that has an attached approval workflow.

10. Add the following `private` variable and method:

```
private SP.FieldCollection _projectAFieldCol;

private SP.FieldChoice ReturnFieldByInternalName
(string internalName)
{
    for (int i = 0; i < _projectAFieldCol.Count; i++)
    {
        if (_projectAFieldCol[i].InternalName == internalName)
        {
            return (_projectAFieldCol[i] as FieldChoice);
        }
    }
    return null;
}
```

11. Replace the code for the `GetListData` method with the following new lines:

```
private void GetListData()
{
    // Runs in the UI Thread
    lblStatus.Content =
        "Lists Connected. Getting List data...";
    // ProjectsListWW is the list of tasks
    _projects =
        _context.Web.Lists.GetByTitle("ProjectsListWW");
    _context.Load(_projects);
    _context.Load(_projects.RootFolder);

    // Just load the necessary field for the List:
    // ProjectA - it contains the workflow approval status
    _projectAFieldCol = _projects.Fields;

    _context.Load(_projectAFieldCol,
        fields => fields.Where(
            field => field.InternalName == "ProjectA")
            .IncludeWithDefaultProperties());

    _context.ExecuteQueryAsync(OnGetListDataSucceeded, null);
}
```

12. Replace the code for the `ShowItems` method with these new lines:

```
private void ShowItems()
{
    // Runs in the UI Thread
    lblStatus.Content = "Showing items...";

    // Get the Workflow Status
    // stored in ProjectA as a FieldChoice
    SP.FieldChoice statusField =
        ReturnFieldByInternalName("ProjectA");

    _projectsList = new List<Project>();
    foreach (SP.ListItem listItem in _projectsItemCol)
    {
        _projectsList.Add(
            new Project()
            {
                ProjectId = Convert.ToInt32(listItem["ID"]),
                Title = listItem["Title"].ToString(),
```

```
                            StartDate =
                                Convert.ToDateTime(listItem["StartDate"]),
                            DueDate = Convert.ToDateTime(listItem["DueDate"]),
                            EstimatedDaysLeft =
                                (Convert.ToDateTime(listItem
                             ["DueDate"]).Subtract(Convert.ToDateTime(listItem
                             ["StartDate"])).Days),
                            Status = listItem["Status"].ToString(),
                            AssignedTo = (listItem["AssignedTo"] as
                                FieldUserValue).LookupValue,
                            NumberOfTasks =
                                Convert.ToInt32(listItem["ItemChildCount"]),
                            Priority = listItem["Priority"].ToString(),
                            ApprovalStatus =
                    statusField.Choices[Convert.ToInt32(listItem["ProjectA"])]
                        });
                }
            dataGridProjects.ItemsSource = _projectsList;
        }
```

13. Build and deploy the solution.

14. Enter the URL for the page that contains the Silverlight Web Part in the web browser. This way, the Silverlight RIA will appear and it will display the value for the `ApprovalStatus` column. The following screenshot shows three rows with `Approved`, `In Progress`, and `Rejected` as their workflow approval status.

Silverlight SharePoint Tasks Viewer

ProjectI	Title	Priority	AssignedTo	NumberOfTasl	ApprovalStatus	Esti
5	Creating a Silverlight 4 UI	(2) Normal	gaston-PC\hillar2010	0	Approved	60
6	Testing Silverlight 4 COM with Lists in SharePoint 201(	(2) Normal	GASTON-PC\gaston	0	In Progress	23
7	Creating a Silverlight 3 UI	(2) Normal	gaston-PC\hillar2010	0	Rejected	2

15. Add new elements to the list, approve and reject them, and refresh the grid for the Silverlight RIA. The `ApprovalStatus` column will display the workflow status attached to the new list.

Understanding workflows' status fields

The GetListData method uses the ClientContext instance to request it to load the default properties for the ProjectA field. We used **Server Explorer** to discover that ProjectA is the internal name for the ProjectApproval field, as learned in the *Browsing SharePoint lists and fields with Visual Studio* section in *Chapter 2*. This field is a FieldChoice instance in the SharePoint Silverlight Client Object Model, and therefore, we use the same technique explained in the previous chapter to retrieve all the possible choices. We added the call to the IncludeWithDefaultProperties extension method without parameters because we just want to retrieve the default properties for the field with ProjectA as its InternalName.

```
_projectAFieldCol = _projects.Fields;

_context.Load(_projectAFieldCol,
    fields => fields.Where(
        field => field.InternalName == "ProjectA")
        .IncludeWithDefaultProperties());
```

This way, we query this field and request its default properties. Finally, the ShowItems method retrieves this field from _projectAFieldCol FieldCollection as a FieldChoice instance, statusField. We have already used another version of the ReturnFieldByInternalName in a previous example. As FieldChoice is the real class for this field instance, it is necessary to cast it to FieldChoice to access the specific field and properties that allow us to retrieve the choices, as shown in the next lines:

```
SP.FieldChoice statusField =
    ReturnFieldByInternalName("ProjectA");
```

The value for the ApprovalStatus string for each Project instance is going to be the result of specifying the integer number stored in the ProjectA field as an index to the Choices string array. This way, we can retrieve the right workflow status title for the number in ProjectA, and display it in the corresponding cell in the bound grid.

```
ApprovalStatus =
    statusField.Choices[Convert.ToInt32(listItem["ProjectA"])]
```

Summary

We learned a lot in this chapter about accessing external databases in a Silverlight RIA included in a SharePoint solution and interacting with workflows. Specifically, we were able to interact with a table in an external data source and we used many of the procedures learned in the previous chapters to work with classic lists. We made the necessary changes to interact with this new type of list and we took advantage of Silverlight 4 Out-of-Browser capabilities to run the RIA in the Windows and/or MAC desktop.

We worked with the new SharePoint 2010 approval workflows and enhanced an existing Silverlight RIA to retrieve workflow status information and display it in a column of a grid. We analyzed the metadata information about fields and lists to display the right values for each of the possible workflow statuses.

Now that we have learned about the creation of dynamic business solutions with external data and workflows on the SharePoint server, we are ready to learn to interact with data consuming the new SharePoint 2010 WCF Data Services, which is the topic of the next chapter.

5
Working with WCF Data Services

In the previous chapters, we learned to interact with data, services, and remote objects from the SharePoint Server. Now, we want to interact with this data by performing read, insert, update, and delete operations with the new SharePoint 2010 WCF Data Services. In this chapter, we will cover many topics that will help us create Silverlight RIAs that run as Silverlight Web Parts to interact with the new data services introduced in SharePoint 2010. We will:

- Query SharePoint 2010 lists in a web browser
- Take advantage of Visual Studio 2010 tools to generate strongly typed Entity Data Models
- Work with SharePoint 2010 WCF Data Services to display data from a list
- Consume SharePoint 2010 WCF Data Services from a Silverlight Web Part
- Perform operations on lists with SharePoint 2010 WCF Data Services
- Insert, delete, and update items items in lists with SharePoint 2010 WCF Data Services
- Use simple tools to observe and debug HTTP requests related to WCF Data Services
- Analyze pages with SharePoint Developer Dashboard

Working with SharePoint 2010 WCF Data Services

So far, we have been working with features provided by the SharePoint 2010 Silverlight Client OM to interact with data in the SharePoint 2010 Server. SharePoint 2010 also exposes data as **WCF Data Services**, formerly known as **ADO.NET Data Services**, which can be consumed by Silverlight 4 applications. WCF Data Services support the **Open Data Protocol** (http://www.odata.org) referred to as **OData**, which defines a data-sharing standard to allow interoperability between heterogeneous clients (data consumers) and producers (services).

We can reach SharePoint 2010 WCF Data Services via regular HTTP requests. They allow us to perform CRUD operations against the service because WCF Data Services expose a data model as a set of queryable **REST (Representational State Transfer)** endpoints and maps four standard HTTP verbs, as summarized in the next table.

CRUD operation	HTTP verb
Create	POST
Read	GET
Update	PUT
Delete	DELETE

> WCF Data Services use Atom and **JSON (JavaScript Object Notation)** as options for the payload format.

We can create a new Silverlight RIA to perform some of the CRUD operations with the existing list of tasks by using the new SharePoint 2010 WCF Data Services instead of the Client OM. WCF Data Services are different than the Client OM and therefore, we will have to learn many new topics. WCF Data Services have a different API and allow us to work with strongly typed lists. Instead, the Client OM forces us to work with weakly-typed lists. Both APIs require the asynchronous execution of queries in Silverlight applications.

In order to access SharePoint 2010 WCF Data Services, you need to make sure that the ADO.NET Data Services Update for .NET Framework 3.5 SP1 for Windows 7 and Windows Server 2008 R2 is installed. It is an update to the Microsoft .NET Framework 3.5 SP1 that provides additional features to extend the functionality offered by ADO.NET Data Services framework. You can download and install it from `http://www.microsoft.com/downloads/details.aspx?familyid=79d7f6f8-d6e9-4b8c-8640-17f89452148e&displaylang=en`.

Querying SharePoint 2010 lists in a web browser

SharePoint 2010 exposes the Web Services in the following URL pattern:

```
http://<site>:<port>/<subsite>/_vti_bin/<web_service>
```

The `ListData` service returns a standard Atom service document that describes collections of information that are available in the SharePoint site. If you want to access the `ListData.svc` WCF Data Service, you will have to replace `<web_service>` with `ListData.svc`, as shown in the next URL pattern:

```
http://<site>:<port>/<subsite>/_vti_bin/listdata.svc
```

Now, considering the aforementioned URL pattern, follow these steps to consume the `ListData.svc` WCF Data Service in your default web browser:

1. Open your default web browser and enter the URL to access the `ListData.svc` WCF Data Service. In this example we will use `http://gaston-pc` as our default SharePoint 2010 site. However, you have to replace it with your SharePoint 2010 site URL. In this case, `http://gaston-pc/_vti_bin/listdata.svc` will display the Data Service Atom feed with all the lists for the `http://gaston-pc` SharePoint site, as shown in the next screenshot. The following lines display the XML result where each `collection` is a SharePoint list that defines a value for its `title` as an Atom field. The highlighted lines show our well-known `ProjectsList2010` list in this SharePoint server:

```xml
<?xml version="1.0" encoding="iso-8859-1" standalone="yes"?>
<service xml:base="http://gaston-pc/_vti_bin/listdata.svc/"
   xmlns:atom="http://www.w3.org/2005/Atom"
   xmlns:app="http://www.w3.org/2007/app"
   xmlns="http://www.w3.org/2007/app">
   <workspace>
```

```
<atom:title>Default</atom:title>
<collection href="Announcements">
  <atom:title>Announcements</atom:title>
</collection>
<collection href="Attachments">
  <atom:title>Attachments</atom:title>
</collection>
<collection href="Calendar">
  <atom:title>Calendar</atom:title>
</collection>
<collection href="CalendarCategory">
  <atom:title>CalendarCategory</atom:title>
</collection>
<collection href="ConvertedForms">
  <atom:title>ConvertedForms</atom:title>
</collection>
<collection href="Project2010ApprovalTasks">
  <atom:title>Project2010ApprovalTasks</atom:title>
</collection>
<collection href="Project2010ApprovalTasksPriority">
  <atom:title>Project2010ApprovalTasksPriority</atom:title>
</collection>
<collection href="Project2010ApprovalTasksStatus">
  <atom:title>Project2010ApprovalTasksStatus</atom:title>
</collection>
<collection href="ProjectApprovalTasks">
  <atom:title>ProjectApprovalTasks</atom:title>
</collection>
<collection href="ProjectApprovalTasksPriority">
  <atom:title>ProjectApprovalTasksPriority</atom:title>
</collection>
<collection href="ProjectApprovalTasksStatus">
  <atom:title>ProjectApprovalTasksStatus</atom:title>
</collection>
<collection href="ProjectsList2010">
  <atom:title>ProjectsList2010</atom:title>
</collection>
<collection href="ProjectsList2010Priority">
  <atom:title>ProjectsList2010Priority</atom:title>
</collection>
<collection href="ProjectsList2010Status">
```

```
      <atom:title>ProjectsList2010Status</atom:title>
    </collection>
    <collection href="ProjectsListWW">
      <atom:title>ProjectsListWW</atom:title>
    </collection>
    <collection href="ProjectsListWWPriority">
      <atom:title>ProjectsListWWPriority</atom:title>
    </collection>
    <collection href="ProjectsListWWStatus">
      <atom:title>ProjectsListWWStatus</atom:title>
    </collection>

    <collection href="UserInformationList">
      <atom:title>UserInformationList</atom:title>
    </collection>
    <collection href="Videos">
      <atom:title>Videos</atom:title>
    </collection>
    <collection href="WebPartGallery">
      <atom:title>WebPartGallery</atom:title>
    </collection>
    <collection href="WebPartGalleryGroup">
      <atom:title>WebPartGalleryGroup</atom:title>
    </collection>
    <collection href="WebPartGalleryRecommendationSettings">
     <atom:title>WebPartGalleryRecommendationSettings</atom:title>
    </collection>
    <collection href="Wfpub">
      <atom:title>Wfpub</atom:title>
    </collection>
    <collection href="WorkflowHistory">
      <atom:title>WorkflowHistory</atom:title>
    </collection>
  </workspace>
</service>
```

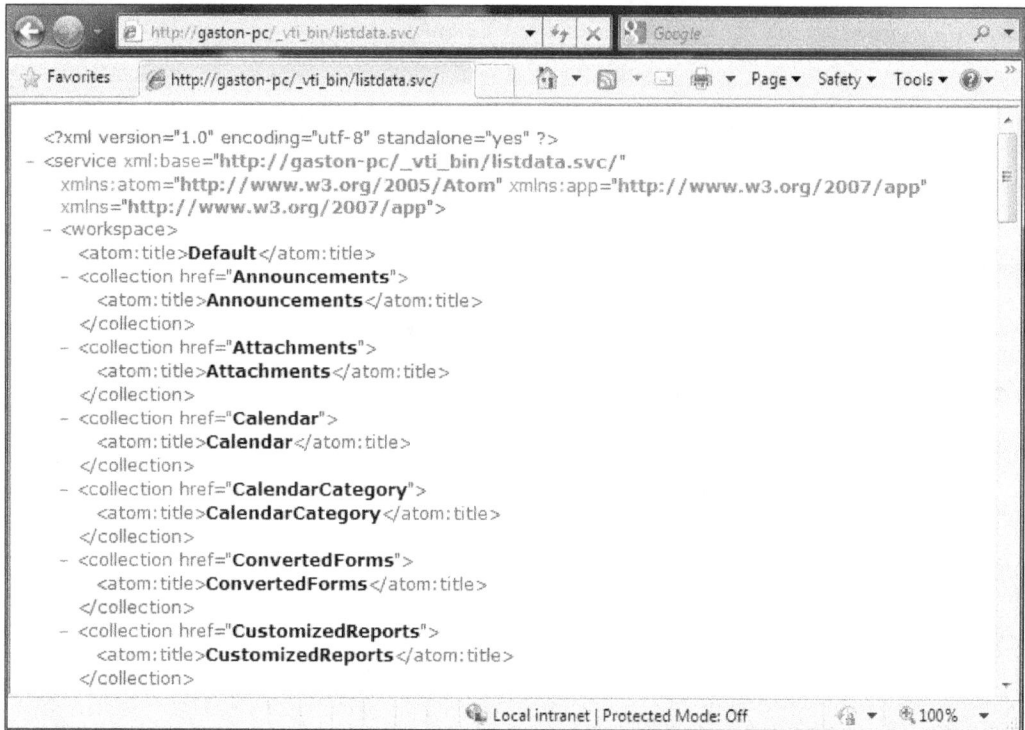

```
<?xml version="1.0" encoding="utf-8" standalone="yes" ?>
- <service xml:base="http://gaston-pc/_vti_bin/listdata.svc/"
  xmlns:atom="http://www.w3.org/2005/Atom" xmlns:app="http://www.w3.org/2007/app"
  xmlns="http://www.w3.org/2007/app">
  - <workspace>
    <atom:title>Default</atom:title>
    - <collection href="Announcements">
      <atom:title>Announcements</atom:title>
    </collection>
    - <collection href="Attachments">
      <atom:title>Attachments</atom:title>
    </collection>
    - <collection href="Calendar">
      <atom:title>Calendar</atom:title>
    </collection>
    - <collection href="CalendarCategory">
      <atom:title>CalendarCategory</atom:title>
    </collection>
    - <collection href="ConvertedForms">
      <atom:title>ConvertedForms</atom:title>
    </collection>
    - <collection href="CustomizedReports">
      <atom:title>CustomizedReports</atom:title>
    </collection>
```

2. Now, add a slash (/) and the name of the list you want to query, to the previously entered URL. In this case, `http://gaston-pc/_vti_bin/listdata.svc/ProjectsList2010` will display the Data Service Atom feed with the titles and the last edit dates of all the items for the `ProjectsList2010` SharePoint list in the `http://gaston-pc` SharePoint site, as shown in the next screenshot. The URL pattern to request the feed for a list is as follows:

   `http://<site>:<port>/<subsite>/_vti_bin/listdata.svc/<listname>`

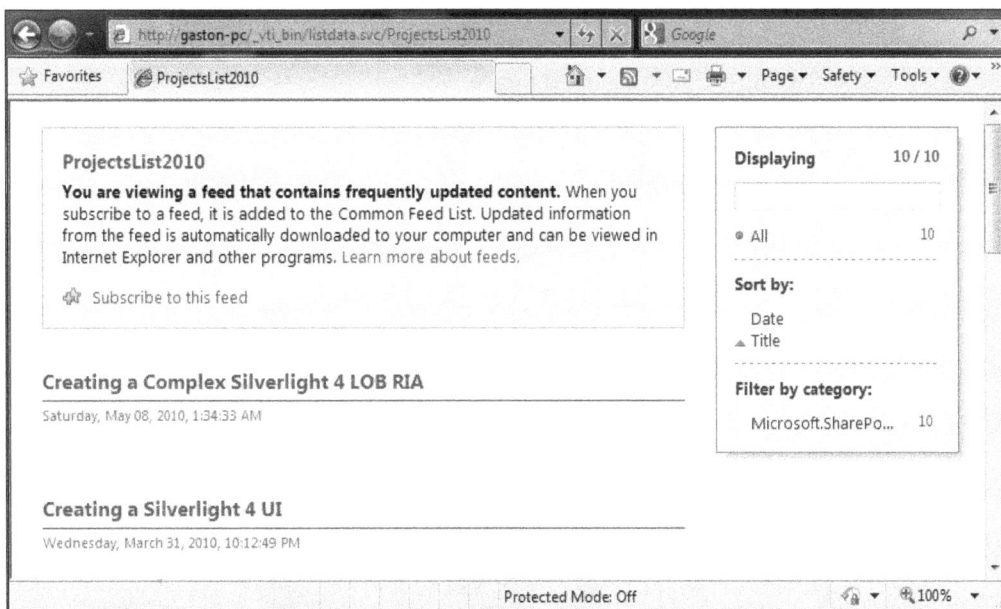

3. The web browser displays the titles and the dates of all the `Microsoft.`
`SharePoint.DataService.ProjectList2010Item` items because it renders
the RSS feed. However, the Data Service Atom feed offers all the properties
or fields for each of the items. Display the source code for the web page in
your web browser. In Internet Explorer, you can do so by pressing the *Alt*
key and then selecting **View | Source** in the main menu, or by clicking on
Page | View Source. The web browser will display a new window with
the XML code received from the server as an Atom feed. The following
lines show code that defines the values for all the fields of a `Microsoft.`
`SharePoint.DataService.ProjectList2010Item` item whose title is
`Creating a Silverlight 4 UI` within `<m:properties>`.

```
<?xml version="1.0" encoding="utf-8" standalone="yes"?>
<feed xml:base="http://gaston-pc/_vti_bin/listdata.svc/"
  xmlns:d="http://schemas.microsoft.com/ado/2007/08/dataservices"
  xmlns:m=
  "http://schemas.microsoft.com/ado/2007/08/dataservices/metadata"
  xmlns="http://www.w3.org/2005/Atom">
  <title type="text">ProjectsList2010</title>
  <id>http://gaston-pc/_vti_bin/listdata.svc/ProjectsList2010</id>
  <updated>2010-05-15T17:41:08Z</updated>
  <link rel="self" title="ProjectsList2010"
    href="ProjectsList2010" />
  <entry m:etag="W/&quot;2&quot;">
```

```
<id>http://gaston-pc/_vti_bin/listdata.svc/ProjectsList2010(1)
  </id>
<title type="text">Creating a Silverlight 4 UI</title>
<updated>2010-03-31T22:12:49-03:00</updated>
<author>
  <name />
</author>
<link rel="edit" title="ProjectsList2010Item"
  href="ProjectsList2010(1)" />
<link rel=
  "http://schemas.microsoft.com/ado/2007/08/dataservices/
  related/Predecessors"
  type="application/atom+xml;type=feed" title="Predecessors"
  href="ProjectsList2010(1)/Predecessors" />
<link rel=
  "http://schemas.microsoft.com/ado/2007/08/dataservices/
  related/Priority"
  type="application/atom+xml;type=entry" title="Priority"
  href="ProjectsList2010(1)/Priority" />
<link rel=
  "http://schemas.microsoft.com/ado/2007/08/dataservices/
  related/Status"
  type="application/atom+xml;type=entry" title="Status"
  href="ProjectsList2010(1)/Status" />
<link rel=
  "http://schemas.microsoft.com/ado/2007/08/dataservices/
  related/Attachments" type="application/atom+xml;
  type=feed" title="Attachments"
  href="ProjectsList2010(1)/Attachments" />
<category term=
  "Microsoft.SharePoint.DataService.ProjectsList2010Item"
  scheme="http://schemas.microsoft.com/ado/2007/08/
  dataservices/scheme" />
<content type="application/xml">
  <m:properties>
    <d:ContentTypeID>0x0108007C7838C285B9704DAA54BEB13213E3BA
      </d:ContentTypeID>
    <d:Title>Creating a Silverlight 4 UI</d:Title>
    <d:PriorityValue>(2) Normal</d:PriorityValue>
    <d:StatusValue>Not Started</d:StatusValue>
    <d:Complete m:type="Edm.Double">0.3</d:Complete>
    <d:AssignedToID m:type="Edm.Int32">6</d:AssignedToID>
    <d:TaskGroupID m:type="Edm.Int32" m:null="true" />
```

```
    <d:Description>&lt;div&gt;It is necessary to create a new
      Silverlight 4 UI to display the active projects in a
      grid. This way, it will be possible to allow the user to
      analyze the active projects with a rich UX.&lt;/div&gt;
    </d:Description>
    <d:StartDate m:type="Edm.DateTime">
      2010-02-16T00:00:00</d:StartDate>
    <d:DueDate m:type="Edm.DateTime">
      2010-02-20T00:00:00</d:DueDate>
    <d:Projects2010Approval m:type="Edm.Int32"
      m:null="true" />
    <d:ID m:type="Edm.Int32">1</d:ID>
    <d:ContentType>Task</d:ContentType>
    <d:Modified m:type="Edm.DateTime">
      2010-03-31T22:12:49</d:Modified>
    <d:Created m:type="Edm.DateTime">
      2010-03-31T22:11:36</d:Created>
    <d:CreatedByID m:type="Edm.Int32">6</d:CreatedByID>
    <d:ModifiedByID m:type="Edm.Int32">6</d:ModifiedByID>
    <d:Owshiddenversion m:type="Edm.Int32">2
      </d:Owshiddenversion>
    <d:Version>1.0</d:Version>
    <d:Path>/Lists/ProjectsList2010</d:Path>
    </m:properties>
  </content>
 </entry>
</feed>
```

4. If you take a look at `<id>` within `<entry>` in the previous code snippet, you will notice a direct URL for this entry. This URL allows you to retrieve this specific `Microsoft.SharePoint.DataService.ProjectList2010Item` item whose `ID` value is 1.

```
<id>http://gaston-pc/_vti_bin/listdata.svc/ProjectsList2010(1)
</id>
```

5. In fact, the URL pattern to request the feed for a specific item is the following, where `<index>` has to be replaced with the value of the `ID` field for the desired `Microsoft.SharePoint.DataService.ProjectList2010Item` item:

```
http://<site>:<port>/<subsite>/_vti_bin/listdata.svc/<listname>
  (<index>)
```

6. Now, add the value of an existing ID as the index enclosed in parenthesis to the existing URL. In this case, `http://gaston-pc/_vti_bin/listdata.svc/ProjectsList2010(26)` will return the Atom feed for the item whose ID value is 26 for the `ProjectsList2010` SharePoint list in the `http://gaston-pc` SharePoint site. Internet Explorer displays an error indicating that it cannot display the feed, as shown in the next screenshot. However, if you display the source code for the web page in your web browser it might show a valid XML document with the requested `entry`. Internet Explorer uses its own default **XSLT (Extensible Stylesheet Language Transformations)** behind the scenes to display XML content, particularly in the case of RSS feeds. The following lines show code that defines the values for all the fields of the requested entry:

```
<?xml version="1.0" encoding="utf-8" standalone="yes"?>
<entry xml:base="http://gaston-pc/_vti_bin/listdata.svc/"
  xmlns:d="http://schemas.microsoft.com/ado/2007/08/dataservices"
  xmlns:m=
  "http://schemas.microsoft.com/ado/2007/08/dataservices/metadata"
  m:etag="W/&quot;4&quot;" xmlns="http://www.w3.org/2005/Atom">
  <id>
    http://gaston-pc/_vti_bin/listdata.svc/ProjectsList2010(26)
  </id>
  <title type="text">Testing the New Feature that Allows a User
    to Update a Title</title>
  <updated>2010-05-08T01:33:31-03:00</updated>
  <author>
    <name />
  </author>
  <link rel="edit" title="ProjectsList2010Item"
    href="ProjectsList2010(26)" />
  <link rel=
    "http://schemas.microsoft.com/ado/2007/08/dataservices/
    related/Predecessors" type="application/atom+xml;type=feed"
    title="Predecessors"
    href="ProjectsList2010(26)/Predecessors" />
  <link rel=
    "http://schemas.microsoft.com/ado/2007/08/dataservices/
    related/Priority" type="application/atom+xml;type=entry"
    title="Priority"
    href="ProjectsList2010(26)/Priority" />
  <link rel=
    "http://schemas.microsoft.com/ado/2007/08/dataservices/
    related/Status" type="application/atom+xml;
    type=entry" title="Status"
    href="ProjectsList2010(26)/Status" />
```

```
<link rel=
  "http://schemas.microsoft.com/ado/2007/08/dataservices/
  related/Attachments" type="application/atom+xml;
  type=feed" title="Attachments"
  href="ProjectsList2010(26)/Attachments" />
<category term=
  "Microsoft.SharePoint.DataService.ProjectsList2010Item"
  scheme="http://schemas.microsoft.com/ado/2007/08/
  dataservices/scheme" />
<content type="application/xml">
  <m:properties>
    <d:ContentTypeID>0x0108007C7838C285B9704DAA54BEB13213E3BA
      </d:ContentTypeID>
    <d:Title>Testing the New Feature that Allows a User to
      Update a Title</d:Title>
    <d:PriorityValue>(2) Normal</d:PriorityValue>
    <d:StatusValue>Not Started</d:StatusValue>
    <d:Complete m:type="Edm.Double">0.17</d:Complete>
    <d:AssignedToID m:type="Edm.Int32">1</d:AssignedToID>
    <d:TaskGroupID m:type="Edm.Int32" m:null="true" />
    <d:Description>&lt;div&gt;&lt;/div&gt;</d:Description>
    <d:StartDate m:type="Edm.DateTime">
      2010-03-28T00:00:00</d:StartDate>
    <d:DueDate m:type="Edm.DateTime">
      2010-04-20T00:00:00</d:DueDate>
    <d:Projects2010Approval m:type="Edm.Int32" m:null="true" />
    <d:ID m:type="Edm.Int32">26</d:ID>
    <d:ContentType>Task</d:ContentType>
    <d:Modified m:type="Edm.DateTime">
      2010-05-08T01:33:31</d:Modified>
    <d:Created m:type="Edm.DateTime">
      2010-04-02T17:51:25</d:Created>
    <d:CreatedByID m:type="Edm.Int32">6</d:CreatedByID>
    <d:ModifiedByID m:type="Edm.Int32">6</d:ModifiedByID>
    <d:Owshiddenversion m:type="Edm.Int32">
      4</d:Owshiddenversion>
    <d:Version>1.0</d:Version>
    <d:Path>/Lists/ProjectsList2010</d:Path>
  </m:properties>
</content>
</entry>
```

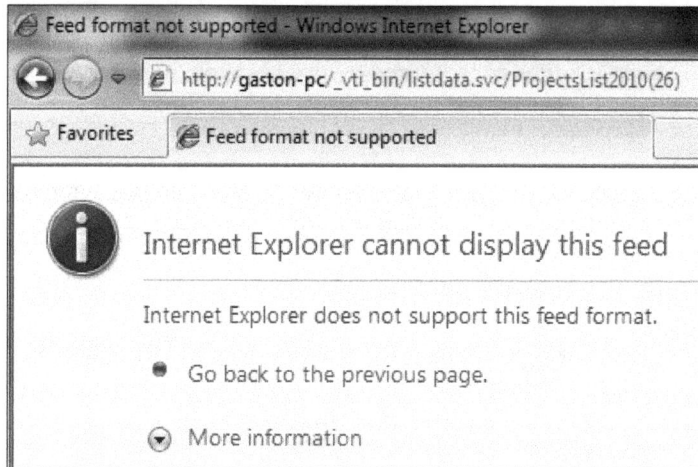

7. In fact, the URL pattern to request the feed for a specific field of an item is the following, where `<field>` has to be replaced with the field's name:

```
http://<site>:<port>/<subsite>/_vti_bin/listdata.
svc/<listname>(<index>)/<field>
```

8. Now, add a slash (/) and the name of one of the fields to the previously entered URL. In this case, `http://gaston-pc/_vti_bin/listdata.svc/ProjectsList2010(26)/PriorityValue` will display the Data Service Atom feed with value for the `PriorityValue` field for the item whose `ID` value is `26` for the `ProjectsList2010` SharePoint list in the `http://gaston-pc` SharePoint site. The web browser will display a simple XML document with the value for the requested field, as shown in the following lines:

```xml
<?xml version="1.0" encoding="utf-8" standalone="yes" ?>
<PriorityValue xmlns=
  "http://schemas.microsoft.com/ado/2007/08/dataservices">(2)
  Normal</PriorityValue>
```

9. You can also perform simple queries in the URL to perform expression-based filtering on a set. For example, you can use the `$filter` query string parameter to retrieve all the `Microsoft.SharePoint.DataService.ProjectList2010Item` items whose `PriorityValue` is equal to `(2) Normal` by entering the following URL, `http://gaston-pc/_vti_bin/listdata.svc/ProjectsList2010?$filter=PriorityValue eq '(2) Normal'`.

We consumed the `ListData.svc` WCF Data Service in our default web browser. We used many URL patterns to request the feed for a specific list, item and field.

Working with SharePoint 2010 WCF Data Services to display data from a list

We can apply other query string parameters but our main goal is to interact with the list in a new Silverlight RIA. Now, we are going to create a new solution in Visual Studio as we learned in the previous chapters. It will include two new projects:

- A Silverlight application project, `SLProjectsCRUD2010WCF`

- An empty SharePoint 2010 project with a module, `SPProjectsCRUD2010WCF`

Follow these steps to create the new Silverlight RIA that accesses the list in the SharePoint Server by using WCF Data Services:

1. Start Visual Studio as a system administrator user.

2. Follow the previously learned steps to create a new **Blank Solution**, `EventsViewer`.

3. Add a new project called `SLProjectsCRUD2010WCF` by going to **Visual C# | Silverlight | Silverlight Application**. Remember to select the options used in the previous examples.

4. Right-click on **References** within the `SLProjectsCRUD2010WCF` project, in **Solution Explorer** and select **Add Service Reference...** from the context menu. A new dialog box will appear.

5. Enter the URL to access the `ListData.svc` WCF Data Service in the **Address** textbox and then click on **Go**. The IDE will download the service information for the entered address; in this case, `http://gaston-pc/_vti_bin/` `listdata.svc`, and **HomeDataContext** will appear in the **Services** tree. Expand **HomeDataContext** and all the names of the lists in the SharePoint site collection will appear within the node, as shown in the next screenshot:

6. Enter `SharePointService` in the **Namespace** textbox and click **OK**. The new service reference, `SharePointService`, will appear in the `Service References` folder within `SLProjectsCRUD2010WCF` in **Solution Explorer**:

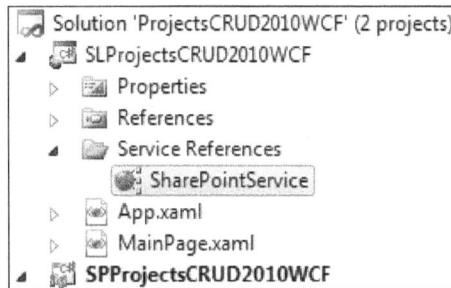

7. Right-click on `SharePointService` and select **View in Object Browser** in the context menu. The IDE will display the main node, `SLProjectsCRUD2010WCF.SharePointService` in the **Object Browser**. Expand this node and the definitions for `HomeDataContext`. The items and the values for the different lists will appear. If you click on `HomeDataContext`, one of its methods is `AddToProjectsList2010` and it allows you to add new items to the `ProjectsList2010` list.

8. If you click on `ProjectsList2010Item` all its methods and properties will appear on the panel located at the right. An instance of this class represents an item in the `ProjectsList2010` list. The `CreateProjectsList2010Item` static method also allows you to add a new item to the list.

The `ProjectsList2010Item` class offers properties for all the fields offered by the list, as shown in the next screenshot, and therefore, you can work with a strongly typed `System.Data.Services.Client.DataServiceContext`, `HomeDataContext`, and strongly typed lists. `HomeDataContext` represents the runtime context of the data service. You will also find the `ProjectsList-2010PriorityValue` and `ProjectsList2010StatusValue` classes that offer access to the values for the `Priority` and `Status` lookup fields.

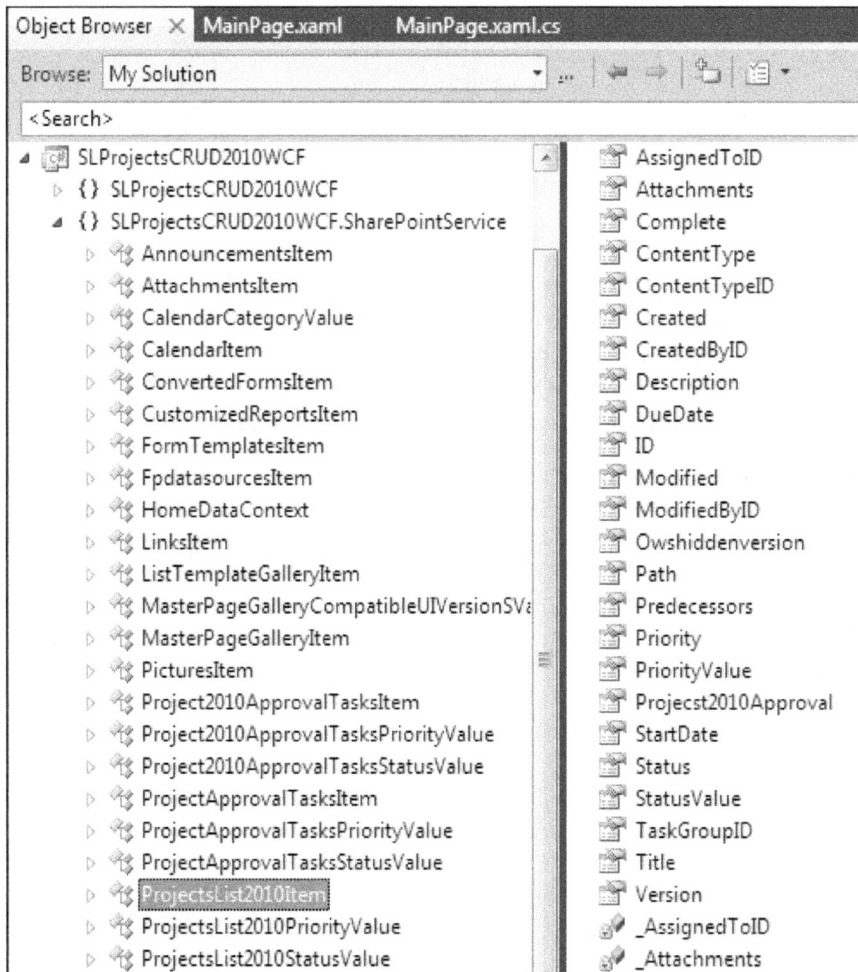

9. Click on the **Show All Files** button in **Solution Explorer** and expand
   `SharePointService`. You will find a `Reference.cs` code file within
   `Reference.datasvcmap`. The IDE generated this code to allow you to work
   with a strongly typed `DataServiceContext` against the SharePoint 2010
   WCF Data Services. This way, you are going to be able to use auto-complete
   features when coding. In fact, you can also use the **Object Browser** to check
   the methods and properties available for each list item class.

> It is also possible to generate the aforementioned `Reference.cs` code
> file by using the `DataSvcUtil.exe` command-line tool. WCF Data
> Services provides this tool that consumes an OData feed and generates
> the client data service classes that are needed to access a data service
> from a .NET framework client application. You can send the root URI
> of the Silverlight 2010 WCF Data Service and the utility requests the
> service metadata document that describes the data model exposed by
> the data service. You can access the `DataSvcUtil.exe` tool from the
> Visual Studio command prompt by selecting **Start | All Programs |
> Microsoft Visual Studio 2010 | Visual Studio Tools | Visual Studio
> 2010 Command Prompt**. If you want to generate a `Reference.cs`
> code file to be included in the Silverlight project for `http://gaston-`
> `pc/_vti_bin/listdata.svc`, you can specify the /uri and /out
> parameters and run the command in the desired destination folder. For
> example, as in this line, in the Visual Studio 2010 Command Prompt,
> `DataSvcUtil /uri:"http://gaston-pc/_vti_bin/listdata.`
> `svc" /language:CSharp /out:"Reference.cs"`. This way, the tool
> will generate the `References.cs` code file with the necessary C# code.
> However, you will have to make changes to the namespaces when you
> add this file to the project.

10. Open `MainPage.xaml`, define new `width` and `height` for the `Grid` as `800`
    and `600` respectively, and add the following controls:

    ○ One `Label` control, `lblStatus`.

    ○ One `DataGrid` control, `dataGridProjects`. Set its
      `AutoGenerateColumns` property to `true`.

    ○ One `Button` control, `butDelete`. Set its `Content` property
      to `Delete`.

11. Open `MainPage.xaml.cs` and add the following two `using` statements.
    `System.Data.Services.Client` represents the .NET framework client
    library that applications can use to interact with WCF Data Services and
    `SLProjectsCRUD2010WCF.SharePointService` is the namespace that
    contains all the classes with the strongly typed SharePoint 2010 Server
    WCF Data Services.

    ```
    using System.Data.Services.Client;
    using SLProjectsCRUD2010WCF.SharePointService;
    ```

12. Add the following `private` variable, `_context`, which will hold a reference
    to an instance of the runtime context of the data service:

    ```
    private SharePointService.HomeDataContext _context;
    ```

13. Add the following method to declare and execute a query request to
    SharePoint 2010 WCF Data Services:

    ```
    private void ShowProjects()
    {
        // Declare the LINQ query
        var projectsQuery = (from p in _context.ProjectsList2010
                select p) as DataServiceQuery
                <SharePointService.ProjectsList2010Item>;

        // Execute the LINQ query
        projectsQuery.BeginExecute(
            (IAsyncResult asyncResult) => Dispatcher.BeginInvoke(() =>
            {
                // Runs in the UI thread
                // EndExecute returns
                IEnumerable<ProjectsList2010Item>
                dataGridProjects.ItemsSource =
                    projectsQuery.EndExecute(asyncResult).ToList();
            }), projectsQuery);
    }
    ```

14. Add the following code to the `Loaded` event, `LayoutRoot_Loaded`, for the
    `LayoutRoot` Grid. You have to replace `"http://gaston-pc/_vti_bin/`
    `listdata.svc/"` with the URL to access the `ListData.svc` WCF Data
    Service.

    ```
    private void LayoutRoot_Loaded(object sender, RoutedEventArgs e)
    {
        // Get the context
        _context =
    ```

```
new SharePointService.HomeDataContext(
    new Uri("http://gaston-pc/_vti_bin/listdata.svc/",
        UriKind.Absolute));
    ShowProjects();
}
```

> In this case, the code uses a hardcoded value for the root URI of the Silverlight 2010 WCF Data Service, `"http://gaston-pc/_vti_bin/listdata.svc/"`. These kinds of values should be placed in a configuration file because they usually have different values for development and deployment uses. In this case, the code used the hardcoded value to simplify the example.

15. Now, follow the steps learned in *Chapter 2*, section *Creating a Silverlight RIA to be linked with a SharePoint module*, to create a new SharePoint module and link it to SLProjectsCRUD2010WCF. Use SPProjectsCRUD2010WCF as the new **Empty SharePoint Project**. Remember to enable Silverlight debugging instead of the default script debugging capabilities.

16. Right-click on the solution's name in **Solution Explorer** and select **Properties** from the context menu that appears. Select **Startup Project** in the list on the left, activate **Single startup project**, and choose SPProjectsCRUD2010WCF in the drop-down list. Then, click **OK**.

17. Build and deploy the solution.

18. Now that the WSP package has been deployed to the SharePoint site, follow the necessary steps to create a new web page, add the Silverlight Web Part, and include the Silverlight RIA in it. Remember that in this case, it isn't necessary to upload the .xap file because it was already deployed with the WSP package.

Consuming SharePoint 2010 WCF Data Services from a Silverlight Web Part

Follow these steps to test the Silverlight Web Part that allows a user to read data from the ProjectsList2010 list by using the client library in Silverlight to access SharePoint 2010 WCF Data Services.

1. Start your default web browser and load the SharePoint page that shows SLProjectsCRUD2010WCF.xap as a Silverlight Web Part, WCFTest.aspx.

2. The Web Part will display the values for all the fields of each item in the `ProjectsList2010` list in the grid:

WCF Test			
ContentTypeID	Title	PriorityValue	StatusValu
0x0108007C7838C285B9704DAA54BEB13213E3BA	Creating a Silverlight 4 UI	(2) Normal	Not Started
0x0108007C7838C285B9704DAA54BEB13213E3BA	Creating a Complex Silverlight 4 LOB RIA	(2) Normal	Not Started
0x0108007C7838C285B9704DAA54BEB13213E3BA	Testing Silverlight 4 COM with Lists in SharePoint 2010	(2) Normal	Not Started
0x0108007C7838C285B9704DAA54BEB13213E3BA	Testing Messages Between Silverlight Web Parts	(2) Normal	Not Started
0x0108007C7838C285B9704DAA54BEB13213E3BA	Testing the New Feature that Allows a User to Update a Title	(2) Normal	Not Started

The code in the `Loaded` event handler for the `LayoutRoot Grid` creates an instance of the `HomeDataContext` for the WCF Data Service reference, `SharePointService`. It sends a new absolute `Uri` as a parameter to its constructor, the URL to access the `ListData.svc` WCF Data Service. The `_context` private variable holds the reference to this instance.

```
_context =
    new SharePointService.HomeDataContext(
        new Uri("http://gaston-pc/_vti_bin/listdata.svc/",
            UriKind.Absolute));
```

> Remember that the `Uri` shouldn't be hardcoded so as to simplify working with different values for development and deployment.

Then, it calls the `ShowProjects` method that declares and executes a query request to the WCF Data Services accessed through `_context`, the runtime context of the data service. First, it declares a LINQ query, `projectsQuery`, cast to `DataServiceQuery<SharePointService.ProjectsList2010Item>`. The `DataServiceQuery<TElement>` class represents a single query request to WCF Data Services, where `TElement` is the type of results returned by the query. In this case, the execution of this query will return an `IEnumerable<ProjectsList2010Item>`. The following code uses the `DataServiceContext` generated by the **Add Service Reference** tool to define a query that retrieves all the items from `ProjectsList2010`:

```
var projectsQuery =
    (from p in _context.ProjectsList2010
     select p) as
    DataServiceQuery<SharePointService.ProjectsList2010Item>;
```

When you type `_context,` in the IDE's code editor, it will offer all the methods and properties for the runtime context of the data service, as shown in the next screenshot. As previously explained, the **Add Service Reference** tool generates classes to represent a strongly typed data model to simplify the consumption of WCF Data Services. Thus, it is easy to access the right list. This is one of the advantages of working with SharePoint 2010 WCF Data Services to query lists.

```
private void ShowProjects()
{
    // Declare the LINQ query
    var projectsQuery = (from p in _context.ProjectsList2010
                    select p) as Da
                                    ProjectsList2010
                                    ProjectsList2010Priority
    // Execute the LINQ query
                                    ProjectsList2010Status
    projectsQuery.BeginExecute(
                                    ProjectsListWW
        (IAsyncResult asyncResult) => Di
                                    ProjectsListWWPriority
        {
                                    ProjectsListWWStatus
            // Runs in the UI thread
                                    ReadingEntity
                                    ReportingMetadata
            // EndExecute returns IEnume
                                    ReportingTemplates
            // Remember to set dataGridP
            dataGridProjects.ItemsSource
```

Then, it is time to execute the query. The Silverlight client library for WCF Data Services only supports the asynchronous execution of queries. Therefore, the code calls the `BeginExecute` method for the `DataServiceQuery<SharePointService.ProjectsList2010Item>, projectsQuery`. This method starts an asynchronous network operation that executes the query. It is a LINQ query and not a CAML query. We learned about CAML queries in *Chapter 2,* in the section *Working with the ClientContext object*, and in *Chapter 4*, section *Applying dynamic filters in a CAML query*. This is another advantage of working with SharePoint 2010 WCF Data Services to query lists, because it isn't necessary to learn CAML and we can use most LINQ expressions against the data model. The biggest disadvantage is the need to run the queries with an asynchronous execution and the lack of support of LINQ joins.

The `BeginExecute` method receives two parameters:

- A `System.AsyncCallBack`, a callback. This is a delegate to invoke when the query completes its asynchronous execution.

- An `Object` used to transfer state between the start of the operation and the callback defined in the first parameter.

The method returns a `System.IAsyncResult` that represents the status of the asynchronous query. Thus, the code calls the `BeginExecute` method with a delegate that receives a `System.IAsyncResult` as a parameter, `asyncResult`, and defines another delegate to run in the UI thread by calling the `Dispatcher.BeginInvoke` method. As we are going to change the data binding properties for the `DataGrid` control, `dataGridProjects`, we have to make sure that the code runs in the UI thread.

The delegate calls the `EndExecute` method for the `DataServiceQuery<SharePointService.ProjectsList2010Item>`, `projectsQuery`. This method ends an asynchronous query request to a data service. It receives a `System.IAsyncResult` that represents the pending asynchronous query request, received as a parameter, `asyncResult`, and returns an `IEnumerable<TElement>`, where `TElement` is the type of results returned by the query. In this case, the `EndExecute` method returns an `IEnumerable<ProjectsList2010Item>`. The results are converted to a `List<ProjectsList2010Item>` by calling the `ToList()` extension method and then it is assigned to the `ItemsSource` property of the `dataGridProjects DataGrid`. The highlighted line runs in the UI thread.

```
projectsQuery.BeginExecute(
    (IAsyncResult asyncResult) => Dispatcher.BeginInvoke(() =>
    {
        dataGridProjects.ItemsSource =
                projectsQuery.EndExecute(asyncResult).ToList();
    }), projectsQuery);
```

The `BeginExecute` method runs in the UI thread but the callback can run in a different thread. Thus, it was necessary to use the `Dispatcher.BeginInvoke` method and add the code in another delegate within the first delegate, the callback. We can call the `EndExecute` method at this point because the callback will run after the asynchronous operation finishes (`asyncResult.IsCompleted` is going to be `true`) and we can collect the results. As we retrieved all the fields for each `ProjectsList2010Item` instance, the `dataGridProjects DataGrid` displays all of them.

The following sequence diagram shows the interaction between the methods defined in `MainPage` that are going to run in the UI thread, the single query request `DataServiceQuery<SharePointService.ProjectsList2010Item>`, `projectsQuery`, the callback that could run in another thread, that is, a worker thread, and the delegate scheduled by the callback to run in the UI thread. This sequence represents the situation in which the asynchronous query has a successful completion.

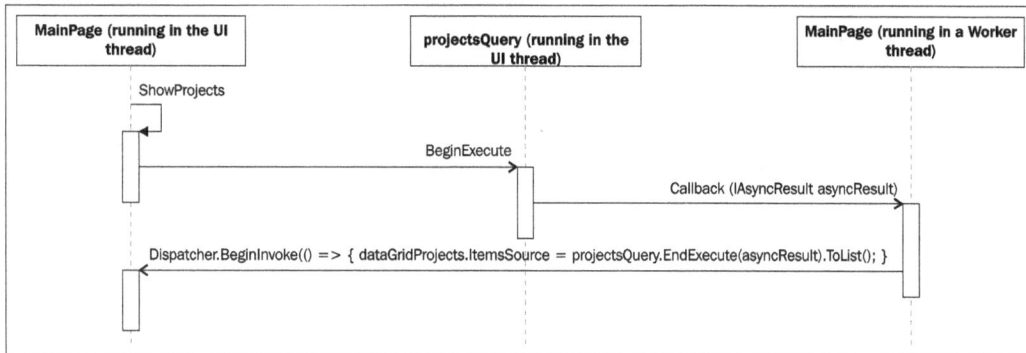

Performing CRUD operations with SharePoint 2010 WCF Data Services

We are now going to improve the Silverlight RIA to display the values for some of the fields in the `ProjectsList2010` list. As we cannot use joins in the queries against SharePoint 2010 WCF Data Services, we will have to combine some complex asynchronous executions to retrieve information for the user assigned to each item. In addition, we will enable the user to perform update and delete operations to the items shown in the grid. In this case, we won't add the messages explained in *Chapter 3* because we will add the insert operation in the same Silverlight RIA in the next sections. Follow these steps to add the new operations to the Silverlight RIA:

1. Stay in Visual Studio as a system administrator user.

2. Add a new class to the project named `Project`, in a new class file, `Project.cs`. Paste the same code that defined the `Project` class in the example created in *Chapter 2*, section *Creating a Silverlight RIA to be linked with a SharePoint module*. This time, we will fill its properties with the values of the fields retrieved from the list of tasks in SharePoint by querying the WCF Data Service model in many asynchronous operations.

```
public class Project
{
    public int ProjectId { get; set; }
    public string Title { get; set; }
    public int EstimatedDaysLeft { get; set; }
    public string Status { get; set; }
    public string AssignedTo { get; set; }
    public int NumberOfTasks { get; set; }
```

```
        public DateTime DueDate { get; set; }
        public DateTime StartDate { get; set; }
        public string Priority { get; set; }
    }
```

3. Add a new class to the project, `ProjectAndUser`. This class will allow us to return a `Project` instance with the username assigned to it as a result of a LINQ query.

```
public class ProjectAndUser
{
    public Project ProjectInstance { get; set; }
    public string AssignedToName { get; set; }
}
```

4. Open `MainPage.xaml.cs` and add the following two `private` variables:

```
private int _projectNumber;
private List<Project> _listProjects;
```

5. Replace the code in the `ShowProjects` method with the following lines. This time, it will run many asynchronous queries to fill all the properties for a new `Project` instance for each item in the `ProjectsList2010` list.

```
// Declare the LINQ query
// IMPORTANT NOTE: DataServiceQuery doesn't support join
var projectsQuery = (from p in _context.ProjectsList2010
                     select
                     new Project()
                     {
                         ProjectId = p.ID,
                         Title = p.Title,
                         StartDate = p.StartDate.Value,
                         DueDate = p.DueDate.Value,
                         EstimatedDaysLeft =
                             (p.DueDate.Value.Subtract(
                                 p.StartDate.Value).Days),
                         Status = p.Status.Value,
                         AssignedTo = p.AssignedToID.ToString(),
                         NumberOfTasks = 0,
                         Priority = p.Priority.Value
                     }) as DataServiceQuery<Project>;

// Execute the LINQ query
projectsQuery.BeginExecute(
    (IAsyncResult asyncResult) =>
```

```
{
    // EndExecute returns IEnumerable<Project>
    _listProjects =
            projectsQuery.EndExecute(asyncResult).ToList();
    _projectNumber = 0;

    for (int i = 0; i < _listProjects.Count; i++)
    {
        var userQuery = (from u in
                _context.UserInformationList
                        where u.ID ==
                Convert.ToInt32(_listProjects[i].AssignedTo)
                        select new ProjectAndUser
                        {
                            ProjectInstance =
                                    _listProjects[i],
                            AssignedToName = u.Name
                        }) as
                DataServiceQuery<ProjectAndUser>;

        // Execute the LINQ query
        var asyncResult2 = userQuery.BeginExecute(
            (IAsyncResult asyncResultUser) =>
                    Dispatcher.BeginInvoke(() =>
            {
                // EndExecute returns
                        IEnumerable<ProjectAndUser>
                var projectAndUser =
                userQuery.EndExecute(asyncResultUser).First();
                projectAndUser.ProjectInstance.AssignedTo =
                        projectAndUser.AssignedToName;

                // Make sure that the increment is an atomic
                        operation
                // In this case, it runs in the UI thread, the
                        main thread
                // and it isn't necessary
                // However, in other cases, if we don't
                        include the Dispatcher.BeginInvoke
                // it would be necessary
                System.Threading.Interlocked.Increment(ref
                        _projectNumber);

                if (_projectNumber == _listProjects.Count)
```

```
                          {
                              //This is the last project
                              dataGridProjects.ItemsSource =
                                  _listProjects;
                          }
                      }), userQuery);
              }
          }, projectsQuery);
```

6. Add the following code to the `Click` event for the `butDelete Button`. This way, when the user clicks on this button, the application will retrieve the `Project` instance selected in the `dataGridProjects DataGrid`, and use its ID to retrieve and delete the item from the list in the SharePoint server.

```
var selectedProject = (dataGridProjects.SelectedItem as Project);

// Declare the LINQ query
var projectsQuery = (from p in _context.ProjectsList2010
        where p.ID == selectedProject.ProjectId
        select p) as
        DataServiceQuery<SharePointService.ProjectsList2010Item>;

// Execute the LINQ query
projectsQuery.BeginExecute(
    (IAsyncResult asyncResult) => Dispatcher.BeginInvoke(() =>
    {
        // EndExecute returns IEnumerable<ProjectsList2010Item>
        var projectItem =
                projectsQuery.EndExecute(asyncResult).First();
        if (projectItem != null)
        {
            try
            {
                // Marks the project as deleted
                _context.DeleteObject(projectItem);
                // Saves the changes
                _context.BeginSaveChanges(
                    (IAsyncResult asyncResultSave) =>
                        Dispatcher.BeginInvoke(() =>
                    {
                        var response =
                        _context.EndSaveChanges(asyncResultSave);
                        lblStatus.Content = "Object deleted";
                        ShowProjects();
                    }), _context);
```

```
    }
    catch (DataServiceRequestException ex)
    {
        // Something went wrong when saving changes
        MessageBox.Show("An error occurred when saving
            changes. " + ex.Message);
    }
}
}), projectsQuery);
```

7. Add the following code to the `CellEditEnded` event for the `dataGridProjects` DataGrid. This way, when the user finishes editing the cell corresponding to the `Title` row, the application will retrieve the `Project` instance selected in the `dataGridProjects` DataGrid, and use its ID to update the value for the `Title` field in the corresponding item in the list in the SharePoint server.

```
if ((e.EditAction == DataGridEditAction.Commit) && (e.Column.
Header.Equals("Title")))
{
    var selectedProject = (dataGridProjects.SelectedItem as
                    Project);

    // Declare the LINQ query
    var projectsQuery = (from p in _context.ProjectsList2010
                    where p.ID == selectedProject.ProjectId
                    select p)
as DataServiceQuery<SharePointService.ProjectsList2010Item>;

    // Execute the LINQ query
    projectsQuery.BeginExecute(
        (IAsyncResult asyncResult) => Dispatcher.BeginInvoke(() =>
        {
            // EndExecute returns IEnumerable<ProjectsList2010Item>
            var projectItem =
                projectsQuery.EndExecute(asyncResult).First();
            if (projectItem != null)
            {
                // Assign the new value for the Title field
                projectItem.Title = selectedProject.Title;
                try
                {
                    // Marks the project as updated
                    _context.UpdateObject(projectItem);
```

```
                    // Saves the changes
                    _context.BeginSaveChanges(
                        (IAsyncResult asyncResultSave) =>
                            Dispatcher.BeginInvoke(() =>
                        {
                            var response =
                        _context.EndSaveChanges(asyncResultSave);
                            lblStatus.Content = "Object updated";
                        }), _context);
                }
                catch (DataServiceRequestException ex)
                {
                    // Something went wrong when saving changes
                    MessageBox.Show( "An error occurred when saving
                        changes. " + ex.Message);
                }
            }
        }), projectsQuery);
    }
```

8. Build and deploy the solution.

9. Load the SharePoint page that shows `SLProjectsCRUD2010WCF.xap` as a Silverlight Web Part, `WCFTest.aspx`.

10. The grid in the Silverlight Web Part will display the data retrieved from `ProjectsList2010`. This time, it will show the values for the properties defined in the `Project` class, as shown in the following screenshot. The `AssignedTo` column shows the usernames.

WCF Test					
ProjectId	Title	EstimatedDaysLeft	Status	AssignedTo	NumberO
1	Creating a Silverlight 4 UI	4	Not Started	gaston-PC\hillar2010	0
2	Creating a Complex Silverlight 4 LOB RIA	5	Not Started	GASTON-PC\gaston	0
13	Testing Silverlight 4 COM with Lists in SharePoint 2010	16	Not Started	gaston-PC\hillar2010	0
20	Testing Messages Between Silverlight Web Parts	3	Not Started	gaston-PC\hillar2010	0
26	Testing the New Feature that Allows a User to Update a Title	23	Not Started	GASTON-PC\gaston	0

11. Now, open a new tab in your web browser and add a new item to the list of tasks in SharePoint by using the list editor. Then, go back to the tab that is displaying the page with the Silverlight Web Part and refresh it. The new item will appear in the grid.

12. Click on the row that you want to delete in the grid and then click on the **Delete** button. The application will mark the corresponding `ProjectsList2010Item` instance as deleted in the WCF Data Services model and then will request the data context to save the changes in an asynchronous operation. Once this asynchronous operation completes its execution, the application will refresh the data shown in the grid. If the operation was successful, the row will disappear from the grid.

13. Double-click on the cell that contains the title that you want to update and you will enter the edit mode.

14. Press the *Tab* key and the application will request the SharePoint server to update the value for the `Title` field of the selected item from the list. If the operation was successful, the status label at the bottom will display the following message, **Object updated**, as shown in the next screenshot:

ProjectId	Title	EstimatedDaysLeft
1	Creating a Silverlight 4 UI	4
2	Creating a Complex Silverlight 4 LOB RIA	5
13	Testing Silverlight 4 COM with Lists in SharePoint 2010	16
20	Testing Messages Between Silverlight Web Parts	3
26	Testing SharePoint 2010 WCF Data Services	23

Object updated

The new version of the `ShowProjects` method declares and executes a query request to the WCF Data Services accessed through `_context`. First, the code declares a LINQ query, `projectsQuery`, cast to `DataServiceQuery<Project>` because it returns a new `Project` instance for each element in the `ProjectsList2010` list. It uses the `ProjectsList2010Item` properties to assign the values for the new `Project` instance properties.

`Priority` and `Status` are fields that offer many choices as their possible values. The `Priority` property for the `ProjectsList2010Item` instance, identified by `p` in the query, is a `ProjectsList2010PriorityValue` and the `Status` property is a `ProjectsList2010StatusValue`. Therefore, it is necessary to access their `Value` property to assign the corresponding string value to the string properties in the new `Project` instance.

```
var projectsQuery = (from p in _context.ProjectsList2010
                     select
                     new Project()
                     {
                         ProjectId = p.ID,
                         Title = p.Title,
                         StartDate = p.StartDate.Value,
                         DueDate = p.DueDate.Value,
                         EstimatedDaysLeft =
                             (p.DueDate.Value.Subtract(
                             p.StartDate.Value).Days),
                         Status = p.Status.Value,
                         AssignedTo = p.AssignedToID.ToString(),
                         NumberOfTasks = 0,
                         Priority = p.Priority.Value
                     }) as DataServiceQuery<Project>;
```

When you type `p.`, in the IDE's code editor, it will offer all the properties and methods for the `ProjectsList2010Item` class that represents the list item in the generated data model, as shown in the next screenshot. As you can work with strongly typed list items, it is easy to access the right property. This is another advantage of working with SharePoint 2010 WCF Data Services to access items from a list.

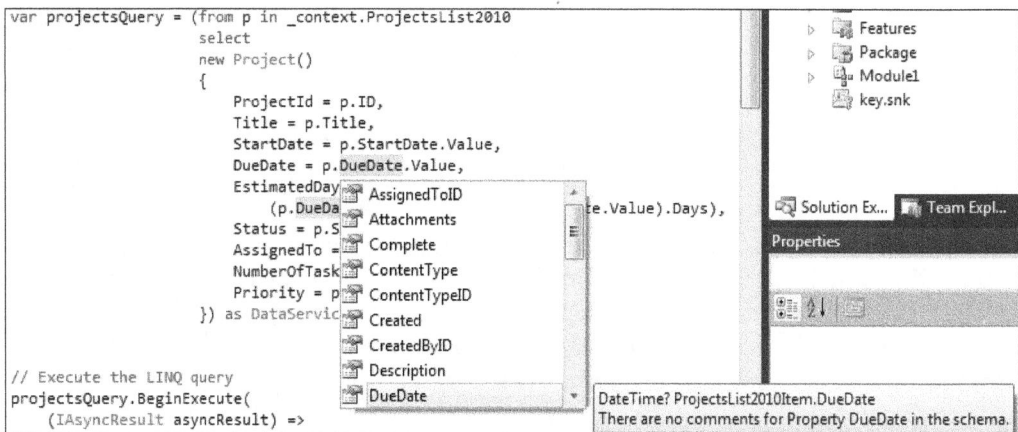

The `AssignedToID` property for the `ProjectsList2010Item` instance, identified by p in the query, offers the `ID` value for the user assigned to this task or project. We need to display the username and not his/her `ID`. The information about the users is available in the `UserInformationList` list but we cannot use a join in the query to retrieve the value for the `Name` field related to the `AssignedToID` value. Thus, we save this `ID` converted to a string in the `AssignedTo` property for the new `Project` instance and then we use this value to query the `Name` for each `Project` instance returned by the query execution.

The code calls the `BeginExecute` method for the `DataServiceQuery<Project>`, `projectsQuery`. The delegate calls the `EndExecute` method and returns an `IEnumerable<Project>`. The results are converted to a `List<Project>` by calling the `ToList()` extension method and then it is assigned to the private `List<Projects>` `_listProjects`. Then, it is necessary to retrieve the related user `Name` value for each `Project` instance. However, as the query for each `Project` instance will have an asynchronous execution, the code is a bit complicated. At this point, the code is running within the callback and it declares and executes a query request to the WCF Data Services accessed through `_context` for each `Project` instance in `_listProjects`. This LINQ query, `userQuery`, is cast to `DataServiceQuery<ProjectAndUser>` because it returns a new `ProjectAndUser` instance with the `Project` instance in `ProjectInstance` and the username in `AssignedToName`.

```
_listProjects = projectsQuery.EndExecute(asyncResult).ToList();
_projectNumber = 0;

for (int i = 0; i < _listProjects.Count; i++)
{
    var userQuery = (from u in _context.UserInformationList
                    where u.ID ==
                        Convert.ToInt32(_listProjects[i].AssignedTo)
                    select new ProjectAndUser
                    {
                        ProjectInstance = _listProjects[i],
                        AssignedToName = u.Name
                    }) as DataServiceQuery<ProjectAndUser>;
```

Then, the loop calls the `BeginExecute` method for the `DataServiceQuery<Proj
ectAndUser>`, `userQuery`, and its callback schedules a new delegate to run in the
UI thread by using the `Dispatcher.BeginInvoke` method. This delegate calls the
`EndExecute` method and returns an `IEnumerable<ProjectAndUser>`. As we expect
just one item as a result for this query, it calls the `First()` extension method to
return the first element of the sequence, a `ProjectAndUser` instance, and assigns
it to the `projectAndUser` local variable. Then, the code assigns the value of the
`projectAndUser.AssignedToName` property to the `AssignedTo` property for the
`Project` instance, `projectAndUser.ProjectInstance`. As the loop will declare and
execute many asynchronous queries, there are going to be many callbacks and the
delegates that they schedule to run in the UI thread. There is no guarantee about the
exact order in which the asynchronous queries are going to finish their execution,
and therefore, we saved a reference to the `Project` instance and the username
for each query result to process. We cannot use `i` or `_projectNumber` to
access `_listProjects` with an index because there is no sequential and ordered
execution; each callback will run after each query finishes its asynchronous operation
and we don't know the exact order.

When the last `ProjectAndUser` instance is processed, it is necessary to assign
`_listProject` to the `ItemsSource` property of the `dataGridProjects` DataGrid.
As the delegate is running in the UI thread, there is no problem changing the
properties for this control. In order to track the number of `ProjectAndUser` instances
processed by these asynchronous operations, each delegate finishes the assignment
to the `AssignedTo` property and `_projectNumber` increments its value. When
`_projectNumber` is equal to `_listProjects.Count`, all the projects have been
processed and it is possible to bind the `List<Project>` to the `DataGrid` because
it will display the right values for all the fields. The code uses an atomic and
thread-safe operation to increment the value of `_projectNumber`, `System.
Threading.Interlocked.Increment`. In this case, this code will run in the UI thread
but in some cases the delegates can run in different worker threads and it is a good
idea to use atomic operations when you need to increment or decrement variables
shared between all these delegates that could run concurrently. Again, in the UI
thread, they won't run concurrently because there is just one UI thread, but in other
cases, it would be necessary to avoid undesired bugs due to concurrency. The next
lines show the code that performs these operations and the delegate that runs in the
UI thread:

```
var asyncResult2 = userQuery.BeginExecute(
    (IAsyncResult asyncResultUser) =>
    Dispatcher.BeginInvoke(() =>
    {
        var projectAndUser =
            userQuery.EndExecute(asyncResultUser).First();
        projectAndUser.ProjectInstance.AssignedTo =
```

```
        projectAndUser.AssignedToName;
    System.Threading.Interlocked.Increment(
        ref _projectNumber);
    if (_projectNumber == _listProjects.Count)
    {
        dataGridProjects.ItemsSource = _listProjects;
    }
}), userQuery);
```

Deleting an item from a list with SharePoint 2010 WCF Data Services

When a user clicks the **Delete** button, the `Click` event handler `butDelete_Click`, runs in the UI thread. The method assigns the value for the data item corresponding to the selected row in the `dataGridProjects DataGrid` to the `selectedProject` local variable. It does so by accessing the `dataGridProjects.SelectedItem` property and casting it to `Project`, because it represents a `Project` instance.

```
var selectedProject =
    (dataGridProjects.SelectedItem as Project);
```

Then, the code declares and executes a query request to the WCF Data Services accessed through `_context`. First, the code declares a LINQ query, `projectsQuery`, cast to `DataServiceQuery<SharePointService.ProjectsList2010Item>`. It selects the `ProjectsList2010Item` item whose `ID` is equal to `selectedProject.ProjectId`.

```
var projectsQuery = (from p in _context.ProjectsList2010
        where p.ID == selectedProject.ProjectId
        select p) as
        DataServiceQuery<SharePointService.ProjectsList2010Item>;
```

Then, it is time to execute the query to retrieve `ProjectsList2010Item`. The code calls the `BeginExecute` method for `DataServiceQuery<SharePointService.ProjectsList2010Item>`, `projectsQuery`, and its callback schedules a delegate to run in the UI thread by using the `Dispatcher.BeginInvoke` method. This delegate calls the `EndExecute` method and returns an `IEnumerable<SharePointService.ProjectsList2010Item>`. As we expect just one item as a result for this query, it calls the `First()` extension method to return the first element of the sequence, a `ProjectsList2010Item` instance, and assigns it to the `projectItem` local variable. If `projectItem` isn't null, there is still an item with the `ID` in the `ProjectsList2010` list and the code starts a `try-catch` block. The code calls the `DeleteObject` method for `_context` sending the `ProjectList2010Item` instance, `projectItem`, as a parameter. This way, the data service context changes the state of the `ProjectList2010Item` instance, `projectItem`, to be deleted.

However, at this point, the operation isn't reflected in the `ProjectsList2010` list. It is necessary to submit the pending changes performed to the data service context states by calling the `BeginSaveChanges` method. The code performs the following sequence:

1. The `BeginSaveChanges` method asynchronously submits the changes and one of its definitions receives two parameters:

    ○   A `System.AsyncCallBack`, a callback. It is a delegate to invoke when the operation completes its asynchronous execution.

    ○   A state `Object` used to pass context data to the callback method.

2. The method returns a `System.IAsyncResult` that represents the status of the asynchronous operation.

3. The code calls the `BeginSaveChanges` method with a delegate that receives a `System.IAsyncResult` as a parameter, `asyncResultSave`, and defines another delegate to run in the UI thread by calling the `Dispatcher.BeginInvoke` method. As we are going to change the `Content` property for a `Label` control, `lblStatus`, we have to make sure that the code runs in the UI thread. The delegate calls the `EndSaveChanges` method for `_context`. This method completes an asynchronous `BeginSaveChanges` operation. It receives a `System.IAsyncResult` that represents the pending asynchronous query request, received as a parameter, `asyncResultSave`, and returns a `System.Data.Services.Client.DataServiceResponse` that indicates the result of the batch operation. In this case, the code doesn't check the results of the `EndSaveChanges` method to simplify the example but catches a `DataServiceRequestException` if something goes wrong.

4. After the call to `EndSaveChanges`, the `lblStatus` Label changes its `Content` property and the code calls the `ShowProjects` method to retrieve the items from the list and refresh the contents of the `DataGrid`.

```
projectsQuery.BeginExecute(
    (IAsyncResult asyncResult) =>
    Dispatcher.BeginInvoke(() =>
    {
        var projectItem = projectsQuery.EndExecute(asyncResult).
                First();
        if (projectItem != null)
        {
            try
            {
```

```
            _context.DeleteObject(projectItem);
            _context.BeginSaveChanges(
                (IAsyncResult asyncResultSave) =>
                Dispatcher.BeginInvoke(() =>
                {
                  var response =
                    _context.EndSaveChanges(asyncResultSave);
                  lblStatus.Content = "Object deleted";
                }), _context);
        }
        catch (DataServiceRequestException ex)
        {
            MessageBox.Show("An error occurred when saving
                changes. " + ex.Message);
        }
    }
}), projectsQuery);
```

Updating an item in a list with SharePoint 2010 WCF Data Services

When the user finishes editing a cell in the `dataGridProjects DataGrid`, the `CellEditEnded` event handler, `dataGridProjects_CellEditEnded`, runs in the UI thread. If the edited column was the one corresponding to the `Title` field and the user committed the edit action, it runs the necessary code to update the corresponding item in the list with the new value for the `Title` field. It uses the values provided in the `EditAction` and `Column.Header` properties from the `DataGridCellEditEndedEventArgs e` parameter to determine that the conditions are satisfied.

```
if ((e.EditAction == DataGridEditAction.Commit) &&
    (e.Column.Header.Equals("Title")))
```

The method assigns the value for the data item corresponding to the selected row in the `dataGridProjects DataGrid` to the `selectedProject` local variable, as previously explained for the delete operation. Then, the code declares and executes a query request to the WCF Data Services accessed through `_context` to retrieve the `ProjectsList2010Item` item whose `ID` is equal to `selectedProject.ProjectId`.

```
var selectedProject =
        (dataGridProjects.SelectedItem as Project);
```

```
var projectsQuery = (from p in _context.ProjectsList2010
                where p.ID == selectedProject.ProjectId
                select p) as
        DataServiceQuery<SharePointService.ProjectsList2010Item>;
```

Then, it is time to execute the query to retrieve `ProjectsList2010Item`. The code performs the following sequence:

1. The code calls the `BeginExecute` method for the `DataServiceQuery<SharePointService.ProjectsList2010Item>`, `projectsQuery`, and its callback schedules a delegate to run in the UI thread by using the `Dispatcher.BeginInvoke` method.

2. This delegate calls the `EndExecute` method and returns an `IEnumerable<SharePointService.ProjectsList2010Item>`. As we expect just one item as a result for this query, it calls the `First()` extension method to return the first element of the sequence, a `ProjectsList2010Item` instance, and assigns it to the `projectItem` local variable.

3. If `projectItem` isn't null, there is still an item with the `ID` in the `ProjectsList2010` list. The code assigns the new value for the `Title` field to `projectItem.Title` and starts a `try-catch` block. It is necessary to update `projectItem.Title` because the `dataGridProjects` DataGrid changed the value of the `Title` property for the `Project` instance but not to the related `ProjectList2010Item` instance that was retrieved with the query from the SharePoint 2010 server. The code calls the `UpdateObject` method for `_context` sending the `ProjectList2010Item` instance, `projectItem`, as a parameter. This way, the data service context changes the state of `projectItem` to modified.

4. However, at this point, the operation isn't reflected in the `ProjectsList2010` list. It is necessary to submit the pending changes performed to the data service context states by calling the `BeginSaveChanges` method. The code calls this method with a delegate that receives a `System.IAsyncResult` as a parameter, `asyncResultSave`, and defines another delegate to run in the UI thread by calling the `Dispatcher.BeginInvoke` method. The delegate calls the `EndSaveChanges` method for `_context`. This method completes the asynchronous `BeginSaveChanges` operation. It receives `asyncResultSave` and returns a `System.Data.Services.Client.DataServiceResponse`. Again, the code doesn't check the results of the `EndSaveChanges` method to simplify the example but catches a `DataServiceRequestException` if something goes wrong.

```
projectsQuery.BeginExecute(
    (IAsyncResult asyncResult) =>
    Dispatcher.BeginInvoke(() =>
```

```
    {
        var projectItem = projectsQuery.EndExecute(asyncResult).
                First();
        if (projectItem != null)
        {
            // Assign the new value for the Title field
            projectItem.Title = selectedProject.Title;
            try
            {
                _context.UpdateObject(projectItem);
                _context.BeginSaveChanges(
                (IAsyncResult asyncResultSave) =>
                Dispatcher.BeginInvoke(() =>
                    {
                        var response =
                            _context.EndSaveChanges(asyncResultSave);
                        lblStatus.Content = "Object updated";
                    }), _context);
            }
            catch (DataServiceRequestException ex)
            {
                MessageBox.Show( "An error occurred when saving
                    changes. " + ex.Message);
            }
        }
    }), projectsQuery);
```

Working with SharePoint 2010 WCF Data Services to insert items

Now, we are going to improve the Silverlight RIA to allow a user to insert a new item to the list in the SharePoint server by using SharePoint 2010 WCF Data Services. In addition, we will use the data model to load the possible choices for the `Priority` and `Status` fields and we will also fill a drop-down list with all the usernames to assign to a new project. Follow these steps to add the new features and operations to the Silverlight RIA:

   1. Stay in Visual Studio as a system administrator user.

2. Open `MainPage.xaml` and add a new `Grid` below the `DataGrid` `dataGridProjects`. Then add the following controls within the new `Grid` and align them as shown in the next screenshot:

  ○ Six `Label` controls aligned at the left with the following values for their `Content` properties:

  - **Title**

  - **Priority**

  - **Status**

  - **% Complete**

  - **Start Date**

  - **Due Date**

  - **Assigned To**

  ○ One `TextBox` control, `txtTitle`.

  ○ One `ComboBox` control, `cboPriority`.

  ○ One `ComboBox` control, `cboStatus`.

  ○ One `ComboBox` control, `cboAssignedTo`.

  ○ One `Slider` control, `sldPercentComplete`. Set `LargeChange` to `10`, Maximum to `100`, and `Minimum` to `0`. This slider will allow the user to set the percentage of the total work that has been completed.

  ○ One `DatePicker` control, `dtStartDate`.

  ○ One `DatePicker` control, `dtDueDate`.

  ○ One `Button` control, `butInsert`. Set its `Title` property to `Insert`.

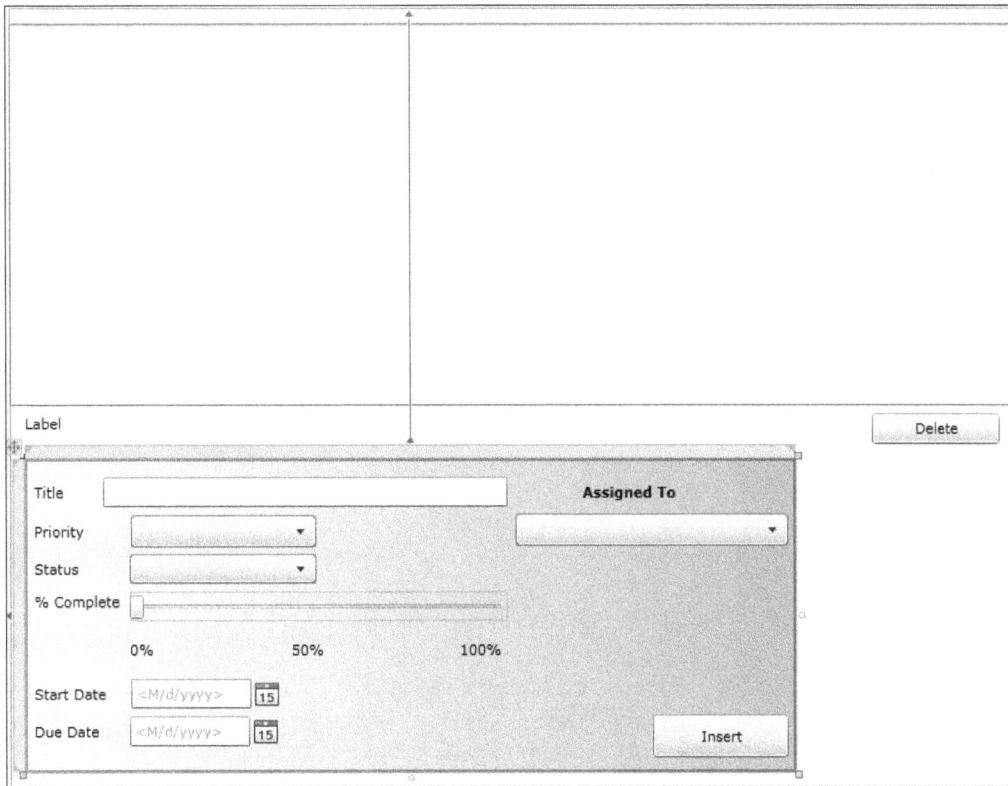

3. Open `MainPage.xaml.cs`. Add the following method to fill the drop-down lists that will display the different options for the user assigned to the new item, the priority, and the status.

```
private void FillComboBoxes()
{
    // Declare the LINQ query
    var priorityValuesQuery = (from value in
                _context.ProjectsList2010Priority
                        select value) as
DataServiceQuery<SharePointService.ProjectsList2010PriorityValue>;

    // Execute the LINQ query
    priorityValuesQuery.BeginExecute(
        (IAsyncResult asyncResultP) => Dispatcher.BeginInvoke(()=>
        {
            // Runs in the UI Thread
            // EndExecute returns
                IEnumerable<ProjectsList2010PriorityValue>
```

```
            var priorityValues =
            priorityValuesQuery.EndExecute(asyncResultP).ToList();

            foreach (ProjectsList2010PriorityValue pValue in
                priorityValues)
            {
                cboPriority.Items.Add(pValue.Value);
            }
        }), priorityValuesQuery);

    // Declare the LINQ query
    var statusValuesQuery = (from value in
            _context.ProjectsList2010Status
                        select value) as
DataServiceQuery<SharePointService.ProjectsList2010StatusValue>;

    // Execute the LINQ query
    statusValuesQuery.BeginExecute(
        (IAsyncResult asyncResultS) => Dispatcher.BeginInvoke(() =>
        {
            // Runs in the UI Thread
            // EndExecute returns
                    IEnumerable<ProjectsList2010StatusValue>
            var statusValues =
                statusValuesQuery.EndExecute(asyncResultS).ToList();

            foreach (ProjectsList2010StatusValue sValue in
                statusValues)
            {
                cboStatus.Items.Add(sValue.Value);
            }
        }), statusValuesQuery);

    // Declare the LINQ query
    var usersQuery = (from value in _context.UserInformationList
                        select value) as
DataServiceQuery<SharePointService.UserInformationListItem>;

    // Execute the LINQ query
    usersQuery.BeginExecute(
        (IAsyncResult asyncResultU) => Dispatcher.BeginInvoke(()=>
        {
            // Runs in the UI Thread
            // EndExecute returns
                    IEnumerable<UserInformationListItem>
```

```
            var users =
                usersQuery.EndExecute(asyncResultU).ToList();

            foreach (UserInformationListItem user in users)
            {
                cboAssignedTo.Items.Add(user);
            }
            // Dispay the value of the Name property
            // for the UserInformationListItem instance
            cboAssignedTo.DisplayMemberPath = "Name";
        }), usersQuery);
}
```

4. Add the following line to the LayoutRoot_Loaded event:

```
private void LayoutRoot_Loaded(object sender, RoutedEventArgs e)
{
    // Get the context
    _context =
        new SharePointService.HomeDataContext(
            new Uri("http://gaston-pc/_vti_bin/listdata.svc/",
                UriKind.Absolute));
    // Fill the comboboxes with the possible choices
    FillComboBoxes();

    ShowProjects();
}
```

5. Add the following line to the Click event for the butInsert Button. This way, when the user clicks on this button, the application will add a new item to the ProjectsList2010 list considering the values entered by the user in the controls.

```
var newProject = new ProjectsList2010Item();

newProject.Title = txtTitle.Text;
newProject.StartDate = dtStartDate.SelectedDate;
newProject.DueDate = dtDueDate.SelectedDate;
newProject.StatusValue = cboStatus.SelectedValue.ToString();
newProject.PriorityValue = cboPriority.SelectedValue.ToString();
newProject.AssignedToID = (cboAssignedTo.SelectedItem as
UserInformationListItem).ID;
newProject.Complete =
    (Math.Round(sldPercentComplete.Value, 0) / 100);

try
{
```

```
        // Add the new project to the list
        _context.AddToProjectsList2010(newProject);
        // Saves the changes
        _context.BeginSaveChanges(
            (IAsyncResult asyncResultSave) =>
              Dispatcher.BeginInvoke(() =>
            {
                // Runs in the UI Thread
                var response =
                  _context.EndSaveChanges(asyncResultSave);
                lblStatus.Content = "Object inserted";
                // Update the projects shown in the grid
                ShowProjects();
            }), _context);
    }
    catch (DataServiceRequestException ex)
    {
        // Something went wrong when saving changes
        MessageBox.Show("An error occurred when saving changes. " +
            ex.Message);
    }
```

6. Build and deploy the solution.

7. Load the `WCFTest.aspx` page that shows `SLProjectsCRUD2010WCF.xap` as a Silverlight Web Part.

8. Enter a value for the **Title**. Select a value for both the **Priority** and the **Status** drop-down lists, use the slider to specify the percentage of the work completed so far, and select both the **Start Date** and the **Due Date** by clicking on the datetime pickers. Then, select a user from the **Assigned To** drop-down list. The following screenshot shows some values and the elegant drop-down list that offers the alternatives for **Assigned To**:

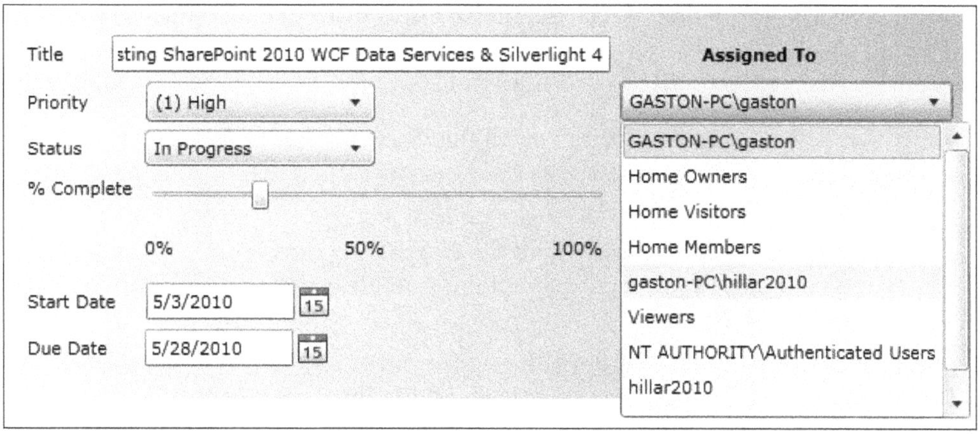

Title	sting SharePoint 2010 WCF Data Services & Silverlight 4		Assigned To
Priority	(1) High ▼		GASTON-PC\gaston ▼
Status	In Progress ▼		GASTON-PC\gaston
% Complete			Home Owners
			Home Visitors
	0% 50% 100%		Home Members
			gaston-PC\hillar2010
Start Date	5/3/2010 `15`		Viewers
Due Date	5/28/2010 `15`		NT AUTHORITY\Authenticated Users
			hillar2010

9. Click on the **Insert** button. The application is going to add the new item to the list and will refresh the grid to show the new row, as shown in the following screenshot:

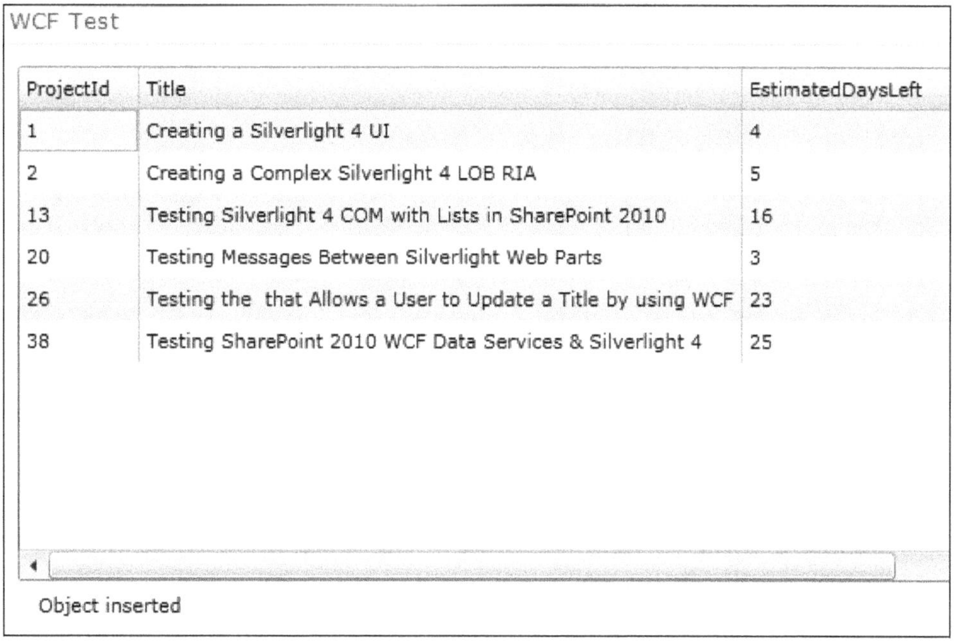

WCF Test

ProjectId	Title	EstimatedDaysLeft
1	Creating a Silverlight 4 UI	4
2	Creating a Complex Silverlight 4 LOB RIA	5
13	Testing Silverlight 4 COM with Lists in SharePoint 2010	16
20	Testing Messages Between Silverlight Web Parts	3
26	Testing the that Allows a User to Update a Title by using WCF	23
38	Testing SharePoint 2010 WCF Data Services & Silverlight 4	25

Object inserted

10. Open or refresh the items for the list in the corresponding SharePoint 2010 page and you will see the new item added to the list with the values entered in the application.

The `FillComboBoxes` method declares and executes three query requests to the WCF Data Services accessed through `_context`, the runtime context of the data service. Then, it uses the results to fill the drop-down lists:

- `priorityValuesQuery` retrieves all the `SharePointService.ProjectsList2010PriorityValue` items and adds their `Value` property to `cboPriority.Items`.

- `statusValuesQuery` retrieves all the `SharePointService.ProjectsList2010StatusValue` items and adds their `Value` property to `cboStatus.Items`.

- `usersQuery` retrieves all the `SharePointService.UserInformationListItem` items and adds the instances to `cboAssignedTo.Items`.

As we want to display the `Name` property for the `UserInformationListItem` in the `cboAssignedTo` ComboBox, the code assigns `"Name"` to its `DisplayMemberPath` property.

```
foreach (UserInformationListItem user in users)
{
    cboAssignedTo.Items.Add(user);
}

cboAssignedTo.DisplayMemberPath = "Name";
```

When the user clicks the **Insert** button, the `Click` event handler runs in the UI thread. This method creates a new `ProjectList2010Item` instance, `newProject`.

```
var newProject = new ProjectsList2010Item();
```

Then, the code completes the value for each field by using its properties and assigning the values written or selected by the user, as shown in the following lines:

```
newProject.Title = txtTitle.Text;
newProject.StartDate = dtStartDate.SelectedDate;
newProject.DueDate = dtDueDate.SelectedDate;
newProject.StatusValue = cboStatus.SelectedValue.ToString();
newProject.PriorityValue = cboPriority.SelectedValue.ToString();
newProject.AssignedToID =
        (cboAssignedTo.SelectedItem as UserInformationListItem).ID;
newProject.Complete =
    (Math.Round(sldPercentComplete.Value, 0) / 100);
```

For the `Status` and `Priority` fields, we can assign the string value in `StatusValue` and `PriorityValue`. However, for the user assigned to this new task or project, we have to complete the `AssignedToID` value with a valid user `ID`. The code casts the `cboAssignedTo.SelectedItem` to `UserInformationListItem` and assigns its `ID`. As the `FillComboBoxes` method filled `cboAssignedTo` with `UserInformationListItem` instances, we can access the `ID` property for the selected instance. The Silverlight RIA doesn't include code to validate the data that is going to be added to the list in the SharePoint server has appropriate values. The code performs the following sequence:

1. The code starts a `try...catch` block.

2. It calls the `_context.AddToProjectsList2010` method with the new `ProjectsList2010Item` instance, `newProject`, as a parameter. This way, the data service context adds the new `ProjectList2010Item` instance and sets its state to `Added`.

3. However, at this point, the operation isn't reflected in the `ProjectsList2010` list. It is necessary to submit the pending changes performed to the data service context states by calling the `BeginSaveChanges` method. The code calls this method with a delegate that receives a `System.IAsyncResult` as a parameter, `asyncResultSave`, and defines another delegate to run in the UI thread by calling the `Dispatcher.BeginInvoke` method. The delegate calls the `EndSaveChanges` method for `_context`. This method completes the asynchronous `BeginSaveChanges` operation. It receives `asyncResultSave` and returns a `System.Data.Services.Client.DataServiceResponse`. Again, the code doesn't check the results of the `EndSaveChanges` method to simplify the example but catches a `DataServiceRequestException` if something goes wrong.

4. After the call to `EndSaveChanges`, the `lblStatus` Label changes its `Content` property.

5. The code calls the `ShowProjects` method to retrieve the items from the list and refresh the contents of the `DataGrid`, with the new item.

```
try
{
    _context.AddToProjectsList2010(newProject);
    _context.BeginSaveChanges(
        (IAsyncResult asyncResultSave) =>
        Dispatcher.BeginInvoke(() =>
        {
            // Runs in the UI Thread
            var response =
                _context.EndSaveChanges(asyncResultSave);
```

```
                    lblStatus.Content = "Object inserted";
                    ShowProjects();
            }), _context);
    }
    catch (DataServiceRequestException ex)
    {
        MessageBox.Show("An error occurred when saving changes. " +
            ex.Message);
    }
```

The `AddToProjectsList2010` method allows you to add a new item to the `ProjectsList2010` list. If you have a different list, the method name is going to follow the same pattern—`AddTo` as a prefix and the list name as a suffix. For example, if the list name is `MyVideos`, the method is going to be `AddToMyVideos`.

> The previous examples focused on the interaction with SharePoint lists by using SharePoint 2010 WCF Data Services as an alternative to the Client OM. However, WCF Data Services are very powerful and they offer many other features that you can also use to work against a SharePoint 2010 server. The concepts of talking to services and communicating with WCF Data Services and REST services are described in-depth in *Microsoft Silverlight 4 Data and Services Cookbook* by Gill Cleeren and Kevin Dockx, Packt Publishing.

Using LINQ to objects to perform joins

We are now going to use another alternative to retrieve information for the user assigned to each item. Intead of running many complex asynchronous executions to retrieve the user related to each item in the `ProjectsList2010` list, we are going to use a LINQ to objects query to perform a join on two lists.

1. Stay in Visual Studio as a system administrator user.

2. Open `MainPage.xaml.cs` and replace the code in the `ShowProjects` method with the following lines. This time, it will run two asynchronous queries to retrieve all the items for the `ProjectsList2010` and `UserInformationList` lists. Then, it will perform a LINQ to objects query to retrieve the `Name` value for the user assigned to each task in the `ProjectsList2010` list.

   ```
   // IMPORTANT NOTE: DataServiceQuery doesn't support join
   // This is another alternative to the previous examples
   // Declare the LINQ query to retrieve all the ProjectsList2010
   list items
   ```

```
var projectsQuery = (from p in _context.ProjectsList2010
                     select p) as
DataServiceQuery<SharePointService.ProjectsList2010Item>;

// Execute the first LINQ query
projectsQuery.BeginExecute(
    (IAsyncResult asyncResultP) =>
    {
        // EndExecute returns IEnumerable<ProjectsList2010Item>
        var listPL2010Item =
                projectsQuery.EndExecute(asyncResultP).ToList();

        // Declare the second LINQ query to retrieve all the users
        // In order to simplify the example,
        // the query doesn't apply a filter to limit the users
        var usersQuery = (from u in _context.UserInformationList
                          select u) as
        DataServiceQuery<SharePointService.UserInformationListItem>;

        // Execute the second LINQ query
        usersQuery.BeginExecute(
            (IAsyncResult asyncResultU) =>
                Dispatcher.BeginInvoke(() =>
            {
                // EndExecute returns
                //     IEnumerable<UserInformationListItem>
                var listUsers =
                    usersQuery.EndExecute(asyncResultU).ToList();

                // In this case
                // p.Status.Value was replaced by p.StatusValue
                // p.Priority.Value was replaced by
                //     p.PriorityValue
                // Now, use LINQ to Objects to perform a join
                // between listUsers and listPL2010Item
                var joinQuery =
                    (from u in listUsers
                     join p in listPL2010Item on u.ID equals
                         p.AssignedToID
                     orderby p.Title
                     select
                     new Project()
                     {
                         ProjectId = p.ID,
                         Title = p.Title,
```

```
                              StartDate = p.StartDate.Value,
                              DueDate = p.DueDate.Value,
                              EstimatedDaysLeft =
                                  (p.DueDate.Value.Subtract(
                                  p.StartDate.Value).Days),
                              Status = p.StatusValue,
                              AssignedTo = u.Name,
                              NumberOfTasks = 0,
                              Priority = p.PriorityValue
                          }

                      );

              listProjects = joinQuery.ToList();

              dataGridProjects.ItemsSource = listProjects;
          }), usersQuery);
      }, projectsQuery);
```

3. Build and deploy the solution.

4. Load the `WCFTest.aspx` page that shows `SLProjectsCRUD2010WCF.xap` as a Silverlight Web Part.

5. The grid in the Silverlight Web Part will display the data retrieved from the list of tasks, `ProjectsList2010`. This time, it will just run two queries to the SharePoint Server to retrieve the data for the grid. The `AssignedTo` column shows the usernames.

The new version of the `ShowProjects` method performs the following sequence:

  ° The code declares and executes a query request to the WCF Data Services accessed through `_context`. First, the code declares a LINQ query, `projectsQuery`, cast to `DataServiceQuery<SharePointService.ProjectsList2010Item>` because it returns each element in the `ProjectsList2010` list.

  ° This delegate calls the `EndExecute` method and returns an `IEnumerable<SharePointService.ProjectsList2010Item>`. The results are converted to a `List<ProjectsList2010Item>` by calling the `ToList()` extension method and assigned to a local variable, `listPL2010Item`.

- ° Then, the code declares a second query request to the WCF Data Services. The new declaration for a LINQ query, `usersQuery`, appears cast to `DataServiceQuery<SharePoi ntService.UserInformationListItem>` because it returns each element in the `UserInformationList` list.

- ° The code calls the `BeginExecute` method for the `DataServic eQuery<SharePointService.UserInformationListItem>`, `usersQuery`, and its callback schedules a delegate to run in the UI thread by using the `Dispatcher.BeginInvoke` method. This time, we are going to make changes to controls and we have to make sure that the code runs in the UI thread.

> In this case, the code isn't applying a filter and the query, `usersQuery`, returns all the users from the SharePoint server. This example tries to offer another alternative to perform a LINQ to objects with the results of two queries to lists on the SharePoint Server. However, we should retrieve only the necessary fields and items from the list. A SharePoint Server could have thousands of users. It is possible to improve the code to return only the necessary fields and to add a filter to request only the necessary users.

6. This new delegate calls the `EndExecute` method and returns an `IEnumerable<SharePointService.UserInformationListItem>`. The results are converted to a `List<UserInformationListItem>` by calling the `ToList()` extension method and assigned to a local variable, `listUsers`.

7. The code declares a LINQ to objects query, `joinQuery`, which performs a join between `listPL2010Item` and `listsUsers`. The join allows the code to access the `Name` value for the `UserInformationListItem` whose `ID` is equal to the `AssignedToID` value for the `ProjectsList2010Item`. The query fills all the properties for a new `Project` instance for each item in the `ProjectsList2010` list joined with `UserInformationListItem`.

8. Finally, the code converts the results for the LINQ to objects query, `joinQuery`, to a `List<Project>`, `listProjects`, by calling the `ToList()` extension method and then it is assigned to the `ItemsSource` property of the `dataGridProjects` DataGrid. Remember that this code runs in the UI thread. In this case, to fill the values for `Priority` and `Status`, the query uses the `PriorityValue` and `StatusValue` properties for the `ProjectsList2010Item`.

Debugging HTTP Requests with Fiddler

If you don't have it yet, you can download and install Fiddler Web Debugger from http://www.fiddler2.com. It is a free tool that simplifies the process of debugging HTTP requests. It is a Web Debugging Proxy that configures itself in such a way that all HTTP requests from WinINet (Windows Internet application programming interface) flow through Fiddler before reaching the target web servers. Likewise, all HTTP responses flow through Fiddler before being returned to the client web browser and the Silverlight RIA. Fiddler logs the requests and the responses, and therefore allows us to understand the underlying communications.

> In this case, we will use Fiddler to debug HTTP requests and responses for SharePoint 2010 WCF Data Services. However, there are other excellent tools that allow us to perform the same tasks. For example, Silverlight Spy (http://firstfloorsoftware. com/silverlightspy) is commercial software that provides a network monitor, which offers similar features than the ones we are going to analyze for Fiddler.

Now, follow these steps to inspect HTTP requests and responses when we insert a new item by using the previously created Silverlight Web Part:

1. Open your default web browser and load the SharePoint page that shows SLProjectsCRUD2010WCF.xap as a Silverlight Web Part, WCFTest.aspx.

2. Now, start Fiddler. It is very important to start Fiddler after the Silverlight Web Part shows all the information in the grid. This way, you will be able to see results similar to the next screenshots.

3. Follow the previously explained steps to insert a new item into the list. After you click on the **Insert** button, check the Fiddler window and you will notice that many requests will appear, as shown in the next screenshot. These HTTP requests were generated by all the operations performed by WCF Data Services in the Silverlight RIA. You will notice that many requests are the result of the queries to retrieve the name for each user to show them in the grid.

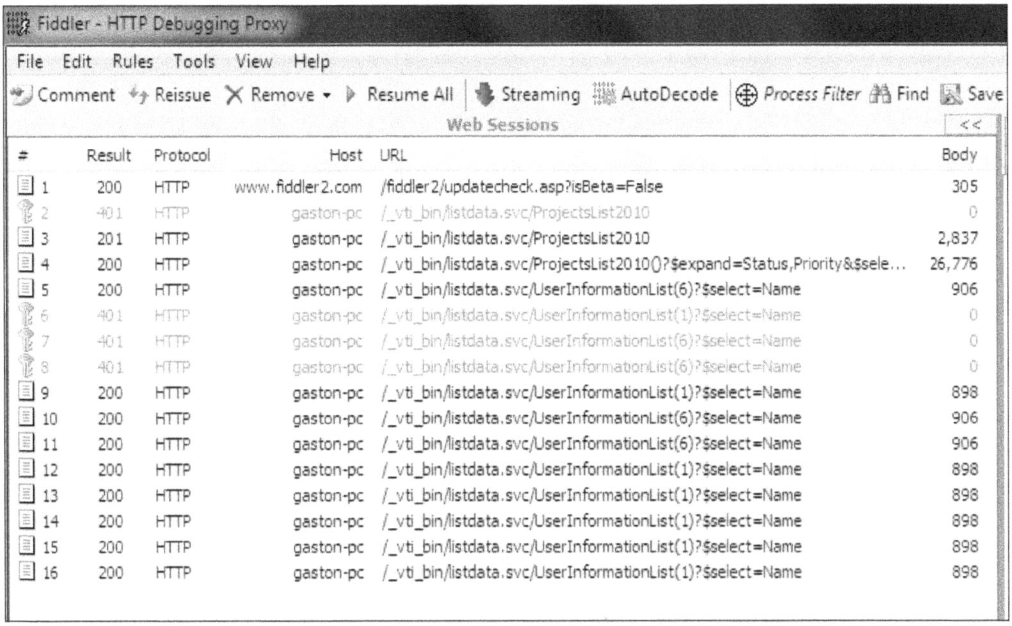

Fiddler - HTTP Debugging Proxy
File Edit Rules Tools View Help
Comment Reissue Remove Resume All Streaming AutoDecode Process Filter Find Save
Web Sessions
Result Protocol Host URL Body
1 200 HTTP www.fiddler2.com /fiddler2/updatecheck.asp?isBeta=False 305
2 401 HTTP gaston-pc /_vti_bin/listdata.svc/ProjectsList2010 0
3 201 HTTP gaston-pc /_vti_bin/listdata.svc/ProjectsList2010 2,837
4 200 HTTP gaston-pc /_vti_bin/listdata.svc/ProjectsList2010()?$expand=Status,Priority&$sele... 26,776
5 200 HTTP gaston-pc /_vti_bin/listdata.svc/UserInformationList(6)?$select=Name 906
6 401 HTTP gaston-pc /_vti_bin/listdata.svc/UserInformationList(1)?$select=Name 0
7 401 HTTP gaston-pc /_vti_bin/listdata.svc/UserInformationList(6)?$select=Name 0
8 401 HTTP gaston-pc /_vti_bin/listdata.svc/UserInformationList(6)?$select=Name 0
9 200 HTTP gaston-pc /_vti_bin/listdata.svc/UserInformationList(1)?$select=Name 898
10 200 HTTP gaston-pc /_vti_bin/listdata.svc/UserInformationList(6)?$select=Name 906
11 200 HTTP gaston-pc /_vti_bin/listdata.svc/UserInformationList(6)?$select=Name 906
12 200 HTTP gaston-pc /_vti_bin/listdata.svc/UserInformationList(1)?$select=Name 898
13 200 HTTP gaston-pc /_vti_bin/listdata.svc/UserInformationList(1)?$select=Name 898
14 200 HTTP gaston-pc /_vti_bin/listdata.svc/UserInformationList(1)?$select=Name 898
15 200 HTTP gaston-pc /_vti_bin/listdata.svc/UserInformationList(1)?$select=Name 898
16 200 HTTP gaston-pc /_vti_bin/listdata.svc/UserInformationList(1)?$select=Name 898

4. Click on the row with `201` in the **Result** column in Fiddler's left panel. If you performed the previous steps and there were no other applications performing HTTP requests, it would be the third row. The Request Headers will display a `POST` HTTP request with the URL to access the `ListData.svc` WCF Data Service, as shown in the next screenshot. The default view for the content located at the bottom of Fiddler's bottom-right panel is **XML** and it will display the values for the fields of the new `ProjectsList2010Item` within the `content` node.

5. Click on the **Raw** button at the top of Fiddler's bottom-right panel. Fiddler will show the **Raw** data of the headers and the **XML** for the HTTP request, as shown in the next screenshot:

```
Transformer   Headers   TextView'   ImageView   HexView   WebView   Auth   Caching   Privacy
Raw    XML

HTTP/1.1 201 Created
Cache-Control: no-cache
Content-Type: application/atom+xml;charset=utf-8
ETag: W/"1"
Location: http://gaston-pc/_vti_bin/listdata.svc/ProjectsList2010(41)
Server: Microsoft-IIS/7.5
SPRequestGuid: 0bb24452-760b-40f9-87ee-5499501fae81
Set-Cookie: WSS_KeepSessionAuthenticated={4a9e96b6-ffbc-4574-9bc1-24694f4ba4f4}
X-SharePointHealthScore: 0
DataServiceVersion: 1.0;
X-AspNet-Version: 2.0.50727
WWW-Authenticate: Negotiate oRswGaADCgEAoxIEEAEAAABDh+CIwTbjqQAAAAA=
Persistent-Auth: true
MicrosoftSharePointTeamServices: 14.0.0.4536
Date: Tue, 18 May 2010 06:07:02 GMT
Content-Length: 2837

<?xml version="1.0" encoding="utf-8" standalone="yes"?>
<entry xml:base="http://gaston-pc/_vti_bin/listdata.svc/" xmlns:d="http://schem
    <id>http://gaston-pc/_vti_bin/listdata.svc/ProjectsList2010(41)</id>
    <title type="text">Testing SharePoint 2010 WCF Data Services &amp; Silverligh
    <updated>2010-05-18T03:07:03-03:00</updated>
    <author>
        <name />
    </author>
    <link rel="edit" title="ProjectsList2010Item" href="ProjectsList2010(41)" />
    <link rel="http://schemas.microsoft.com/ado/2007/08/dataservices/related/Pred
    <link rel="http://schemas.microsoft.com/ado/2007/08/dataservices/related/Prio
    <link rel="http://schemas.microsoft.com/ado/2007/08/dataservices/related/Stat
    <link rel="http://schemas.microsoft.com/ado/2007/08/dataservices/related/Atta
    <category term="Microsoft.SharePoint.DataService.ProjectsList2010Item" scheme
    <content type="application/xml">
        <m:properties>
            <d:ContentTypeID>0x0108007C7838C28589704DAA548EB13213E3BA</d:ContentTypeI
            <d:Title>Testing SharePoint 2010 WCF Data Services &amp; Silverlight 4</d
            <d:PriorityValue>(1) High</d:PriorityValue>
            <d:StatusValue>In Progress</d:StatusValue>
            <d:Complete m:type="Edm.Double">0.24</d:Complete>
            <d:AssignedToID m:type="Edm.Int32">1</d:AssignedToID>
            <d:TaskGroupID m:type="Edm.Int32" m:null="true" />
            <d:Description m:null="true" />
            <d:StartDate m:type="Edm.DateTime">2010-05-03T00:00:00</d:StartDate>
            <d:DueDate m:type="Edm.DateTime">2010-05-28T00:00:00</d:DueDate>
            <d:Projcst2010Approval m:type="Edm.Int32" m:null="true" />
            <d:ID m:type="Edm.Int32">41</d:ID>
            <d:ContentType>Task</d:ContentType>
```

```
Find...                                                    View in Notepad
```

We can check what is going on with SharePoint 2010 WCF Data Services with the help of Fiddler. We can work with WCF Data Services in a Silverlight Web Part and combine the debugging features learned in the previous chapters with Fiddler as well.

Analyzing Web Parts with SharePoint Developer Dashboard

We are going to use another alternative to retrieve information for the user assigned to each item. We can avoid running many complex asynchronous executions to retrieve the user for each item in the ProjectsList2010 list. Follow these steps to retrieve the user related to each item in the ProjectsList2010 list by using a LINQ to objects query to perform a join on two lists.

1. Stay in Visual Studio as a system administrator user.

2. Open `MainPage.xaml.cs` and replace the code in the `ShowProjects` method with the following lines. This time, it will run two asynchronous queries to retrieve all the items for the `ProjectsList2010` and `UserInformationList` lists. Then, it will perform a LINQ to objects query to retrieve the `Name` value for the user assigned to each task in the `ProjectsList2010` list.

```
// IMPORTANT NOTE: DataServiceQuery doesn't support join
// This is another alternative to the previous examples

// Declare the LINQ query to retrieve all the ProjectList2010 list
items
var projectsQuery = (from p in _context.ProjectsList2010
                     select p)
as DataServiceQuery<SharePointService.ProjectsList2010Item>;

// Execute the first LINQ query
projectsQuery.BeginExecute(
    (IAsyncResult asyncResultP) =>
  {
        // EndExecute returns IEnumerable<ProjectsList2010Item>
        var listPL2010Item =
            projectsQuery.EndExecute(asyncResultP).ToList();

        // Declare the second LINQ query to retrieve all the users
        // In order to simplify the example,
        // the query doesn't apply a filter to limit the users
        var usersQuery = (from u in _context.UserInformationList
                     select u) as
        DataServiceQuery<SharePointService.UserInformationListItem>;

        // Execute the second LINQ query
        usersQuery.BeginExecute(
            (IAsyncResult asyncResultU) =>
                Dispatcher.BeginInvoke((() =>
          {
            // EndExecute returns
IEnumerable<UserInformationListItem>
            var listUsers =
                usersQuery.EndExecute(asyncResultU).ToList();

            // In this case
            // p.Status.Value was replaced by p.StatusValue
            // p.Priority.Value was replaced by
                p.PriorityValue
            // Now, use LINQ to Objects to perform a join
            // between listUsers and listPL2010Item
```

```
var joinQuery =
    (from u in listUsers
     join p in listPL2010Item on u.ID equals
         p.AssignedToID
     orderby p.Title
     select
     new Project()
     {
         ProjectId = p.ID,
         Title = p.Title,
         StartDate = p.StartDate.Value,
         DueDate = p.DueDate.Value,
         EstimatedDaysLeft =
             (p.DueDate.Value.Subtract(
                 p.StartDate.Value).Days),
         Status = p.StatusValue,
         AssignedTo = u.Name,
         NumberOfTasks = 0,
         Priority = p.PriorityValue
     }

    );

    listProjects = joinQuery.ToList();

    dataGridProjects.ItemsSource = listProjects;
}), usersQuery);
}, projectsQuery);
```

3. Build and deploy the solution.

4. Load the SharePoint page that shows `SLProjectsCRUD2010WCF.xap` as a Silverlight Web Part, `WCFTest.aspx`.

5. The grid in the Silverlight Web Part will display the data retrieved from `ProjectsList2010`. This time, it will run just two queries to the SharePoint Server to retrieve the data for the grid. The `AssignedTo` column shows the usernames.

The new version of the ShowProjects method performs the following sequence:

- ° The code declares and executes a query request to the WCF Data Services accessed through _context. First, the code declares a LINQ query, projectsQuery, casted to DataServiceQuery<SharePointService.ProjectsList2010Item> because it returns each element in the ProjectsList2010 list.

- ° This delegate calls the EndExecute method and returns an IEnumerable<SharePointService.ProjectsList2010Item>. The results are converted to a List<ProjectsList2010Item> by calling the ToList() extension method and assigned to a local variable, listPL2010Item.

- ° Then, the code declares a second query request to WCF Data Services. The new declaration for a LINQ query, usersQuery, appears casted to DataServiceQuery<SharePointService.UserInformationListItem> because it returns each element in the UserInformationList list.

- ° The code calls the BeginExecute method for the DataServiceQuery<SharePointService.UserInformationListItem>, usersQuery, and its callback schedules a delegate to run in the UI thread by using the Dispatcher.BeginInvoke method. This time, we are going to make changes to controls and we have to make sure that the code runs in the UI thread.

In this case, the code isn't applying a filter and the query, usersQuery, returns all the users from the SharePoint server. This example tries to offer another alternative to perform a LINQ to objects with the results of two queries to list on the SharePoint server. However, we should retrieve only the necessary fields and items from the list. A SharePoint Server could have thousands of users. It is possible to improve the code to return only the necessary fields and to add a filter to request only the necessary users.

6. This new delegate calls the EndExecute method and returns an IEnumerable<SharePointService.UserInformationListItem>. The results are converted to a List<UserInformationListItem> by calling the ToList() extension method and assigned to a local variable, listUsers.

Analyzing pages and Web Parts with SharePoint Developer Dashboard

When the Web browser renders a SharePoint page with its Web Parts, there is a lot of activity in the SharePoint Server and its related components. When a Silverlight application is part of a Web Part, it can use the Client OM or the WCF Data Services to interact with SharePoint, and therefore, it is very difficult to imagine all the things that happen in the server to render a complex SharePoint page.

SharePoint 2010 introduced a new instrumentation framework, the **Developer Dashboard**. It offers diagnostic information that can help us troubleshoot performance problems and explains what is going on behind the scenes in the SharePoint server.

Activating the Developer Dashboard On Demand display mode

By default, Developer Dashboard is switched off. It isn't convenient to enable Developer Dashboard for all the pages because it would add an overhead for all the requests to the SharePoint Server and consume additional server resources.

> The Developer Dashboard provides information that might compromise security on the SharePoint Server. Thus, it is very important to use this feature very carefully in production servers and to restrict the users that can see this information.

It is possible to enable the Developer Dashboard in two different display modes:

- On: The Dashboard information will be visible at the bottom of all the SharePoint pages that use the default master page.
- OnDemand: An icon will appear on the upper-right corner of the SharePoint pages. When the user clicks on this icon, the Dashboard information will toggle on and off.

The administrator can activate the OnDemand mode for all the users in the farm by following these steps:

1. Start the SharePoint 2010 Management Shell as a system administrator.

2. Run the following command:

   ```
   stsadm -o setproperty -pn developer-dashboard -pv ondemand
   ```

3. Open your default web browser and load the SharePoint page that shows `SLProjectsCRUD2010WCF.xap` as a Silverlight Web Part, `WCFTest.aspx`.

4. The icon to toggle the Developer Dashboard visibility will appear on the upper-right corner of the SharePoint page, as shown in the next screenshot:

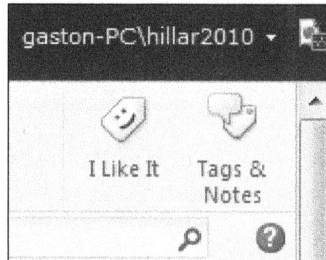

It is also possible to activate the `OnDemand` mode for specific users by specifying a mask for `RequiredPermissions` in `[Microsoft.SharePoint.Administration.SPWebService]::ContentService.DeveloperDashboardSettings`. The SharePoint administrator can run a PowerShell script to specify this mask and activate the `OnDemand` mode. The following lines show a PowerShell script that produces the same effect as the previously explained Management Shell command. The SharePoint administrator can replace the highlighted line with the desired mask to limit the users.

```
$DevDashboardSettings = [Microsoft.SharePoint.Administration.
SPWebService]::ContentService.DeveloperDashboardSettings;
$DevDashboardSettings.DisplayLevel = 'OnDemand';
$DevDashboardSettings.RequiredPermissions ='EmptyMask';
$DevDashboardSettings.TraceEnabled = $true;
$DevDashboardSettings.Update()
```

The SharePoint administrator can check the values by entering the following line:

```
[Microsoft.SharePoint.Administration.SPWebService]::ContentService.
DeveloperDashboardSettings
```

The Management Shell will display the current values for the different settings. The following lines show an example of the values after running the previous commands. It is very important to check the value for the `RequiredPermissions` property.

```
DisplayLevel                  : OnDemand
TraceEnabled                  : True
RequiredPermissions           : EmptyMask
MaximumSQLQueriesToTrack       : 50
MaximumCriticalEventsToTrack  : 50
AdditionalEventsToTrack       : {}
```

```
Name                            :
TypeName                        : Microsoft.SharePoint.Administration.
SPDeveloperDashboardSettings
DisplayName                     :
Id                              : 09b01680-93bd-44be-ac45-c3c917dd0512
Status                          : Online
Parent                          : SPWebService
Version                         : 403589
Properties                      : {}
Farm                            : SPFarm Name=SharePoint_Config_083dcd97-
8bb0-4325-8de3-072258fdd4e6
UpgradedPersistedProperties     : {}
```

Understanding the Developer Dashboard

Now, follow these steps to visualize the information provided by the Developer Dashboard for our sample application.

1. Click on the icon to toggle the Developer Dashboard visibility. The web page will display the Developer Dashboard at the bottom.

2. Scroll down the web page and you will find the Developer Dashboard information, as shown in the next screenshot. The Dashboard groups the information in seven sections.

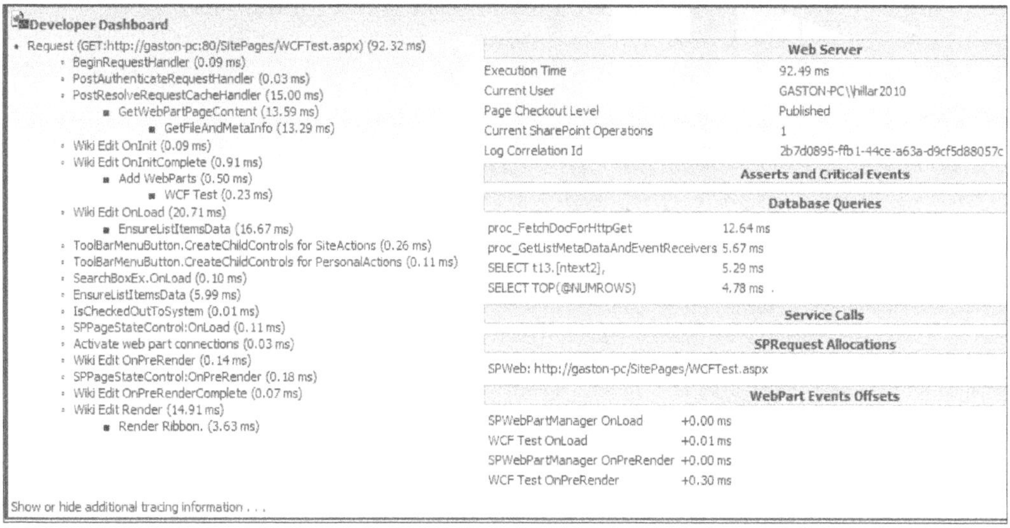

° **Developer Dashboard**: This appears on the left and displays all the SharePoint request (SPRequest) objects generated from the page render and their execution time.

° **Web Server**: This appears as the first section on the right and summarizes basic information on the page render:

   Execution time is the time required to render the page. **Current User** is the user who is logged in to the SharePoint server. **Page Checkout Level** shows whether the page is checked out (Published) or not. **Current SharePoint Operations** shows the number of active SharePoint requests (SPRequest) across all the active threads. **Log Correlation Id** is useful if you want to view the corresponding trace level events for this page render in the **Unified Logging Service (ULS)** logs.

° **Asserts and Critical Events**: It includes details for critical events and errors. It is possible to access the corresponding call stack by clicking on the desired item for this section.

° **Database Queries**: This displays all the database queries that occurred during the page render with their execution times. It is possible to click on one of the queries and a dialog box will display the full SQL query in **Query Text**, the call stack that originated the SQL query in **Callstack**, and its detailed I/O footprint in **IO Stats**. The following screenshot shows the information offered by this dialog box for the proc_FetchDocForHttpGet query.

- ° **Service Calls**: This displays calls to Web Services on a backend and their response times.

- ° **SPRequest Allocations**: This displays the SharePoint request (SPRequest) objects allocated in the current operation. The higher the number of objects, the more memory usage on the server. If you see too many objects allocated, you might want to check the code for the Silverlight application to avoid keeping SharePoint objects alive when it isn't necessary.

- ° **WebPart Events Offsets**: This displays the time offset of a Web Part event since the same event is in its parent control (WebPartManager).

3. Once you finish checking the information shown in the Developer Dashboard, click on the icon to toggle the Developer Dashboard visibility off. The web page won't display the Developer Dashboard at the bottom.

> The information offered by the Developer Dashboard isn't restricted to WCF Data Services usage. We can also take advantage of this information for our previous examples that used the Client OM.

We learned to use the Developer Dashboard to obtain diagnostic information that can help us troubleshoot performance problems. This new instrumentation framework explains what happens behind the scenes in the SharePoint Server and allows use to solve performance bottlenecks.

Deactivating the Developer Dashboard

The administrator can deactivate the Developer Dashboard for all the users in the farm by following these steps:

1. Start the SharePoint 2010 Management Shell as a system administrator.

2. Run the following command:

```
stsadm -o setproperty -pn developer-dashboard -pv off
```

3. Open your default web browser and load the SharePoint page that shows SLProjectsCRUD2010WCF.xap as a Silverlight Web Part, WCFTest.aspx.

4. The icon to toggle the Developer Dashboard visibility won't appear on the upper-right corner of the SharePoint page.

> Don't leave the Developer Dashboard activated for a production SharePoint server. Remember that it can compromise the server's security.

Summary

We learned a lot in this chapter about developing Silverlight 4 applications in SharePoint 2010 sites that interact with data in lists by performing insert, update, and delete operations with WCF Data Services. Specifically, we created a new Silverlight 4 RIA that allowed us to view, update, delete, and insert new items in a remote SharePoint list through HTTP requests. We were able to work with a strongly typed data model that represented the different lists and field choices.

We were able to explore an alternative to the SharePoint Silverlight Client Object Model when we have to interact with SharePoint lists. We are now able to take advantage of the powerful SharePoint 2010 WCF Data Services and we can choose between them and the Silverlight Client OM according to our applications' needs.

We used Fiddler to inspect communication between the Silverlight RIA and the SharePoint Server. Finally, we analyzed the performance and resource usage information for pages and Web Parts with SharePoint Developer Dashboard. This way, our debugging experience can be improved with this new powerful instrumentation framework.

Now that we have learned about the interaction with the SharePoint Server through SharePoint 2010 WCF Data Services in Silverlight 4, we are ready to learn to add rich media and animations to business applications by working with enhanced Silverlight User eXperiences, which is the topic of the next chapter.

6
Interacting with Rich Media and Animations

We want to take advantage of Silverlight 4 features to work with rich media and perform animations. In this chapter, we will cover many topics related to retrieving digital assets from SharePoint libraries through the SharePoint Silverlight Client Object Model and consuming them in a Silverlight RIA. We will:

- Create and manage asset libraries in SharePoint 2010
- Access the digital assets in a SharePoint library from a Visual Web Part and a Silverlight RIA
- Create a SharePoint Visual Web Part that sends parameters and renders a Silverlight RIA
- Link a SharePoint Visual Web Part to a Silverlight RIA
- Add a SharePoint Visual Web Part in a web page
- Work with multiple interactive animations and effects
- Display and control videos
- Add background music from the assets library
- Change themes in Silverlight and SharePoint

Bringing life to business applications and complex workflows

So far, we have been able to interact with data from the SharePoint Server through the SharePoint Silverlight Client Object Model and WCF Data Services. Sometimes, we need to share, manage, and consume rich media, related to data.

SharePoint 2010 improves rich media management by introducing asset libraries and we can take advantage of this new feature by consuming it in a Silverlight RIA through the SharePoint Silverlight Client OM. Silverlight 4 offers outstanding features to create amazing User eXperiences (**UX**) when combining rich media with effects and animations.

Creating asset libraries in SharePoint 2010

SharePoint Server 2010 introduced a new asset library specially designed for managing and sharing digital assets and rich media files such as images, audio, and video. It is possible to combine workflows, routing, rules, and policies with asset libraries. However, in this case, we will focus on creating simple asset libraries to allow us to store images, videos, and audio files and we will consume them through the SharePoint Silverlight Client Object Model.

We will combine a new SharePoint Visual Web Part with a Silverlight RIA to allow users to select their desired asset library and to browse its images and videos with interactive animations and dazzling effects. The SharePoint Visual Web Part will display a drop-down list with the available asset libraries that store images, videos, or audio files and when the user selects one of them, the Silverlight RIA will use the capabilities offered by the Client OM to retrieve and display the digital assets. This way, with this new composite Web Part, it is going to be possible to create a new asset library and to upload the necessary images and videos to display, and the desired background music as an audio file. The Web Part will allow a user to interact with any asset library.

First, follow these steps to create two asset libraries in a SharePoint site:

1. Open your default web browser, view the SharePoint site, and log in with your username and password.
2. Click **Site Actions | More Options...** in the ribbon and the **Create** dialog box will appear.

3. Select **Library** under **Filter By:** and then **Asset Library** in **Installed Items**, as shown in the following screenshot:

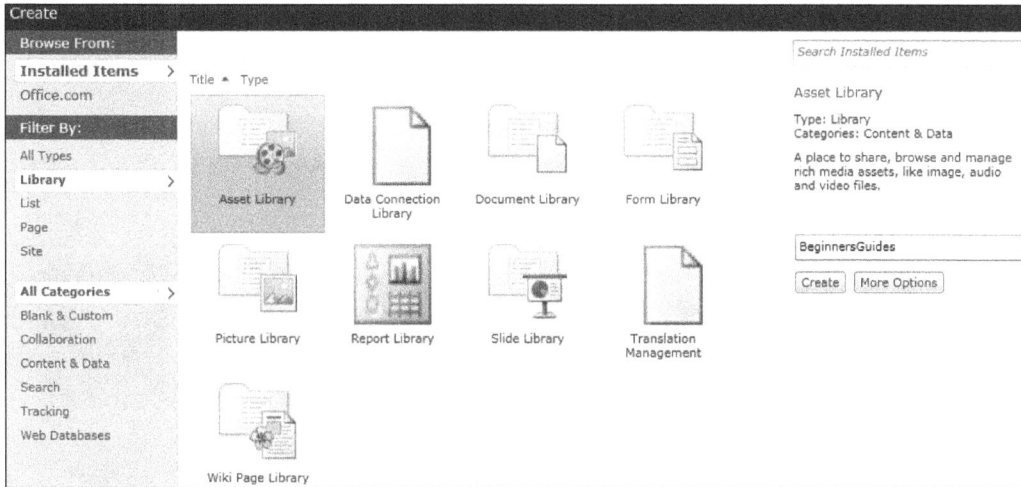

4. Enter `BeginnersGuides` in the **Name** textbox.

5. Click on **More Options**. SharePoint will display a new panel with additional options for the new asset library.

6. Enter `Beginner's Guides` in **Description** and select **Yes** in **Display this list on the Quick Launch?**

7. Click on **Create**; SharePoint will create the new asset library with no digital assets and it will appear in the Quick Launch for the SharePoint site.

8. Now, follow the aforementioned steps (1 to 7) to create another asset library. Use `Cookbooks` as the **Name** and **Description** for this new asset library.

Adding content to an assets library

Follow these steps to prepare and add images, videos, and audio files to the previously created asset libraries.

1. Prepare two folders, BeginnersGuides and Cookbooks. Add many JPG and/ or PNG images to these folders. Add a **WMV (Windows Media Video)** video file and an **MP3** audio file to both folders. The following screenshot shows an example of the contents of the BeginnersGuides folder with 17 JPG images, a WMV video file, and an MP3 audio file:

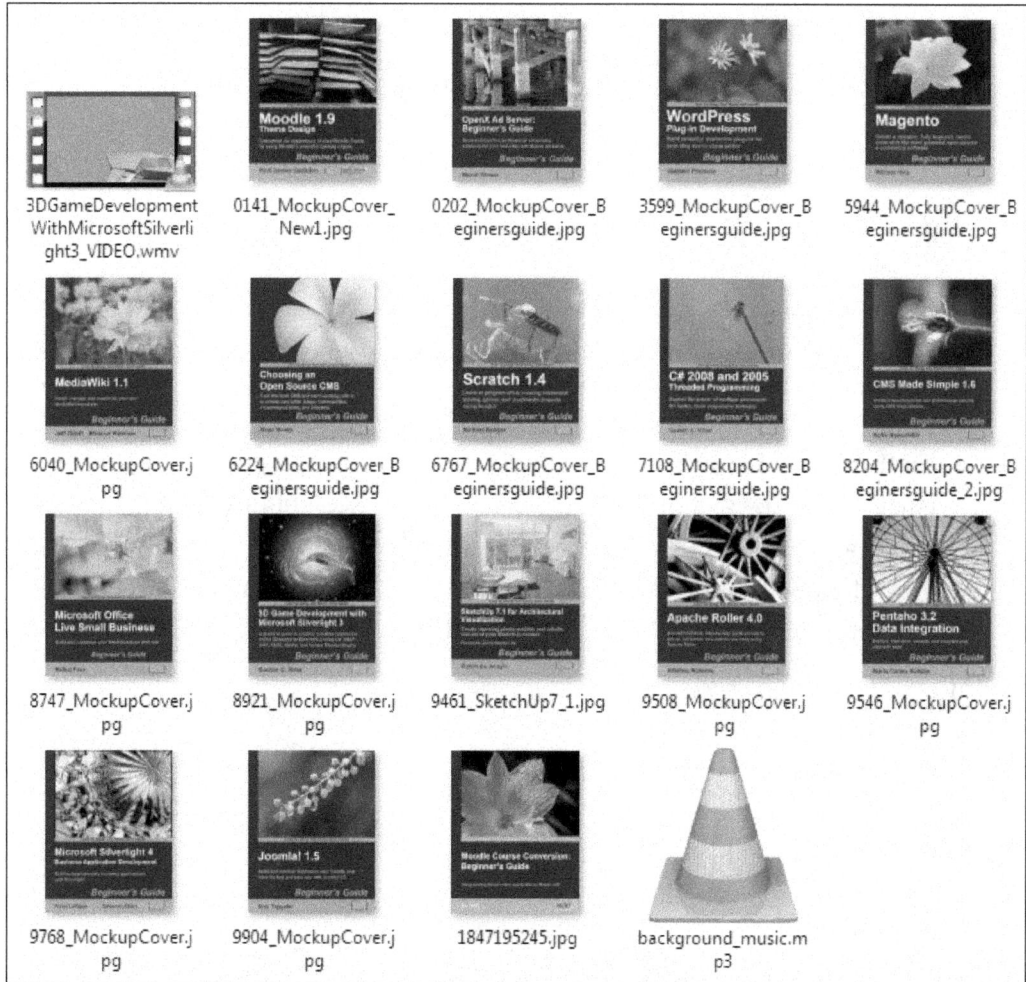

> By default, SharePoint 2010 establishes 50 MB as the maximum upload file size setting. This setting specifies the maximum size of a file that a user can upload to the server. If a user tries to upload a file larger than the specified maximum upload size, the upload will fail.

2. Click on the hyperlink for the `BeginnersGuides` asset library in the Quick Launch for the SharePoint site.

3. Click on **Add new item**. The **Upload document** dialog box will appear. Click on **Upload Multiple files...** and a panel to which to drag files and folders will appear.

4. Open an Explorer window and navigate to your `BeginnersGuides` folder. Select all the files within the folder and drag-and-drop them in the **Drag files and folder here** panel within the **Upload Document** dialog box. All the file names will appear in the panel.

5. Click on **OK** and SharePoint will upload all the dropped files to the previously created asset library. Click on **Done** and the new digital assets will appear in the asset library. By default, SharePoint will display a thumbnail preview for the image files:

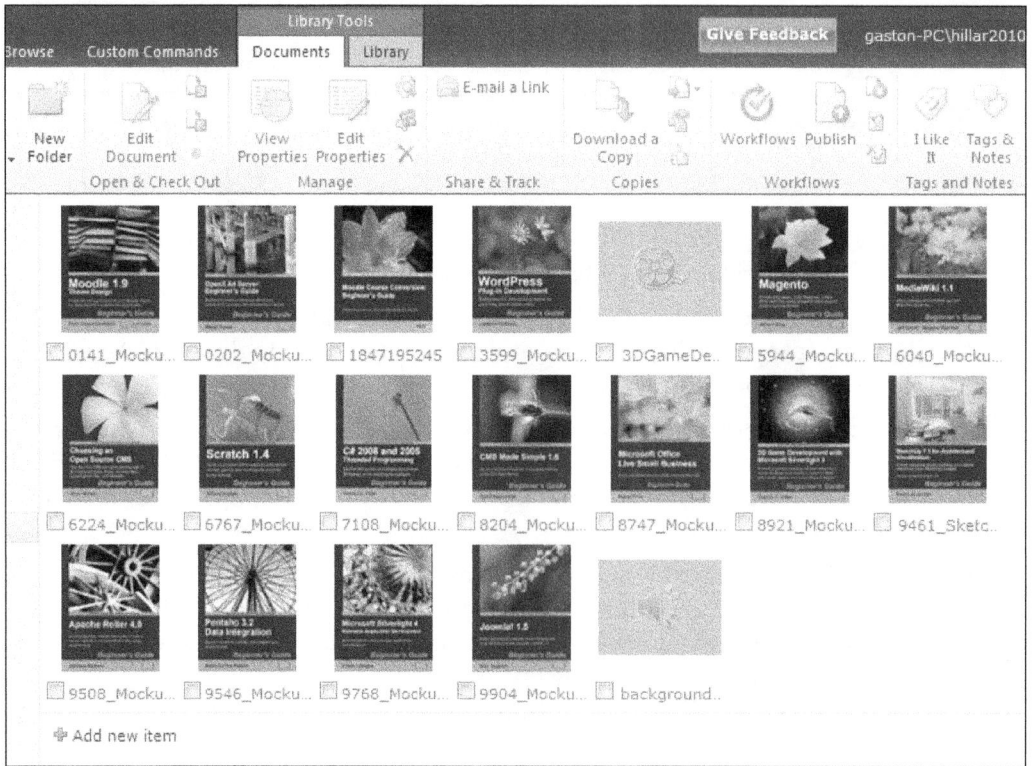

6. Click on one of the thumbnails for the images and a bigger thumbnail will appear with detailed properties for the digital asset:

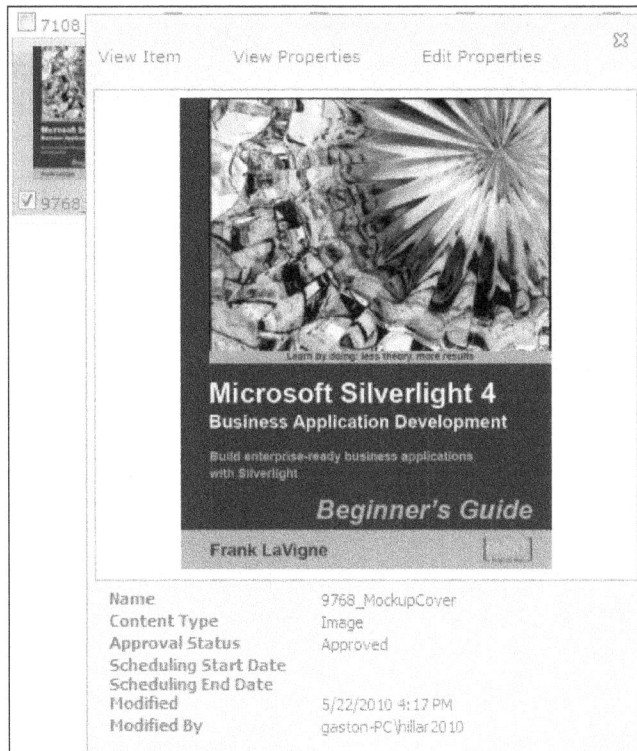

7. Click on **Edit Properties**, located at the top of the bigger thumbnail preview; a new dialog box will appear and you will be able to edit many properties related to the digital asset. The **Content Type** drop-down list will display **Image**, because SharePoint automatically recognized the digital asset as an image. As we uploaded many images dragging and dropping them to the panel, SharePoint assigned the name but it didn't set values for Title, Keywords, Comments, Author, and Copyright. You can use this dialog box to set the values for these properties in order to organize the contents of the asset library. Then, click on **Save**.

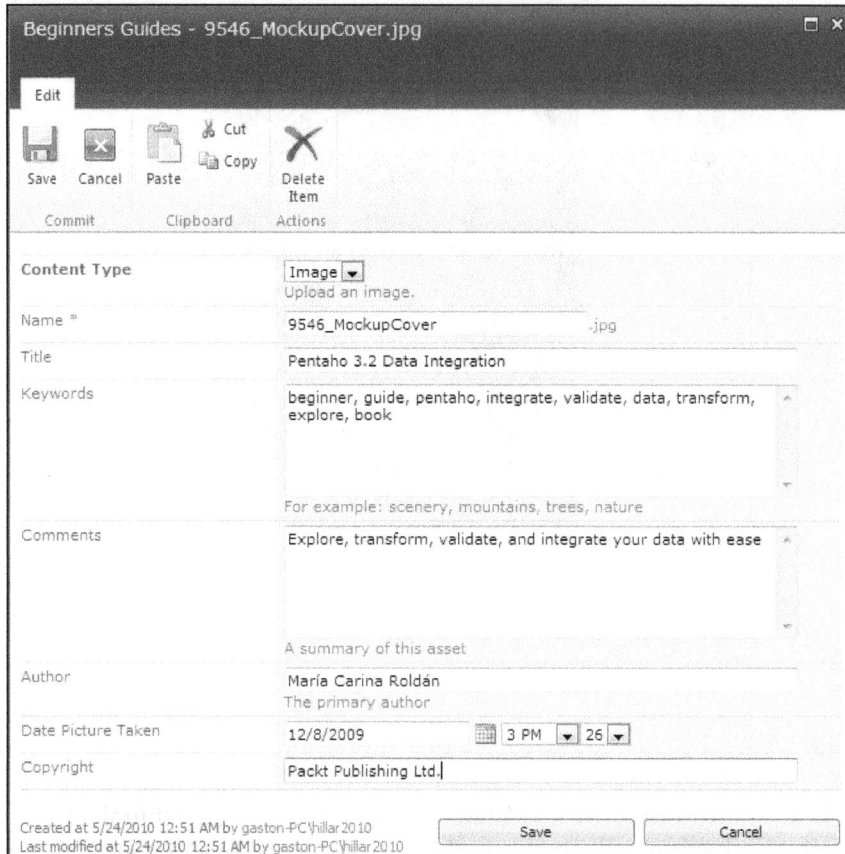

8. Now, follow the aforementioned steps (1 to 7) to add an audio file, images, and videos to the other asset library, Cookbooks. Remember to upload the files stored in the Cookbooks folder.

We added images, videos and audio files to the two asset libraries, BeginnerGuides and Cookbooks, in the SharePoint site. Now, we can browse the asset libraries' structure and then create an interactive Silverlight RIA capable of consuming the uploaded digital assets.

Browsing the structure for SharePoint Asset Libraries

Once we have created the two asset libraries in SharePoint, we can use Server Explorer in Visual Studio to analyze the new asset libraries' structures.

1. Start Visual Studio as a system administrator user.

2. Activate the **Server Explorer** palette by clicking on **View | Server Explorer**.

3. Click on the expand button for **SharePoint Connections** and then on the expand button for the SharePoint server. You will be able to browse its different nodes.

4. Expand **Lists and Libraries** and then **Document Libraries** for the Site Collection in which you created the new asset libraries. Remember that the default Site Collection is **Home**. There are asset libraries and document libraries within **Document Libraries** and therefore, it is going to be necessary to use a smart filter to display the right asset library names in the drop-down list that the user will use to select the desired asset library with pictures, videos, and audio files.

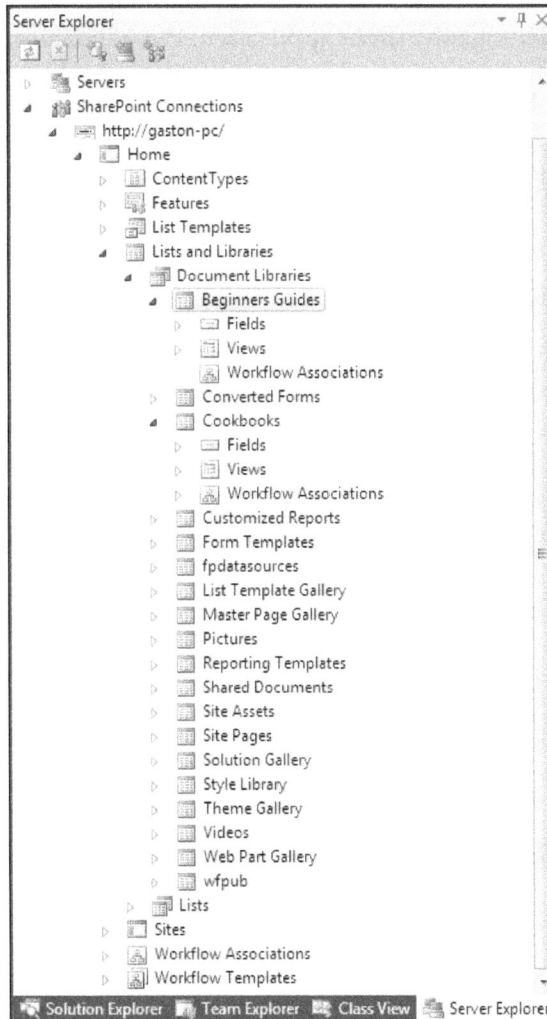

Controlling the rich media library by using controls in a Visual Web Part

This time, we are going to create a new solution in Visual Studio that will include two new projects:

- A SharePoint 2010 Visual Web Part, SPAssetsBrowserWebPart
- A Silverlight application project, SLAssetsBrowser

SharePoint is built on top of **ASP.NET**, and therefore, a **Visual Web Part** inherits key features from the ASP.NET Web Part architecture. The Visual Web Part will display the available asset libraries with videos, pictures, and/or audio files in a SharePoint site and it will send the selected asset library as a parameter to the Silverlight host control that will render the Silverlight application. We will take advantage of one of the new project templates in Visual Studio 2010, the Visual Web Part project template, which enables us to visually design a Web Part that can be deployed to SharePoint. The necessary steps to display a Silverlight application within the Visual Web Part are a bit complex but the flexibility offered by this combination is worth the effort.

Follow these steps to create the new Visual Web Part that accesses the available asset libraries in a SharePoint site:

1. Stay in Visual Studio as a system administrator user.
2. Select **File | New | Project...** Expand **Other Project Types** and select **Visual Studio Solutions** under **Installed Templates** in the **New Project** dialog box. Then, select **Blank Solution**, make sure that **.NET Framework 4** version is selected, and enter AssetsBrowser as the project's name and click **OK**. Visual Studio will create a blank solution with no projects.

3. Right-click on the solution's name in **Solution Explorer** and select **Add | New Project...** from the context menu. Expand **Visual C#** and then expand **SharePoint** and select **2010** under **Installed Templates** in the **Add New Project** dialog box. Then, select **Visual Web Part**, enter `SPAssetsBrowserWebPart` as the project's name, and click **OK**. The **SharePoint Customization Wizard** dialog box will appear.

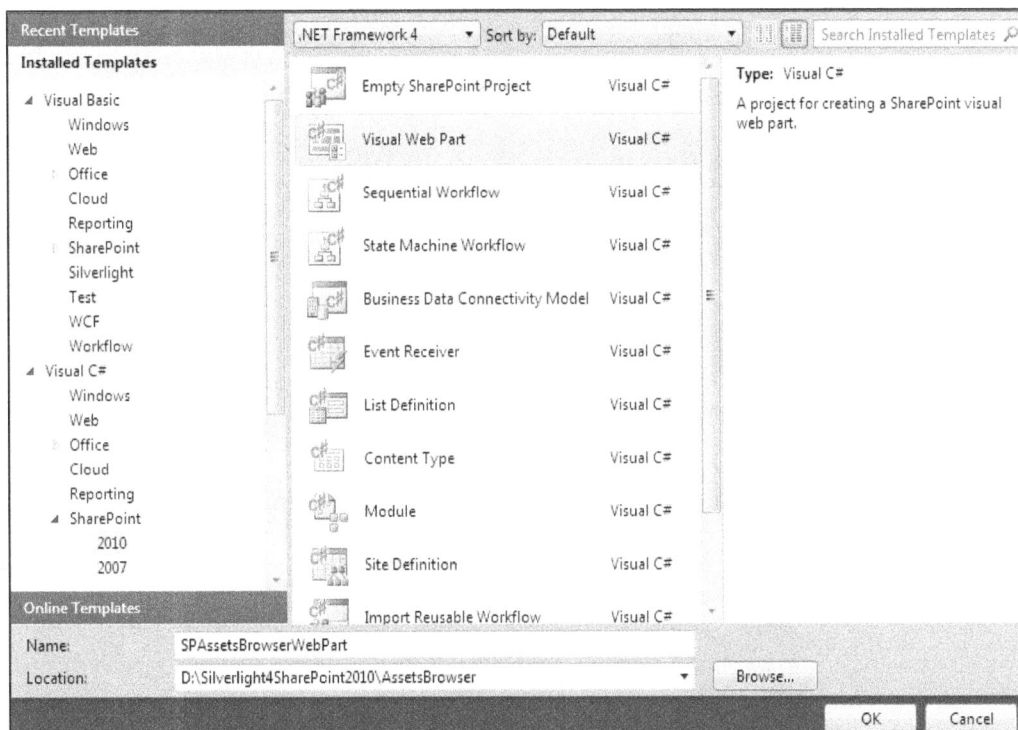

4. Enter the URL for the SharePoint server and site in **What local site do you want to use for debugging?**

5. Click on **Deploy as a farm solution**. Sandboxed solutions don't support the Visual Web Parts and therefore, it is necessary to deploy projects that include them as a **farm solution**. Then, click on **Finish** and the new `SPAssetsBrowserWebPart` empty SharePoint 2010 Visual Web Part project will be added to the solution. The code editor will open the source code for the `VisualWebPart1UserControl.ascx UserControl` (`System.Web.UI.UserControl`). This `UserControl` defines the UI for the Visual Web Part and it has a code-behind file, `VisualWebPart1UserControl.ascx.cs`.

6. Right-click on the `VisualWebPart1` folder in **Solution Explorer** and select **Delete** in the context menu. Click **OK** in the confirmation dialog box.

7. Now, right-click on the recently added project's name in **Solution Explorer**, `SPAssetsBrowserWebPart`, and select **Add | New Item...** in the context menu. Expand **Visual C#** and then expand **SharePoint** and then select **2010** under **Installed Templates** in the **New Item** dialog box. Then, select **Visual Web Part**, enter `AssetsBrowserWebPart` in **Name**, and click **OK**. The code editor will open the source code for the `AssetsBrowserWebPart.ascx` UserControl (`System.Web.UI.UserControl`). Its new code-behind file is `AssetsBrowserWebPartUserControl.ascx.cs`. Renaming a Visual Web Part can be a very complex process and therefore, it is easier to delete the default `VisualWebPart1` folder and add a new Visual Web Part item with the desired name. This way, Visual Studio will create the container folder and all its related files with the new name.

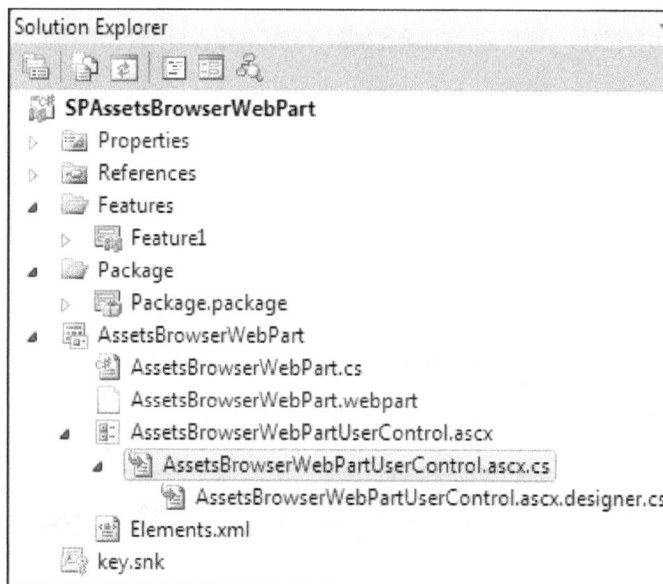

```
Solution Explorer
  ▦  SPAssetsBrowserWebPart
  ▷  ▦  Properties
  ▷  ▦  References
  ▲  ▦  Features
     ▷  ▦  Feature1
  ▲  ▦  Package
     ▷  ▦  Package.package
  ▲  ▦  AssetsBrowserWebPart
        ▦  AssetsBrowserWebPart.cs
        ▦  AssetsBrowserWebPart.webpart
     ▲  ▦  AssetsBrowserWebPartUserControl.ascx
        ▲  ▦  AssetsBrowserWebPartUserControl.ascx.cs
              ▦  AssetsBrowserWebPartUserControl.ascx.designer.cs
        ▦  Elements.xml
     ▦  key.snk
```

8. Switch to the **Design** view for the `AssetsBrowserWebPart.ascx` UserControl and use the **Toolbox** to drag-and-drop the following server controls. The names for the server controls are assigned in the `ID` property in the **Properties** window.

    ° One `Label` control, `Label1`. Set its `Text` property to `Select the Asset Library to display`.

- One `DropDownList` control, `cboDocumentLibraries`. Set its `AutoPostBack` property to `true`. This way, the page will automatically **post back** to the server after the user changes the selection for this drop-down list.

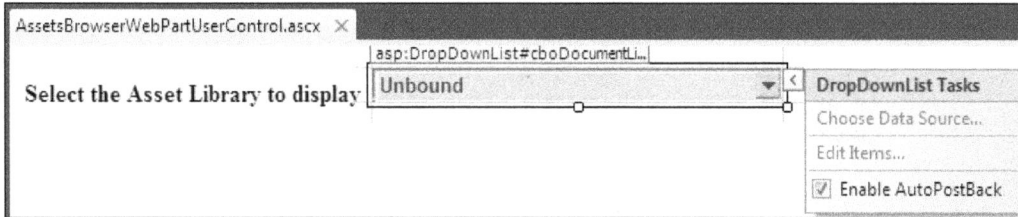

9. Now, open the code-behind file for the `AssetsBrowserWebPart.ascx` UserControl, `AssetsBrowserWebPartUserControl.ascx.cs` and add the following `using` statements.

```
using Microsoft.SharePoint;
using Microsoft.SharePoint.WebControls;
```

10. Add the following public property for the `AssetsBrowserWebPartUserControl` partial class.

```
public string SelectedList { get; private set; }
```

11. Add the following lines to the `Page_Load` event. This code will run at the server when a user requests the Visual Web Part for the first time and each time a postback occurs. Thus, it is necessary to run different code when it is a postback by checking the Boolean value of the `IsPostBack` property. When the code runs for the first time (`IsPostBack == false`), it will add the titles for the lists of `SPBaseType.DocumentLibrary` type with at least one item (`libraryList.RootFolder.ItemCount > 0`) and with content types of `Picture`, `Image`, `Audio`, or `Video`.

```
if (!IsPostBack)
{
  var _context = SPContext.Current;
  var documentLibraries =
  _context.Web.GetListsOfType(SPBaseType.DocumentLibrary);
  foreach (SPList libraryList in documentLibraries)
  {
    if ((libraryList.RootFolder.ItemCount > 0) &&
      ((libraryList.ContentTypes[0].Name == "Picture") ||
      (libraryList.ContentTypes[0].Name == "Image") ||
      (libraryList.ContentTypes[0].Name == "Audio") ||
```

```
    (libraryList.ContentTypes[0].Name == "Video")))
    {
      // The list has at least 1 element
      cboDocumentLibraries.Items.Add(
      new ListItem(libraryList.Title));
    }
  }
  // Select the first item in the dropdown list
  cboDocumentLibraries.SelectedIndex = 0;
}
SelectedList = cboDocumentLibraries.SelectedValue;
```

12. Go back to the **Design** view for `AssetsBrowserWebPartUserControl.`
    `ascx` and define a `SelectedIndexChanged` event handler for the
    `cboDocumentLibraries` DropDownList and add the following code in it.
    This way, when the user selects a different item in the drop-down list, the
    `SelectedList` property will hold the name for the new list that has been
    selected.

    ```
    SelectedList = cboDocumentLibraries.SelectedValue;
    ```

13. Now, open the `AssetsBrowserWebPart.cs` code file within the
    `AssetsBrowserWebPart` folder. This file defines the `AssetsBrowserWebPart`
    class as a subclass of `WebPart`. Its original code defines a path for the
    `UserControl`, `AssetsBrowserWebPartUserControl.ascx`, that this `WebPart`
    subclass will load and add to the `Controls ControlCollection`. This way,
    the `WebPart` renders the `UserControl`. The following lines show the original
    code for this file.

    ```
    using System;
    using System.ComponentModel;
    using System.Web;
    using System.Web.UI;
    using System.Web.UI.WebControls;
    using System.Web.UI.WebControls.WebParts;
    using Microsoft.SharePoint;
    using Microsoft.SharePoint.WebControls;
    namespace SPAssetsBrowserWebPart.AssetsBrowserWebPart
    {
      [ToolboxItemAttribute(false)]
      public class AssetsBrowserWebPart : WebPart
      {
        // Visual Studio might automatically update this path when you
        change the Visual Web Part project item.
    ```

```
    private const string _ascxPath = @"~/_CONTROLTEMPLATES/
SPAssetsBrowserWebPart/AssetsBrowserWebPart/
AssetsBrowserWebPartUserControl.ascx";
    protected override void CreateChildControls()
    {
      Control control = Page.LoadControl(_ascxPath);
      Controls.Add(control);
    }
  }
}
```

14. Add the following private variable to the `AssetsBrowserWebPart` class. This variable will hold a reference to the `Control` instance cast as `AssetsBrowserWebPartUserControl`. This way, it will be possible to access the value for the `SelectedList` public property to send it as a parameter to the Silverlight host control in the `OnPreRender` method.

```
private AssetsBrowserWebPartUserControl _control;
```

15. Add the following lines in the `CreateChildControls` method to save the reference to the `AssetsBrowserWebPartUserControl` instance.

```
protected override void CreateChildControls()
{
  Control control = Page.LoadControl(_ascxPath);
  Controls.Add(control);
  _control = (control as AssetsBrowserWebPartUserControl);
  base.CreateChildControls();
}
```

16. Override the `OnPreRender` event to add the Silverlight host control that will load and display the Silverlight RIA and it will send the selected asset library title as a parameter. The highlighted lines define the `.xap` file location and the parameter called `Name`.

```
protected override void OnPreRender(EventArgs e)
{
  var name = _control.SelectedList;
  string webUrl = SPContext.Current.Web.Url;
  string renderHost = @"<div id='silverlightControlHost'>
  <object data='data:application/x-silverlight-2,'
type='application/x-silverlight-2' width='100%' height='100%'>
  <param name='source' value='/_catalogs/wp/SLAssetsBrowser.xap'/>
  <param name='background' value='white' />
  <param name='minRuntimeVersion' value='4.0.50303.0' />
```

```
<param name='autoUpgrade' value='true' />
<param name='initParams' value='Name=" + name.Trim() + @"' />
<a href='http://go.microsoft.com/fwlink/?LinkID=149156
&v=4.0.50303.0' style='text-decoration:none'>
<img src='http://go.microsoft.com/fwlink/?LinkId=161376'
alt='Get Microsoft Silverlight' style='border-style:none'/>
</a>
</object><iframe id='_sl_historyFrame' style='visibility:hidden;
height:0px;width:0px;border:0px'></iframe></div>";
LiteralControl host = new LiteralControl(renderHost);
Controls.Add(host);
base.OnPreRender(e);
}
```

The values for the `renderHost` string define a Silverlight control host. You can check the test page generated by Visual Studio for the Silverlight application to find the most up to date definition.

Once you have built your application, click on the **Show All Files** button in **Solution Explorer**. Then, expand the `Bin\Debug` folder for your Silverlight project. You will find many folders and files; open the HTML file that ends with `TestPage`. `html`, in our example, `SLAssetsBrowserTestPage.html`. You can copy from `<div id="silverlightControlHost">` to `</div>` and you can assign this value to `renderHost` to create a Silverlight host control. However, you have to change the following line that defines the path for the `.xap` file:

```
<param name="source" value="SLAssetsBrowser.xap"/>
```

It has to be replaced with the path for the `.xap` file inside the SharePoint `_catalogs/wp` folder.

```
<param name='source' value='/_catalogs/wp/SLAssetsBrowser.xap'/>
```

In this case, then, it was necessary to add a parameter after the last `param name`, because we want to send a specific value to the Silverlight RIA.

Creating a Silverlight RIA rendered in a SharePoint Visual Web Part

Follow these steps to create the new Silverlight RIA that loads the images, videos, and audio from the asset library selected in the Visual Web Part that renders this application and sends the selected name as a parameter:

1. Stay in Visual Studio as a system administrator user.

2. Select **File | New | Project....** Expand **Visual C#** and select **Silverlight** under **Installed Templates** in the **New Project** dialog box. Then, select **Silverlight Application**, enter `SLAssetsBrowser` as the project's name, choose **Add to Solution** in the **Solution** drop-down list, and click **OK**.

3. Deactivate the **Host the Silverlight application in a new Web site** checkbox in the **New Silverlight Application** dialog box and select **Silverlight 4** in **Silverlight Version**. Then, click **OK**. Visual Studio will add the new Silverlight application project to the existing solution.

4. Follow the necessary steps to add the following two references to access the SharePoint 2010 Silverlight Client OM:

   ° `Microsoft.SharePoint.Client.Silverlight.dll`

   ° `Microsoft.SharePoint.Client.Silverlight.Runtime.dll`

5. Open `App.xaml.cs` and add the following `using` statement:

```
using Microsoft.SharePoint.Client;
```

6. Replace the code in the `StartUp` event handler with the following lines. The code stores the value for the `Name` parameter, specified by the Visual Web Part in the string that creates the Silverlight host control, in the `parameterName` local variable. Then, it creates a new instance of `MainPage` sending this value as a parameter to the constructor.

```
private void Application_Startup(object sender, StartupEventArgs e)
{
    string parameterName = e.InitParams["Name"];

    this.RootVisual = new MainPage(parameterName);
    ApplicationContext.Init(e.InitParams,
      System.Threading.SynchronizationContext.Current);
}
```

7. Select **Start | All Programs | Microsoft Silverlight 4 Toolkit April 2010 | Binaries** and Windows will open the folder that contains the Silverlight Toolkit binaries. By default, they are located at `C:\Program Files (x86)\Microsoft SDKs\Silverlight\v4.0\Toolkit\Apr10\Bin` in 64-bit Windows versions, and at `C:\Program Files\Microsoft SDKs\ Silverlight\v4.0\Toolkit\Apr10\Bin` in 32-bit Windows versions. Remember that we installed Silverlight Toolkit (Updated for Silverlight 4 compatibility) in *Chapter 1, Integrating Silverlight 4 with SharePoint 2010*, in *Setting up the development environment*.

8. Add a reference to `System.Windows.Controls.Toolkit.dll`. Remember that it is located in the aforementioned `Bin` sub-folder. This way, we will have access to the `WrapPanel` control.

9. Open `MainPage.xaml` and activate the **Toolbox**. Right-click on the **All Sivlerlight Controls** header and select **Choose Items...** in the context menu. The **Choose Toolbox Items** dialog box will appear with the **Silverlight Components** tab activated. Make sure that the checkbox located at the left of the **WrapPanel** item in the **Name** column is checked. This way, the **Toolbox** will display the `WrapPanel` control and you will be able to add it by dragging and dropping it to the desired location within the design view.

10. Define a new width and height for the `Grid`, `800` and `600`, and add the following controls. The following lines show the XAML that defines all the controls and some effects for the `lblLibraryName` Label and the `wrapPanel` WrapPanel.

    ○ One `Label` control, `lblLibraryName`, located at the top

    ○ One `ScrollViewer` control, `scrollViewer`

    ○ One `WrapPanel` control, `wrapPanel`, within the `ScrollViewer` control

    ○ One `Label` control, `lblStatus`, located at the bottom

    ○ One `ProgressBar` control, `pgbLoadingStatus`, located at the bottom

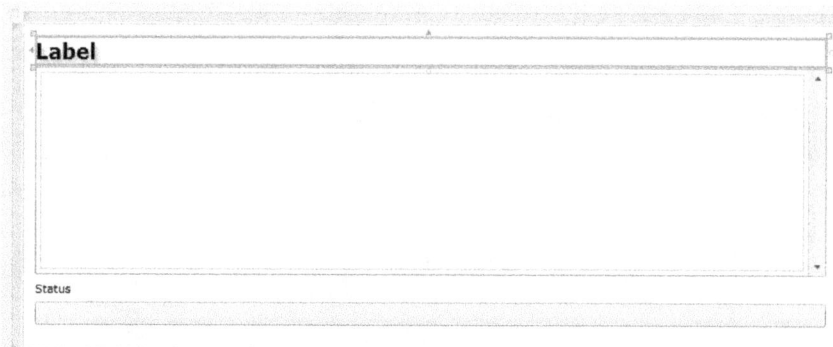

```xml
<UserControl x:Class="SLAssetsBrowser.MainPage"
 xmlns="http://schemas.microsoft.com/winfx/2006/xaml/presentation"
            xmlns:x="http://schemas.microsoft.com/winfx/2006/xaml"
        xmlns:d="http://schemas.microsoft.com/expression/blend/2008"
xmlns:toolkit="http://schemas.microsoft.com/winfx/2006/xaml/
presentation/toolkit"
    xmlns:mc="http://schemas.openxmlformats.org/markup-
compatibility/2006"
    mc:Ignorable="d"
    d:DesignHeight="600" d:DesignWidth="800"  xmlns:sdk="http://
schemas.microsoft.com/winfx/2006/xaml/presentation/sdk">
    <Grid x:Name="LayoutRoot" Loaded="LayoutRoot_Loaded"
Width="Auto" Height="Auto">
    <sdk:Label Height="28" HorizontalAlignment="Left"
Margin="12,12,0,0" Name="lblLibraryName" VerticalAlignment="Top"
Width="776" FontSize="20" FontWeight="Bold" >
        <sdk:Label.Effect>
          <DropShadowEffect ShadowDepth="5" Color="Orange" />
        </sdk:Label.Effect>
    </sdk:Label>
    <ProgressBar Height="22" HorizontalAlignment="Left"
Margin="12,554,0,0" Name="pgbLoadingStatus"
VerticalAlignment="Top" Width="776" />
    <sdk:Label Height="22" HorizontalAlignment="Left"
Margin="12,534,0,0" Name="lblStatus" VerticalAlignment="Top"
Width="776" Content="Status" />
        <ScrollViewer Height="487" HorizontalAlignment="Left"
Margin="12,41,0,0" Name="scrollViewer" VerticalAlignment="Top"
Width="776">
        <toolkit:WrapPanel Name="wrapPanel" Width="Auto"
Height="Auto" RenderTransformOrigin="0.497,0.493">
          <toolkit:WrapPanel.Effect>
            <DropShadowEffect ShadowDepth="10"/>
          </toolkit:WrapPanel.Effect>
        </toolkit:WrapPanel>
      </ScrollViewer>
    </Grid>
</UserControl>
```

11. You can also define the effects in Expression Blend without having to edit the XAML code. You can do so by right-clicking on `MainPage.xaml` and selecting **Open in Expression Blend...** in the context menu. This way, you will be able to work with the additional effects offered by this tool.

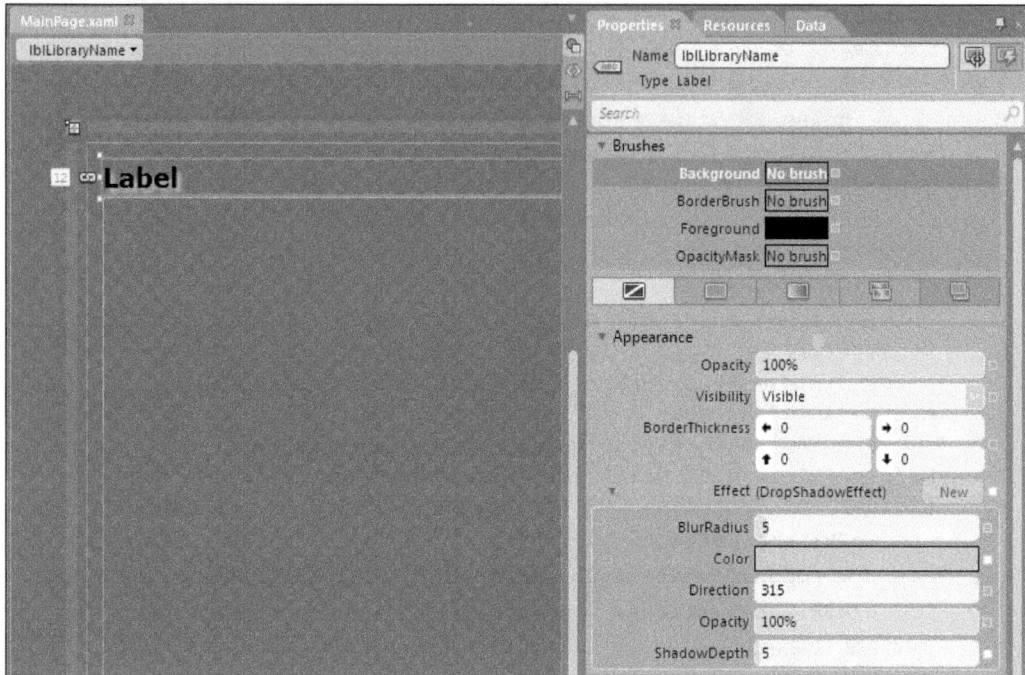

> There are many open source projects that provide additional effects that you can use in your RIAs, such as Silverlight.FX, http://projects.nikhilk.net/SilverlightFX.

12. Open `MainPage.xaml.cs`. Now, it is necessary to add a `using` statement to include the `Microsoft.SharePoint.Client` namespace, as we want to work with the SharePoint Silverlight Client OM. We also have to work with the `BitmapImage` class, included in `System.Windows.Media.Imaging`.

Add the following lines of code:

```
using Microsoft.SharePoint.Client;
using SP = Microsoft.SharePoint.Client;
using System.Windows.Media.Imaging;
```

Add the following seven private variables:

```
private ClientContext _context;
private SP.List _documents;
private string _assetLibraryName;
private int _maxImageWidth = 150;
```

```
private int _imageMargin = 5;
// The background music can be added just once
private bool _backgroundMusicAdded = false;
// The current document to load
private int _documentToLoad;
```

13. Replace the `MainPage` constructor with this new constructor that receives the asset library name as a parameter, assigns its value to the `_assetLibraryName` private variable, and displays it in the `lblLibraryName` Label.

```
public MainPage(string assetLibraryName)
{
  InitializeComponent();
  _assetLibraryName = assetLibraryName;
  lblLibraryName.Content = assetLibraryName;
}
```

We are going to work with three media file types, `Audio`, `Video`, and `Picture`. Add the following code to define an enumeration and a method that returns the media file type according to the received file name's extension:

```
private enum MediaFileType
{
  Audio,
  Video,
  Picture
}

private MediaFileType GetMediaFileType(string fileName)
{
  switch (System.IO.Path.GetExtension(fileName).ToUpper())
  {
    // It isn't necessary to add break;
    // after each line because the code
    // exits with the return statement
    case ".JPG":
    return MediaFileType.Picture;
    case ".JPEG":
    return MediaFileType.Picture;
    case ".GIF":
    return MediaFileType.Picture;
```

```
        case ".WMA":
        return MediaFileType.Audio;
        case ".MP3":
        return MediaFileType.Audio;
        case ".AAC":
        return MediaFileType.Audio;
        case ".WMV":
        return MediaFileType.Video;
        case ".MP4":
        return MediaFileType.Video;
        default:
        return MediaFileType.Picture;
    }
}
```

14. Add the following event handlers that will define and start animations when the user right-clicks on a button that displays an image or a video:

```
private void imageButton_MouseRightButtonDown(object sender,
MouseButtonEventArgs e)
{
  // This ensures that Silverlight won't show up
  // the default Silverlight context menu
  e.Handled = true;
  var hlButton = (sender as HyperlinkButton);
  var image = hlButton.Content as Image;
  // Add a doubleAnimation for a MaxWidth animation
  var doubleAnimMaxWidth = new DoubleAnimation();
  doubleAnimMaxWidth.Duration =
    new Duration(TimeSpan.FromSeconds(6));
  doubleAnimMaxWidth.From = image.ActualWidth;
  doubleAnimMaxWidth.To = scrollViewer.ActualWidth -
    (_imageMargin * 2);
  doubleAnimMaxWidth.FillBehavior = FillBehavior.HoldEnd;
  // Create a new Storyboard to handle the MaxWidth animation
  var storyboardMaxWidth = new Storyboard();
  storyboardMaxWidth.Children.Add(doubleAnimMaxWidth);
  Storyboard.SetTarget(doubleAnimMaxWidth, image);
  Storyboard.SetTargetProperty(doubleAnimMaxWidth,
   new PropertyPath("MaxWidth"));
  storyboardMaxWidth.AutoReverse = true;
  storyboardMaxWidth.RepeatBehavior = new RepeatBehavior(1);
  // Add a doubleAnimation for a MaxHeight animation
```

```
var doubleAnimMaxHeight = new DoubleAnimation();
doubleAnimMaxHeight.Duration = new
  Duration(TimeSpan.FromSeconds(6));
doubleAnimMaxHeight.From = image.ActualHeight;
  doubleAnimMaxHeight.To = scrollViewer.ActualHeight -
    (_imageMargin * 2);
doubleAnimMaxHeight.FillBehavior = FillBehavior.HoldEnd;
// Create a new Storyboard to handle the MaxHeight animation
var storyboardMaxHeight = new Storyboard();
storyboardMaxHeight.Children.Add(doubleAnimMaxHeight);
Storyboard.SetTarget(doubleAnimMaxHeight, image);
Storyboard.SetTargetProperty(doubleAnimMaxHeight,
  new PropertyPath("MaxHeight"));
storyboardMaxHeight.AutoReverse = true;
storyboardMaxHeight.RepeatBehavior = new RepeatBehavior(1);
// Start the previously defined storyboards
storyboardMaxWidth.Begin();
storyboardMaxHeight.Begin();
}


private void videoButton_MouseRightButtonDown(object sender,
MouseButtonEventArgs e)
{
  // This ensures that Silverlight won't show up
  // the default Silverlight context menu
  e.Handled = true;
  var hlb = (sender as HyperlinkButton);
  var element = hlb.Content as MediaElement;
  // Add a doubleAnimation for a MaxWidth animation
  var doubleAnimMaxWidth = new DoubleAnimation();
  doubleAnimMaxWidth.Duration = new
    Duration(TimeSpan.FromSeconds(9));
  doubleAnimMaxWidth.From = element.ActualWidth;
  doubleAnimMaxWidth.To = scrollViewer.ActualWidth -
    (_imageMargin * 2);
  doubleAnimMaxWidth.FillBehavior = FillBehavior.HoldEnd;
  // Create a new Storyboard to handle the MaxWidth animation
  var storyboardMaxWidth = new Storyboard();
  storyboardMaxWidth.Children.Add(doubleAnimMaxWidth);
  Storyboard.SetTarget(doubleAnimMaxWidth, element);
```

```
Storyboard.SetTargetProperty(doubleAnimMaxWidth,
  new PropertyPath("MaxWidth"));
storyboardMaxWidth.AutoReverse = true;
storyboardMaxWidth.RepeatBehavior = new RepeatBehavior(1);
// Add a doubleAnimation for a MaxHeight animation
var doubleAnimMaxHeight = new DoubleAnimation();
doubleAnimMaxHeight.Duration = new
  Duration(TimeSpan.FromSeconds(9));
doubleAnimMaxHeight.From = element.ActualHeight;
doubleAnimMaxHeight.To = scrollViewer.ActualHeight -
  (_imageMargin * 2);
doubleAnimMaxHeight.FillBehavior = FillBehavior.HoldEnd;
// Create a new Storyboard to handle the MaxHeight animation
var storyboardMaxHeight = new Storyboard();
storyboardMaxHeight.Children.Add(doubleAnimMaxHeight);
Storyboard.SetTarget(doubleAnimMaxHeight, element);
Storyboard.SetTargetProperty(doubleAnimMaxHeight,
  new PropertyPath("MaxHeight"));
storyboardMaxHeight.AutoReverse = true;
storyboardMaxHeight.RepeatBehavior = new RepeatBehavior(1);
// Start the previously defined storyboards
storyboardMaxWidth.Begin();
storyboardMaxHeight.Begin();
}
```

Add the following event handler that will restart the reproduction of a video after it ends:

```
private void media_MediaEnded(object sender, RoutedEventArgs e)
{
  var media = (sender as MediaElement);
  // It is necessary to stop it or to set its Position to
TimeSpan.Zero
  media.Stop();
  // Play again
  media.Play();
}
```

15. Add the following two methods that add and return a `HyperlinkButton` to the `wrapPanel` WrapPanel with an image and a video:

```
private HyperlinkButton AddImage(string url)
{
  var image = new Image();
```

```
       image.MaxWidth = _maxImageWidth;
       image.Stretch = Stretch.Uniform;
       var bitmapImage = new BitmapImage(new Uri(url,
         UriKind.Absolute));
       image.Source = bitmapImage;
       var imageButton = new HyperlinkButton();
       imageButton.Visibility = System.Windows.Visibility.Collapsed;
       imageButton.Margin = new Thickness(_imageMargin);
       imageButton.Content = image;
       imageButton.NavigateUri = new Uri(url);
       imageButton.MouseRightButtonDown += new
         MouseButtonEventHandler(imageButton_MouseRightButtonDown);
       imageButton.TargetName = "_blank";
       imageButton.Cursor = Cursors.Hand;
       // Add the new Hyperlink button with the image
       // to the WrapPanel wrapPanel
       wrapPanel.Children.Add(imageButton);
       return imageButton;
    }

private HyperlinkButton AddVideo(string url)
{
  MediaElement media = new MediaElement();
  media.MaxWidth = (_maxImageWidth * 3);
  media.Stretch = Stretch.UniformToFill;
  media.Source = new Uri(url, UriKind.Absolute);
  media.AutoPlay = true;
  media.MediaEnded += new RoutedEventHandler(media_MediaEnded);
  var videoButton = new HyperlinkButton();
  videoButton.Visibility = System.Windows.Visibility.Collapsed;
  videoButton.Margin = new Thickness(_imageMargin);
  videoButton.Content = media;
  videoButton.NavigateUri = new Uri(url);
  videoButton.MouseRightButtonDown += new
    MouseButtonEventHandler(videoButton_MouseRightButtonDown);
  videoButton.TargetName = "_blank";
  videoButton.Cursor = Cursors.Hand;
  // Add the new Hyperlink button with the video
  // to the WrapPanel wrapPanel
  wrapPanel.Children.Add(videoButton);
  return videoButton;
}
```

16. Add the following method that defines and starts animations for the `HyperlinkButton` that displays an image or a video received as a parameter:

```
private void AddImageVideoAnimation(HyperlinkButton hlButton)
{
  // Add a projection to the button
  var projection = new PlaneProjection();
  hlButton.Projection = projection;
  // Add a doubleAnimation for a Projection's RotationZ animation
  var doubleAnimProjectionZ = new DoubleAnimation();
  doubleAnimProjectionZ.Duration = new
    Duration(TimeSpan.FromSeconds(5));
  doubleAnimProjectionZ.From = 0.0;
  doubleAnimProjectionZ.To = 360.0;
  doubleAnimProjectionZ.FillBehavior = FillBehavior.HoldEnd;
  // Create a new Storyboard to handle the Projection's RotationZ
animation
  var storyboardProjectionZ = new Storyboard();
  storyboardProjectionZ.Children.Add(doubleAnimProjectionZ);
  Storyboard.SetTarget(doubleAnimProjectionZ, projection);
  Storyboard.SetTargetProperty(doubleAnimProjectionZ,
    new PropertyPath("RotationZ"));
  // Add a doubleAnimation for a Projection's RotationY animation
  var doubleAnimProjectionY = new DoubleAnimation();
  doubleAnimProjectionY.Duration = new
    Duration(TimeSpan.FromSeconds(3));
  doubleAnimProjectionY.From = -45.0;
  doubleAnimProjectionY.To = 45.0;
  doubleAnimProjectionY.FillBehavior = FillBehavior.HoldEnd;
  doubleAnimProjectionY.RepeatBehavior = RepeatBehavior.Forever;
  doubleAnimProjectionY.AutoReverse = true;
  // Create a new Storyboard to handle the Projection's RotationY
animation
  var storyboardProjectionY = new Storyboard();
  storyboardProjectionY.Children.Add(doubleAnimProjectionY);
  Storyboard.SetTarget(doubleAnimProjectionY, projection);
  Storyboard.SetTargetProperty(doubleAnimProjectionY,
    new PropertyPath("RotationY"));
  // Add a doubleAnimation for an Opacity animation
  var doubleAnimOpacity = new DoubleAnimation();
  doubleAnimOpacity.Duration = new
    Duration(TimeSpan.FromSeconds(5));
  doubleAnimOpacity.From = 0.0;
```

```
doubleAnimOpacity.To = 1.0;
doubleAnimOpacity.FillBehavior = FillBehavior.HoldEnd;
// Create a new Storyboard to handle the Opacity animation
var storyboardOpacity = new Storyboard();
storyboardOpacity.Children.Add(doubleAnimOpacity);
Storyboard.SetTarget(doubleAnimOpacity, hlButton);
Storyboard.SetTargetProperty(doubleAnimOpacity,
  new PropertyPath("Opacity"));
// Start the previously defined storyboards
storyboardProjectionZ.Begin();
storyboardOpacity.Begin();
storyboardProjectionY.Begin();
hlButton.Visibility = System.Windows.Visibility.Visible;
}
```

17. Add the following method that plays an audio file as background music for the application. It will just play background music once, no matter the number of times it is called.

```
private void AddBackgroundMusic(string url)
{
  if (_backgroundMusicAdded)
  {
    // Background music already loaded
    return;
  }
  _backgroundMusicAdded = true;
  MediaElement backgroundMusic = new MediaElement();
  LayoutRoot.Children.Add(backgroundMusic);
  backgroundMusic.Volume = 0.8;
  backgroundMusic.Source = new Uri(url);
  backgroundMusic.Play();
}
```

18. Now, it is necessary to add code to connect to the SharePoint server, connect to the lists, retrieve data from the assets library name stored in _assetLibraryName, request its files, and process each picture, video, and audio file to add it to the wrapPanel WrapPanel. These methods will run in the UI thread. Replace "http://gaston-pc" with the SharePoint website's URL.

```
private void Connect()
{
  // Runs in the UI Thread
```

```
    lblStatus.Content = "Started";
    // Replace http://gaston-pc with
    // your SharePoint 2010 Server URL and Site
    _context = new SP.ClientContext(new Uri("http://gaston-pc",
UriKind.Absolute));
    _context.Load(_context.Web);
    _context.ExecuteQueryAsync(OnConnectSucceeded, null);
}

private void ConnectLists()
{
    // Runs in the UI Thread
    lblStatus.Content = "Web Connected. Connecting to Lists...";
    _context.Load(_context.Web.Lists);
    _context.ExecuteQueryAsync(OnConnectListsSucceeded, null);
}

private void GetListData()
{
    // Runs in the UI Thread
    lblStatus.Content = "Lists Connected. Getting List data...";
    _documents = _context.Web.Lists.GetByTitle(_assetLibraryName);
    _context.Load(_documents);
    _context.Load(_documents.RootFolder);
    // Request the files
    _context.Load(_documents.RootFolder.Files);
    _context.ExecuteQueryAsync(OnGetListDataSucceeded, null);
}

private void LoadItems()
{
    // Runs in the UI Thread
    lblStatus.Content = String.Format("Loading {0} items...",
      _documents.RootFolder.Files.Count);
    pgbLoadingStatus.Maximum = _documents.RootFolder.Files.Count;
    pgbLoadingStatus.Value = 0;
    _documentToLoad = 0;
    // Clear the WrapPanel children
    wrapPanel.Children.Clear();
    foreach (File file in _documents.RootFolder.Files)
    {
```

```
        _context.Load(file);
        _context.ExecuteQueryAsync(
        OnLoadItemsSucceeded,
        OnLoadItemsFailed);
    }
}


private void ShowItem()
{
    // Runs in the UI Thread
    lblStatus.Content = String.Format("Processing item # {0}",
        _documentToLoad);
    string fileName =
    _documents.RootFolder.Files[_documentToLoad].Name;
    string Url = _context.Url + _documents.RootFolder.Files
        [_documentToLoad].ServerRelativeUrl;
    switch (GetMediaFileType(fileName))
    {
        case MediaFileType.Audio:
        AddBackgroundMusic(Url);
        break;
        case MediaFileType.Picture:
        var imageButton = AddImage(Url);
        AddImageVideoAnimation(imageButton);
        break;
        case MediaFileType.Video:
        var videoButton = AddVideo(Url);
        AddImageVideoAnimation(videoButton);
        break;
    }
    // Update the progress bar
    pgbLoadingStatus.Value++;
    _documentToLoad++;
    if (_documentToLoad >= _documents.RootFolder.Files.Count)
    {
        // All documents loaded
        lblStatus.Content = "Displaying animations for all the
documents.";
    }
}
```

19. Most of the methods added in the previous step execute asynchronous queries to the SharePoint server. Both the successful and failed requests fire asynchronous callbacks that are going to run in another thread, different from the UI thread. Hence, if you have to update the UI, it is necessary to invoke the code to run in the UI thread. The following methods, which are going to be fired as asynchronous callbacks, schedule the execution of other methods to continue with the necessary program flow in the UI thread:

```
private void ShowErrorInformation(ClientRequestFailedEventArgs
args)
{
  MessageBox.Show("Request failed. " + args.Message + "\n" +
    args.StackTrace + "\n" +
  args.ErrorDetails + "\n" + args.ErrorValue);
}

private void OnConnectSucceeded(Object sender,
  SP.ClientRequestSucceededEventArgs args)
{
  // This callback isn't called on the UI thread
  Dispatcher.BeginInvoke(ConnectLists);
}

private void OnConnectListsSucceeded(Object sender, SP.ClientReque
stSucceededEventArgs args)
{
  // This callback isn't called on the UI thread
  Dispatcher.BeginInvoke(GetListData);
}

private void OnGetListDataSucceeded(Object sender, SP.ClientReques
tSucceededEventArgs args)
{
  // This callback isn't called on the UI thread
  Dispatcher.BeginInvoke(LoadItems);
}

private void OnLoadItemsFailed(Object sender,
SP.ClientRequestFailedEventArgs args)
{
  // This callback isn't called on the UI thread
  // Invoke a delegate and send the args instance as a parameter
  Dispatcher.BeginInvoke(() => ShowErrorInformation(args));
}
```

```
private void OnLoadItemsSucceeded(Object sender, SP.ClientRequestS
ucceededEventArgs args)
{
  // This callback isn't called on the UI thread
  Dispatcher.BeginInvoke(ShowItem);
}
```

20. Add the following line to the LayoutRoot_Loaded event:

```
Connect();
```

We created a new Silverlight RIA that receives an asset library name as a parameter from the Visual Web Part that renders this application. When the user selects an asset library from a drop-down list in the Visual Web Part, the Silverlight RIA will load the images, videos, and audio from the chosen asset library. We added the necessary code to create an application that displays the images and videos with many animations and effects.

Linking a SharePoint Visual Web Part to a Silverlight RIA

Follow these steps to link the previously created Visual Web Part, AssetsBrowserWebPart, with this new Silverlight RIA, SLAssetsBrowser. This way, the Silverlight RIA will be part of the package that contains the Visual Web Part.

1. Stay in Visual Studio as a system administrator user.

2. Expand the SharePoint Visual Web Part folder, AssetsBrowserWebPart, in the **Solution Explorer**.

3. Now, right-click on AssetsBrowserWebPart and select **Properties** in the context menu that appears. You will see the values for its properties in the **Properties** panel.

4.. In the **Properties** palette, click the ellipsis (**...**) button for the **Project Output References** property. The **Project Output References** dialog box will appear.

5. Click on **Add** below the **Members:** list. The SharePoint 2010 Visual Web Part's project name, SPAssetsBrowserWebPart, will appear as a new member.

6. Go to its properties, shown on the list located at the right. Select the Silverlight application project's name, SLAssetsBrowser, in the **Project Name** drop-down list.

7. Select `Element File` in the **Deployment Type** drop-down list. The following value will appear in **Deployment Location**, `{SharePointRoot}\Template\ Features\{FeatureName}\AssetsBrowserWebPart\`. The following screenshot shows the dialog box with the explained values:

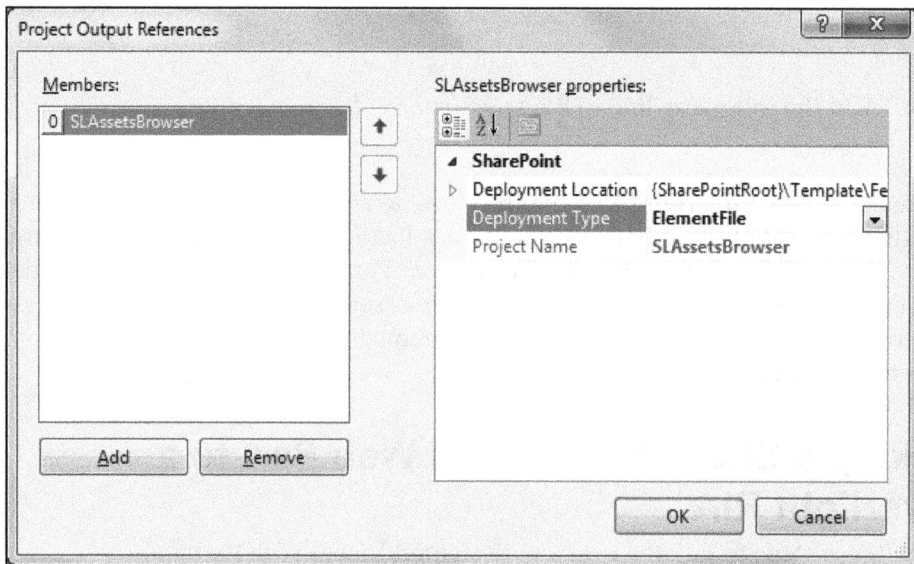

8. Click **OK**. The SharePoint Visual Web Part project now includes a reference to the Silverlight application project, `SLTasksViewer`. However, it is still necessary to add a line to the `Elements.xml` file to make the Silverlight RIA be part of the Visual Web Part.

9. Open the `Elements.xml` file. The following lines are the initial contents of this XML file. They describe the elements that compose this SharePoint 2010 Visual Web Part.

```xml
<?xml version="1.0" encoding="utf-8"?>
<Elements xmlns="http://schemas.microsoft.com/sharepoint/" >
  <Module Name="AssetsBrowserWebPart" List="113"
    Url="_catalogs/wp">
    <File Path="AssetsBrowserWebPart\AssetsBrowserWebPart.webpart"
Url="AssetsBrowserWebPart.webpart" Type="GhostableInLibrary" >
      <Property Name="Group" Value="Custom" />
    </File>
  </Module>
</Elements>
```

10. Add the highlighted line before `</Module>`. The new contents of this XML file will include a reference to the linked Silverlight project `.xap` file, `SLAssetsBrowser.xap`. This is a new element for this SharePoint 2010 Visual Web Part. During the deployment process, the `SLAssetsBrowser.xap` file will be located in the `AssetsBrowserWebPart` folder in the **SharePoint package file**, also known as the **WSP package**, because it has a `.wsp` extension. Thus, the WSP package will also deploy the Silverlight application to the SharePoint server.

```xml
<?xml version="1.0" encoding="utf-8"?>
<Elements xmlns="http://schemas.microsoft.com/sharepoint/" >
  <Module Name="AssetsBrowserWebPart" List="113" Url="_catalogs/
wp">
    <File Path="AssetsBrowserWebPart\AssetsBrowserWebPart.webpart"
Url="AssetsBrowserWebPart.webpart" Type="GhostableInLibrary" >
      <Property Name="Group" Value="Custom" />
    </File>
    <!-- Added -->
    <File Path="AssetsBrowserWebPart\SLAssetsBrowser.xap"
      Url="SLAssetsBrowser.xap" />
    <!-- EOF Added -->
  </Module>
</Elements>
```

11. Remember to enable Silverlight debugging instead of the default script debugging capabilities.

12. Right-click on the solution's name in **Solution Explorer** and select **Properties** from the context menu that appears. Select **Startup Project** in the list on the left, activate **Single startup project**, and choose the SharePoint Visual Web Part project's name in the drop-down list below it, `SPAssetsBrowserWebPart`. This way, the solution is going to start with the SharePoint project and not with the Silverlight application. This is very important because it will allow us to debug the Silverlight application when it runs in a SharePoint site. Then, click **OK**.

13. Expand **Features | Feature1** in Solution Explorer and double-click on `Feature1.feature`. Visual Studio will display a new panel with the feature title, description, scope, and its items. The feature will include three files in the **Items in the feature** list, `AssetsBrowserWebPart`, `AssetsBrowsersWebPartUserControl.ascx` and `Elements.xml`.

Feature1.feature ×	

Title: SPAssetsBrowserWebPart Feature1

Description: My Visual WebPart Feature

Scope: Site ▾

Items in the Solution:

Items in the Feature:

AssetsBrowserWebPart (SPAssetsBrowserWebPart)
VisualWebPart

▲ Files
    AssetsBrowserWebPart.webpart
    AssetsBrowserWebPartUserControl.ascx
    Elements.xml

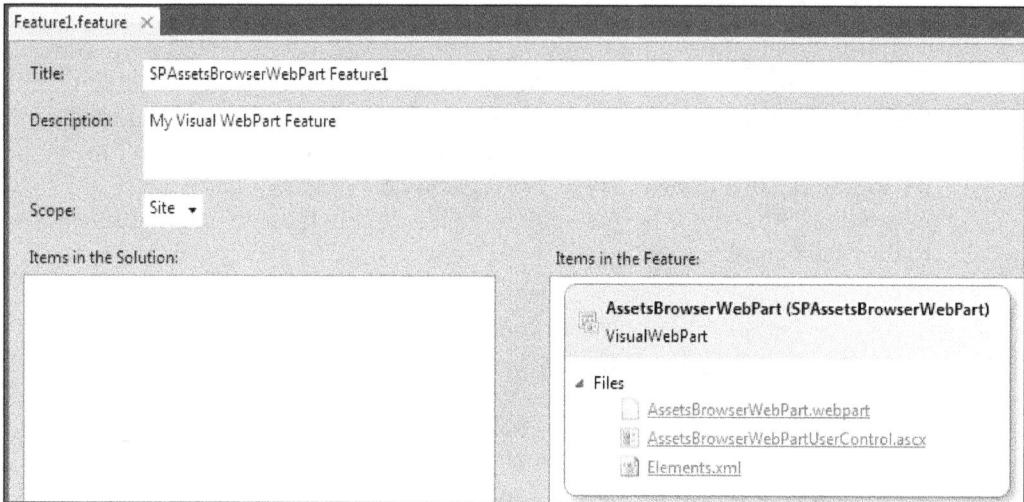

14. Build and deploy the solution.

Adding a SharePoint Visual Web Part in a Web Page

Now that the WSP package has been deployed to the SharePoint site, follow these steps to create a new web page and add the Visual Web Part that includes and renders the Silverlight RIA. In this case, it isn't necessary to upload the `.xap` file, because it was already deployed with the WSP package.

1. Open your default web browser, view the SharePoint site, and log in with your username and password.

2. Click **Site Actions | New Page** and SharePoint will display a new dialog box requesting a name for the new page. Enter `AssetsBrowser` and click on **Create**. SharePoint will display the editing tools for the new page.

3. Click **Insert | Web Part** in the ribbon and a new panel will appear. Select **Custom** in **Categories** and then the previously deployed Visual Web Part name, AssetsBrowserWebPart, in **Web Parts**.

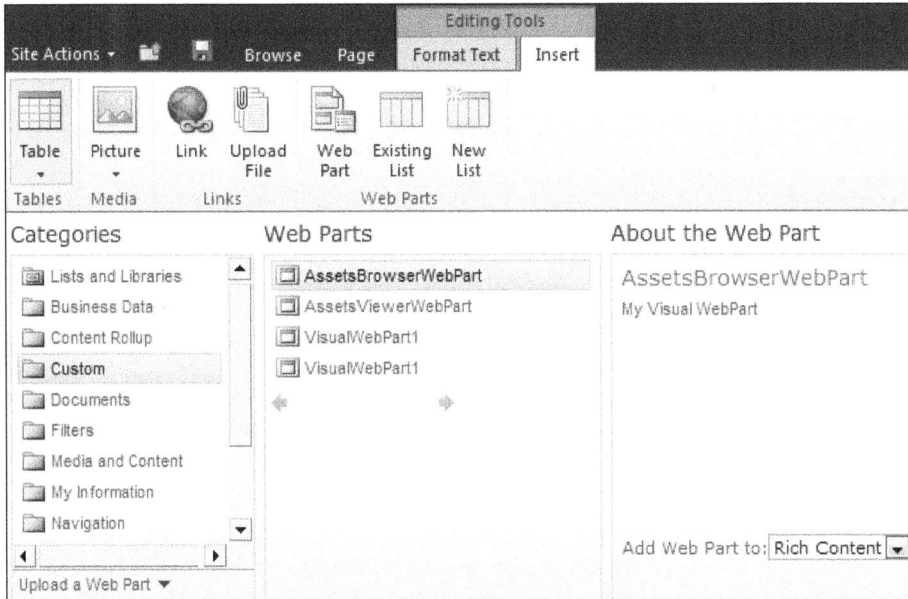

4. Click **Add**. The **Select the Asset Library to display** legend and the drop-down list will appear. Click on the down arrow, located at the top, and then select **Edit Web Part**. The **AssetsBrowserWebPart** pane will appear at the right. It will enable us to define many properties that affect the appearance and behavior for this Visual Web Part that renders a Silverlight RIA.

5. Enter Assets Browser in **Title**.

6. Click on **Yes** in **Should the Web Part have a fixed height?** and enter 700 in **Pixels**.

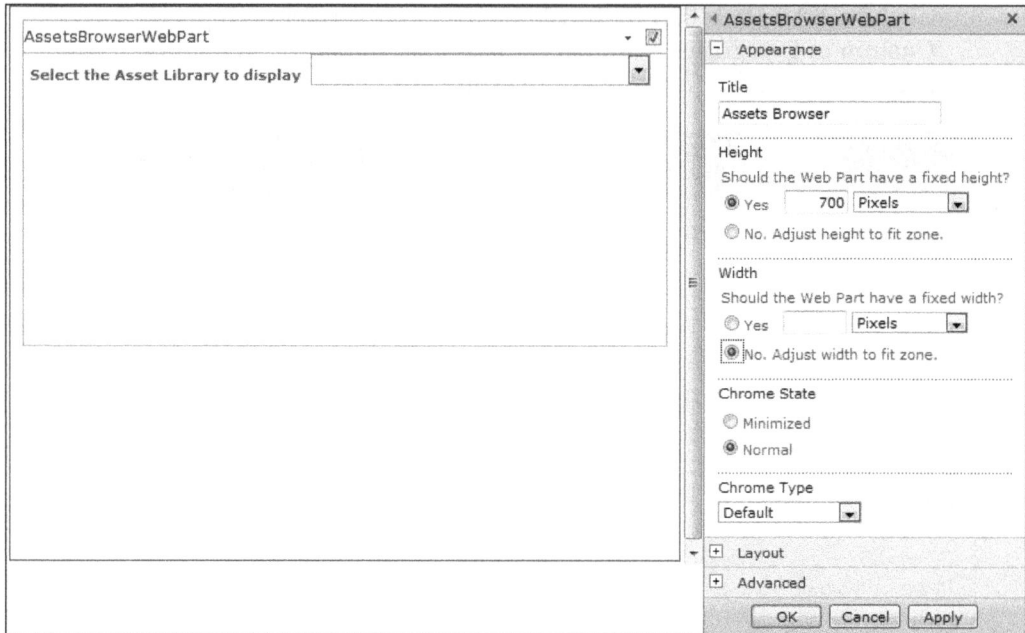

7. Click on **No. Adjust width to fit zone.** in **Should the Web Part have a fixed width?**, and then on **OK**.

8. Click on the **Save** button in the ribbon. Now, the new page will appear displaying the previously created Visual Web Part. This Web Part is going to display the drop-down list of asset libraries with pictures, videos, and audio files. The Silverlight RIA will appear below the drop-down list displaying the images and videos found in the first asset library in the drop-down list with interactive animations and dazzling effects. It is going to load and then it will display its different status values in the label located at the bottom:

    ° **Started**

    ° **Web Connected. Connecting to Lists...**

    ° **Lists Connected. Getting List data...**

    ° **Loading n items...**

    ° **Processing item #x...**, where x is the number of picture, video or audio file being processed

    ° **Displaying animations for all the documents. (this should be Bullet end)**

The following screenshot shows this value for the label and the Silverlight RIA displaying the images and videos for the chosen asset library.

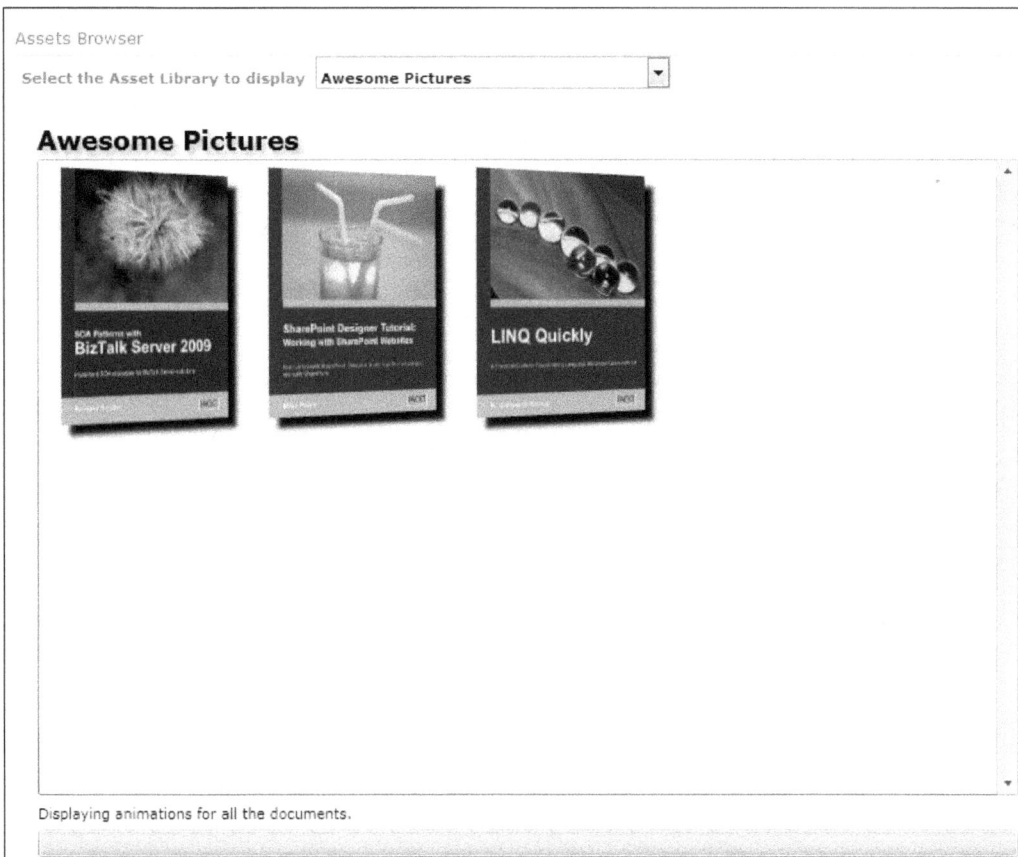

9. Now, go back to Visual Studio and open the code-behind
   file for AssetsBrowserWebPartUserControl.ascx,
   AssetsBrowserWebPartUserControl.ascx.cs. Insert a breakpoint in
   the first line of the Page_Load event handler, if (!IsPostBack). Insert
   another breakpoint in the line of code of the cboDocumentLibraries_
   SelectedIndexChanged event handler, SelectedList =
   cboDocumentLibraries.SelectedValue;.

```
        protected void Page_Load(object sender, EventArgs e)
        {
            if (!IsPostBack)
            {
                var _context = SPContext.Current;
                var documentLibraries = _context.Web.GetListsOfType(SPBaseType.DocumentLibrary);
                foreach (SPList libraryList in documentLibraries)
                {
                    if ((libraryList.RootFolder.ItemCount > 0) &&
                        ((libraryList.ContentTypes[0].Name == "Picture") ||
                         (libraryList.ContentTypes[0].Name == "Image") ||
                         (libraryList.ContentTypes[0].Name == "Audio") ||
                         (libraryList.ContentTypes[0].Name == "Video")))
                    {
                        // The list has at least 1 element
                        cboDocumentLibraries.Items.Add(new ListItem(libraryList.Title));
                    }
                }
                // Select the first item in the dropdown list
                cboDocumentLibraries.SelectedIndex = 0;
            }
            SelectedList = cboDocumentLibraries.SelectedValue;
        }

        protected void cboDocumentLibraries_SelectedIndexChanged(object sender, EventArgs e)
        {
            SelectedList = cboDocumentLibraries.SelectedValue;
        }
    }
}
```

10. Open `AssetsBrowserWebPart.cs` and insert a breakpoint in the first line of the `OnPreRender` event handler.

11. Select **Debug | Start Debugging** from the Visual Studio's main menu or press *F5* to start debugging the solution.

12. Visual Studio will display a new window for your default web browser with the server and Site Collection in which you deployed the WSP package.

13. Enter the URL for the previously added page that contains the Visual Web Part in the web browser. This way, the ASP.NET code for the Visual Web Part will start running and Visual Studio will stop in the breakpoint established in the `Page_Load` event handler in the code-behind file, `AssetsBrowserWebPartUserControl.ascx.cs`.

14. Inspect the value for `IsPostBack` and it will be `false`, because it is the first time that the Visual Web Part is rendered. Thus, the method will run the code to add the titles of the document libraries that have pictures, images, audio, or video files. The first item for the `cboDocumentLibraries DropDownList` will be selected as the default library and the `SelectedList` property is going to save the selected title. Run the code step-by-step to understand the execution flow.

15. Then, Visual Studio will stop in the breakpoint established in the `OnPreRender` event handler, in `AssetsBrowserWebPart.cs`. The `renderHost` string will include a line that defines the value for the `Name` parameter. This parameter will specify a string with the value stored in the `SelectedList` public property. In this method, the code defines a new `LiteralControl` instance initialized with the `renderHost` string and adds it to the Controls `ControlCollection`.

16. Press *F5* and the web browser will display the Silverlight RIA with the first asset library contents.

17. Now, select a different asset library to display in the drop-down list located at the top of the Visual Web Part. This way, the ASP.NET code for the Visual Web Part will start running again, performing a postback, and Visual Studio will stop in the breakpoint established in the `Page_Load` event handler in the code-behind file, `AssetsBrowserWebPartUserControl.ascx.cs`.

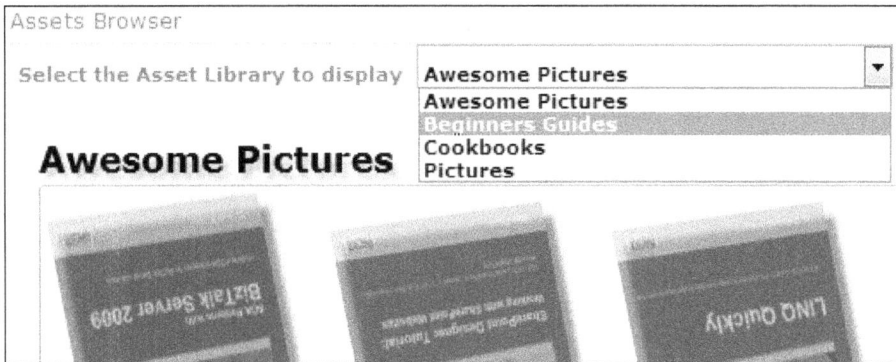

18. Inspect the value for `IsPostBack` and it will be `true` because it is a postback for the `UserControl`. Thus, the method won't run the code to add the titles of the document libraries to the drop-down list. It will just run the line that sets the `SelectedList` property to the selected title. Run the code step-by-step to understand the execution flow.

19. Then, Visual Studio will stop in the breakpoint established in the `OnPreRender` event handler, in `AssetsBrowserWebPart.cs`. The `renderHost` string will include a line that defines the new value for the `Name` parameter, held in the previously explained `SelectedList` public property. This way, the new `LiteralControl` instance will add a Silverlight RIA with a different parameter value.

20. Press *F5* and the web browser will display the Silverlight RIA with the new asset library contents. The images and the videos will appear with animations and effects.

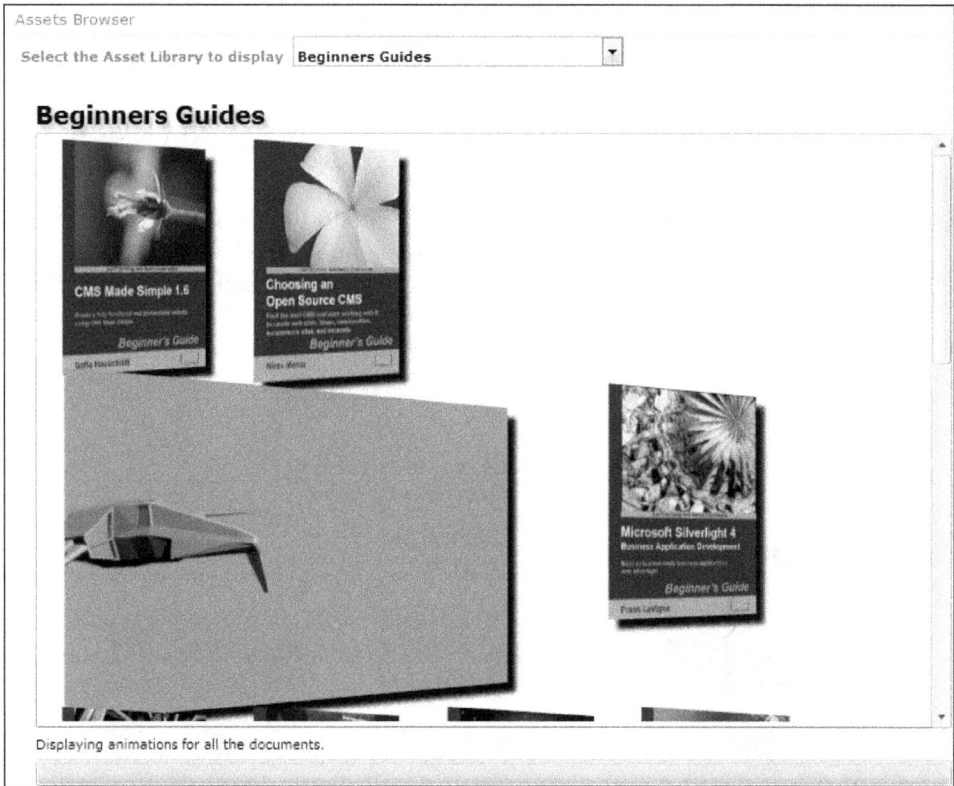

We added the SharePoint Visual Web Part to a new Web page in the SharePoint Site Collection. Then, we used Visual Studio to debug the Visual Web Part and we learned how Visual Web Parts renders a Silverlight RIA with parameters. We inserted many breakpoints to analyze the postback performed by the UserControl within the Visual Web Part.

Organizing controls in a containing box

The Silverlight RIA displays a WrapPanel control, wrapPanel, within a ScrollViewer, scrollViewer. The WrapPanel control works as a container and it locates its child elements in sequential positions from left to right, in columns, when its Orientation property is set to Horizontal. At the edge of the containing box, it breaks the content to the next row and therefore, it simplifies the organization of HyperlinkButton controls.

As we don't know the number of rows that will be necessary to display all the pictures and videos in the `WrapPanel` control, the `ScrollViewer` control defines a scrollable viewport. When the content of the `WrapPanel` is not entirely visible, the `ScrollViewer` will display scrollbars to allow the user to move the content area that is visible. The visible content is known as, **viewport** and all of the content included in the `ScrollViewer` is known as the **extent**.

The XAML markup in `MainPage.xaml` defines a `DropShadowEffect` for the `WrapPanel` control, with its `ShadowDepth` property set to `10`. This way, all the `HyperlinkButton` controls added as `wrapPanel`'s children will inherit this effect and will drop a shadow with a depth of `10` pixels.

```
<ScrollViewer Height="487" HorizontalAlignment="Left"
Margin="12,41,0,0" Name="scrollViewer" VerticalAlignment="Top"
Width="776">
  <toolkit:WrapPanel Name="wrapPanel" Width="Auto" Height="Auto"
RenderTransformOrigin="0.497,0.493">
    <toolkit:WrapPanel.Effect>
      <DropShadowEffect ShadowDepth="10"/>
    </toolkit:WrapPanel.Effect>
  </toolkit:WrapPanel>
</ScrollViewer>
```

Reading files from an assets library

The `GetListData` method requests the asset library, a special list, specified in `_assetLibraryName`, and loads it, its `RootFolder Folder`, and its `RootFolder.Files FileCollection`.

```
_documents = _context.Web.Lists.GetByTitle(_assetLibraryName);
_context.Load(_documents);
_context.Load(_documents.RootFolder);
_context.Load(_documents.RootFolder.Files);
```

After the successful asynchronous execution of the queries, the `LoadItems` method clears the children for the `wrapPanel WrapPanel`. Then, it runs an asynchronous query to load each `File` in the asset library, `_documents, RootFolder.Files FileCollection`.

```
wrapPanel.Children.Clear();
foreach (File file in _documents.RootFolder.Files)
{
  _context.Load(file);
  _context.ExecuteQueryAsync(
          OnLoadItemsSucceeded,
            OnLoadItemsFailed);
}
```

Each successful asynchronous query will schedule the `ShowItem` method to run in the UI thread. The first time this method is called, `_documentToLoad` is set to `0` and the code in this method will increment `_documentToLoad` each time it finishes processing a file. The method retrieves the file name, stored in the `Name` property for the `File` instance to determine the media file type and saves it in the local `fileName` string. Then, it computes an absolute `Url` to access the file, `_context.Url` concatenated with the `ServerRelativeUrl` property for the `File` instance, and saves it in the local `Url` string.

```
string fileName = _documents.RootFolder.Files[_documentToLoad].Name;
string Url = _context.Url + _documents.RootFolder.Files[_
documentToLoad].ServerRelativeUrl;
```

Working with interactive animations and effects

A `switch` statement considers the results of the `GetMediaFileType` method that receives the `fileName` string as a parameter. As previously explained this method determines the media file type according to the extension and returns a `MediaFileType` as a result.

If the file type is `MediaFileType.Picture`, the method calls the `AddImage` method with the `Url` string as a parameter and it saves the `HyperlinkButton` instance returned by this method in `imageButton`. Then, it calls the `AddImageVideoAnimation` with `imageButton` as a parameter.

```
case MediaFileType.Picture:
  var imageButton = AddImage(Url);
  AddImageVideoAnimation(imageButton);
    break;
```

The `AddImage` method creates a new `Image` instance, sets values for its `MaxWidth` and `Stretch` properties, creates a `BitmapImage`, `bitmapImage`, with the absolute `Uri` from the URL received as a parameter, `url`, and assigns `bitmapImage` to the `image.Source` property.

```
var image = new Image();
image.MaxWidth = _maxImageWidth;
image.Stretch = Stretch.Uniform;
var bitmapImage = new BitmapImage(new Uri(url, UriKind.Absolute));
image.Source = bitmapImage;
```

Then, the code creates a new invisible `HyperlinkButton`, `imageButton`, and sets its `Content` property to the previously created `Image` instance, `image`. When `imageButton` becomes visible, it will show the bitmap image. The `NavigateUri` property for `imageButton` is set to a new `Uri` from the URL received as a parameter, `url`. The `TargetName` property is set to `_blank`, and therefore, when the user clicks the `HyperlinkButton`, the web browser will open a new window and will display the image from the URL.

The code attaches an event handler to the `MouseRightButtonDown` event that occurs when the user clicks the right mouse button and the mouse pointer is over the `Hyperlinkbutton`. It assigns a new `MouseButtonEventHandler` that will fire the `imageButton_MouseRightButtonDown` method. This method runs an animation for the `Hyperlinkbutton`.

```
var imageButton = new HyperlinkButton();
imageButton.Visibility = System.Windows.Visibility.Collapsed;
imageButton.Margin = new Thickness(_imageMargin);
imageButton.Content = image;
imageButton.NavigateUri = new Uri(url);
imageButton.MouseRightButtonDown += new MouseButtonEventHandler(imageB
utton_MouseRightButtonDown);
imageButton.TargetName = "_blank";
imageButton.Cursor = Cursors.Hand;
```

Finally, it is necessary to add the `HyperlinkButton` as a child to the `wrapPanel` `WrapPanel` and return the instance. As previously explained, `wrapPanel` will take care of organizing the layout of all the `HyperlinkButton` instances added as children.

```
wrapPanel.Children.Add(imageButton);
return imageButton;
```

At this point, the `HyperlinkButton` is invisible, because its `Visibility` property was set to `System.Windows.Visibility.Collapsed`. However, when the `AddImage` method returns, the `AddImageVideoAnimation` receives the `HyperlinkButton` control as a parameter, `hlButton`, and brings life to the image that it displays.

Firstly, it adds a `PlaneProjection` instance to the `HyperlinkButton`, `hlButton`, by setting its `Projection` property to a new `PlaneProjection` instance, `projection`. `PlaneProjection` is a subclass of the `Projection` class. The latter allows describing how to project a 2D object in the 3D space by using perspective transforms. Then, the code will run an animation with the values that define the perspective transform for `hlButton`.

```
var projection = new PlaneProjection();
hlButton.Projection = projection;
```

> The `RotationX`, `RotationY`, and `RotationZ` properties for a `PlaneProjection` instance specify the number of degrees to rotate the `HyperlinkButton` in the space. The `LocalOffsetX` and `LocalOffsetY` properties specify the distance the `HyperlinkButton` is translated along each axis of the `HyperlinkButton`'s plane.

Then, the code defines three `DoubleAnimation` (`System.Windows.Media.Animation.DolubleAnimation`) instances and adds them as children of their corresponding `Storyboard` (`System.Windows.Media.Animation.Storyboard`) instances. A `DoubleAnimation` instance allows us to animate the value of a `Double` property between two target values specified by their `From` and `To` properties. It uses a linear interpolation over a specified duration, specified by the `Duration` property. Each `Storyboard` instance defines a container timeline that provides object and property targeting information for its child `DoubleAnimation` instance. The code creates the `DoubleAnimation` and `Storyboard` instances summarized in the following table:

DoubleAnimation instance	Storyboard instance	Animates	From	To	Duration (seconds)
doubleAnim ProjectionZ	storyboard ProjectionZ	projection. RotationZ	0.0	360.0	5
doubleAnim ProjectionY	storyboard ProjectionY	projection. RotationY	45.0	45.0	3
doubleAnim Opacity	storyboard Opacity	hlButton. Opacity	0.0	1.0	5

The following lines create the `doubleAnimProjectionZ DoubleAnimation` and set its properties. The `FillBehavior` property is set to `FillBehavior.HoldEnd` to specify that the animation must hold its value after it reaches the end of its active period. This way, the target property for this animation will remain at its end value after the animation ends and it won't revert to its non-animated value.

```
var doubleAnimProjectionZ = new DoubleAnimation();
doubleAnimProjectionZ.Duration = new Duration(TimeSpan.
FromSeconds(5));
doubleAnimProjectionZ.From = 0.0;
doubleAnimProjectionZ.To = 360.0;
doubleAnimProjectionZ.FillBehavior = FillBehavior.HoldEnd;
```

The next lines create the `Storyboard` instance and add `doubleAnimProjectionZ` as a child. Then, it is necessary to set the target object and the target property by calling the static methods `Storyboard.SetTarget` and `Storyboard.SetTargetProperty` with `doubleAnimProjectionZ` as its first parameter.

```
var storyboardProjectionZ = new Storyboard();
storyboardProjectionZ.Children.Add(doubleAnimProjectionZ);
Storyboard.SetTarget(doubleAnimProjectionZ, projection);
Storyboard.SetTargetProperty(doubleAnimProjectionZ, new
PropertyPath("RotationZ"));
```

The animations defined in `doubleAnimProjectionZ` and `doubleAnimOpacity` will run just one. However, `doubleAnimProjectionY` will run forever and it will auto reverse its execution, because its `RepeatBehavior` is set to `RepeatBehavior.Forever` and `Autoreverse` to `true`. Once it reaches the value specified by `To` for `projection.RotationY`, it will start a new animation from this value to the value specified by `From`, in the reverse direction.

```
doubleAnimProjectionY.RepeatBehavior = RepeatBehavior.Forever;
doubleAnimProjectionY.AutoReverse = true;
```

Once the method defines all the properties for the `DoubleAnimation` and `Storyboard` instances, it applies the animations associated with each Storyboard to their targets and initiates them by calling the `Begin` method.

```
storyboardProjectionZ.Begin();
storyboardOpacity.Begin();
storyboardProjectionY.Begin();
hlButton.Visibility = System.Windows.Visibility.Visible;
```

It is also possible for a single `Storyboard` instance to have many `DoubleAnimation` or other `Animation` subclasses as children. In this case, we used an independent `Storyboard` instance for each animation, because we want to have full control over each one to allow us to start and/or stop each animation to experience different alternatives for the UX in the future. However, if we just need to start all the animations at the same time, we can create a single `Storyboard` instance, add all the `DoubleAnimation` instances as their children, set the `Target` and `TargetProperty` for each `DoubleAnimation`, and call the `Begin` method.

When you open the page that contains the Visual Web Part, the Silverlight RIA will display all the hyperlink buttons that display images and videos with dazzling movements. `doubleAnimProjectionY` will run forever. The following screenshot shows one of the frames for the animations:

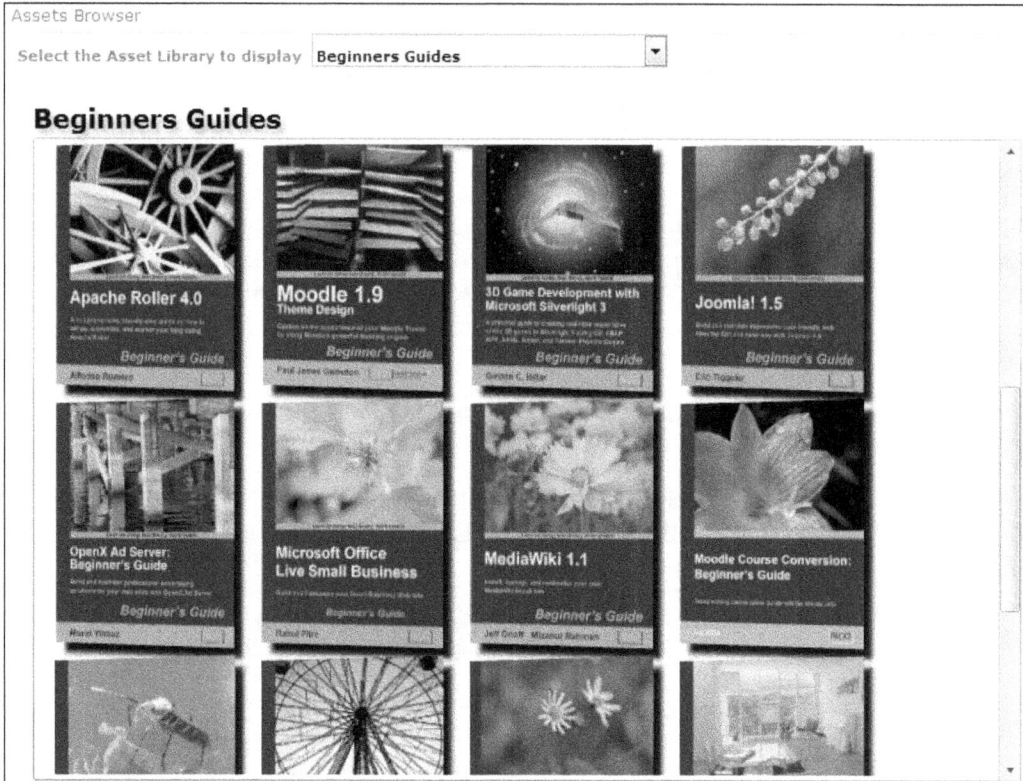

When you click on a dancing image, an animated `Hyperlink` button, the web browser will open a new window with the image displayed with its full size. When you right-click on a dancing image, the code in the `imageButton_MouseRightButtonDown` method will run and the image will go on performing the same animation but it will also grow and then stretch. The container `WrapPanel` will make sure that the different elements displayed reorganize as the hyperlink button grows and stretches. The following picture shows one of the frames for the animation.

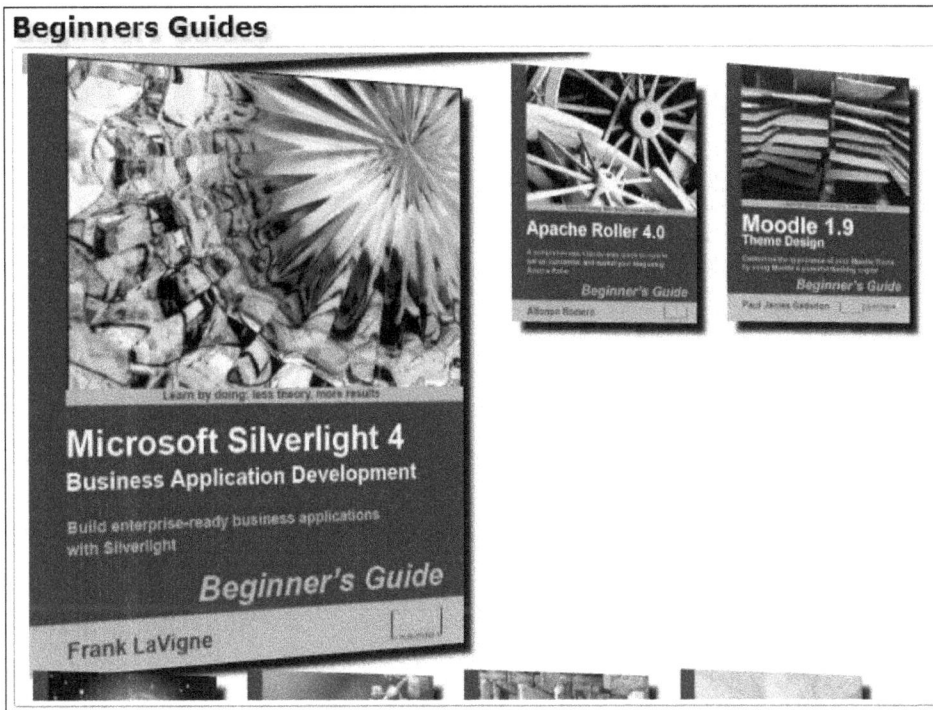

The `imageButton_MouseRightButtonDown` method receives two parameters, `object sender` and `MouseButtonEventArgs e`. The first line sets the `Handled` property for `e` to `true`. This way, it ensures that Silverlight won't show the default Silverlight context menu that appears when the user right-clicks within the Silverlight application area.

```
e.Handled = true;
```

As we attached this method as an event handler for the `MouseRightButtonDown` event for a `HyperlinkButton`, `sender` can be cast to `HyperlinkButton`, `hlb` and we can access its `Content` property to access its associated `Image` and store its reference in `image`.

```
var hlButton = (sender as HyperlinkButton);
var image = hlButton.Content as Image;
```

Then, the code defines two `DoubleAnimation` instances and adds them as children of their corresponding `Storyboard` instances. The code creates the `DoubleAnimation` and `Storyboard` instances summarized in the following table.

DoubleAnimation instance	Storyboard instance	Animates	From	To	Duration (seconds)
doubleAnim MaxWidth	storyboard MaxWidth	image. MaxWidth	image. Actual Width	scrollViewer. ActualWidth - (_imageMargin * 2)	6
doubleAnim MaxHeight	storyboard MaxHeight	image. MaxHeight	Image. Actual Height	scrollViewer. ActualHeight - (_imageMargin * 2)	6

Both `DoubleAnimation` instances have their `AutoReverse` property set to `true` and `RepeatBehavior` set to `RepeatBehavior(1)`. This means that the image will grow and then it will auto-reverse the animation to stretch to its original width and height.

Once the method defines all the properties for the `DoubleAnimation` and `Storyboard` instances, it applies the animations associated with each `Storyboard` to their targets and initiates them by calling the `Begin` method.

```
storyboardMaxWidth.Begin();
storyboardMaxHeight.Begin();
```

You can right-click on many images and the animation will run for all these images. The following screenshot shows one of the frames for the animation.

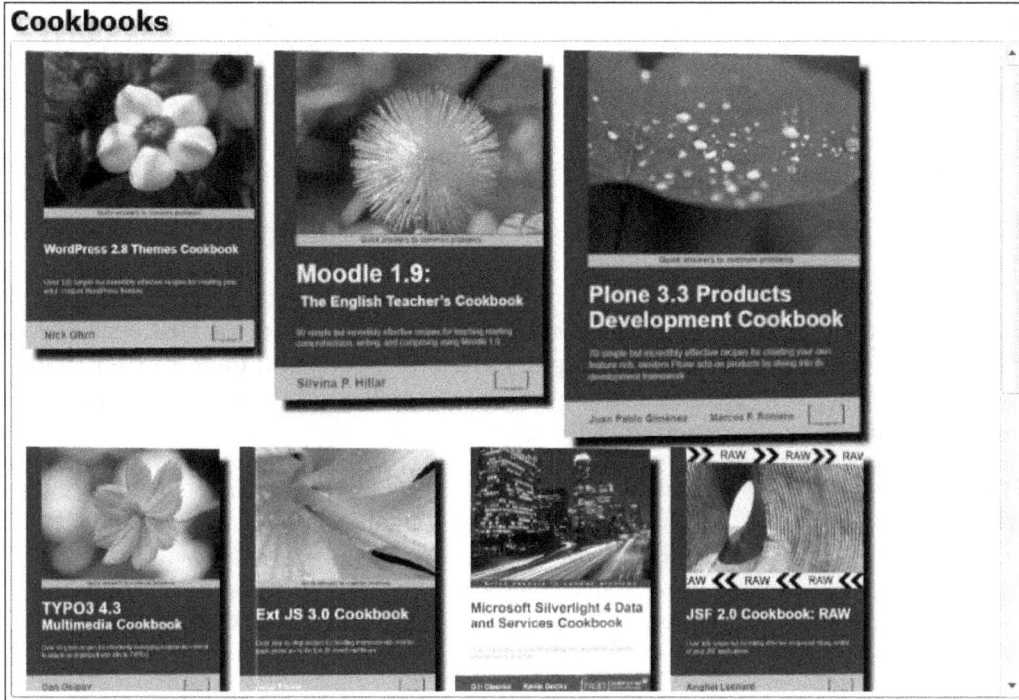

Adding and controlling videos

When the file type is `MediaFileType.Video`, the `ShowItem` method calls the `AddVideo` method with the `Url` string as a parameter and it saves the `HyperlinkButton` instance returned by this method in `videoButton`. Then, it calls the `AddImageVideoAnimation` with `videoButton` as a parameter.

```
case MediaFileType.Video:
  var videoButton = AddVideo(Url);
  AddImageVideoAnimation(videoButton);
  break;
```

The `AddVideo` method creates a new `MediaElement` instance, `media`, and sets values for its `MaxWidth` and `Stretch` properties. Then, it assigns the absolute `Uri` from the URL received as a parameter, `url`, to the `media.Source` property.

```
MediaElement media = new MediaElement();
media.MaxWidth = (_maxImageWidth * 3);
media.Stretch = Stretch.UniformToFill;
media.Source = new Uri(url, UriKind.Absolute);
```

Then, the code sets the `AutoPlay` property to `true` to automatically start the playback of the video specified in the `Source` property. The code attaches an event handler to the `MediaEnded` event that occurs when the video finishes. It assigns a new `RoutedEventHandler` that will fire the `media_MediaEnded` method. This method plays the video again from the beginning and therefore, the video is going to play forever while the Silverlight RIA performs all the animations.

```
media.AutoPlay = true;
media.MediaEnded += new RoutedEventHandler(media_MediaEnded);
```

Then, the code creates a new invisible `HyperlinkButton`, `videoButton`, and sets its `Content` property to the previously created `MediaElement` instance, `media`. When `videoButton` becomes visible, it will show the video being reproduced. The `NavigateUri` property for `videoButton` is set to a new `Uri` from the URL received as a parameter, `url`. The `TargetName` property is set to `_blank` and therefore, when the user clicks the `HyperlinkButton`, the web browser will open the video from the URL in the default player associated with the file extension.

The code attaches an event handler to the `MouseRightButtonDown` event that occurs when the user clicks the right mouse button and the mouse pointer is over the `Hyperlinkbutton`. It assigns a new `MouseButtonEventHandler` that will fire the `videoButton_MouseRightButtonDown` method. This method runs the previously explained animation for the `Hyperlinkbutton`. This animation is very similar to the one explained for the `imageButton_MouseRightButtonDown` method.

```
var videoButton = new HyperlinkButton();
videoButton.Visibility = System.Windows.Visibility.Collapsed;
videoButton.Margin = new Thickness(_imageMargin);
videoButton.Content = media;
videoButton.NavigateUri = new Uri(url);
videoButton.MouseRightButtonDown += new MouseButtonEventHandler(videoB
utton_MouseRightButtonDown);
videoButton.TargetName = "_blank";
videoButton.Cursor = Cursors.Hand;
```

Finally, it is necessary to add the `HyperlinkButton` as a child to the `wrapPanel` `WrapPanel` and return the instance.

```
wrapPanel.Children.Add(videoButton);
return videoButton;
```

At this point, the `HyperlinkButton` is invisible, because its `Visibility` property was set to `System.Windows.Visibility.Collapsed`. However, when the `AddVideo` method returns, the `AddImageVideoAnimation` receives the `HyperlinkButton` control as a parameter, `hlButton`, and brings life to the video that it displays, as explained for the images.

The following screenshot shows one of the frames for the animated `HyperlinkButton` reproducing the video and growing after the user right-clicked on it:

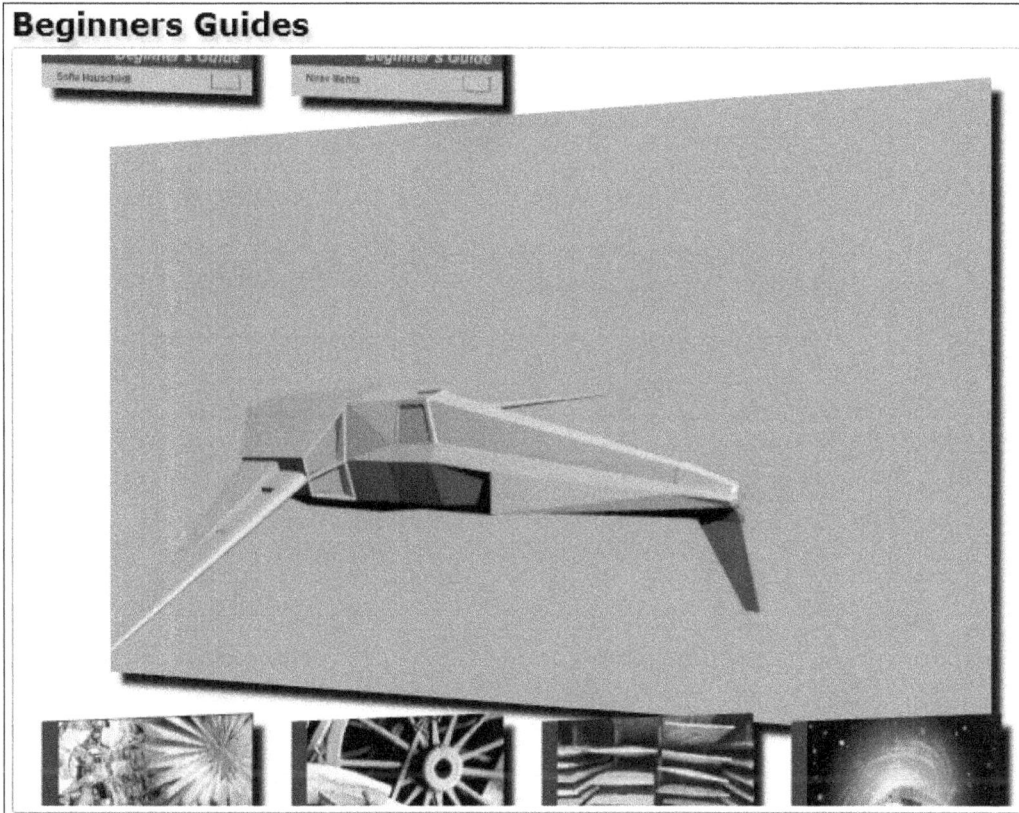

We defined the horizontal reproduction area for the video to be `_maxImageWidth * 3` pixels and we assigned the `UniformToFill` value to the `Stretch` property. Thus, the `MediaElement` resizes the original to fill the container's dimensions while preserving the video's native aspect ratio.

The following screenshot shows the results of using the four possible values in the `Stretch` property with the same original video:

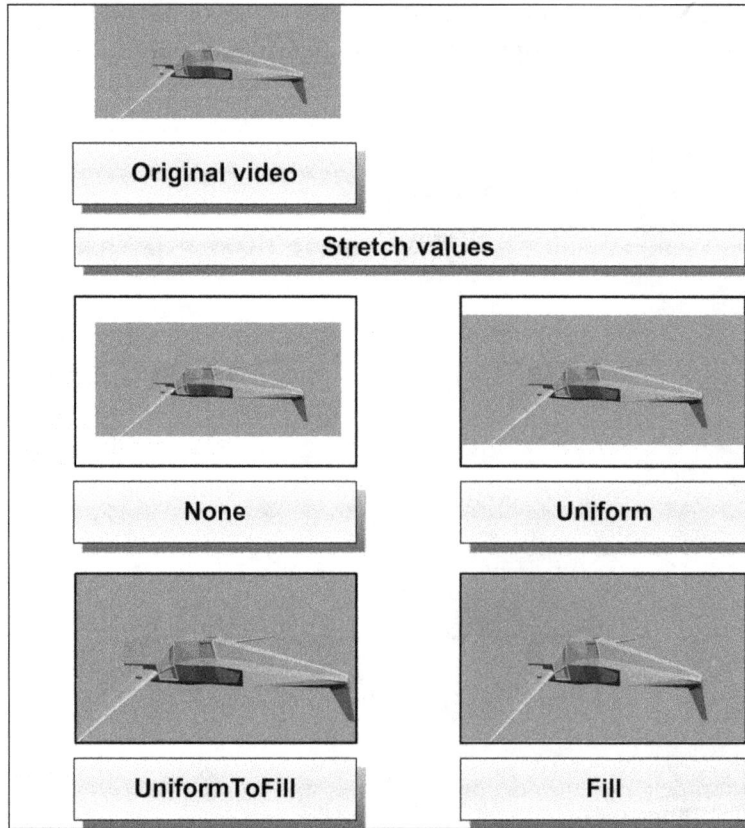

The following table explains the results of using the aforementioned values:

Stretch value	Description	Aspect ratio
None	The video preserves its original size.	Preserved
Uniform	The video is resized to fit in the destination dimensions.	Preserved
UniformToFill	The video is resized to fill the destination dimensions. The video content that does not fit in the destination rectangle is clipped.	Preserved
Fill	The video is resized to fill the destination dimensions.	Not preserved

Video formats supported in Silverlight 4

Silverlight 4 supports the video encodings shown in the following table:

Encoding name	Description and restrictions
None	Raw video
YV12	YCrCb(4:2:0)
RGBA	32-bit Red, Green, Blue, and Alpha
WMV1	Windows Media Video 7
WMV2	Windows Media Video 8
WMV3	Windows Media Video 9
WMVA	Windows Media Video Advanced Profile (non-VC-1)
WMVC1	Windows Media Video Advanced Profile (VC-1)
H.264 (ITU-T H.264 / ISO MPEG-4 AVC)	H.264 and MP43 codecs; base main and high profiles; only progressive (non-interlaced) content and only 4:2:0 chroma sub-sampling profiles

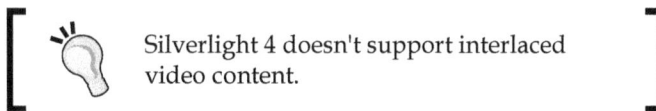

> Silverlight 4 doesn't support interlaced video content.

If we want to use a video with an encoding that does not appear in the previously shown table in a Silverlight RIA, we will have to convert it to one of the supported formats before uploading it to a SharePoint assets library.

Adding and controlling sounds and music

When the file type is `MediaFileType.Audio`, the `ShowItem` method calls the `AddBackgroundMusic` method with the `Url` string as a parameter.

```
case MediaFileType.Audio:
    AddBackgroundMusic(Url);
    break;
```

The `AddBackgroundMusic` method checks whether it was called before (`_backgroundMusicAdded == true`) before running the rest of the code, because it doesn't want to reproduce two audio files as the background music. If `_backgroundMusicAdded` is `true`, it assigns `true` to `_backgroundMusicAdded`.

The code creates a new `MediaElement` instance, `backgroundMusic`, adds it to a parent container, `LayoutRoot`, and sets its `Volume` property to 80% (`0.8`). The `Volume` ranges from 0 to 1. It uses a linear scale.

```
_backgroundMusicAdded = true;
MediaElement backgroundMusic = new MediaElement();
LayoutRoot.Children.Add(backgroundMusic);
```

Then, it assigns the absolute `Uri` from the URL received as a parameter, `url`, to the `backgroundMusic.Source` property and calls the `Play` method to start reproducing the audio file with the specified volume level. The background music will be reproduced just once.

```
backgroundMusic.Volume = 0.8;
backgroundMusic.Source = new Uri(url);
backgroundMusic.Play();
```

Audio formats supported in Silverlight 4

Silverlight 4 supports the audio encodings shown in the following table:

Encoding name	Description and restrictions
LPCM	Linear 8 or 16-bit Pulse Code Modulation.
WMA Standard	Windows Media Audio 7, 8, and 9 Standard.
WMA Professional	Windows Media Audio 9 and 10 Professional; Multichannel (5.1 and 7.1 surround) is automatically mixed down to stereo. It supports neither 24-bit audio nor sampling rates beyond 48 kHz.
MP3	ISO MPEG-1 Layer III.
AAC	ISO Advanced Audio Coding; AAC-LC (Low Complexity) is supported at full fidelity (up to 48 kHz). HE-AAC (High Efficiency) will decode only at half fidelity (up to 24 kHz); Multichannel (5.1) audio content is not supported.

If we want to use an audio file with an encoding that does not appear in the previously shown table, we will have to convert it to one of the supported formats before uploading it to a SharePoint assets library.

Changing themes in Silverlight and SharePoint

We learned about the themes included in Silverlight Toolkit in *Chapter 1*, in the *Browsing themes with sample controls* and in *Creating Rich User eXperiences (UX)* sections. The Visual Web Part is a great candidate for applying the themes included in Silverlight's Toolkit to offer the user a more exciting UI.

1. Stay in Visual Studio as a system administrator user.

2. Add a reference to `System.Windows.Controls.Theming.Toolkit.dll`. Remember that it is located in the `Bin` sub-folder explained in *Chapter 1*, within the *Creating Rich User eXperiences (UX)* section.

3. Add a reference to the DLL for `System.Windows.Controls.Theming. ShinyRed` in the `Themes` sub-folder. This way, we are going to be able to apply the `ShinyRed` theme.

4. Add the following line to include the namespace that defines the theme in the `UserControl` defined in `MainPage.xaml`:

    ```
    xmlns:shinyRed="clr-namespace:System.Windows.Controls.
    Theming;assembly=System.Windows.Controls.Theming.ShinyRed"
    ```

5. Add the following line before the definition of the main `Grid`, `LayoutRoot`:

    ```
    <shinyRed:ShinyRedTheme>
    ```

6. Add the following line after the definition of the main `Grid`, `LayoutRoot`:

    ```
    </shinyRed:ShinyRedTheme>
    ```

7. This way, the `ShinyRed` theme will be applied to the main `Grid`, `LayoutRoot`, and all its child controls. Build and deploy the solution and open the page that displays the Visual Web Part. The Silverlight RIA looks really more attractive. However, the colors displayed by the rest of the SharePoint UI don't match the `ShinyRed` theme colors.

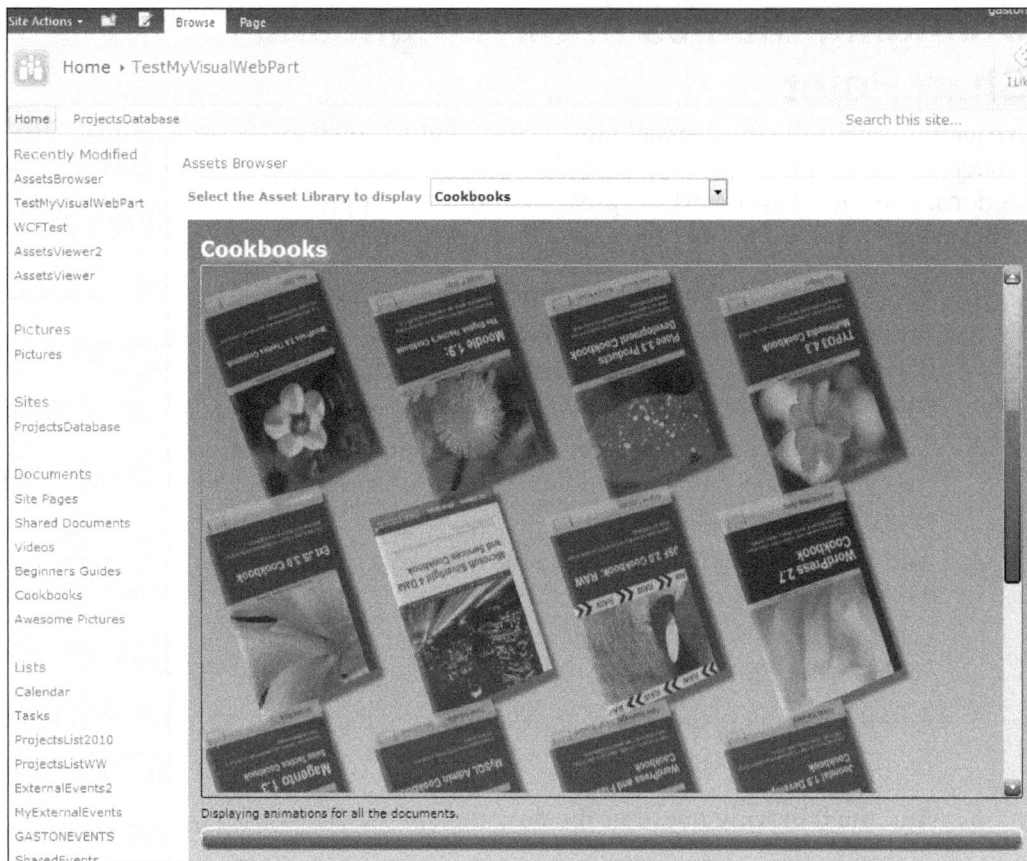

8. Click **Site Actions | Site Settings** and a list of customization options organized by categories will appear.

9. Click on **Site theme** under **Look and Feel**. A page that allows us to change the fonts and color scheme for our site will appear.

10. Select the `Municipal` theme in the list located at the right. This theme uses a color scheme that is appropriate for Silverlight applications that use the `ShinyRed` theme.

11. Click on **Preview** and the web browser will open a new window with your site's home page with the new color schemes and fonts that the selected theme defines.

12. Close this window and click on **Apply**. SharePoint will apply the new theme to the pages that haven't been individually themed. The new theme won't affect the site's layout.

13. Now, refresh the page that displays the Visual Web Part and the combination of a new SharePoint theme with the theme applied to the Silverlight RIA will look really nice.

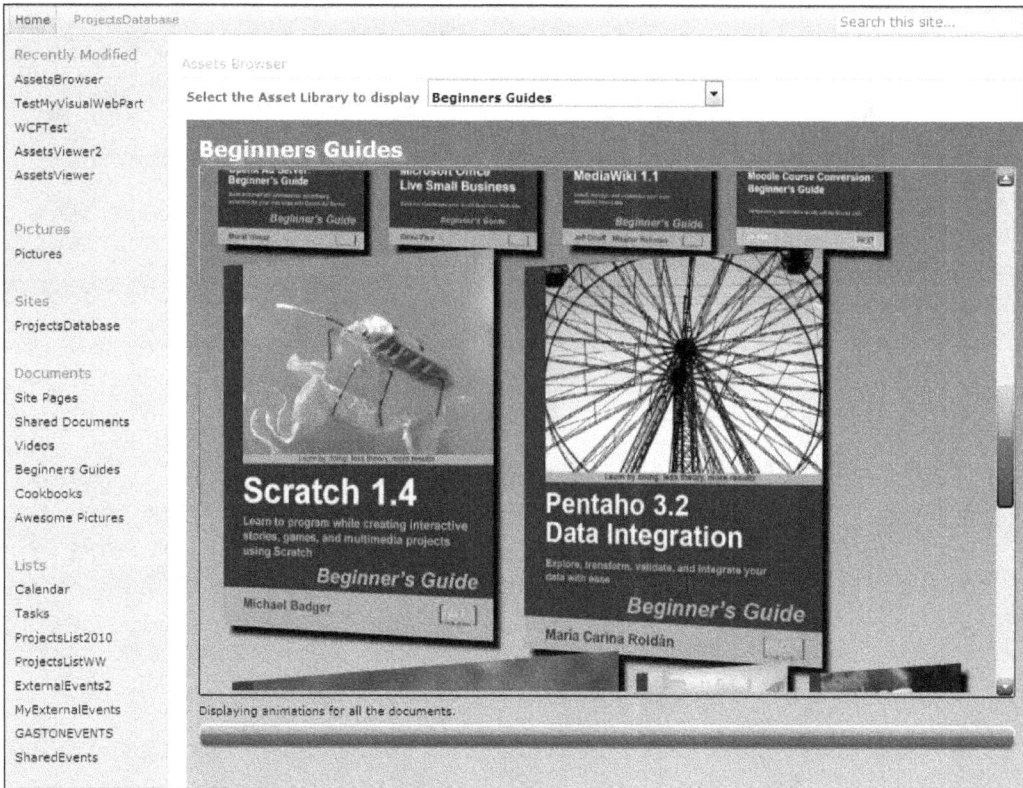

Summary

We learnt a lot in this chapter about accessing asset libraries in a Silverlight RIA rendered in a SharePoint Visual Web Part. Specifically, we were able to send parameters to the Silverlight control host to define the desired asset library to display. We used many of the procedures learned in the previous chapters to work with classic lists but this time we consumed files. We took advantage of Silverlight 4 rich media features to add effects and interactive animations to the images and videos.

We have learned many alternatives to integrate Silverlight 4 with SharePoint 2010 and we have understood the great possibilities offered by Silverlight RIAs in SharePoint sites. Now, we are ready to create enhanced Silverlight User eXperiences combined with the powerful SharePoint 2010 services.

Index

Symbols

_context.ExecuteQueryAsync method 59, 97
_context.Web.CurrentUser.Id property 101
.xap file 35
 ExternalEvents 140

A

AddBackgroundMusic method 307
AddFieldChoicesToComboBoxes method
        105
AddFieldChoicesToComboBox method 107
AddImage method 296
AddItem method 100
AddItemToList method 90, 91, 99, 100
AddToProjectsList2010 method 236
ADO.NET Data Services. *See* WCF Data
        Services, SharePoint 2010
asset library, SharePoint 2010
   content, adding to 258-261
   creating 256
   creating, steps 256, 257
   structures, browsing 262, 263
AssetsBrowserWebPart class 269
AssignedTo property 222
AutoGenerateColumns property 23
AutoPostBack property 267

B

backgroundMusic.Source property 308
BCS 134
BDC 134
BeginInvoke method 60

BeginSaveChanges method 235
BitmapImage class 274
Business Connectivity Services. *See* BCS
Business Data Catalog. *See* BDC
butDelete_Click method
   LayoutRoot_Loaded 157

C

CAML 63
class
   AssetsBrowserWebPart 269
   BitmapImage 274
   classProject 64
   Projection 297
ClientContext object
   working with 61
ClientRequestFailedEventHandler 59
CLR 60
Collaborative Application Markup
        Language. *See* CAML
Common Language Runtime. *See* CLR
ConnectAndAddItemToList method 89, 91,
        99
ConnectAndFillComboBoxes method 107
ConnectLists method
Connect method 54
Content property 152
Count property 80
CreateChildControls method 269
Create, Read, Update, and Delete. *See*
        CRUD
CRUD 86

D

DataGridCellEditEndedEventArgs e parameter 129
dataGridProjects_CellEditEnded method 127
dataGridProjects.SelectedItem property 130, 223
Developer Dashboard
  deactivating 252
  enabling, in different modes 247
  information, visualizing 249-252
  OnDemand mode, activating 247, 248
  Web Parts, analyzing 245
development environment
  preparing 9
  setting up 10, 11
  Silverlight 4 Offline Documentation (in CHM format), downloading 11
  Silverlight 4 Tools for Visual Studio 2010, downloading 10
  Silverlight Toolkit rich controls, discovering 12-14
  Silverlight Toolkit (Updated for Silverlight 4 compatibility), downloading 11
  themes browsing, sample controls used 15
Dispatcher.BeginInvoke method 100, 226, 246
DisplayMemberPath property 234
downloading
  Expression Blend for .NET 11
  Silverlight 4 Offline Documentation (in CHM format) 11
  Silverlight Toolkit (Updated for Silverlight 4 compatibility 11

E

EndSaveChanges method 235
event
  LayoutRoot_Loaded 156
  MouseRightButtonDown 297
  OnPreRender 269
ExecuteQueryAsync method 59, 61, 99
ExecuteQuery method 61

Expression Blend for .NET
  downloading 11
Extensible Stylesheet Language Transformations. *See* XSLT
extent 295
external database, Silverlight RIA
  accessing 134
  BCS calls, impersonating 167-171
  BCS consumption, from Silverlight Web Part 163-165
  BCS related security issues 166, 167
  CAML query included fields, specifying 158-163
  data sources, interacting with 150-158
  dynamic filters, applying in CAML query 171-174
  external content type, creating 139-148
  new database, creating 134-139
  SharePoint list browsing, external content fields used 149, 150
  SharePoint list browsing, external content used 149, 150
  Silverlight RIAs, running outside Web Browser 174-178

F

Fiddler
  HTTP Requests, debugging 240-243
FieldValueType property 49
FillBehavior property 298
FillComboBoxes method 234

G

GetByTitle method 63, 100
GetItemById method 130
GetItems method 63
GetListData method 56, 63
GetMediaFileType method 296

H

HasExternalDataSource property 149
HTTP Requests
  debugging, Fiddler used 240-243

I

imageButton_MouseRightButtonDown
    method 297, 301
InitializeGrid method 24
interactive animations
  working with 296-303
InternalName property 49
ItemCount property 63, 158
ItemsSource property 24, 26, 239

J

JavaScript Object Notation. *See* JSON
JSON 192

L

LayoutRoot_Loaded event 156
Line-Of-Business. *See* LOB
LoadItems method 63
LOB
  about 86
  as independent WebParts 119-121
  expanding, with delete operations 121-124
  expanding, with update operations 126-129
  item, deleting from list 124
  item, updating in list 129-131
LookupId property 101

M

media_MediaEnded method 304
method
  _context.ExecuteQueryAsync 59, 97
  AddBackgroundMusic 307
  AddFieldChoicesToComboBoxes 105
  AddItem 100
  AddItemToList 90-100
  AddToProjectsList2010 236
  BeginInvoke 60
  BeginSaveChanges 235
  ConnectAndAddItemToList 89-99
  ConnectAndFillComboBoxes 107
  Connect 54
  ConnectLists 54
  CreateChildControls 269

dataGridProjects_CellEditEnded 127
Dispatcher.BeginInvoke 100, 246
EndSaveChanges 235
ExecuteQuery 61
ExecuteQueryAsync 59, 99
FillComboBoxes 234
GetByTitle 63, 100
GetItems 63
GetListData 56, 63
GetItemById 130
GetMediaFileType 296
imageButton_MouseRightButtonDown
  297, 301
InitializeGrid 24
LoadItems 63
media_MediaEnded 304
methodShowItems 54
OnConnectListsSucceeded 56
OnConnectSucceeded 56, 59
OnGetListDataSucceeded 56
OnLoadItemsSucceeded 56
OnConnectSucceeded 91
OnUpdateFailed 127
OnUpdateSucceeded 127
ReturnFieldByInternalName 105
ShowErrorInformation 97
MouseRightButtonDown event 297

N

NavigateUri property 297

O

OData 192
OnConnectListsSucceeded method 56
OnConnectSucceeded method 56, 59, 91
OnGetListDataSucceeded method 56
OnLoadItemsSucceeded method 56
OnPreRender event 269
OnUpdateFailed method 127
OnUpdateSucceeded method 127
OOB 178
Open Data Protocol. *See* OData
Out-of-Browser. *See* OOB

P

parameter
  DataGridCellEditEndedEventArgs e 129
Project class 64
Projection class 297
property
  _context.Web.CurrentUser.Id 101
  AutoGenerateColumns 23
  AutoPostBack 267
  AssignedTo 222
  Content property 152
  Count 80
  dataGridProjects.SelectedItem 223
  DisplayMemberPath 234
  FieldValueType 49
  HasExternalDataSource 149
  InternalName 49, 126
  ItemCount 63
  ItemsSource 24, 239
  LookupId 101
  NavigateUri 297
  RequiredPermissions 248
  RootFolder 63
  SchemaXml 103, 185
  SelectedList 292, 293
  selectedProject.Title 130
  Title 50
  ViewXml 63
  TargetName 297
property 130
  dataGridProjects.SelectedItem 130

R

Representational State Transfer. *See* REST
RequiredPermissions property 248
REST 192
ReturnFieldByInternalName method 105
RIAs 7
Rich Internet Applications. *See* RIAs
RootFolder property 63

S

SchemaXml property 103, 185
SelectedList property 292, 293
selectedProject.Title property 130
ServerRelativeUrl property 296
SharePoint
  themes, changing 309-312
SharePoint 2010
  asset library, creating 256
  rich media management, improving 256
  WCF Data Services, working with 192
SharePoint 2010 server
  preparing 16, 17
  Site Collection, browsing 18-20
SharePoint, debugging. *See* Silverlight,
    debugging
SharePoint package file 287
ShowErrorInformation method 97, 157
ShowItems method 54
Silverlight 4
  supported audio formats 308
  supported video formats 307
Silverlight, debugging
  32-bit application, differences 81
  64-bit application, differences 81
  multiple browser support applications,
    preparing 82
  scalability 82
  Visual Studio 2010 multi-monitor support,
    using 80
  Web Part, debugging 75-80
Silverlight integration, with SharePoint
  benefits 8, 9
  SharePoint solution, creating 9
Silverlight LOB RIA
  creating 20-27
  rich user experience, creating 27, 28
  Silverlight 4 RIA, building 29, 30
SilverlightProjects.xap file 30
Silverlight RIA
  linking, to Visual Web Part 285-288
  external database, accessing 134
  themes, modifying 309-312

Silverlight RIA, included in a SharePoint solution
asynchronous operations, working with 98-101
complex LOB applications, creating 112, 113, 116
data, managing 86
item insertion, Silverlight Web Part used 94-97
LOB systems, as independent WebParts 119-121
LOB systems, expanding with delete operations 121-124
LOB systems, expanding with update operations 126-129
multiple Silverlight Web Parts in same page, interacting with 117, 118
Silverlight Client Object Model, working with 86-93
specific field information, retrieving 102-112
Silverlight RIA included in SharePoint solution, deploying 44
asynchronous methods, working with 58-60
callbacks, working with 58-60
ClientContext object, working with 61-65
default deployment configuration 71, 72
external database accessing 134
SharePoint lists browsing, Visual Studio used 47-51
SharePoint module, linking to Silverlight RIA 65-70
Silverlight RIA, creating 51-57
tasks list, creating 44-46
Silverlight RIA, rendered in SharePoint Visual Web Part
creating 271-285
Silverlight Toolkit (Updated for Silverlight 4 compatibility
downloading 11
Silverlight Web Part
adding 30
adding, for displaying Silverlight RIA 33-38
client and server code 41
multiple Silverlight RIAs, working with 39-41
Silverlight RIA, adding to shared document 30-33
WCF Data Services, consuming from 209-212
Sql Server Configuration Manager 135
StartUp event handler 53

T

TargetName property 297
Title property 50

U

ULS 250
Unified Logging Service. *See* **ULS**

V

videos
adding 303-306
controlling 303-306
formats, in Silverlight 4 307
viewport 295
ViewXml property 63
Visual Web Part
about 264
adding, in Web page 288-294
controls, organizing 294, 295
creating 264-270
files, reading from assets library 295, 296
linking to Silverlight RIA 285-288

W

WCF Data Services, SharePoint 2010
consuming, from Silverlight Web Part 209-212
CRUD operations, performing 213-223
items, inserting 227-236
LINQ to objects used, for perform join 236-239
list item, deleting 223-225
list item, updating 225-227
user information, retrieving 236-239
web browser list, querying 193-202
working with 192

working with, for data dispaly 203-209
Web Parts
   analyzing, Developer Dashboard used 245
Windows Media Video. *See* **WMV**
WMV 258
workflow
   attaching, to tasks list in Sharepoint
      180-182
   displaying, Silverlight RIA used 185-188
   interacting with 179
   items, inserting 182-184
   status field 189
WSP package 68, 287

X

XSLT 200

[PACKT] PUBLISHING enterprise

professional expertise distilled

Thank you for buying
Microsoft Silverlight 4 and SharePoint 2010 Integration

About Packt Publishing

Packt, pronounced 'packed', published its first book "Mastering phpMyAdmin for Effective MySQL Management" in April 2004 and subsequently continued to specialize in publishing highly focused books on specific technologies and solutions.

Our books and publications share the experiences of your fellow IT professionals in adapting and customizing today's systems, applications, and frameworks. Our solution based books give you the knowledge and power to customize the software and technologies you're using to get the job done. Packt books are more specific and less general than the IT books you have seen in the past. Our unique business model allows us to bring you more focused information, giving you more of what you need to know, and less of what you don't.

Packt is a modern, yet unique publishing company, which focuses on producing quality, cutting-edge books for communities of developers, administrators, and newbies alike. For more information, please visit our website: www.packtpub.com.

About Packt Enterprise

In 2010, Packt launched two new brands, Packt Enterprise and Packt Open Source, in order to continue its focus on specialization. This book is part of the Packt Enterprise brand, home to books published on enterprise software – software created by major vendors, including (but not limited to) IBM, Microsoft and Oracle, often for use in other corporations. Its titles will offer information relevant to a range of users of this software, including administrators, developers, architects, and end users.

Writing for Packt

We welcome all inquiries from people who are interested in authoring. Book proposals should be sent to author@packtpub.com. If your book idea is still at an early stage and you would like to discuss it first before writing a formal book proposal, contact us; one of our commissioning editors will get in touch with you.

We're not just looking for published authors; if you have strong technical skills but no writing experience, our experienced editors can help you develop a writing career, or simply get some additional reward for your expertise.

WCF 4.0 Multi-tier Services Development with LINQ to Entities

ISBN: 978-1-849681-14-8   Paperback: 348 pages

Build SOA applications on the Microsoft platform with this hands-on guide updated for VS2010.

1. Master WCF and LINQ to Entities concepts by completing practical examples and applying them to your real-world assignments

2. The first and only book to combine WCF and LINQ to Entities in a multi-tier real-world WCF service

WCF 4.0 Multi-tier Services Development with LINQ to Entities

Mike Liu

Refactoring with Microsoft Visual Studio 2010

ISBN: 978-1-849680-10-3   Paperback: 315 pages

Evolve your software system to support new and ever-changing requirements by updating your C# code base with patterns and principles

1. Make your code base maintainable with refactoring

2. Support new features more easily by making your system adaptable

3. Enhance your system with an improved object-oriented design and increased encapsulation and componentization

Refactoring with Microsoft Visual Studio 2010

Peter Ritchie

Please check **www.PacktPub.com** for information on our titles